Edited by: Captain W. Rick Rubel U.S. Navy (retired)
Dr. George R. Lucas, Jr. U.S. Naval Academy

Case Studies in Ethics for Military Leaders

Cover Art: Courtesy of Comstock

Pearson Learning Solutions, 501 Boylston Street, Suite 900, Boston, MA 02116
A Pearson Education Company
www.pearsoned.com

Printed in the United States of America

4 5 6 7 8 9 10 V092 16 15 14 13 12

000200010270778877

JL/LP

ISBN 10: 1-256-16618-9
ISBN 13: 978-1-256-16618-4

Chief Warrant Officer Hugh W. Thompson

1944-2006

Exemplar of Moral Courage at My Lai

CONTENTS

Preface: Case Studies in Military Ethics
Dr. George R. Lucas, Jr.

This volume of case studies in military ethics is intended to address a serious deficiency in the teaching and study of military ethics. In other areas of applied or professional ethics (such as business, medicine, or law) students and practicing professionals rely upon a *large and established body of case literature* to orient them to the variety of ways that "things can go terribly wrong" in the normal practice of their craft, or to alert them to the difficult moral responsibilities that will be laid upon them during a time of crisis. Health care professionals, for example, rely in their education upon the reading of numerous troubling and difficult cases, drawn from actual experience. These cases acquaint future physicians with a range of issues concerning, how to respond effectively and appropriately to dilemmas involving allocation of scarce medical resources, how to set appropriate limits and expectations on their own power and authority to combat illness, and most importantly, how to treat patients and the public with the respect and care they deserve.

In military ethics, by contrast, there was (before this volume) no substantial body of authentic case-study literature drawn broadly from the experiences of practicing professionals, or capturing the range of organizational dilemmas routinely faced by military officers and enlisted personnel during the normal course of their duties. Likewise, there has not been a well-established tradition of teaching moral values and moral reasoning to students and practitioners within the military profession through the disciplined and effective use of a recognizable case-study method.

Instead, what those in the military profession have relied upon for our teaching and training are what soldiers call "war stories" and sailors call "sea stories." These are accounts, drawn from the battlefield and the fleet, of interesting and complicated circumstances requiring junior or senior officers to make difficult leadership decisions and moral choices. Often, those choices are not well made, and the decisions come back to haunt the subsequent careers of the individuals who make them. In others instances, it may seem as if simple good luck, or a special but inexplicable sense of judgment and foresight, helped the individual in question to "do the right thing."

In all these instances, however, those of us listening to (or reading about) these "sea stories" are confronted with important questions such as:

- What *is* the right decision in each instance?
- How *does* the individual officer decide?

These are the questions with which the study of ethics and moral reasoning ought to begin. Yet, by themselves, the simple re-telling of "sea stories" is not very helpful or instructive in answering such questions, or in helping improve the abilities of officers to handle the difficult moral conflicts they most certainly will encounter. In particular, we require sufficient structure and context in such stories, as well as authentic detail, in order to enable us to determine:

- what the options or choices might be,
- how one might discern better from worse alternatives,
- what role the larger organization and its values, leadership style, and reward system are likely to play in affecting the behavior of its individual members, and

- what the likely outcome or consequences of each of the possible decisions would be for the individual officer, as well as for his or her comrades-in-arms and specific branch of military service.

These are the kinds of substantive details that distinguish a well-written case study from a mere war story or sea story. Studying good cases drawn from actual professional line experience helps the officer, or officer-in-training, become aware of the kinds of moral conflicts that can arise in the course of the performance of professional duties. Studying such cases should also help the officer to *improve his or her ability to reason* about particular circumstances, and so to choose thoughtfully and wisely when confronted with a moral crisis, rather than merely be overwhelmed by it. Finally, studying a range of cases arising in the pursuit of one's profession will also help to clarify the core values and traditions of the military profession itself, and explain the moral obligations that these values and traditions place specifically upon each and every one of those who wears the uniform.

The cases in this volume are designed to address this urgent educational and professional need. They span a wide range of history and experience in all four of the branches of military service: the Navy, Army, Air Force, and the Marine Corps. Some cases illustrate heroic and inspiring behavior, while others record disappointing and ultimately unacceptable conduct. Still others present dilemmas, very typical of genuine moral dilemmas, in which a single "right" answer may prove elusive, and the case itself therefore prove frustrating. All of the cases, however, provide a great deal of useful, practical illustration concerning the range of moral dilemmas that military personnel will encounter during their careers, and also about the high standards of professional conduct to which they may rightfully and realistically expect to be held. In that sense, these cases collectively re-enforce the "informed consent" for the individual members of an all-volunteer military force. That is, they serve to acquaint each and every one of us with the strict moral standards to which military professionals will be held, as well as with the high moral calling their profession proudly represents.

This volume of case studies is designed to stand alone as a resource for those in the military, and others in business or other professions interested in military experience. The individual cases may be read alone, or read and discussed with others, and otherwise used as independent resources for individual or group study and reflection.

This volume may also be used with its companion volume, *Ethics and the Military Profession: the Moral Foundations of Leadership* (also edited by myself and Captain Rick Rubel) to provide a college-level course of study in moral theory and practice. The cases in this volume can be paired with readings in moral philosophy in that volume to help bring abstract theory "to life" in actual professional practice, or to illustrate how a particular approach to moral reasoning (e.g., utilitarianism) may "play out" in actual practice to help an officer reason through a complex situation, or deliberate about a difficult individual decision.

Many of the cases presented in this volume are what is termed "decision-forcing" cases. That is, the cases place the reader in the position of the principal decision-maker in the case, equipped only with the knowledge and information and perspective that the original participant possessed at the time. The cases then require a decision or response from the reader. In these instances, a case sequel is supplied in the appendix of this volume that narrates subsequent events as these actually transpired. By and large, the remaining cases are "narrative" or historical in structure: they attempt to provide a distinct, chronological summary of some complex event, such as the Tailhook or Aviano incidents, for the reader's consideration and reflection.

There is no pre-established or set manner in which this pairing need occur, and leaders, mentors, or individual military or civilian instructors should feel free to be creative in associating one or more cases with a set of readings and discussions. For example: the case study of U. S. Army Captain Lawrence Rockwood in Haiti could serve to supplement readings and discussions of the role of an individual's conscience or religious beliefs in military life, or as an illustration of the formal obligations laid upon each officer by the Constitution, with its separation of powers and civilian control of the military. The famous case of Marine Corps Lieutenant Colonel Oliver North in the "Iran Contra" affair obviously fits well in the latter context of discussing conflicts of loyalties and the dilemmas associated with the Constitutional obligations of military service. It might also be paired with the "Aviano case" or even with the "Tailhook" case to illustrate how organizations and their members often try to escape the consequences of difficult choices by hiding or denying them (a familiar organizational strategy that invariably backfires).

Readers and instructors alike should beware of some common pitfalls of thinking, for example, that all cases are examples of bad behavior to be avoided, or that such behavior and its analysis and discussion amount to an implied criticism of the organization or service in which the event occurred. It is truly a great mystery (which study and reflection on these cases might help us unravel) why "good people" sometimes do "bad things." It is an even greater challenge to understand how and why organizations with good leadership and sound core values may yet end up mired in scandal and controversy. It is sometimes painful, but always useful, to try and confront such deep and profound dilemmas. It is never helpful, by contrast, to avoid or deny them.

Most importantly, not all case studies are of this "negative" sort: witness the courage shown by Chief Warrant Officer Hugh Thompson during the terrible massacre of non-combatants in My Lai during the Vietnam War, as described in the case study included in this volume. These and other inspiring cases help us confront difficult dilemmas in the knowledge that it is possible both to know and, despite severe odds, to do "the right thing." CWO Thompson's career and actions in 1968, culminating thirty years later in the award of the coveted Soldier's Medal, underscore the stringent demands and high moral calling of the military profession. Accordingly, it is to him that this volume is dedicated.

Introduction

Getting to the Moral Point of the Case

Captain Rick Rubel (USN, Ret)
Distinguished Military Professor of Ethics
U. S. Naval Academy (Annapolis)

In using this book of case studies in Military Ethics, the reader; whether a student, a military officer, or interested civilian, should strive to use the cases to reach a deep level of understanding about themselves and how they would reason through the situation in the case.

On the surface of the case lie the facts of the situation, and the possible options one may have available to them. Below that surface is a *moral dilemma*; the difficult choice between right or wrong, or between two wrongs, or two rights. Even deeper below the dilemma, is the underlying *moral point* to the case. It is only through the analysis of this *moral point* that one can understand their own moral reasoning, take away the value of the case, and begin the process of learning about themselves. One should be able to come away from the case with the answer to the question, "What kind of reasoning did I use here, and will this type of reasoning work in all similar situations?" Since a case cannot be provided for every possible situation in military ethics, the reader must ask these questions of universality and consistency in order to obtain the full benefit from the cases.

Ethics in the First Person

In reading, analyzing and discussing the cases in this volume, what is desired is to engage the reader or student in the living details of leadership and ethics, to involve them in what our colleague, Professor Deni Elliot, terms "ethics in the first person." We need to ask, in each circumstance, what would *I* do? How would *I* decide? What do *I* think should be done, or should not have been done? And why? What are the reasons in favor of (and against) *my* proposed solution or choice? What can *I* learn from reading and studying the case? What can *I* take away from our encounter that will prepare *me* for the moral dilemmas and the hard choices I will most certainly face in the future?

Moral Obligations and Conflict of Mission

As human beings, we all have a moral obligation to do what is right. The source of moral obligations, however, will vary for different people. Our sense of moral obligation may arise from straightforward external motivations, such as the fear of punishment, or the hope of reward. Or we may derive our sense of obligation internally, from our religious commitments, or our intuitive belief in a natural order, or our intuitive recognition of our moral duties.

As military officers, however, we have an additional and distinct source of moral obligation. At the very instant we drop our right hand and complete our Oath of Office we have incurred a new and enormous obligation. This new obligation is not always clear to the new officer or officer candidate. In the relatively short oath we use words such as: "solemnly," "faithfully," "allegiance," and "God," and we agree to fight "*all* enemies. . . ." This directly implies that we (the military) do not get to choose who we fight. And importantly, we swear that we will support and defend the Constitution of the United States. Before we can proceed in the study of military ethics, we must clearly understand what it means to take an oath to a 214-year-old document. Implicitly, we are agreeing to the values and principles upon which our country was founded. But more importantly, and explicitly, we are taking an oath to the Constitution that sets up our form of government. We are agreeing to the civilian control of the military (the President is our Commander-in-Chief), to the process of declaring war (the military will not start its own wars), and the process of elections (the military will serve, not take control).

After taking this solemn oath, we are then given a Commission as an officer. This further obligates us; but this document specifically, and *individually* ties us to the President. We serve at his/her pleasure, and he will give us orders "from time to time."

By taking the oath and accepting the commission, we have agreed to serve. The nature of service to any great cause requires selflessness. This selflessness in turn implies that we will make our decisions based on higher loyalties than ourselves. This new, official obligation will inevitably come into conflict with our personal moral beliefs. In a perfect world, all of our orders and missions will fall within the sphere of what we believe to be morally acceptable. But in the real world, we may be asked to perform a mission or follow an order that seems "wrong," and we then have to decide what is "right". Thus, Conflict of Mission is the subject of many of the cases that follow.

The Ethical Decisions of Command

In preparation for the responsibilities of command, one will be asked to examine the "three-way-moral-problem": the Mission (vs) the risk to our sailors or troops (vs) the risk to innocent civilians. The moral basis of this complicated formula is that we are obligated not to harm innocent non-combatants.

As a point of command leadership, we need to ensure that all of the orders we give our men and women are within the sphere of *their* morals, so they can live with their moral conscience in the aftermath. In making multi-dimensional decisions of command, it is often a choice between two or more options that have both uncertain and negative consequences. How does one combine the practical aspects of their decision with their intuitive sense of moral duty? The decision process may start with the question, "Is this legal?" If it is not legal, one should probably not proceed further. If legal, the next question that follows should be "It is moral?" And if there is more than one option, "How do I decide?" Making the best decision will probably involve more than just choosing the "lesser of the evils." The decision should be based on a thorough review of all considerations, including your mission, your morals, your religion, and your duty to protection of your people, and the innocents. In the review of one's moral position, one has to be able to explain (to themselves) their own moral reasoning. This is where the moral theories of our companion book should help in working through these very difficult cases. The difficult part of the decision task is to determine which of all the considerations is the most important. Sometimes the most important will be the greater good for the whole. Other times, it will be the principle that cannot be compromised. And sometimes the major consideration will be, "Can one live the rest of their life with the decision?"

Dealing With Moral Conscience

In preparing young men and women to defend their country, it is important to recognize that decisions in the military *uniquely* involve life and death. With the gravity of those decisions comes a heavy moral burden. The instructors of military ethics have a responsibility not only to prepare the future officers for the moral decision, but also to prepare them for how to handle the aftermath of that decision; their moral conscience. I have found that at the end of some of the case discussions, asking the midshipmen the question: "Can you live with that decision?" often brings a deep stare and introspection that begins their examination of their moral conscience.

To relate a short anecdote, I had a student several years ago who was a former marine enlisted. When talking about moral conscience, he asked, "So, sir, when I get the enemy in my sights, you want me to stop and deal with my moral conscience?" I said "No. I want you to deal with your moral conscience today, in class, so when you get the enemy in your sights, you have already dealt with it." These cases will allow you to "deal with it" in class.

Character and Moral Courage

Beyond the moral decision of the case, and the more difficult question of "how did you decide," is a point of character and moral courage. This is often harder to understand than the underlying moral theories. One way to look at this, is that for someone to actually *perform the right action*, there are two components that must be fulfilled. The first one is to "*know* what is right." This will involve using the moral reasoning, values, and obligations discussed above. But the second component is to have the character to actually *do* the right thing. This is the critical point in the process when you have determined what is right, but have trouble actually doing it. We have all experienced this point, and this could be considered the *point of moral courage*.

It is harder to find cases of positive moral courage than to find cases of senior officers who did the wrong thing and got caught. I believe this is because acts of positive moral courage often go unnoticed, while headlines are made from high-visibility blunders. As a related point of discussion, I ask my classes, "Why is it usually harder to do the right thing?" I cannot prove that it is harder, but this question always brings a simple nod of understanding.

The Practice of Military Ethics

In using case studies for applied military ethics, there may be no single right answer. Importantly, the student should be able to defend his or her answer using good moral reasoning. There are, however, wrong answers. When core values, such as truth, honor and integrity, are traded off for consequential outcomes, or blind obedience to illegal orders, that decision should be challenged.

This case study book for military ethics is the practice ground for military careers. It provides a chance for students to "scrimmage" with their instructor and their class-roommates. It provides a chance to make mistakes in moral reasoning in an academic forum. And most importantly, it provides a chance to prepare future officers for the awesome responsibilities they will face in their careers.

I

The Ethical Dimensions
of Command

Leave No One Behind[1]
Captain Rick Rubel, USN (Ret)
Edited by Commander Lee Schonenberg, USN

Many military organizations adhere to the code, "Leave no one behind."

This phrase creates a deep individual commitment among service members, which will, in turn, strengthen the fighting spirit and morale of a unit. It helps to assure families of service members that their loved ones will not be left behind—alive or dead; they will be brought home.

But this code also places a heavy moral burden on a Commanding Officer (CO).

He or she must ask: How many healthy service members will I risk to bring home one wounded service member or a body? This becomes one of the most difficult moral decisions of command—losing an unknown number of lives to uphold the important code, "Leave no one behind."

This case is a peacetime scenario—which probably occurs more frequently than the wartime scenario and has the exact same moral decision at its core.

He was one of those rare naval aviators who was universally admired. In both social and official situations, he always seemed to ask the right question find that balance between friendliness and professionalism. When he walked into the squadron ready-room, people would sit up a little straighter—not because he required it, but because they admired him, and they wanted his respect.

As CO of Helicopter Antisubmarine Squadron NINE (HS-9), Cmdr. James "Fox" Davis, USN, knew his men and women, and he understood his mission. The squadron's many missions included antisubmarine and anti-surface operations, combat search and rescue, and logistics support for the carrier battle group. Their everyday, embedded mission was search and rescue (SAR). As CDR Davis used to say with pride: "On a *good day* we catch a submarine. On a *great day* we save a life." The SAR mission was well-respected in the fleet, not only because the HH-60H "Seahawk" would be there to pick you up out of danger, but also because its aircrew often would selflessly risk their lives to make a dangerous pick-up.

Davis knew the fine line between bravado and professionalism. He instilled in his squadron the importance of following NATOPS (safety of flight rules) and that if you have to take risks, make sure you understand, plan for, and minimize those risks while performing your duty.

HS-9 was three months into a six-month deployment on the carrier, and they had established a superb record with the carrier air wing commander (CAG). The CAG is the commander of all the aircraft squadrons and is responsible for aircraft operations to the battle group commander. The squadron CO worked for the CAG, and although the CAG was an F/A-18 "fighter-jock," he treated his HS skipper with private and public respect. Davis' squadron also was respected by the CAG and battle group staffs not only for getting the job done but also for taking care of their people and even for getting routine administrative paperwork in on time—a trait not all that common among naval aviators.

---

[1] This is a composite case of scenarios based on a true story. The names have been changed so that the decisions made are not attributed to a known officer.

Every Tuesday afternoon at 1330 during the deployment, the squadron skipper held training with his pilots and crews. They would review basic procedures and talk about operational and emergency flight parameters. In aviation terms, they discussed flight "envelopes"—the parameters of safe flight and which of these areas a pilot could trade off in emergency situations of mechanical failure or weather conditions. His pilots felt comfortable enough with their skipper to ask hypothetical questions, such as, "Skipper, what if we were in the situation where. . . ."

In normal flight operations, an HH-60H would be airborne in a "primary search and rescue" position to immediately rescue a downed pilot or man overboard. On this day, they were transiting the North Atlantic and, as was often the case in October, the weather was terrible and unpredictable. Depending on where you were in relation to the land and islands, you could find a sudden change in the weather in both wind speed and wave height.

With winds at 45 knots and waves and swells over 30 feet, all aircraft were either struck down to the hangar bay or tied down on the flight deck. The air boss called Davis and asked him to keep helo (call-sign) Troubleshooter 615 on the flight deck in an "alert 30" launch status, but with double tie-downs and extra straps on the wildly bouncing rotor blades. Davis complied, but he knew that if the helo was needed, it would take quite a bit longer to get it ready.

Fox Davis was in his stateroom trying to do paperwork while the carrier rolled and pitched. On his desk, Davis had a small communications panel with several phones. His squadron duty officer Lt. "Puck" Evans had just reported to him that the alert 30 was set with Troubleshooter 615 and Lt. Cmdr. "Chipper" Morrison as aircraft commander. The alert 60 also was set with Troubleshooter 722 and Lt. "Pigpen" Phillips and his crew.

At that moment, two of Davis' desk phones rang at the same time. Davis was a bit startled, because one call appeared to be coming from the air boss and the other from his squadron ready room. "This can't be good!" he thought.

He answered the call from the air boss first: "Fox, here."

"Fox, we have a confirmed man overboard from the destroyer *USS Mahan*. They have a DR [dead reckoning] plot on his position, five miles from us."

"What are the weather conditions?" Davis asked, as he tried to turn on his closed-circuit TV to see the topside camera picture. He tried all channels but could not get a picture on the screen.

"That's the problem," the air boss said. "We have about zero-zero conditions [visibility] and 45-knot winds and 30-foot swells." (This explained why Davis couldn't get a picture on his closed circuit TV.)

Davis knew he would be asked for a recommendation at the end of this call, so in his mind he began to go through the flight envelopes, helicopter launch and recovery parameters, hypothermia tables (how long a person can survive in this water), and qualifications of his crew. After reviewing those considerations, the image of the sailor in the water trying to survive caused him to quickly say, "Let's launch 615 and reset 722 as an alert 15 standby. I'll assemble the rescue coordination team in CVIC [carrier information center]."

Within seconds, "NOW LAUNCH THE ALERT HELO!" came over the 1MC speakers.

By the time Davis got down the passageway to the ready room, Chipper Morrison, his copilot, hoist operator, and a rescue swimmer in full water survival gear ran past him with flight helmets in hand. Davis didn't want to stop them with a long talk, because he knew they were trying to focus on the rescue mission, and they were well trained—they knew what to do.

Within 12 minutes—18 minutes ahead of schedule—Troubleshooter 615 lifted off the flight deck with almost zero-zero visibility, disappearing into the fog and rain at about 30 feet of altitude. Every second counts. They established radio communication with the *USS Mahan* and were directed to the estimated position of the man in the water. They radioed back that the visibility was about 50 feet, and there was no ceiling. In other words, they could see less than 50 feet around them.

In the calculus of finding a lone sailor in 30-foot waves, high winds, and reduced visibility, the odds for success on this mission were very low, but there was a chance. This mission was well out of safe flight parameters (NATOPS), but a human life was at stake. Davis sent his executive officer to the information center, and he went to the ready room to be with his pilots. In the ready room, time almost stood still as they waited for news from 615. The alert 15 crew of Troubleshooter 722 was standing by in the aircraft, with their 'fingers on the engine start button'. Davis tried to look calm for his squadron pilots, but he knew this mission was at, or beyond, the limit of his crew's and aircrafts capabilities.

He thought to himself, "With these conditions, they are working very hard just to stay out of the water themselves, making finding the man overboard very difficult."

Then the phone in the ready room rang, "Fox, this is the air boss." His voice was steady but very serious. "Mahan says that 615 spotted something in the water, and on the way down to a hover, caught a gust or a large wave, and they believe 615 went in the water. Mahan hasn't heard from them in over two minutes and the helo is not on radar."

This is every squadron commanding officer's nightmare call.

There was a long pause on the phone, as the air boss understood that Davis would need to assess the information. After a few seconds came the inevitable question:

"Skipper, do you want to launch 722 to go after them?"

As Davis focused on this question, all the sounds in the ready room were filtered out by his concentration. Time seemed to stop as he considered what to do. Should he risk another flight crew to save the first crew in the water? Maybe he should "cut his losses" and declare it was unsafe to fly. He knew he was well outside safe flight parameters. He had many people to answer to, including his CAG, his pilots, and their families. CAG certainly would not want to lose another plane or crew. But his squadron pilots certainly would want to make another rescue attempt. His squadron would want to launch every flyable helicopter to save their squadron-mates. (Often, in these situations, the CO is the only one to hold a crew back from a high-risk rescue.) They were trained to save lives, and he knew they would be ready to go in an instant. "What about the families?" he thought. But if I send another crew, and they go down, how will I explain to their families that we flew in these conditions—twice?

All his years of flight training allowed him to stay cool and think calmly under stress. But his flight training never prepared him for this decision. In vivid detail, he thought, "Every second counts for survivability. A perfectly good helicopter went down because of the weather. Will 722 have a better chance, or could they go down too?"

While the air boss waited on the phone for an answer, CDR Fox Davis tried to decide the right thing to do.

Questions for Discussion

1. What are the unknowns that might effect your decision if you had the information? (In real life almost all decisions are made with unknowns.)

2. If you were the CO, in making the decision to launch or not launch the second helo:
   a. What are the major considerations?
   b. Would the people above you (CAG, Strike Group Commander, Navy, NATOPS, USN) want you to (launch or not launch?
   c. Would the people below you want to launch or not launch? (Your pilots, their crews, the squadron, the families of the men in the first helo, in the second helo?)
   d. To which do you have a higher obligation?

3. If you were the decision maker, would you launch the second helo?

4. Is the code "Leave no One Behind" a good code, or does it unnecessarily risk human life?

Incident at Shkin
Captain Bob Schoultz, USN (Ret)

I

Their mission was to confirm or deny the presence of Taliban and/or Al Qaeda leadership and prepare for a potential raid on the compound. The Special Forces had been sent in to observe the compound near the village of Shkin after a predator unmanned aerial vehicle had observed suspicious activity at the compound, flying unseen and unheard for a full day overhead. But the Special Forces, like the predator, were unable to tell just what was happening in the compound. Cpt Smith, the team leader of the Special Forces team on the site, had been able to confirm the presence of what appeared to be Al Qaeda and/or Taliban soldiers, but had not yet seen signs of 'leadership.' They had observed armed patrols leaving the compound, moving around the perimeter and then re-entering the compound. They had also observed other activity indicative of a 'military' presence—an armed sentry inside the compound and at least one gathering of armed men in what appeared to be some type of formation. The roof-mounted microwave antennae and mast-mounted antennae in the compound were other indicators that this was not your standard Afghani farmer's compound, housing a large extended family. So they waited and watched.

Intelligence indicated that this old compound was more than merely another military outpost for Taliban or Al Qaeda; it had the potential of offering up some key Taliban or Al Qaeda leaders. Earlier reports had indicated that it had been used as a meeting place for high-level leadership, and being only seven and a half kilometers from the Pakistani border, it was a very convenient staging area for equipment and men, entering and leaving Afghanistan through Pakistan. At one point, intelligence indicated that Osama bin Laden had been scheduled to meet with his doctor at this compound, but the intelligence was determined to be unreliable. It was clear that the compound was a potentially significant Taliban/Al Qaeda outpost and merited close observation.

II

Early on the night of 13 January, after several days on site, Cpt Smith and his team finally observed something unusual, and reported it immediately. Previous Special Forces Teams observing the target had observed regular vehicular traffic coming into the village of Shkin from the border with Pakistan. On this particular night, they observed headlights of a single vehicle leave the specific compound they had been watching, move to the Pakistani border, and flash its lights. In the clear mountain air, the SF team was able to clearly distinguish the headlights of twelve vehicles return down the steep mountain roads from the border to the vicinity of the compound. Several of the vehicles remained at the compound, while others dispersed to other compounds in and around Shkin. Cpt Smith watched carefully for any other unusual activity. It was difficult; at night and from over 2 kilometers away, they couldn't see much, even with their night vision devices. In this part of Afghanistan, by ten o'clock at night, there was scarcely a light to be seen in the whole region, and this night was no different. Soon after the vehicles arrived in Shkin, Cpt Smith and his men were not able to observe any activity—all was dark.

Unbeknownst to Cpt Smith, his report of this unusual activity had received a lot of attention back at Central Command in Florida, and staff officers at some level decided to take the initiative.

Reprinted by permission of the author.

III

Cpt Smith's boss was a Navy Seal, Captain Hansen, who was in charge of the Joint Special Operations Task Force (JSOTF), located in Qandahar, responsible for Special Operations support to operations in southern Afghanistan. Capt Hansen was aware of the potential importance of Cpt Smith's most recent report, but was surprised when approximately an hour and a half after getting the report from Cpt Smith, he was contacted by Central Command (CENTCOM). His staff was notified that a B1 bomber was enroute with precision guided munitions, with the mission to strike the compound and the concentration of Taliban and Al Qaeda vehicles located there. The bombs were scheduled to be on target in two hours. The CENTCOM planners had asked him and his staff how quickly he could put a team on target after the strike to exploit it for intelligence value.

Capt Hansen quickly got his key staff and commanders together and determined that they could potentially put a team on the target a few hours after the strike. It would be difficult and risky, given the very short notice and the distance between where his forces currently were located and the Shkin compound. He would have to redirect forces already planning or conducting other assigned missions, and they would have little time to plan or prepare. But it could be done. However, as he and his staff discussed this surprising development, they sensed that this mission just didn't make sense. He knew from the reports that there were numerous noncombatants living in the compound, and while he also suspected that the vehicles that Cpt Smith had reported could be very significant, they still didn't know who was in those vehicles or what they were doing. Also, he knew that there was no "large" concentration of vehicles at the Shkin compound as the CENTCOM staffers has indicated. They must have misunderstood the report from the field.

Capt Hansen decided that he needed to talk to someone in authority back at CENTCOM to make sure they knew what they were doing. After his communicators got him the secure connection to Tampa, a sergeant at CENTCOM advised him that the only person of authority in the headquarters at the time was Brigadier General (BG) Jones, and he was not available, being in the middle of an important briefing. Capt Hansen directed the sergeant to interrupt the General and tell him that Capt Hansen urgently needed to speak to him.

Within two minutes, Brigadier General Jones was on the phone. Capt Hansen explained to him what was happening, and shared with him his concerns about the mission that was underway. BG Jones was surprised and was completely unaware of the attack that had just been directed. He agreed with Capt Hansen that this strike was inappropriate given the lack of specific information concerning the target, and said he would take action to cancel it. But, he said, the vehicles that were observed may be very significant. He asked Capt Hansen if he could get his forces into the compound and exploit the potential opportunity. It was certainly possible that someone of importance had arrived that night.

Capt Hansen responded that they had a plan on the shelf for an assault, that they would dust it off and make sure it still fit the circumstances. He believed they could assault the target, capture and/or neutralize any resistance with acceptable risk, but he would have to get back to him. BG Jones then had to break off the conversation, explaining that he had to hurry to cancel the airstrike. The strike was cancelled thirty minutes prior to its scheduled time-on-target. Very soon thereafter, CENTCOM sent the JSOTF an execute order to conduct a raid against the compound as soon as feasible.

When he had been asked to put a team on the compound to exploit the planned airstrike, Capt Hansen had hesitated. Cpt Smith's SF team on site, did not have enough men or firepower. He would have had to divert another team, and they would have had to go into the compound unrehearsed and poorly prepared. It was doable, but very risky.

But an assault against the compound was different from putting a team onto a target that had just been bombed. An assault against an enemy position is always very risky. Capt Hansen decided that he would delay until the following night, while Cpt Smith stayed on target and watched. If Cpt Smith observed anything critical, he could speed up the time line if necessary, but his forces needed the extra 24 hours to reposition troops, put the team together, study the terrain and the intelligence, and make sure they went in ready. By waiting 24 hours, he was risking the possibility of missing any leadership that might have arrived that night, but he significantly reduced the risk to his own forces of executing an inadequately prepared and rehearsed plan.

IV

As the strike plan came together, a total of 60 men and 6 helicopters would assault the target. Prior to the assault, Cpt Smith and his team would move in closer to the target to better observe and report on activity in and around the compound, and would watch and report any threats they might see during the raid. By that night, all was ready. Insertion onto the target was scheduled for 2200. The helicopters departed Qandahar and flew together most of the distance to the compound, and then separated about 10 miles out, to allow each to fly at low level his own separate route, to land simultaneously at each helicopter's designated Helicopter Landing Zone (HLZ) around the compound. As the helicopters approached the compound, three of the helicopters missed their designated HLZ's due in part to a navigational equipment error, and due in part to 'brown outs' from dust raised on approaching their HLZ's, which caused the helicopters to drift several hundred yards while trying to find better landing spots. As a consequence, only one of the six SF Teams was able to achieve the surprise they desired.

Immediately upon landing, this one SF Team exited its helicopter and approached the compound to breach an entry. The twelve men burst into the compound, and immediately encountered numerous hostile personnel who had been awakened by the helicopters and the noise. The OIC verbally took control of this group with a small security element while the rest of his team began clearing the buildings inside the compound. On entering their first building, they had to fight hand-to-hand to control and detain two combative males, who were found with two females and a number of children in a room with posters on the wall of Osama bin Laden, and a large quantity of weapons. They found a wide variety of weapons to include mortars, Rocket Propelled Grenades (RPG), a wide variety of ammunition and a 4X4 vehicle. As they continued searching, they discovered a bunker with a large amount of ammunition and anti-tank mines.

Meanwhile one of the other teams had landed so far away that, after exiting the helicopter, they entered what they thought was an outbuilding of the compound complex, and found themselves in a mosque with one person inside praying. The SF soldiers 'flex-cuffed' this individual with the plastic handcuffs they carry, and left him there, while they reoriented themselves and moved on to the compound. On their way to the compound they saw two people hiding in a ditch sprint away into the darkness and escape. They did not fire and continued moving to the compound.

Finally reaching the compound, almost 10 minutes after the first team had arrived, they breached the closed northern gate and entered, moving immediately to buildings nearest their gate. The door to the first building was locked, and they had to breach their way through it. Inside they found a large box covered with a blanket. They moved immediately into the next room where they encountered seven women and six young children sitting against the far wall of the room. The SF soldiers secured the women and children with flex cuffs and returned to the first room and opened the large box. The box contained a wealth of documents, passports, photos as well as numerous Ak47's, RPG's, mortar tubes with sights, and a collection of old rifles.

Leaving several men to guard the box and the women and children, the SF soldiers continued clearing buildings. They found the door to the next building locked, and as they prepared to breach the door with a shotgun, one of the soldiers noticed through a crack in the door what appeared to be a woman on her knees on the other side of the door, listening. The soldier stopped the breacher from shooting the locking mechanism, which would likely have killed or seriously wounded the woman. Two men were then able to mechanically breach the door—that is, with crow bars and force—and found the woman with a number of children and three men sitting next to a large safe. One of the men was hostile and combative and required one of the SF sergeants to wrestle him into submission, while his fellow assaulters ensured that the other two males remained passive. The safe was found to contain 198,000 Pakistani rupees, two AK47's, four RPG's, and binoculars.

Another of the SF teams had also landed a good distance from the compound, and struggling with the rough terrain in the darkness, approached the compound as quickly as they could. On their way to the compound, they came upon an individual who immediately fled. After yelling and firing a warning shot the individual stopped, was searched and flex-cuffed. As they neared the compound, they came upon an outbuilding and prepared to enter it. Prior to entering a room or building, soldiers frequently throw in a "flash-bang"—a small explosive charge which creates enough light and noise ("flash-bang") to temporarily stun and disable anyone in the room. In the first building they entered, a flash-bang managed to set the building on fire and it burned to the ground, but not before four males ran from the building. Two were able to get away by leaping into a ditch and disappearing into the dark, but two were caught and put up a violent struggle before being subdued.

The SF Team then proceeded to and entered the compound and began clearing buildings that the other SF Teams had not yet cleared. In the first building they entered, they found numerous documents along with weapons, women, children, a young man and an older man. The older man became very combative and had to be subdued.

One thing that surprised the SF soldiers during this mission was that women knew to immediately put their hands together in front of them to be flex-cuffed whenever the soldiers approached them. During previous assaults in Afghanistan, women usually became hysterical upon seeing US soldiers and were frequently combative and resistant. They had been told to expect to be raped by the Americans, and to have their children taken away from them. Apparently the word had quickly circulated within Afghanistan that the US soldiers would not rape nor mistreat women nor their children, but would simply flex-cuff them, which they were more than ready to accept.

Once the compound was secured, the FBI agents who had accompanied the soldiers identified the men they wanted to further interrogate, and hung a chem.-lite around their necks, to distinguish them from those to be left behind. The SF team collected all of the munitions and weapons for the Explosive Ordnance Disposal team to destroy prior to extraction, which they did, resulting in a large explosion. The helicopters were then called back in, and at 2315, a little over an hour after the helicopters had landed to insert the assaulters, they took off, taking with them seven males who the FBI had determined warranted further interrogation.

V

Prior to the assault, Cpt Smith and his team had moved their Observation Point (OP) closer to the compound in order to better provide support to the raid. After the assault, Cpt Smith and a small number of his men were directed to stay behind to continue to watch the site for any further developments. The day after the assault, as they watched the locals carefully approach the compound to investigate the events of the night before, they saw one group of what appeared to be local farmers head into the hills in their direction. As they passed within one hundred meters of their position, the locals spotted the OP and approached. The locals were clearly agitated and began gesturing angrily and aggressively, signaling that they wanted the SF soldiers to leave. Cpt Smith then had one of his snipers stand up and point his weapon at the approaching men, which had the intended effect; they calmed down, became more conciliatory and approached the position in a friendly manner. Ever watchful and suspicious, Cpt Smith had one of his sergeants who spoke Arabic try to talk to them. No dialogue or communication was possible, since these Afghanis did not speak Arabic. As the farmers left, Cpt Smith reported the contact to higher headquarters. A short while later, as he and his men were preparing to move their OP, they observed the farmers returning; they had brought with them one of the village elders who spoke Arabic. He had come to bargain, offering to house, feed, and provide water to the men in the OP, if they promised to never bomb his village. Later that night, Cpt Smith and the rest of his men were extracted by helicopter back to the headquarters.

VI

The post operation analysis indicated that the operation against the compound at Shkin was an intelligence coup. Though the operation had not captured key Taliban or Al Qaeda leadership, the prisoners and documents that they did capture proved of great value for later operations.

Questions for Discussion

1. Did Capt Hansen have a moral or legal obligation to contact CENTCOM and inquire about the planned strike?

2. Should he have been held accountable had he not made that effort?

3. Did CENTCOM assume too much risk in choosing to put ground forces against this target instead of bombs? What could have gone wrong? Why did they choose to assume this risk?

4. If the B1 had not been stopped and the compound had been bombed, would this have been a war crime? Why or why not?

5. If it were later determined later that Osama bin Laden had been in the vehicles coming from the border, and been at the compound on the night of the scheduled strike, would you still agree with the decision to cancel the strike? What about Capt Hansen's decision to wait 24 hours to conduct the raid?

6. The SF soldiers had many opportunities to shoot to kill. Why were they reluctant to do so? Did they assume too much risk?

7. What were the advantages of conducting this operation the way it was conducted? What were the disadvantages? What were the risks?

Rescuing the Boat People[1]

Captain Rick Rubel

Lt. David Soleski moved his sunglasses out of the way, so he could look through his binoculars. As he looked at "Skunk Charlie-Delta" (surface contact) he mumbled out loud to his Junior Officer of the Deck (JOOD), "Looks like another junk going nowhere, fast." Lt Soleski was the Officer of the deck of the U.S. Navy Austin Class Amphibious Transport Dock (LPD). As officer of the deck, he was the Captain's watch officer on the bridge responsible for the operation and safety of the ship. At this moment, they were transiting the South China Sea, near Singapore, one of the busiest seaways in the world. The Navy indexes their surface contacts by starting with "A" each morning and going through the alphabet, and they were already up to C-D, and it was only 1420. The OOD was doing his best to weave in and out of the surface traffic, trying to keep all shipping more that 4000 yards away from his warship.

The Junior Officer of the Deck, Ensign Davis, answered Lt Soleski, "Sir, CIC has this guy, skunk Charlie-Delta, with no zero speed, currently at 6000 yards."

"Very well." Said the OOD, and he continued to watch.

As the contact got closer the two officers observed a large number of people in the boat, standing and waving at the ship. They were not waving greetings, but were quite frantic, and appeared to waving pieces of white cloth or material. Lt Soleski was hoping he could keep skunk C-D more that 4000 yards away from the ship so he didn't have to notify the Captain, who was down in his cabin. "It'll be close to 4000 yards CPA (closest point of approach)," he told his JOOD. As the boat approached 4500 yards from them, and as both officers were still looking through their binoculars, they were both startled, and both said out loud at the same time, "Did you see that? It looked like one of them jumped in the water!"

The OOD reached for his phone, "Captain, this is Lt Soleski, Officer of the Deck. I have a contact off the port bow, bearing 220 degrees true, at 4500 yards, with zero speed. It appears to be a junk with a lot of people waving." The Captain didn't see the problem with that description and said, "Ok, proceed on your course and speed." The OOD then quickly added, "Sir, they are waving frantically at us, and we think we just saw one of the people jump into the water." After a short pause, the Captain, said, "I'll be right up to the bridge."

As the Captain walked from his Cabin to the bridge, a trip he could make with his eyes closed, he huffed under his breath, "We don't have time for this." The ship was transiting from its homeport of Sasebo, Japan to Bahrain. They had been assigned an important operation to assume the flagship for minesweeping operations in the Persian Gulf. Two months prior, USS Roberts had been struck with a mine, so minesweeping operations were a high priority. Also, they were carrying 900 Marines to the Gulf, including a Force Recon Team. They were slightly behind PIM (planned intended motion) but should be able to catch up over the next few days.

---

[1]This case is based on the story of Capt Al Balian, Commanding Officer, USS Dubuque (LPD-8). The sources of the case are from: "Rescuing the Boat People" case written by Paul E. Roush, CBS *60 Minutes* interview of Capt Balian by Diane Sawyer, and NROTC Holy Cross University case "The BOLINAO Affair: A Case Study of USS Dubuque (LPD-8)." The story-line in the case is added for narrative.

"The Captain's on the Bridge!" announced the Quartermaster of the Watch, as required, when the C.O. arrived a little out of breathe after climbing two sets of ladders. On his chest he wore several Viet Nam Campaign ribbons, a Silver Star, and a Purple Heart. He was familiar with this situation since he had rescued refugees twice before.

"What do you have, Dave?" he asked the OOD.

"Sir, we have this Chinese-type junk at about 3800 yards, and we think we saw someone jump into the water." The messenger of the watch handed the C.O. his binoculars without being asked. "Let's get closer to them and slow down."

"Aye, sir. Left standard rudder, make turns for 10 knots." the OOD ordered the helmsmen, and lee helm.

As the ship pulled within 500 yards of the junk and stopped, the waving became more frantic, and visibly, about a dozen more people jumped into the water. As the swimming refugees slowly worked their way towards the ship, a great deal of activity began on the ship as sailors grabbed lifejackets to prepare to throw to the swimmers as they got closer. As they watched the swimmers get tired and flounder, it was hard to tell if any of them went under the waves. When the swimmers reached 100 yards or so from the ship life jackets started to be thrown in the water. The Captain asked, "Who said to throw life jackets in the water? That'll just encourage more of them to jump in the water." The OOD took that to mean stop throwing life jackets, so he put out that word.

The Captain then picked up the 1MC and ordered, "Don't let the refugees aboard the ship." The crew then began to stop some of the refugee swimmers from boarding the ship, by pulling in the lines that were in the water.

The Captain noticed, "They look Vietnamese. Have ICFN Phan come to the bridge." Seaman Phan spoke Vietnamese, so when he arrived on the bridge the Captain gave him the 1MC (topside) microphone and said, "Tell them not to board our ship, and to go back to their own boat." The Seaman translated the captain's orders, but it came out very choppy as he struggled to find the words from his childhood.

The Captain then told the OOD to have the XO and Operations officer come to the bridge. He told the XO to put a small team together in the ship's Motor Whale Boat (MWB), along with Phan, and to go over to the check out the junk. "Do not board the junk. We don't know what's going on there, and I don't want to put anyone at risk. Take a grunt with you for small arms protection."

The Operations Officer reported to the Captain, and was asked to summarize the standing orders from higher authority that govern this situation. The OPS Officer ran down below and came back within a few minutes with a summary of the OPORDERS and regulations:

1. *U.S. Navy Regulation 0925.* "A Commanding Officer must render assistance to any person found at sea in danger of being lost."

2. *COMSEVENTHFLT OPORDER 201.* "The natural inclination of mariners, the customs and traditions of the sea, and reference (a) [Navy Regulations] require U.S. Navy ships to render aid to vessels and persons found in distress. In those instances wherein relief of persons in life endangering circumstances cannot be accomplished; by repair to boats, reprovisioning or navigational assistance, rescue is normally by means of embarkation."

3. *CINCPACFLT OPORDER 201.* "If refugees encountered at sea are experiencing, or are apt to experience undue hardship or if circumstances (*e.g.* adverse weather, pirates in vicinity, unseaworthy vessel, etc.) are such that death may ensue, refugees may be embarked."

Although events were moving slowly, things were becoming a bit chaotic. It took about 20 mins to get the team together and launch the MWB. A few minutes after the MWB left the side of the ship the XO reported back on the radio, "Captain, it looks like they have a make-shift sail about 5 feet by 6 feet and we have asked them several times, and they say they don't have an engine. The boat seems seaworthy, it only has a slight list to starboard. And I think that's because all the refugees are on the same side, and is trimmed (fore and aft) about right. There are about 60 people on the boat, including women and children. The people look a bit emaciated and are pretty desperate looking. To be honest, sir,

Seaman Phan is struggling with their dialect and we have to ask everything several times, and may get a different answer each time we ask the same question. They left Viet Nam 7 days ago, heading for the Philippines. Also, about 20 people have died so far on the trip. Over"

The Captain asked through his radio, "Do you see any bodies in the water?"

"I don't see any, sir." as the XO looked around.

The Captain had seen this before; refugees risking everything to leave their country. He thought to himself about what he should do. The instructions that Ops provided were not completely definitive, and since the boat seemed seaworthy, maybe he was not required to embark them. He has orders to transit for an important mission in Bahrain. If he spent much more time with this junk, he would be endangering his mission. If he picked up the refugees and embarked them, he could be endangering his crew, with unknown diseases, and security concerns. And with a MAG of Marines onboard there was no extra space. Also, if he picked them up, he would have to find a country to accept them, and that is not an easy diplomatic problem to solve without a lot of time.

On the other had, he was concerned about the report that 20 of them had already died. He reasoned that they had traveled over 250 miles in seven days, they should be able to go the remaining 200 miles in about the same amount of time. So, maybe if he gave them provisions, they would be fine.

The reader knows what the Captain knew at the time.

1. List the information you know for sure.
2. List what you can infer from the facts in #1.

If you were the Captain:

3. What are your options?
4. What are your primary, secondary, and tertiary considerations?
5. What would you do?

1) makeshift boat of 60 people, 20 have died. Small sail. Required to embark people who maybe @ risk. Travel time. Risk and hardship of bringing them obeard. Diplomatic Issue. Important mission @ hand.

2) These people are refugees fleeing Vietnam. They have little provisions and more of them will die if they dont help them. They could not reach land @ all.

3) - Leave them
   - Provide Provisions to continue on
   - Take them back to the ship

4) 1) the mission in Bahrain
   2) Safety of Crew
   3) safety + welfare of the refugees

5) Quarantine the boat people on the ship and negotiate with nearby countries to host them

Interdiction in Afghanistan
Captain Bob Schoultz

I

It was 2000 hours, March 2002 in the Joint Special Operations Task Force (JSOTF) headquarters in Afghanistan, and LCDR Reynolds had just returned from the chow tent where he had lingered talking with some of the other officers on the JSOTF staff. LCDR Reynolds was a Seal officer in charge of the Seals assigned to the JSOTF conducting Special Operations during Operation Enduring Freedom. Upon returning to the headquarters building to catch up on paper work and review intelligence reports, he was summoned by the JSOTF Operations Officer, LTC Thompson, who wanted to talk to him about a mission they had just received.

LTC Thompson handed LCDR Reynolds an intelligence report and a copy of an email that had just arrived from the Operations Officer of the Land Forces Component Commander (LFCC). The email directed the JSOTF Commander to provide a concept of operations for interdicting a vehicle convoy of Al Qaeda and Taliban terrorists that was expected to be moving down a road about 70 miles to the south the next morning sometime after 0730, apparently trying to escape Afghanistan into Pakistan. It was believed that the convoy might include some key Taliban or Al Qaeda leadership. The LFCC wanted the mission concept in two hours. This meant essentially that the staff wanted to know if the JSOTF thought they could undertake the mission, what support they would need, and whether their plan could be deconflicted with other ongoing missions. LTC Thompson had already contacted MAJ Mark Wyatt, the XO of the Army H47 Helicopter squadron who would be over momentarily to look at the mission with LCDR Reynolds and his men. The mission was to interdict the convoy, and to capture if possible or kill if necessary any suspected members of Al Qaeda or Taliban who they might encounter.

II

LCDR Reynolds knew he had limited time to plan, rehearse, and go over contingencies with his team. Tight time-lines had become standard, but they were all fully aware of the increased risk they assumed when they had less time to prepare. A tight time-line meant less time to consider and plan for the numerous 'what ifs,' to carefully check the intelligence, and make sure that everyone knew the plan and its various 'branches and sequels.' A recent tragedy could at least in part be attributed to a very abbreviated planning and rehearsal timeline. In a high risk, high stakes operation, a Seal reconnaissance team had been ambushed on insertion by Al Qaeda forces who had been undetected during the pre-mission reconnaissance. The team had been surprised, and two of their friends and teammates had been killed as well as a number of rangers, under the relentless fire of the enemy. The deaths of these teammates were fresh in the minds of his men, and had only steeled their resolve to do whatever it took to find and kill these terrorists. But the enemy was not to be underestimated—LCDR Reynolds and his men knew that their planning must be thorough, and in quick reaction, emergent missions, they always had to weigh the trade-off between the opportunities presented by late-breaking intelligence, and the increased risk of a short planning cycle.

Reprinted by permission of the author. This case study is a fictionalized account based on an incident that actually happened. Some details have been modified, but the key portions of the incident happened as described.

The risks to rapid and short-fused planning, however, had taken an ugly twist two days earlier, when LCDR Reynolds and his team had seen first hand the tragic but unintended consequences that can come from fast-paced operations and decisions made with incomplete or inadequate intelligence. Several days earlier overhead surveillance had seen armed men around a walled compound and corroborating intelligence had indicated that a this compound would be used for a meeting of high level Taliban officials. A precision guided missile was launched and struck the main building of the compound during the window when the meeting was scheduled to take place. LCDR Reynolds and his men had been staged to go into the compound minutes after the missile struck to gather any intelligence that remained, capture and treat any wounded, and to determine whether any of the dead or wounded were key Taliban or Al Quada leaders. When they arrived, they found the dead on target had been non-combatants—farmers and their families who were living in the compound. The weapons that were found were personal fire arms that virtually all rural Afghanis possessed and carried for self protection. LCDR Reynolds and his men were shaken by the gruesome results of this miscalculation: elderly people, farmers, women, children, with no apparent connection to the enemy. After determining that there was no exploitable intelligence on the target, he and his men returned to base and reported to his superiors what had happened including his dismay at the mistake. He then refocused his efforts on being ready for his next mission. Part of preparing for the next mission involved dealing with the psychic effects of this one; he contacted the chaplain, told him what had happened, and asked him to talk to the men. Afterward, he knew that having the chaplain meet with them had made a difference, to some of the men more than others, but it felt like the right thing to have done after witnessing, and in a sense participating in the tragic consequences of a mistake in war.

III

After receiving the mission to interdict the convoy from LTC Thompson, LCDR Reynolds knew what to do and started going into his mission planning routine, which had become almost automatic. He was the mission commander, and MAJ Wyatt and the H47s would be under his tactical command. This was just like the seemingly hundreds of exercises he'd conducted, and similar to many of the missions he'd recently conducted during this war. The years of training were paying off. His team was gelling into the type of unit he and every other military officer wants to lead: they only needed to be pointed in the right direction, with a good mission concept and clear commander's intent, and then the plan and preparation just seemed to come together. If everything went as planned and as rehearsed, his role in the execution of the operation would be minimal—communicate with higher headquarters and keep the squad leaders informed about any new developments, and let the squad leaders execute the plan. But of course, nothing ever goes exactly as planned, and it would be his job to make immediate adjustments to whatever unforeseen circumstances they would find, and understand the ripple effect that changes to the plan inevitably caused. That was what he got paid for.

Intelligence indicated that ongoing allied operations were putting significant pressure on Al Qaeda and Taliban forces in Southeast Afghanistan. This increasing pressure was making local Al Qaeda and Taliban movement and operations more and more difficult. Allied forces had received an intelligence tip that some senior leaders, with a group of their armed supporters, would be attempting to escape into Pakistan by vehicle soon after first light the following day. The enemy had already realized that allied aircraft routinely and easily targeted vehicles moving at night; consequently, the terrorists were now seeking to blend in with the normal daylight traffic on the roads. It appeared that Taliban and Al Qaeda were having some success in escaping into Pakistan blending in with the stream of refugees coming out of Afghanistan.

The intelligence indicated that a convoy of three vehicles would be leaving a particular village the next morning and moving toward Pakistan. The vehicles would be SUV's of the Toyota Land Cruiser type and/or compact pick up trucks full of people traveling south on the one road leading to Pakistan. Intelligence sources indicated that normally, the terrorists put their heavily armed men in lead vehicles as an armed reconnaissance element, while the leadership with their personal armed guards would follow some distance behind, maintaining communications with the lead vehicles about any difficulties encountered. Also, and particularly worrisome, were the indicators that the terrorists were probably carrying "Man-portable Air Defense Systems" (MANPADS), specifically, Soviet-era SA-7 shoulder-fired missiles, which are particularly effective against helicopters, especially during daylight when helicopters can easily be seen.

In short order, his men had worked out a plan with Maj Wyatt and his team. Also the intelligence planners had coordinated with the assigned overhead surveillance; Navy P-3 aircraft would be watching the road and it would be their mission to find and track the targeted vehicles. A very difficult part of the mission was to 'interdict' the convoy in such a way as to achieve complete surprise, while still offering the opportunity for the occupants of the vehicles to surrender without putting his own men at risk. "Capture if possible, kill if necessary" is always tricky, and frequently requires a split second decision, some clear indicator of hostile intent, but also an intuitive sense of threat. But capturing the occupants would be a great coup; he and his men knew that the key to unraveling the terrorist network in Afghanistan was intelligence, and the people in this convoy represented a potential gold mine of intelligence. The Seals would capture them if they could, but if the terrorists resisted with lethal force, as they usually seemed to do, then the Seals were to shoot to kill.

IV

LCDR Reynolds went to see Col Smith, the JSOTF commander to discuss his perspective or any limitations he might have for this mission. With the tragedy of the mission a couple of days previously still on his mind, LCDR Reynolds also wanted to know how certain they were of the intelligence, and whether the rules of engagement had changed. The rules of engagement define the circumstances under which lethal force can be used, and what are the restrictions in the use of that force. Col Smith replied that he understood the intelligence to be quite reliable and the rules of engagement hadn't changed. If the vehicles they encounter demonstrate hostile intent, by displaying or firing weapons, they are legitimate targets. Col Smith believed that the reason higher headquarters wanted the JSOTF to send helos and Seals to do this mission, rather than targeting them from a distance, was because of the desire not to repeat the mistake of two days ago, with which LCDR Reynolds was only too familiar. That said, he reminded LCDR Reynolds that his tactics had to take into account the desire to bring back prisoners if at all possible, while not taking undue risk. In other words, bring back prisoners if you can, but not if it means taking significant risks with the lives of any of your men. Col Smith reiterated to LCDR Reynolds that the rules of engagement gave him all the guidance he needed.

That was what LCDR Reynolds wanted to hear. He felt the rules of engagement as they stood made sense, and gave him and his team the latitude to exercise their professional judgment to complete the mission and stay alive. Rapid assessment of hostile intent in a fast moving tactical environment is a standing requirement, and they had rehearsed and talked through a wide variety of situations many times. He and his men knew the value of prisoners, but they also knew the value of aggressiveness and firepower to staying alive in a gunfight. Their tactics, their survival, and their mission success depended on "Surprise, Speed, and Violence of Action"—there was no room for timidity. Yet they had recently witnessed the tragic results of "Surprise, Speed and Violence of Action" exercised without good judgment—in other words, aggressiveness and firepower misapplied.

V

The plan came together quickly—it had to. MAJ Mark Wyatt would be the lead helo pilot for this mission LCDR Reynolds would be in his helo. There would be a total of three helos, referred to as chalk one (with MAJ Wyatt and LCDR Reynolds), and chalks two and three which would carry the rest of the Seals, led by LCDR Reynolds' Assistant Officer in Charge and Platoon Chief respectively. They talked through the contingencies with the pilots and went over the map, and had the intel guys coordinate with the P3's doing the overhead surveillance.

The plan was submitted and quickly approved. The plan was simple and made sense, and at any rate, there was little time to debate it. Their plan had them taking off at 0645 the next morning and flying to a point near the road where they would loiter at a low altitude, visually and audibly sheltered from the road by the mountains, and wait for a cue from the P3 watching the road. When the P3 saw what appeared to be the convoy, it would notify the helos, and vector them to the vehicles on the road. The helos would then move in under the cover of the mountains and surprise the convoy, quickly determine whether to take the vehicles under fire, or if in doubt, land and put the Seals on the ground, and let the Seals make the final determination. The helos would be available to provide cover fire or extraction, as required.

Everyone was very aware of the threat of shoulder fired SA-7's, to which the helos were very vulnerable. An SA-7 missile, in the hands of a reasonably proficient operator, could spell disaster. In daylight however, helos are also easy prey and vulnerable to small arms fire, and bullets from an AK47 can puncture the skin of their aircraft killing and wounding pilots and passengers. A couple of lucky shots from an AK47 can also bring down a helo and kill everyone on board. As the events in Mogadishu and "Blackhawk Down" had made clear, being in a low-flying helo, near the enemy in daylight is very risky business.

VI

Early the next morning, all went as planned. LCDR Reynolds even got a couple of hours of sleep prior to his meeting at 0530 with his squad leaders and the helo pilots, to go over the plan and review details, one final time prior to launch. The Seals embarked the three H47's, and after all systems checked out and the pilots had established communications with the P3, they took off and headed for the designated loiter point. After about an 40 minutes of flight time, they arrived at the loiter point, again checked in with the P3 and began flying in low slow circles, far enough away from the road so as not to be heard, yet close enough to respond quickly when called by the P3.

LCDR Reynolds had been through this drill many times before. Sitting in the helo, with the headset on, partially listening to the relaxed banter of the pilots, he was lost in his own thoughts with the muffled hum and shake of the helo in the background of his awareness. Waiting for the call. Waiting. He mentally walked through the plan for the operation and its various contingencies; how they would make their approach to the convoy, how quickly they would have to determine threat level and response. How far back would the trail vehicle be with the so-called leaders? Would they stumble upon one of the key leaders of the Taliban or Al Qaeda? Did they really have SA-7's?

He pushed from his mind what would happen if the bad guys could get off a shot at the helos with an SA-7 before they could be neutralized. Worrying about it wouldn't do anything. He knew the pilots were very concerned as well; they had discussed it during the planning. But LCDR Reynolds also knew they had a lot going for them on this op—the confidence and skill that comes from extensive training and lots of experience. Surprise, Speed, Violence of Action—their keys to survival, the keys to success.

Approximately 20 minutes after arriving at the loitering point, LCDR Reynolds heard on the head set that the P3 had spotted what appeared to be the target convoy: two pickup trucks traveling together, followed about a mile back by another pick up truck. It would be about 20 minutes before the vehicles reached that section of the road where LCDR Reynolds and the helo pilots had determined that the terrain gave them the greatest advantage for surprise, and the bad guys the least opportunities for escape, on vehicle or on foot. After discussing it briefly with MAJ Wyatt, LCDR Reynolds advised the Seal Leading Petty Officer (LPO) in his helo what he had just heard, and the LPO alerted the rest of the Seals. The Seals then seemed to come alive. Up to that point, they had been sitting in the back with their eyes closed, some probably dozing lightly, some probably rehearsing the mission in their heads, some probably thinking of things completely unrelated to this operation. But now all the men were alert and focused, checking their gear one more time, adjusting their position to be better prepared to exit the helo in a hurry.

MAJ Wyatt continued to get information from the P3. The convoy was continuing down the road toward the interdiction point. After about 10 minutes, the P3 crew advised MAJ Wyatt that it was time to leave the loiter position and begin moving toward the road. LCDR Reynolds advised his LPO and the LPO passed it on to the men in the helo.

As the helos approached the interdiction point, they stayed very low to the ground, flying at about 50 feet, to minimize the chances that the "wop, wop, wop" of their approach would get over the mountains and alert the convoy. At about 2 minutes out, the P3 passed on some disturbing news. "We've lost the trail vehicle. We haven't seen it for several minutes—last we saw it was about 3 miles back. It might be masked by the mountains between us and them. But two vehicles are on final into your target zone and will be there in a couple of minutes."

"Damn!" LCDR Reynolds thought. Quick decision time. The plan had been for him and MAJ Wyatt to break off from chalks two and three in the last twenty seconds, and to go to the trail vehicle, to permit a simultaneous hit on the lead and trail vehicles. He was going to the trail vehicle, because that was where the real valuable targets would be—the leaders. LCDR Reynolds quickly considered the possibility of his helo flying thru the mountains searching for the trail vehicle while chalks one and two were taking care of the lead vehicles. There was no telling where that vehicle could be or what it could be doing. Even though the primary target was the leadership in the trail vehicle, with this new uncertainty, LCDR Reynolds did not want to take off on a potential wild goose chase, splitting his force, now that the plan may be coming unraveled at the last minute.

He told MAJ Wyatt he wanted to keep all three helos together until they had a better idea what they were up against. Or at least until the P3 found the third vehicle. MAJ Wyatt concurred and told the chalks one and two that the plan had changed and that they would stay together and all hit the lead vehicles. They then started their climb up and over the final hill that lay between them and the road, and presumably the two lead vehicles. LCDR Reynolds ensured that the word was passed to the Seals in chalks two and three. Everyone in the helos was on full alert, the pilots and crew calmly passing information back and forth, the Seals on their feet, looking out the windows, weapons at the ready, on safe.

VII

As they popped over the summit of the hill, they saw about a five hundred feet below them and to the left, two pick up trucks approaching from the north. LCDR Reynolds suddenly experienced that familiar jolt of adrenaline, a combination of stress, excitement, responsibility and complete focus. The helos came over the crest of the hill and headed down low and fast, directly toward the vehicles, approaching at full speed, circling from left to right, counter-clockwise. LCDR Reynolds stared intently at the occupants in the back of the pick up truck, looking for any sign of hostile intent. First the front vehicle, and then the rear vehicle stopped when they saw and heard the helos, and he saw men get out and begin running. Then LCDR Reynolds thought he saw weapons and muzzle flashes. LCDR Reynolds was looking over the shoulder of the left door gunner, who also saw the weapons and muzzle flashes, and immediately opened up on the lead vehicle with his mini gun, shifting to the second vehicle as soon as he could get a good shot at it. At about that time, the second helo picked up the lead vehicle and started cutting it to pieces. LCDR Reynolds saw more muzzle flashes and then saw men fall. No sign of anyone setting up to fire an SA-7. The helos passed the vehicles flying fast and low and putting out a huge volume of fire. The two pick up trucks were being cut to pieces, and men who had not been able to get out of the vehicles in time were being chewed up as well. Those who had left the trucks were scrambling in chaos and disorder, some firing at the helos, several of them falling victim to the withering fire coming from the door gunners. LCDR Reynolds saw that this part was going well. Now, where was the trail vehicle with the leadership?

As his helo was turning to circle the vehicles and make an approach from the other side, LCDR Reynolds felt that chalks two and three could handle this. He said to MAJ Wyatt on the headset, "Mark, I think they've got this under control. Let's go find the trail vehicle. What do you think?" "Roger," he responded. " I'll advise chalk two to take control here," at which point he pulled up out of the pattern and told the pilot of chalk two that he and LCDR Reynolds were detaching to go look for the other vehicle. The P3 had just called to tell them that they still had no sign of the third vehicle. MAJ Wyatt told the P3 what he was doing, and then he turned and headed up the road down which they had seen the two vehicles coming.

VIII

LCDR Reynolds called his LPO up to him, took off his head set, and yelled over noise of the helo to tell him what they were doing. The LPO nodded and then went to the back of the helo to tell the other Seals who, still very tense and focused, were looking toward him with some anticipation. They knew that something was up. LCDR Reynolds then moved to the door gunner on the right side of the aircraft, since the helo was flying with the road on the right side. The longer it took to find the vehicle, the greater the risk. They had to assume that the trail vehicle had heard the helos and the gunfire, and perhaps even had radio communication from the lead vehicles. That gave the bad guys plenty of time to set up on the helo—they would certainly be expecting them. These were the leaders, and they would have the most devoted soldiers with them as bodyguards, and probably the best weapons, possibly to include SA-7's. Helos are big, easy targets in daylight, especially if you know that they are coming. The right door gunner had not expended any ammunition on the assault on the other two vehicles—he was keyed up, ready, and had a full load of ammo.

As the H47 flew down the narrow valley that hugged the road, there was an intense and anxious silence on the headsets. The pilots, crew and LCDR Reynolds knew that this was where they were most vulnerable. Though they may not achieve complete surprise, they hoped to overwhelm the bad guys by hitting them suddenly and with overwhelming firepower. But they had to be lucky and good.

As the H47 turned a corner in the valley, they looked up a narrow canyon. LCDR Reynolds saw the pick up truck just as he heard MAJ Wyatt calmly say, "There they are." What looked like a truck full of people was stopped on the side of the road about 200 yards ahead to the right. The door gunner had a clear shot, and he quickly swung his mini-gun and took aim.

IX

LCDR Reynolds suddenly sensed something wasn't right. Just as the truck came into view, just as the door gunner swung his weapon in the direction of the truck, just as MAJ Wyatt said, "There they are," LCDR Reynolds in an instant realized that no one was running from the vehicle, and he thought he saw someone in the truck (a woman?) hold something up high as if to display it to the helo. He grabbed the door gunner and yelled "NO!" and held his fist in front of the door gunner's face in the signal for "Stop what you're doing!" The door gunner was confused, but he followed the order and didn't shoot. The helo continued toward the truck, low and fast as LCDR Reynolds looked hard at the truck, looking for signs of hostile intent. In the two long seconds it took to get to and pass the truck, they noticed that this was different from the other vehicles. No one left the truck. No one ran for cover. It was hard to tell whether these people were armed or not, given the speed and approach angle of the helo. The helo sped past the truck so close that the people in the bed of the truck were ducking from the rotor wash, and LCDR Reynolds saw that he had been right—it had been a woman he'd seen, and what she was holding up appeared to be a baby. He didn't see any weapons yet or anyone displaying hostile intent. That didn't mean they weren't bad guys, and that they weren't a threat. LCDR Reynolds told MAJ Wyatt to circle around and land in front of the vehicle, far enough away to be safe, but close enough for the Seals to quickly envelope the vehicles, clarify the situation, and take appropriate action.

After speeding by the vehicle, MAJ Wyatt exhaled. When he didn't hear the door gunner firing, he thought the weapon had jammed and that they were 'done for'. He flew the H47 at full throttle farther down the road, banked around a bend in the road, and then ascended to fly over a hill to come back to a position several hundred yards in front of the vehicle. He was ever mindful of the possibility that an SA-7 was being prepared for the first clear shot. LCDR Reynolds dashed back to his LPO and told him that the Seals would debark and move in to observe the vehicle—it wasn't clear if these were hostiles. He then moved back to the front of the helo so that he could get oriented prior to landing.

The helo flared and landed fast. The Seals quickly debarked out the rear ramp and moved to outside the rotor-wash to set up a hasty perimeter in the nearest cover. The H47 lifted off the ground, turned 180 degrees away from the direction of the vehicle, and took off. The Seals patrolled to the vicinity of the pick up truck and observed the passengers not moving, sensing their danger. The LCDR Reynolds was able to signal to the passengers to move away from the pick up truck. He then had his team search the pickup truck and its passengers, and determined that they were not Taliban nor Al Qaeda leadership, nor was there any evidence that they had any connection to them. Either the intel had been wrong about the three-vehicle convoy, or the situation had changed since the source had reported it. It didn't matter. These people did not fit the profile of Taliban or Al Qaeda and happened to be in the wrong place at the wrong time.

LCDR Reynolds realized that he had narrowly avoided making a tragic mistake. He was still worried about a possible trail vehicle, and called MAJ Wyatt to ask him if he had any other information. MAJ Wyatt had been in touch with the P3, and had gone to altitude himself to see if he could see any other vehicles, and there was nothing. LCDR Reynolds then got on the radio with the Seals who were on the ground at the site of the two lead vehicles. They had already debarked the helos, taken control of the site with no resistance, and they were inspecting the dead and wounded. All were males and had been carrying arms. Eight were dead, the three wounded were being treated, and they had taken two unscathed prisoners, who had survived the initial assault, and had stood with their hands raised when the Seals approached. This was all good news.

LCDR Reynolds then had his LPO direct the civilians to sit down and to remain where they were. They were still sitting on the ground away from their pick up truck when the Seals were picked up by the helo and flown to join their teammates at the site of the two lead vehicles.

Part C:

Col Smith, the JSOTF Commander had heard that his helo pilots believed that LCDR Tom Reynolds had taken undue risk during an operation from which they had just returned, and that this was causing some tension between the Seals and Army helo crews. Col Smith had heard what had happened and was familiar with the events of the operation, but knew he needed to get the story directly from his two commanders. He called MAJ Wyatt and LCDR Reynolds into his office to get the issues out on the table.

LCDR Reynolds and MAJ Wyatt walked into his office, and after Col Smith indicated that he understood that there was some disagreement about how the operation had been conducted, MAJ Wyatt, clearly emotional, addressed the issue right up front:

"Sir, we could have all been killed, and lost the bird. We were a sitting duck. We're real lucky Tom was right, because if he'd been wrong, we would have a lot of dead Americans and this war would look a lot different right now." MAJ Mark Wyatt stepped back and exhaled slowly.

Col Smith looked at LCDR Reynolds and indicated it was his turn to speak.

"Sir, he's right—we could have all been killed—if I'd been wrong. But I wasn't. I was in charge. And I was right. I made the call based on what I saw, and what I sensed, and I stand by it. It was clearly the right thing to do. We knew we were at risk, but we still have to do the right thing."

Mark Wyatt jumped on him. "Right Tom, but all the indicators were there that these were bad guys, and you didn't KNOW, and my guys and yours were sitting ducks for several seconds, and that put not only all of us, but potentially the whole focus of everything we're doing here at risk. Can you imagine what this task force would be doing right now if those had been bad guys we had taken an SA-7 right down the throat? I don't want to kill innocent people either, but if you had been wrong, nobody, I mean NOBODY, would forgive you. And we'd all be dead."

"Mark—it just didn't feel right—and, we saw no hostile intent."

"We didn't have time to see hostile intent, Tom! When we took off after that third vehicle, my understanding was that we were going hunting. We knew we had flushed the bad guys, and at that point, we were in a gunfight. When we came around that bend in the road, it was either them, or us. When you stopped my gunner, and I didn't hear the guns, I figured it was us. I expected a flash and woosh and then lights out."

"You two calm down and come back and see me when you get your stuff squared away," interrupted Col Smith. He knew that he was the one who had to take responsibility for risk, and if there was something unclear about risk, he needed to resolve it. "I'm going to have to think about this, and talk to the lawyers. Now get out of here and get some rest. We've got a bunch of other things hopping and we'll need you to be focused."

MAJ Wyatt and LCDR Reynolds left the Colonel's office and agreed to get together in a couple of hours after they had taken care of their men and their gear, and sorted out the other details from their mission. MAJ Wyatt was clearly still upset as he walked away to rejoin the other pilots preparing their reports.

As LCDR Tom Reynolds walked back to where his men were working, he thought about what his friend Mark Wyatt had said. He had gambled and won, but he had bet the whole farm—not just his farm, but the lives of everyone else in the helo, as well as the future capability of the Special Operations Task Force.

Questions for Discussion

1. List the all points in the case when a decision was made whether to fire, or not fire.

2. What was each of these decisions base on?

3. How does an officer weight the risk to his/her people versus the risk to non-combatants?

4. How important do you believe was LCDR Reynolds' experience at the compound several days prior to this mission in his decision not to fire? Do you think he would have made the same decision had he not had that experience?

5. Did the attack on the compound violate the Laws of Armed Conflict principles of discrimination and proportionality? Would an attack on the third vehicle, had it occurred, been a violation of these same principles?

6. Did LCDR Reynolds' decision show exceptionally good judgment, was it an obvious call, or was he just lucky?

7. Should LCDR Reynolds be praised for his decision? Are there any dangers to giving too much positive recognition to military officers who make that decision?

8. What were LCDR Reynolds' moral obligations here, to his country, to his troops, to the non-combatants?

9. If LCDR Reynolds had not stopped the door gunner, and had they killed or wounded the non-combatants in the third vehicle, would that have justified a court martial? Are there any legal vs moral issues here?

USS *Vincennes*—Friend or Foe?

Edited by Captain Rick Rubel

On the USS *Vincennes*, it was 0633 local time, on the morning of July 2. The phone buzzed in Captain Will Rogers's cramped sleeping quarters as the captain was shaving. Already, just two hours after the sunrise, the 100-degree heat of the sun was overwhelming the ship's air-conditioning systems. Fine-grained sand whipped across the gulf from the Arabian Desert, creating a yellowish haze. Rogers picked up the phone. It was the duty officer in the ship's combat information center, the nerve center two decks below Rogers's sea cabin: "Skipper, you better come down to CIC."

Some 50 miles to the northeast, the U.S. Navy frigate Montgomery was coming through the western entrance of the Strait of Hormuz. Every day, tankers bearing half the world's imported oil wend their way through the strait, only 32 miles wide at its choke point. The recent Iran-Iraq War had turned the strait into a gauntlet. Gunboats of the Iranian Revolutionary Guard, had been attacking tankers and merchantmen bound to and from Kuwait, Iraq's main ally in the war. Anxious to keep Kuwait's oil flowing, the United States had agreed to provide escort to Kuwait tankers registered under the U.S. flag.

On this July morning, the Montgomery spotted a half-dozen Revolutionary Guard launches venturing out from the island hideouts. At 0633, he ordered "all ahead flank." and the cruiser's four massive gas-turbine engines cranked up to 80,000 horsepower and sent the warship smashing through the waves at 30 knots.

At 0722, the *Vincennes*'s SH-60B Seahawk helicopter lifted off and sped north; within 20 minutes it was circling over the Iranian gunboats. The pilot of Ocean Lord 25, Lt. Mark Collier, found the gunboats hovering around a German cargo vessel, the Dhaulagiri. They weren't shooting. It was a common harassment tactic.

In the cockpit of Ocean Lord 25, pilot Mark Collier followed the gunboats north, as they retreated toward their island lair. He later explained that he wanted to drop down and see how many men were aboard the launches, and how they were armed. He almost found out the hard way. As he banked around them, Collier saw what he later describes as "eight to ten bursts of light" and "sparks . . . just a big spark" in the sky 100 yards from his helo. He thought for a moment it was the sun glinting off of a boat, but then he saw puffs of smoke. "Did you see that?" Collier, called out to Petty Officer Scott Zilge. "Yeah," Zilge replied. "Let's get out of here. That was an airburst of antiaircraft fire." As Colier dropped the helo to the safety of 100 feet, the aircraft's commander, Lt. Roger Huff, sitting in the co-pilot's seat, radioed the *Vincennes*: "Trinity Sword. This is Ocean Lord 25. We're taking fire. Executing evasion."

In the combat information center it was immediately recognized that the gunboats had committed a hostile act. Under the navy's "rules of engagement" in the gulf, Rogers could order hot pursuit. "General Quarters," he snapped. "Full power." Once again, the *Vincennes* forged north at 30 knots.

Aegis cruisers were not designed for small-craft battles. They were built to take on the Soviet Navy in the North Atlantic. The Aegis's ultra-high tech radar system is designed to track scores of incoming missiles and aircraft in a major sea battle. The Iranian launches were so small that as they bobbed on the swell, they flickered in and out of the *Vincennes*'s surface search radar, showing up not as separate targets but as a single symbol on the radar screen. Impatiently, Rogers turned to his tactical action officer (TAO), Lt. Cmdr. Victor Guillory. "Can the bridge see anything?" he demanded. The bridge reported that it could occasionally glimpse the wakes of a few boats as flashes through the haze.

Capt Rogers reported to Bahrain that the gunboats were gathering speed and showing hostile intent. Again, he announced his intention to open fire. With the Captain's permission, Commander Guillory ordered the *Vincennes's* guns to fire when ready. Two minutes later the ship's five-inch gun opened up on its first target, a launch 8,000 yards away.

Some 55 miles to the northeast, at precisely 0945:30, Iran Air Capt. Mohsen Rezaian announced to the tower at Bandar Abbas airport that his A300 Airbus was ready for takeoff. A minute later, he throttled up his two General Electric CF6 engines and lifted the airline into the haze. His course would take the plane and its human cargo southwest to Dubai, in the United Arab Emirates. Though Rezaian could not know it, his flight path would also go almost directly over the USS *Vincennes*.

The CIC of an Aegis cruiser looks like a luxury video arcade. Rows of operators hunch over radio consoles, each monitoring one element of the battle. Talking to each other in muffles voices through headsets and mouthpiece microphones, they exchange information and follow standard commands. All the information from their screens is integrated by the mighty Aegis computer into, the "big picture"—thrown up as symbols on maps displayed on four giant 42-inch-by-42-inch screens at the head of the room where the captain and his two "battle mangers" sit. The $400 million Aegis system can track every aircraft within 300 miles. Its computers tag each contact with the symbol for "friendly," "hostile" or "unidentified." In a war at sea, Aegis is expected to seek and identify all airborne threats to an entire carrier battle group, to display the speed and direction of each, and to rank them by the danger they present. The Aegis Weapon System is so powerful that it can not only track up to 200 incoming enemy aircraft or missiles, but also can automatically command missiles to shoot them down.

At 0947, the *Vincennes's* powerful Spy radar picked up a distant blip—a plane lifting off from the airport at Bander Abbas. The blip was in fact Iran Air's Flight 655 on its twice-a-week milk run to Dubai. But since Bander Abbas is a military as well as a civilian airport, any flight out over the gulf were automatically "tagged" by the navy ships as "assumed hostile." At his computer console in the *Vincennes's* CIC, Petty Office Andrew Anderson saw the blip for an incoming bogey go up on one side of the big blue screens. Anderson's job in "Air Alley," the row of operators who handled air warfare, was to identify any air traffic within range of the ship. He told the Aegis system to query the incoming plane: Identify, Friend or Foe? By standard practice, all planes carry a transponder that automatically answers the IFF query with Mode 1 or 2 (military), or Mode 3 (civilian). Anderson got a Mode 3 "Commair" (commercial airliner) from his console. He reached beside his console for the navy's listing of commercial flights over the gulf. But as he scanned the schedule, he missed Flight 655. Apparently, in the darkness of the CIC, as its lights flickered every time the *Vincennes's* five-inch gun fired off another round at the Iranian gunboats, he was confused by the gulf's four different time zones.

Anderson turned to the petty officer next to him in Air Alley, John Leach, and wondered aloud if the blip could be an Iranian warplane—an F-4 or F-14 perhaps? Their boss in Air Alley, Lt. Clay Zocher, overheard the two enlisted men talking, Zocher was already nervous. He had stood this watch only twice before during General Quarters and he'd never mastered the computer routines for his console. He was worrying at the moment about an Iranian P-3 patrol plane that was making its way down the Iranian coastline. Could the P-3 be coordinating an attack on the *Vincennes* with the unidentified bogey? Zocher decided to pass the chatter in Air Alley up the chain of command to his boss, Lt. Cmdr. Scott Lustig, the *Vincennes's* Tactical Commander for Air Warfare.

Lustig ordered Zocher to send the incoming plane a warning: "Unidentified aircraft . . . You are approaching a United States naval warship in international waters." It was the standard challenge, broadcast over the international distress frequencies routinely monitored by military and commercial aircraft. Briefly, Lustig considered another option. On the display screen in front of him Lustig could see that the Forestall's F-14s were circling just five minutes away. There was enough time—barely—to call them in to check out the bogey.

Aboard the *Vincennes*, it was now 0949 and Captain Rogers was totally consumed with his firefight against the gunboats. He was shouting for the five-inch-gun crew to load faster, and ordered hard-right rudder to bring his stern gun to bear. The ship shuddered and heeled to starboard.

Military theorists write about "friction", the inevitability of error, accident and miscalculation in the stress of combat. The architects of modern warfare have tried to use the technology to minimize battle-field blindness. But the large amount of electronic data in a combat information center can be just confusing. Officers and men communicate by headphones over several channels, with left and right ears usually listening to different circuits. Rogers and his key officers in the CIC were all on the same circuit.

At 0950, someone called out that the incoming plane was a "possible Astro"—the code word for an enemy F-14. No one was ever able to find out who. In Air Alley, the operators thought the word came from the technicians in the ship's electronic-warfare suite. The technicians thought the warning came from Air Alley. Galvanized by this warning, Petty Officer Anderson again beamed out an IFF query. Ominously, the response he now got back this time was different; his console flashed Mode 2: "military aircraft." Only much later did the investigators figure out that Anderson had forgotten to reset the range on his IFF device. The Mode 2 did not come from the Airbus, climbing peacefully above the gulf, but from an Iranian military plane, probably a military transport, still on the runway back in Bander Abbas.

"Possible Astro!" Anderson sang out, at a moment of near chaos in the CIC. It was 0951. Having swung full circle, Rogers was now bringing his reloaded forward gun to bear on the Iranian launches. The gun fired off 11 rounds—and jammed. The skipper again ordered the rudder hard over. The stern swung around, and in the CIC, papers and books toppled of consoles as the ship heeled over. At his station to Rogers's left, Lustig looked at his screen. The incoming plane was 32 miles away. "What do we do?" he asked Rogers. (His commanding officer was not too overwhelmed by the Iranian speed-boats to forget the woeful example of Capt. Glenn Brindel, the skipper of the USS *Stark*. A year earlier, Brindel had been in the head when his ship was struck and almost sunk by a pair of anti-ship missiles fired by the pilot of a lone Iraqi Mirage F-1)

Rogers decided that the *Vincennes* fire control radar would "lock on" any possible hostile plane that got within 30 miles. At 20 miles, the *Vincennes* would shoot it down. Rogers was not absolutely sure that his ship did face an enemy warplane . The plane seemed too high—some 7,000 feet—for an attack approach. At his rear, another officer, Lt. William Mountford, warned "possible commair." Three more times, the warnings went out: "Iranian fighter . . . you are steering into danger and are subject to United States naval defensive measures."

Then something happened that psychologists call "scenario fulfillment"—you see what you expect, and often you expect what you train for. Petty Officers Anderson and Leach both began singing out that the aircraft, now definitively tagged on the big screen as an F-14, was descending and picking up speed. The tapes of the CIC's data later showed no such thing. Anderson's screen showed that the plane was traveling 380 knots at 12,000 feet and climbing. Yet Anderson was shouting out that the speed was 455 knots, the altitude 7,800 feet and descending. The information from the various consoles didn't seem to match, and didn't to fit together with a clear understanding of the CIC team.

Rogers had to make a decision. An F-14 could do little damage to the *Vincennes*. The version that Washington sold to its ally the Shah of Iran in the early 1970's was purely a fighter plane, not config-ured to strike surface targets. Still, if Rogers meant to attack it with a missile, he had to fire before the aircraft closed much within 10 miles. At 0954:05, with the plane 11 miles away, Rogers reached up and switched the missile firing key to "free" the ship's SM-2 antiaircraft missiles. In Air Alley, Zocher had been given the green light to fire, and take track 1105 with missiles. In the CIC, the lights dimmed momentarily, like a prison's during an electrocution.

Some 10 miles away, Captain Rezaian of Iran Air was calmly reporting to Bander Abbas that he had reached his first checkpoint crossing the gulf. He heard none of the *Vincennes* warnings. His four radio bandwidths were taken up with air-control chatter.

"Have a nice day," the tower radioed. "Thank you, good day," replied the pilot. Thirty seconds later, the first missile blew the left wing off his aircraft.

The Aegis weapons system performed just as it was designed to do.

On the *Vincennes's* bridge, cameraman Rudy Pahayo was still filming. His audio captured a bab-ble of voices: "Oh, dead!" "Coming down!" "We had him dead on!" One voice commanded: "Hold the noise down, knock it off!" Another shouted, "Direct hit!" then a lookout came in from the wing of the bridge. The target couldn't have been an F-14, he said. The wreckage falling from the sky, he murmured to the *Vincennes's* executive officer, Cmdr. Richard Foster, is bigger than that.

A few miles away, on the bridge of the Montgomery, crewmen gaped as a large wing of a commercial airliner, with an engine pod still attached, and plummeted into the sea. Aboard the USS *Sides*, 19 miles away, Captain Carlson was told that his top radar man reckoned the plane had been a commercial airliner. Carlson almost vomited, he said later.

On the *Vincennes*, there was an eerie silence. The five-inch guns ceased their pounding. None of the Revolutionary Guard boats had come within 5,000 yards of the cruiser. No one was sure how many had been hit; perhaps one, perhaps more. Rogers gave the order to head south, out of Iranian waters.[1]

Sequel:

On July 3, 1988, an American warship shot down an Iranian airliner, killing 290 civilians.

The destruction of Iran Air Flight 655 was a human tragedy.

It damaged America's world standing. It might have caused Iran to delay the release of the American hostages in Lebanon. It may have given the mullahs a motive for revenge and provoked Tehran into playing a role in the December 1988 bombing of Pan Am 103. For the U.S. Navy it was a professional embarrassment. The navy's most expensive surface warship, designed to track and shoot down as many as 200 incoming missiles at once, had blown apart an innocent civilian airliner in its first time in combat.

Questions for Discussion

1. Situation
    a. What was the situation in the Gulf during this time frame?
    b. What was the mission of the Navy during this time?
    c. What was the mission of the USS *Vincennes*?

2. What was the tragic outcome of the events on *Vincennes* on that day in the case?

3. What were the factors that contributed to the tragedy?

4. If you were radar console operator (petty officer) on the air-tracking console that saw that IFF and altitude of the air contact "didn't look exactly right," would you have spoken up to stop the firing sequence?
    *   What is your moral obligation to speak up?
    *   What criteria would you use to determine when to speak up?
    *   If you say nothing are you morally responsible for what happens?
    *   If you tell your LT. that something doesn't look right, and he doesn't pass that information forward, are you morally absolved of all responsibility?

5. *As a leader*, do you want your people to speak up and even stop the firing sequence? Or do you want them to always do as they are told?
    a. When do you want them to speak up and stop the firing sequence?
    b. Develop a set of criteria for when you would want your people to speak up and when you want them to execute the firing sequence. (if they speak up for everything, the ship may never be able go fire a missile)

6. Should the CO create the command environment where people feel free to discuss the combat situation as it unfolds?

---

[1] Edited from *Newsweek* Magazine, July 13, 1992.

Who Lives? Who Dies?*

Colonel Paul E. Roush, USMC (Ret)

A non-commissioned officer (NCO) on duty at Headquarters, Combined Action Group (CAG), Phu Bai, Viet Nam, roused Lieutenant Colonel (LtCol) John Miller from a deep sleep shortly before 4:00 AM. The news was not good. Radio traffic from a Combined Action Company (CACO) indicated that a large force of Viet Cong guerrillas had attacked a Combined Action Platoon (CAP) in Thua Thien Province. Initial reports held out little hope for survival of the marines and Vietnamese soldiers in the CAP "A" 6/9 compound in Phu Loc village.

LtCol Miller was the commanding officer of the CAG, responsible for the CAP's throughout the two northern provinces of the Republic of Viet Nam (RVN). His CAG headquarters was co-located with the headquarters of the Third Marine Division at PhuBai. He struggled to put the pieces together, based on very limited information.

Apparently, when a barrage of shoulder-fired rocket rounds and satchel charges began to detonate in the compound, the marine manning the radio watch in the CAP "A" 6/9 compound had immediately notified the CACO of the attack. All contact with the CAP was lost shortly after the initial communication. The CACO relayed the information on to the Phu Bai CAG.

LtCol Miller's concern from the moment word of the attack came to him was saving the marines in CAP "A" 6/9. A quick check of the patrol overlays indicated that a portion of the CAP was out on patrol during the time of the attack, but he had no means of contacting that element.[1] He had a sick feeling in the pit of his stomach as he considered his options. First he asked for artillery fire to support the marines under attack, but his request was denied because the rules of engagement (ROE) did not permit firing on populated areas.[2] The time involved in alerting, mounting-out, and transporting a helicopter-borne force of adequate size to the site of the attack ruled out that option. Time was of the absolute essence because such attacks were carefully coordinated, violent, and quick. He requested that the infantry battalion at the Third Marine Division headquarters at Phu Bai commit a reaction force along the main road to the village of Phu Loc, a distance of about five miles. Based on the battalion commander's recommendation, the Division Operations Officer denied the request, on the bases that communications had been lost with the CAP, and the possibility that the attacking Viet Cong may have placed mines or ambushes or both along the only road to the village.

The next senior person in the chain of command was the Combined Action Director at Headquarters, III Marine Amphibious Force (111 MAF), Colonel Bill Elliott. When LtCol Miller notified the Director about the events at CAP "A" 6/9, his frustration over the failure of local marine tactical units to come to the aid of his marines was evident. He also made it clear that he intended to put an operational CAP back into the same compound within a matter of hours.

---

[1] CAG regulations required each CACO to forward patrol routes for each of its CAPs to ensure coordination with other friendly units that might be moving in the same area at the same time. This was a means of reducing the likelihood of casualties from friendly fire and ensuring that patrols did not become too predictable.

[2] Rules of engagement are the formal rules that set forth the circumstances and limitations under which U.S. forces may initiate or continue combat engagements with the enemy. In exceptional cases artillery fire could be brought to bear on populated areas, but only with the advance approval of the Vietnamese District Chief. Obtaining that approval was likely to require so much time that it was ineffectual in an attack on CAPs.

*This case was produced by the Center for the Study of Professional Military Ethics, U.S. Naval Academy.

When the CAP "A" 6/9 marines who were out on patrol during the attack returned to their compound, they learned that their five marine comrades, including the squad leader, as well as the Popular Force (PF)[3] soldiers who were in the compound, had all been killed. The compound itself had been substantially destroyed. They reestablished radio contact with the CACO headquarters. LtCol Miller and the CACO commanding officer arrived on site shortly thereafter and began working out the details for rebuilding and continuing to operate CAP "A" 6/9.

The Combined Action Program

This imaginative program integrated PF soldiers native to a given area with U. S. Marines, in order to provide security to hamlets and villages in cleared or semi-cleared areas.[4] From a single platoon in May 1965, the program had grown by the summer of 1967 to 75 platoons.[5] The basic unit in the Combined Action Program was the Combined Action Platoon (CAP), which included 14 U.S. Marines, a U.S Navy corpsman, and 35 PF's.[6] The arrangement was a cooperative one. Neither element commanded the other.[7]

The missions of the CAPs would be ambitious under any circumstances, but they were especially daunting, given that the senior marine in the CAP was the squad leader, an enlisted marine with the rank of sergeant. Most sergeants were twenty-two years old, or younger, and only about half of them were high school graduates. The missions were spelled out in I Corps Coordinator Instruction 5401.3 G/drb dated 16 July 1967:

a. Destroy the communist Viet Cong infrastructure within the village or hamlet area of responsibility.

b. Provide public security and help maintain law and order.

c. Protect the friendly political/social infrastructure.

d. Protect bases and communication lines within the village and hamlets in which they are located by conducting day and night patrols and ambushes in their assigned areas.

e. Contribute to combined operations with Regional Forces and other Popular Force, Army of the Republic of Viet Nam, or Free World Military Assistance Forces in their activity area.

f. Participate in civic action and conduct propaganda against the Viet Cong.

g. Participate in Revolutionary Development activities to the maximum extent possible with the accomplishment of the foregoing missions/tasks.

---

[3]The Popular Force soldier is the lowest paid soldier in the Vietnamese Armed Forces. He must augment his pay by working part of the time in or near the hamlet/village where he is located in order to provide the basic living essentials for his family. The Vietnamese District Chief routinely delivers a food supplement from USAID to the PFs.

[4]A cleared area would indicate an area in which organized, armed resistance by anti-government forces would not be likely. Such resistance would be encountered only in exceptional circumstances. Operation in a semi-cleared area would entail somewhat more risk, but would still permit relative freedom of operation.

[5]Headquarters III Marine Amphibious Force I Corps Coordinator Instruction 5401.2 3G/drb dated 16 July 1967. (Subject: I Corps/III MAF Combined Action Program Joint Policy).

[6]Headquarters III Marine Amphibious Force Order 3121.4a 3G/WRC/drb dated July 17 1967. (Subject: Standing Operating Procedure for the Combined Action Program).

[7]Command and control of the CAPs was rather complex. A number of CAPs (normally three to five) constituted a Combined Action Company (CACO). The CACO headquarters was commanded by a U.S. Marine Corps officer—normally a Captain—and located at the headquarters of the Vietnamese District Chief. The CAPs were under the direct control of the Vietnamese District Chief in the district in which the CAP was located. This control was exercised by means of a Combined Action Team (CAT), located at the district headquarters. The CAT included the command elements of a given CACO and the Vietnamese equivalent that was responsible for the PF platoons. The CACOs within a specified area (in this case, the two northern provinces of the Republic of Viet Nam (Thua Thien and Quang Tri) were placed under the command of a Combined Action Group (CAG), commanded by a U.S. Marine Corps Lieutenant Colonel. The CAGs reported to the CG, III MAF through his III MAF Combined Action Director.

LtCol John Miller

From the time he had assumed command of the Phu Bai CAG just two months earlier, LtCol Miller was deeply committed to those missions. From the very beginning, he made his presence felt. He spent much of his time away from the headquarters, visiting as many of the more-than-thirty CAPs as he could, ignoring the threats of ambushes and mines along the roads, occasionally accompanying the troops on their patrols and ambushes. Not a single marine doubted that the "old man" cared for him, understood the risks he faced, and was willing to share those risks. He had gotten to know the Vietnamese district chiefs throughout Thua Thien and Quang Tri provinces. He initiated a system of food supplements for the Vietnamese soldiers in the CAPs, when they performed well in combat. When these local soldiers behaved heroically, LtCol Miller took steps to present them with American decorations for valor. On one occasion he arranged for the visiting Commanding General, Fleet Marine Force, Pacific to present the bronze star medal for valor to a PF soldier from one of the CAPs near the Third Marine Division headquarters, inviting all the Vietnamese officials from the region to attend the ceremony. He increased significantly the patrolling and ambush activity of the CAPs in order to enhance local security.

The Response

Within days of the attack on CAP "A" 6/9, CG, III MAF sent a related message to all subordinate commands.[8] It was clear to LtCol Miller that the message was in response to his frustrations when he spoke to Col Elliott the morning of the attack. The message made pointed reference to the events that contributed to the disaster in Phu Loc village. It made three points. First, it said that coordinated assaults of highly trained, sapper-type[9] Viet Cong units posed an extremely serious threat to CAPs. Second, it directed nearby tactical units to come to the assistance of CAPs under attack. Third, it called for the use of artillery fire in the event of an attack on a CAP.

When LtCol Miller read the message he had mixed reactions. On the one hand he was pleased that the subject was being addressed. On the other, he recognized that the message was simply an injunction to "do better" and "try harder." It involved no fundamental change. LtCol Miller was convinced that fundamental change was necessary if the Combined Action Program were to succeed.

The heart of the matter, from LtCol Miller's perspective, was his concern that friendly forces could not move quickly enough to respond to the kind of attack faced by CAPs, no matter how strong the urging from headquarters. The Viet Cong approach was to plan meticulously, including repeated rehearsals of the attack. They would then mass forces in numbers that were overwhelmingly superior to the number of defenders in CAP compounds. When the element of surprise is factored in, the combination is very potent, indeed. The compounds themselves were so small—typically, the approximate size of a basketball court—that any breach in the perimeter defense put the attackers close to the center of the compound.

Obviously, the time available for effective response is very limited, which magnifies the importance of artillery support. While it would require perhaps an hour to alert, provide briefings for, and move a reaction force comprising marine infantrymen to the scene of the attack, artillery does not suffer the same constraints. Artillery weapons can fire over a distance of fifteen or more miles. A single exploding projectile (a "round," in artillery terminology) shatters into hundreds of lethal, jagged, metal fragments, capable of producing many casualties. An artillery barrage of a hundred rounds, for example, could have disastrous consequences for an attacking force caught in the open. Calculation of firing data, orientation of the artillery weapons (howitzers, in most cases), and preparation of the rounds would take approximately five minutes. The rounds would arrive on target in less than a minute from the time of firing.

On the surface, the use of "artillery as a reaction force" seemed a reasonable option. There were, however, several major obstacles. One was the delay involved in obtaining permission to use artillery in this way. The existing rules of engagement allowed its use in populated areas only with approval of the local Vietnamese authorities on a case-by-case basis. Since nearly all CAPs were located

[8]CG, III MAF msg 120328Z Sep 67.

[9]Sapper units are units whose capabilities include expertise in breaching (i.e., breaking through) fortified positions.

in populated areas, the injunction from III MAF seemed to LtCol Miller to be hollow, for the following reason. Gaining approval to fire required going up the military chain of command, then down the chain of command of the Vietnamese leadership, then back up the Vietnamese chain and back down the military chain. Even without the problems of locating all the appropriate authorities in the middle of the night, and overcoming the communication and language barriers, the system required so much time that using artillery was essentially a non-option. By the time it materialized, the attack would be over and the local villagers would be the only targets. In other words, from LtCol Miller's perspective, the III MAF message asked subordinate commands to do what was not possible to do. Even if all those problems could be resolved, there would still remain an even larger problem; namely, the potential for a large number of civilian casualties as a collateral effect of the use of artillery.

A particular issue kept making its way into LtCol Millers consciousness. It concerned the behavior of the local Vietnamese civilians. Almost inevitably, some number of them would be aware of the massing of Viet Cong attackers prior to such an attack. Villagers knew, for example, that elements of the Viet Cong were in the hamlet several hours prior to the attack on CAP "A" 6/9, but they remained silent. If they had sounded the alarm, the odds of the CAP's survival would have been much higher. Unfortunately, the likelihood of Viet Cong retaliation against the local populace would increase by an order of magnitude as a consequence of such action. The Vietnamese civilian, in other words, is in a very tenuous position. However much he may want the CAP to succeed, he wants even more for himself, his family, and his neighbors to stay alive. To be sure, he wants the increased security, the access to medical care, and the improved quality of life from completed civic action projects, all of which are benefits that the CAP brings.[10] More than that, however, he wants to avoid being executed by the Viet Cong for collaborating with the government or the American forces.

LtCol Miller understood all that, but he also knew that the success of the Combined Action Program depended on support of the local populace. Should the people become convinced that the CAPs were unable to protect them, they would neither support nor participate in the combined action effort. If swift and effective Viet Cong attacks on CAPs were to continue without countervailing reaction from RVN and US forces, the Viet Cong would be seen as invincible in the minds of the local populace.

After mentally rehearsing these considerations, LtCol Miller still had to conclude that the use of artillery was the only potentially useful reaction force available, if it could be done in a timely manner. While tactical units were generally not close enough to transport troops to the CAP in time to thwart the attack, they did include artillery batteries that could place huge volumes of fire on top of a CAP compound that was under attack. This firepower was capable of causing a large number of casualties among attacking troops, who, by definition, are relatively exposed, while dug-in defenders had at least some chance of survival. Even if the CAP were overrun in such a scenario, the number of Viet Cong casualties could be high enough to discourage future attacks on other CAP compounds. Further, if the artillery caused substantial Viet Cong casualties, their evacuation from the site might slow the Viet Cong egress enough to allow tactical units to arrive in time to inflict additional casualties.

Obviously the down side of the proposal remained its prohibition in the existing rules of engagement. LtCol Miller knew that there was likely to be significant property destruction and some—perhaps many—casualties among the civilians living in the vicinity of the CAP compound if artillery were used as he contemplated. He knew that the villagers wanted to be neutral in the conflict engulfing their land. From his perspective, however, there was no way their current behavior could be considered neutral. He believed that it was important to put the onus of choice on the local populace. What was happening seemed to him a mere facade of neutrality. The villagers were making choices that favored the Viet Cong. The location of the CAP compound adjacent to or within the hamlet denies or delays the artillery support for the CAP marines, given the rules of engagement. The silence of the villagers during the pre-attack staging phase denies the CAP the opportunity to prepare for the attack and the time needed to alert reaction forces. In essence, the kind of "neutrality" the villagers practiced denied firepower and mobility to the CAPs, while leaving intact all Viet Cong advantages.

---

[10] Examples of the kind of civic action projects routinely undertaken by the CAPs included constructing wells, market places, schools, dispensaries, midwife hospitals, and wash ramps; establishing trash and human waste disposal points; training local people to perform routine medical services; and arranging visits by physicians and dentists to provide enhanced health care. In some villages there was a significant reduction in disease during the CAPs tenure there.

LtCol Miller reasoned that it was necessary to force the local Vietnamese civilian to choose. Peaceful coexistence with the Viet Cong while having a CAP compound in his village or hamlet should not be an option. He should be free to choose to accept or reject the placement of the CAP in his village or hamlet, which means that he can choose either to enjoy or to forego the benefits that the CAP brings to him, his family, and his community. He already knows that the Viet Cong are the ones who initiate the attack, and that use of artillery would be in response to such attack. LtCol Miller believed that the U.S. response to any Viet Cong attack must be effective enough to convince the villager that the Viet Cong cannot prevail over the long haul.

Within a week after receiving the III MAF message concerning reaction forces for the CAP's, LtCol Miller had composed a letter that he addressed to The Deputy Commanding General, III MAF, via the Director, Combined Action Program, in which he provided details of the above analysis. The letter included three recommendations:[11]

> Recommendation #1. "that a policy be established whereby instantaneous artillery support in the immediate area of all CAP's be approved in writing by Vietnamese authorities down to the District Level and by CG, III MAF." If approved, this recommendation would eliminate the delay that currently prevents the application of timely artillery fire. In essence, an attack by the Viet Cong would elicit a rapid and deadly response without the need for any further authorization.

> Recommendation #2. "that the policy be publicized by Vietnamese officials down to the smallest hamlet to ensure that all the people are aware that future attacks will be met with commensurate force. They must realize that their best hope lies in reporting the presence of any Viet Cong force in the vicinity of a CAP." This recommendation, if approved, would force the village or hamlet to choose which risks it prefers. On the one hand, there is risk of harm at the hands of the Viet Cong for cooperation with the CAP. On the other, there is risk from U.S. artillery fire in the event of a Viet Cong attack on the CAP. The basic thrust of this recommendation is that the consequences of an artillery response to a Viet Cong attack are likely to be more painful than the Viet Cong response to the villagers' cooperation with the CAP.

> Recommendation #3. "that this policy be carried out, regardless of the location of any future attack, to convince the population that a negative neutrality is detrimental to themselves, their property, the Combined Action Program, and the established government. Consequently, the Viet Cong will know that the people cannot be utilized as protective shields. Delineation of opposing forces will become more pronounced as animosity grows between the people and the enemy." This recommendation means that the villagers cannot coexist peacefully with both the Viet Cong and the Combined Action Program. They will have to choose one side or the other, and can no longer straddle the fence.

LtCol Miller read his letter yet again. He rehearsed in his mind the competing arguments. He knew the magnitude of the issues he was raising. He knew he was recommending a course of action that could be a public affairs nightmare. It was not hard to imagine a scenario in which scores of old men, women, and children would be killed or wounded as a result of artillery fire deliberately brought to bear on a village.

On the other hand, denial of his request could cause a public outcry, should such a denial become known publicly. Denial could easily be interpreted as a Marine Corps decision to withhold help from young enlisted marines who might be saved with the artillery support, and who certainly would die if it were not forthcoming. It is one thing to say that the isolation of CAPs makes it very difficult to get help to them in time, but it is quite another to say that help is readily available in the form of artillery support, but that it will be withheld in order to minimize risk to the local villagers.

---

[11] Lt Col Miller's rationale and recommendations were set forth in Headquarters, Phu Bai Combined Action Group letter 6/RJK/jkl dated Sep 1967 (Subject: Reaction Forces for Combined Action Platoons).

LtCol Miller had another nagging concern. The marines who constitute the squads in the Combined Action program are all volunteers. They attend a two-week school at the CAG headquarters before being assigned to one of the CAPs. It was LtCol Miller's responsibility to provide that training. What was he going to tell those marine volunteers? Should they hear that their lives would be sacrificed in order to avoid harming Vietnamese civilians? What would be the effect on morale in the CAPs?

LtCol Miller was a passionate advocate for the Combined Action Program, and was convinced it was pursuing the right missions. Progress was evident. The CAPs were making a difference. He believed, however, that the program could not survive if it lost the support of the local people in the hamlets and villages. The question to be resolved is this: what will cause the people to withhold that support? Is it their perception that the CAPs cannot defend themselves, let alone the villages? Is it fear for their own survival if defense of the CAPs requires placing artillery fire in the heart of their community when a CAP is attacked? Is it some combination of these and other reasons?

Even though he believed that the Vietnamese civilians were less than fully innocent, LtCol Miller knew there were serious legal and moral questions in his recommended approach. Violations of the Law of War are also violations of the Uniform Code of Military Justice (UCMJ), the legal regulations governing the U.S. Armed Forces. The Law of War draws heavily upon the provisions in the Hague and Geneva Conventions. That law requires parties to a conflict to distinguish between the civilian population and combatants. Specifically, it prohibits attacks that may be expected to cause incidental loss of civilian life, injury to civilian objects, or a combination thereof, which would be excessive in relation to the concrete and direct military advantage anticipated. It specifies that non-combatants cannot be deliberately attacked at any time. On the other hand, the case could be made that firing to protect one's troops who are under attack is not an attack upon the civilians. Any casualties could, it seemed, be viewed as collateral damage. Also, the concrete and direct advantage LtCol Miller anticipated was nothing less than success for the missions assigned the CAPs. He did not want to expose himself, his seniors, and his subordinates to charges of war crimes, but he wanted to do everything he could to protect the lives of his marines and to make the mission succeed.

These were the stakes as he pondered whether or not to send his recommendations forward.

Come Right: Conflicts of Priority
Captain Rick Rubel

I was the Officer of the Deck (OOD) on a Guided Missile Destroyer (DDG).

I had just been promoted to LTJG and had recently been qualified by the Captain as Officer of the Deck for Formation steaming. Because I had been qualified early, I was anxious to show the Captain that I would do a good job. As OOD, I was responsible for the operation of the bridge watch team, and as Conning Officer I was responsible for giving the helm and engine orders to the helmsman. Legally, the conning officer is the only officer on the ship who can give these orders to the helmsman.

It was 1035, on a clear day with high clouds, and good visibility. We were in formation with a nuclear powered Aircraft Carrier (CVN), on a course of 025 deg T at 15 Knots. While conducting Tic-Tacs (tactical maneuvering exercises) we found ourselves 250 yards off the port Bow of the CVN. (This is much too close to safely station from a CVN, but the Officer in Tactical Command of the exercise (OTC) had ordered us to that station.)

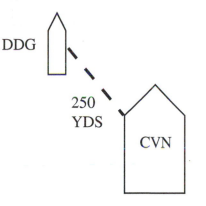

The next tactical signal was sent by the OTC, and then "executed". In order to execute this tactical signal, we were required to maneuver the ship to another station in relation to the CVN. (Note: when a signal is executed, all Commanding Officers want to smartly turn the ship to it's new course in keeping with smart ship-handling.)

> At this point the Captain yelled to me, "Come Right!"
> I quickly said back to the Captain, "I can't, Sir."
> He immediately repeated his order, "Come Right!"
> I repeated, "I can't, Sir."
> He then took two quick steps over to me and yelled, "Damn it, Come Right!"

Stop the situation here.
What would you have done if you were me?

Points to Consider

1. I had determined that if we had turned right, we would have had a collision with the CVN in approximately 15–20 seconds. By the time our ship's bow started swinging to the right, it would probably be too late to avoid collision.

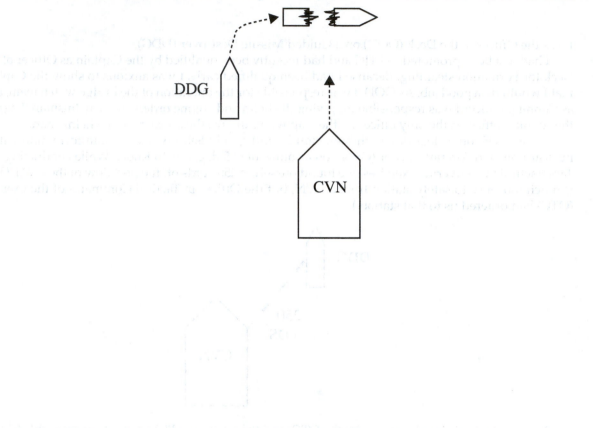

II

The Moral Dilemmas
of Modern Warfare

Life or Death:
The Marcus Luttrell Story
of "The Lone Survivor"[1]
Captain Rick Rubel

Marcus Luttrell was raised in North Texas. His father, a patriotic Viet Nam veteran, taught him to love his country and work hard for what he believed. His father also told his two sons at an early age about a group of "elite warriors" and their courage, patriotism, strength and determination—their refusal to accept defeat. Marcus even asked a local retired Green Beret to train him when he was 14 years old, to prepare him for the day he would become a SEAL. While the other high school boys were involved with after-school activities and sports, Marcus was lifting weights, running, learning martial arts, and training under his Green Beret taskmaster. He molded Marcus into a determined man who could push through bodily pain to achieve his objective. After his brother became a Navy SEAL, there was never a doubt in Marcus' mind that he would follow in his brother's footsteps.

At 23 Marcus enlisted and headed off to U.S. Navy boot camp, immediately followed by BUD/S training (Basic Underwater Demolition/ SEALs). In the grueling SEAL training, almost 65 per cent of the original class dropped out. The motto "Never, never, ever quit" applied to the extraordinary remaining men, who refused to give in to pain and exhaustion. They had the concept of teamwork drilled into their heads until it became their nature to support their teammates through the worst hardships ever developed in human training.

Afghanistan Missions

After graduating from BUD/S and serving in Iraq for several tours, Marcus Luttrell was assigned to SEAL Delivery Vehicle Team ONE. Marcus Luttrell lived, trained, and fought alongside his SEAL teammates. In the SEALs, the lines between officer and enlisted are more informal as they develop close personal bonds during the intensity of training and combat. Marcus Luttrell, additionally, had been trained to be the team corpsman to render medical aid.

In March, 2005, he deployed with his unit to the U.S. Base in Bagram, Afghanistan. Similar to his Iraq missions, their job was to drop into areas behind enemy lines (although the lines were not clear) and gather intelligence on high-value Taliban. Their goal was to capture these high-value men and turn them over to the interrogators to get valuable information. In some cases, their mission was to kill specific enemy leaders. When going into dangerous regions, they moved by night with the most modern night-vision equipment available. During the day, they worked to remain undetected. As the SEALs like to say, they "own the night." Since their unit numbers were small, they relied on camouflage, stealth, and quiet as their advantages over the larger Taliban forces. They would often fly into the

---

[1] *Lone Survivor*, Marcus Luttrell, Little, Brown and Co., 2007.

Pashtun region of Afghanistan, a region near the Pakistani border that is primarily tribal and does not generally recognize any central government. The strong Muslim culture, shaped by centuries of fighting numerous conquerors, made this area a perfect haven for the Taliban to regroup, recruit, and launch attacks on the Afghan government and U.S. forces.

Operation Redwing

After detailed planning, Operation Redwing was approved on June 28, 2005. Petty Officer Marcus Luttrell and his three SEAL teammates, LT Michael Murphy, PO Matthew Axelson, and PO Danny Dietz boarded a CH-47 to be inserted in the Hindu Kush Mountains in the Pashtun region to search for a Taliban leader named Ben Sharmak. It was believed that capturing him would provide information about other Taliban strongholds and bomb-makers; killing him might reduce the armed threat in the region.

During the preparation phase, LT Murphy and Marcus Luttrell were worried about the aerial photos of the mission area. The terrain they would be dropped into did not seem well-suited for camouflage and concealment. They also noted that their selected observation point (the side of a steep mountain) was several miles from the only flat area that could serve as a helo drop site.

In the darkest part of the moonless night, after several deceptive maneuvers (called "touch and goes" to confuse the enemy who may be watching), they were inserted into the drop zone. After a period of quiet, motionless listening, they believed they were alone on the high, flat field. They gathered their equipment and made their way up the mountain to their pre-selected area where they could observe the small town below. The hike in full battle gear was harder and took longer than they had anticipated—about seven hours. When they reached their observation area, it was almost dawn. As they settled into concealed positions, they realized that they could not see the town. So they left their concealed positions and found a spot with good observation potential, but less concealment. From their new position, they could see, but it would be hard to launch an offense or maintain a defense because the high ground above gave them little chance for escape. However, their mission was to observe the town and find Taliban Ben Sharmak, and this position would support that.

Life or Death

After a short time of waiting and watching, an unusual thing happened. Marcus looked up and saw an Afghan man approaching. Marcus stood and pointed his rifle; the man stopped. Even stranger, about a hundred goats soon surrounded the four SEALs and the goatherd they had just confronted. Two more Afghans joined them—a boy of 14 and another man.

The SEALs asked the men if they were Taliban, and they immediately said, "No Taliban. No Taliban." Marcus noted that the men glared and scowled at him with obvious dislike.

The SEALs spent the next hour or so discussing among themselves what to do with the three Afghan goatherds. First, they discussed the Geneva Convention, which protects unarmed civilians. They also seemed to agree that the strictly tactical military decision would be to kill them. There was no way to determine if the men were associated with the Taliban, but the glares and scowls indicated that they were not friendly to the American cause. The worst-case scenario for the SEALs' mission would be for them to be detected. They did not have rope or duct tape to bind the men, and they reasoned that even if they did, someone would come looking for them— and the goatherds' location would be obvious from the hundred goats that would remain in their vicinity. They quickly rejected the option of binding them.

PO Axelson thought they should kill the men, telling his boss LT Murphy, "Just give me the word." LT Murphy reasoned that if they killed the men, someone would find the bodies (because of the goats), and the Taliban would play this to the Arab media. Once the press had the story, the SEALs would be tried for murder back in the United States. Initially, Marcus Luttrell thought from the military view it made no sense to let the goatherds go and allow the team to be discovered. Knowing that they were outnumbered by Sharmak's army 140 to 4, they would be killed if their location was compromised.

The team agreed to get some guidance from headquarters. Things went from bad to worse as their radio inexplicably would not connect with HQ.

At this point, LT Murphy outlined their three options:

1. Kill the goatherds quietly with knives and throw them off the cliff.
2. Kill them right where they were and cover up the bodies.
3. Turn them loose and "get the hell out of here."

LT Murphy pointed out that with option 1 or 2 they would all have to remain silent forever so they would not be tried for murder in the United States.

PO Axelson insisted, "We're not murderers. No matter what we do. We're on active duty behind the enemy lines, sent here by our superior commanders. We have the right to do everything we can to save our own lives. The military decision is obvious. To turn them loose would be wrong."

At this point, LT Murphy took a vote. Axelson quickly voted to kill them. LT Murphy favored letting them go. Danny Dietz basically abstained from the vote by just saying, "I don't [care] what we decide, just tell me what to do."

Then they asked Marcus Luttrell what he thought. He fully understood his comrades' arguments, but as he said later, "My Christian soul was whispering something in the back of my mind. It would be wrong to execute these unarmed men in cold blood. And the idea of doing that and then covering our tracks and slinking away like criminals, denying everything, would make it worse."

Finally, Marcus Luttrell cast the tie-breaking vote by saying, "We gotta let them go." They motioned to the three men to leave. Although the SEALs and their captives did not share a common language, the Afghan men knew what they had been discussing—their fate—life or death.

After the Decision

After watching the goatherds walk out of site, Marcus immediately said to himself, "We must be crazy. Let's get out of here!"

The SEALs quickly re-positioned to a different site. About 10 minutes after they had settled in, *their worse fear came true.* They looked up to the ridge and saw 80 to 100 well-armed Taliban fighters coming down the ridge toward them. This was serious, and they now knew they would be fighting for their lives, just as they recently discussed. The problem was that their firing position was not good, neither defensively or offensively. To get away from the overwhelming enemy, they would have to go down the mountain, and in some cases, off the cliffs.

The four men fought a horrific gun battle that lasted most of the day. They fought like American warriors, like Navy SEALs, like teammates, and like close friends. As the Taliban sprayed a high volume of inaccurate AK47 fire and rocket propelled grenades (RPGs), the SEALs took sharp aim, conserved ammo, and used teamwork. As they continued to fight and retreat down the mountain, they fell several hundred feet down steep cliffs. The volume of Taliban firepower was relentless, wounding the SEAL team.

LT Murphy was shot in the stomach and the back, but continued to fight as he bled to death. PO Axelson continued to fight with several body wounds. After killing about 40 to 50 of the enemy and with three of the SEALs mortally wounded, they tried to make a last stand. In an extraordinary act of heroism, LT Murphy took out his cell phone to call HQ. To get reception, he had to stand up on a bluff in the open. In his call, he explained the desperate situation. His final words on the phone were, *"Roger that, Sir. Thank you."*—professional up to the end. Shortly after, he was fatally shot in the chest.

As Marcus watched his best friend die, there was little he could do to help, even though he was the corpsman of the team. He was shot in the leg, bleeding from both entry and exit wounds. He had broken some vertebrae in his back during one of the falls and could not stand up on both feet. Then he watched as his other two best friends and teammates, Axelson and Dietz, were killed by relentless enemy fire. He was the lone survivor of the SEAL team. To get away from the AK-47s and RPGs, he jumped down steep cliffs, falling hundreds of feet at a time.

Marcus Luttrell didn't know until later, but the Special Forces put together a quick response to LT Murphy's cell phone call for help. Seven SEALs and seven Rangers, along with commanding officer LCDR Kristensen, immediately volunteered to save their fellow Americans and boarded an MH-47. As they were landing in the drop zone near the firefight, an enemy RPG was fired into the back of the helo, causing an explosion that killed everyone aboard.

Pashtun Hospitality

Bleeding, thirsty, and numb, Marcus Luttrell crawled on his hands and knees for hours, looking for water. Some local Pashtun tribesmen, apparently not Taliban, found him. In an unusual tribal custom, the town elders not only took him into their houses to heal his wounds and feed him, but they also invoked a tribal custom (unique to that area) called "lokhay." Lokhay literally means "put on a pot," and this goes far beyond normal hospitality. Since the Pashtun region is remote and tribal, recognizing no central government, the people have maintained this extraordinary "all or nothing" custom when encountering strangers for hundreds of years. If they vote to let you go, you are on your own. But if they extend this ultimate hospitality of lokhay, you have essentially become part of their "family" and will be protected even if they have to fight to *their* deaths. The village that was sheltering Marcus was surrounded by Taliban for days during his recovery. His hosts made good on their promise to protect him, as they moved him from house to house.

After days of recovery with food and medicine, Marcus was able to put together a makeshift battery arrangement for his distress radio. He sent a one-way message asking for rescue. After dodging the Taliban for a few more days, he was rescued by Army Rangers.

Aftermath

After returning to the United States and receiving medical attention, he was awarded the Navy Cross by the president in the Oval Office. His three teammates also received the Navy's highest honors posthumously, including the Congressional Medal of Honor for LT Murphy.

He then fulfilled his final promise to his three best friends. He traveled to San Diego, Long Island, and Las Vegas to tell the families of his fallen teammates that they all died heroically, serving the country they loved.

Questions for Discussion

1. Did the Navy SEALs make the right decision to let the Afghan goatherds go free? Why or why not?
    a. Do you agree with PO Axelson's statement? "We're not murders. No matter what we do. We're on active duty behind the enemy lines, sent here by our superior commanders. We have the right to do everything we can to save our own lives. The military decision is obvious. To turn them loose would be wrong."
    b. Does this allow military fighters to do anything to defend themselves?
    c. Should there be a consequence short of trial for murder for this kind of situation?
2. Should they have taken a vote, or should the lieutenant have made the decision?
3. Is there any way to avoid these kinds of situations?

Abu Ghraib
Captain Rick Rubel

Case I:

Do we want our troops to be morally responsible, or do we want them to do as they are told?

Consider the following:

You are a Private in the Army and have just arrived in Iraq to join your first unit, the 800th Military Police (MP) Brigade. You arrived in Iraq this morning, and your trip from the airport was eye-opening as you observed dozens of U.S. military and Iraqi civilian vehicles burned out along the side of the road. Iraqi men along the route stared motionlessly at your vehicle as you passed by them. When you arrived at the prison, you received a short 10-minute brief from your Sergeant who basically told you, "You've been to MP school. You know what to do."

As you follow the directions to go to the cell block office for your first duty, you walk down the corridors with cells on both sides full of Iraqi prisoners. This is certainly the strangest walk of your life. The smell of human feces and urine is just about enough to make you vomit. The prisoners look at you with sullen, sunken eyes—eyes that have both anger and hatred in them. They taunt you by spitting on you and saying in clear English, "I will kill you. I will kill your family." as they reach out and try to grab you. There is a muffled tension in the air which can only be described as the smell of blood.

In the cell block office, you meet the Specialist in charge of the block who introduces you to an American wearing plain khaki pants and a shirt with no insignias or markings. They both tell you that your job during this 8-hour watch is to harass detainees #150216 and #150849. They say that they think both of these guys set off an improvised explosive device, and killed a few soldiers. You ask them what that means and they tell you, "It just means break their spirit . . . you know so they will talk. Keep them awake, smack them around a bit, and get inside their heads . . . you know . . . make them feel less like a man . . . more like a weasel."

You think to yourself, "They didn't teach me this at the 22-week Military Police school at Fort Wood, Missouri. But if they're all doing this, it must be good . . . to make them talk . . . to find out who burned up all those vehicles I saw along the side of the road."

What do you do, Private?

Case II:

I. Introduction

Beginning in September, 2003, Abu Ghraib prison became a U.S. operated holding facility for various Iraqi prisoners. One of the primary "missions" of the prison was to obtain valuable intelligence from prisoners who would help the U.S. win the war against terrorism and insurgency. As this mission was pursued, there were numerous breakdowns in leadership, organization, legal interpretations and compliance, and individual morals. These breakdowns led to documented abuses of prisoners by a number of guards. These abuses included sexual humiliation, sexual exploitation and assault (guards having sex with female prisoners), and the beatings and deaths of other prisoners.

II. Background

The Prison: Abu Ghraib is a large 280-acre facility located twenty miles west of Baghdad. During the regime of Saddam Hussein, it was reported that over 4000 people were executed in that facility and many more were tortured. After the fall of Baghdad in April, 2003, the U.S. used the facility to detain several categories of prisoners. This included common street criminals, security detainees, insurgents, terrorists, and "high value" leaders of the insurgency.[1]

Organization: In June, 2003, The 800th Military Police Brigade, Commanded by Brigadier General Janice Karpinski, was placed in charge of the prison. Since one of the missions of the prison became gathering intelligence, the 205th Military Intelligence Brigade was assigned to the prison to interrogate prisoners.

Mission: The function of the prison was to provide a safe, secure, and humane environment that supports the expeditious collection of intelligence.[2] As the post-war insurgency and terrorism grew in the last half of 2003, the pressures to obtain more intelligence from the prisoners grew proportionally. In this type of counter-insurgency operation, *intelligence is everything* and can directly save many lives outside the prison walls.

It was the job of the 205th Military Intelligence Brigade to interrogate the prisoners and obtain this valuable information. As a rule, the Military Police only gather passive intelligence (information over-heard), but do not participate in interrogation sessions. In established procedures there is a clear separation between the role of the Military Police guards, whose job is to secure the compound, and the role of the Military Intelligence, whose job is to obtain strategic and operational intelligence.[3]

The Rules: The rules governing the treatment of Prisoners of War are derived from the "1949 Geneva Convention Relative to the Treatment of Prisoners of War." In part, this document defines Prisoners of War (POWs) as captured enemy personnel in various categories. These categories include;

- Members of the Armed Forces
- Members of a Resistance Movement—which must have a command and rank structure, identifying badges or insignias; but does not include soldiers operating on their own
- Levee en Masse–individuals who are defending their home country—but this status only applies until the land is occupied, and the individuals must adhere to the Law of Armed Conflict and carry arms openly.

The Geneva Convention specifically excludes the coverage of 'Terrorists.'

At a minimum, the Convention requires that all prisoners "Must be humanely treated and are entitled to respect for the persons and their honor. This includes protection from acts of violence, intimidation and public curiosity." With respect to interrogations, the convention says, no physical or mental torture, or any form of coercion may be inflicted on prisoners of war to secure information of any kind whatever, and they may not be threatened, insulted, or abused.[4]

III. Abuses at the Prison

Numerous incidents of "sadistic, blatant, and wanton criminal abuses were inflicted on several detainees." Documented abuses by guards included:[5]

- Punching, slapping, kicking, and jumping on their bare feet with boots

---

[1] The New Yorker. Annals of National Security, "Torture at Abu Ghraib", Seymour Hersh 5/10/05

[2] The US Army report on Iraqi prisoner abuse; executive Summary of Article 15-6 investigation of the 800th Military Police Brigade, Maj Gen Antonio Taguba, Background -2

[3] The US Army report on Iraqi prisoner abuse; executive Summary of Article 15-6 investigation of the 800th Military Police Brigade, Maj Gen Antonio Taguba, Background B.6-b

[4] Geneva Convention, 1949, Summary

[5] The US Army report on Iraqi prisoner abuse; executive Summary of Article 15-6 investigation of the 800th Military Police Brigade, Maj Gen Antonio Taguba, Background–Part One -5

- Photographing and videotaping naked male and female detainees
- Forcibly arranging detainees in various sexually explicit positions for photos
- Forcing detainees to remain naked for several days at a time and forcing male prisoners to wear women's underwear
- Forcing male detainees to masturbate themselves while being photographed
- Arranging naked detainees into a human pile and take pictures
- Posing with a detainee with a dog's leash around his neck
- Breaking chemical lights and pouring dangerous phosphoric acid on them
- Beating detainees with a broom handle and a chair
- Sodomizing a detainee with a chemical light and broom stick
- Allowing military dogs to threaten and bite detainees
- Taking photos of dead Iraqi detainees while making gestures

IV. Breakdowns

From the long list of documented abuses above, it is clear that there were many distinct breakdowns at the Abu Ghraib prison. These breakdowns can be grouped in four categories:

A. Organizational Breakdowns

When the 205th Military Intelligence Brigade was assigned to the prison to gain intelligence, the relationship between them and the 800th Military Police Brigade was not clearly defined. Since they were co-located, the prison guards were not sure if they should follow the instructions of the Intelligence Officers who were trying to obtain valuable information. There was evidence in investigation reports that although there were no organizational orders, there were "lower level" instructions to guards to "set conditions for detainees for subsequent Military Intelligence interrogations." Specifically, "They did not have authorities and procedures in place to affect a unified strategy to detain, interrogate, and export information from detainees in Iraq."[6]

In one instance, a Military Police guard, SGT Davis, said that he heard a Military Intelligence officer tell another guard, SSG Fredrick, "Loosen this guy up for us. Make sure he has a bad night. Make sure he gets the treatment."[7]

This organizational confusion was made even more complicated by the use of civilian contractors from several U.S. corporations. These men and women wore generic civilian clothing, and had free access to all the cell blocks, but the guards were never sure of their status within the organization.

B. Leadership breakdowns

Beginning at the top, BGen Janice Karpinski, was cited in the investigation for failure of leadership. Her failures included; not demanding that her unit follow Standard Operating Procedures (SOP) and the Geneva Convention, and not actively walking around her prison command and knowing what was going on there. She was also cited for failure to remove ineffective officers, and failure to follow "Basic Soldier Standards." In her interview with the senior investigator, she (emotionally) completely refused to "either understand or accept that many of the problems inherent in the 800th MP Brigade were caused or exacerbated by poor leadership. . ."[8] General Karpinski was Relieved for Cause: for dereliction of duty.

---

[6] The US Army report on Iraqi prisoner abuse; executive Summary of Article 15-6 investigation of the 800th Military Police Brigade, Maj Gen Antonio Taguba, Background–Part One -1

[7] The US Army report on Iraqi prisoner abuse; executive Summary of Article 15-6 investigation of the 800th Military Police Brigade, Maj Gen Antonio Taguba, Background–Part One -1.11.b

[8] The US Army report on Iraqi prisoner abuse; executive Summary of Article 15-6 investigation of the 800th Military Police Brigade, Maj Gen Antonio Taguba, Background–Part Two -14

Other officers were relieved of command for lack of leadership and failure to adequately train their troops. Secretary of Defense Donald Rumsfeld said that he offered his resignation to the President twice over the Abu Ghraib situation, but was asked to stay on the job.[9]

C. Legal confusion

The prison detained several categories of prisoners. There were common Iraqi criminals awaiting trial, captured insurgents, and terrorists. The Geneva Convention invokes different protection for each of these categories. Particularly, insurgents without a command structure and terrorists do not specifically fall under captured combatant protection. It could be argued that all detainees should be treated with equal respect and dignity; but it could also be argued that some categories do not have the specific coverage of the 1949 Convention.

D. Moral Breakdowns

The final area of breakdowns that led to the abuses was moral breakdowns. <u>In the presence of organizational, leadership, and legal breakdowns, the final remaining source of decision-making is the individual moral reasoning of the soldier.</u>

Within the scenes of abuse at Abu Ghraib, this case will examine five individuals/groups who handled the same situation very differently.[10]

1. The Sadist: Spc. Charles A. Graner, 35 years old, from Unitown, Pa, was accused of numerous acts of abuse against the detainees. He was reported to have piled up naked men, jumped on their bare hands and feet with his boots, and "merrily whistled, sang, and laughed while brutalizing the prisoner and forcing some to eat pork and drink alcohol" (against their Muslim religion). He was also convicted in a court martial of punching a prisoner until he became unconscious.[11] When the Military Intelligence Officers realized that Graner would work the prisoners over, they continued to ask him to abuse the prisoners. Graner was found guilty of all charges, including conspiracy to maltreat detainees, cruelty, and maltreatment, as well as charges of assault, indecency, adultery, and obstruction of justice. On January 15, 2005, he was sentenced to ten years in federal prison. In several testimonies, it was reported that Graner seemed to enjoy the abusive acts, and invented many of them himself for photo opportunities, while he posed and smiled.

2. Immature, Dependent Followers and onlookers:

Private First Class Lynndie England, 21 years old from Ashby WV, was reported, and charged with, severe abuse and humiliation of detainees. Although reportedly she did not directly, physically injure any detainees, she can be seen in photos with a dog collar around a naked Iraqi, and force one to masturbate himself. She can be seen in other photographs posing with naked prisoners. Given the sensitivities of Muslims and Arabs to sexuality, nudity, and women, these actions can be seen as particularly degrading. Other army guards can be seen in pictures of prisoners being abused standing by as onlookers, on edge of the scene watching.

England was convicted of one count of conspiracy, four counts of maltreating detainees and one count of committing an indecent act. She was sentenced to three years in prison and given a dishonorable discharge.

3. Participated, but confused about mission:

Staff Sergeant Ivan Fredrick was the senior enlisted at the prison. Although he took part in the scenes of abuse he was quoted to have said, "I questioned some of the things I saw . . . such things as leaving inmates in their cells with no clothes on or in female underpants . . . I ques-

---

[9] CNN Interview with Larry King , February 4, 2005

[10] Dr. Al Piece discussed very similar categories of behavior in his remarks at the U.S. Naval Academy in September, 2004

[11] *The New Yorker*. Annals of National Security, "Chain of Command," Seymour Hersh 5/17/04

tioned this and the answer I got back was, 'This is how Military Intelligence (MI) wants it done.'"

He also said, "We had no support, no training whatsoever, and I kept asking my chain of command for certain things. . . like rules and regulations. And it just wasn't happening."

SSGT Fredrick pleaded guilty on 20 October, 2004 to conspiracy, dereliction of duty, and maltreatment of detainees, and was sentenced to 8 years in prison.

SSGT Fredrick was clearly conflicted. Unlike the first two categories, he believed the actions he observed were wrong, but could not get the mission confirmation he needed from his superiors.

4. Refusal to participate:

Not everyone participated in the abuse. An army Captain who was stationed at the prison said he was approached by an intelligence officer who requested that his MPs keep a group of detainees awake around the clock until they talked. He said, *"No. We will not do that."*

The Intelligence officer asked him, "What's the problem? We're stressed and all we are asking you is to keep them awake."

The Captain said, "How? You've received training on that. My soldiers don't know how to do that. And when you ask an eighteen-year-old to keep someone awake and he doesn't know how to do that, he's going to get creative."

The Captain's superior backed him up, and the request was withdrawn by Military Intelligence.[12]

5. Reporting the Abuse:

Specialist Joseph M. Darby, 24 year old from Corriganville, Maryland is credited with turning over the pictures to authorities. He said in his testimony, "I knew I had to do something. I didn't want to see any more prisoners abused. . . because I knew it was wrong."

Other soldiers saw the abuse, but apparently tolerated, and eventually accepted it. An example of this was that the photo of the naked pyramid was a screen saver on many of the guard's computers.

Darby left the disk of photos with a letter describing the scenes with Criminal Investigation Division (CID).

Joseph Darby is described as "One that didn't go along with his peers. . . he didn't worry about what people thought." "He was just doing his job." A friend said about Joe Darby, "Growing up, he didn't have much at all. But he was brought up properly. He was brought up to know right from wrong."[13]

Questions for Discussion

1. *If you were the guard in the scenario in Case I who was told by the Intelligence officer to "harass the prisoner,"*
    (a) *What questions would you want to ask the Sergeant telling you to harass the prisoner?*
    (b) *list the reasons why you* <u>would</u> *consider doing what the intelligence officer told you to do*
    (c) *List the reasons why you would consider* <u>not</u> *doing what he told you to do*
    (d) *What would you do? What is your primary consideration from all the reasons on the two lists?*

2. *What are the character attributes that would contribute to someone responding to this situation as:*
    (a) *The Sadist*
    (b) *The Immature, Dependent Follower*
    (c) *The ones Confused about Mission and participated*
    (d) *The ones who Refused to participate*
    (e) *The Reporter of the abuse*

---

[12] *The New Yorker.* Annals of National Security, "Chain of Command," Seymour Hersh 5/17/04

[13] CBS News.com, Who's who person, 4 May, 2004

3. *So what was different about Joseph Darby that caused him to report the abuse, and eventually stop it?*

4. *Given the pressure to obtain information from the "high value" detainees, was the order to harass them legal/illegal? How do we determine this?*
   Was the order moral/immoral? How do we determine this?

5. *Do we want our troops to be morally responsible, or do we want them to do as they are told?*

6. *When should we expect our troops to challenge our orders?*

The case writer appreciates the editorial assistance received from: Dr. Albert Pierce, Dr. Shannon French, Dr. Chris Eberle, Dr. Patricia Cook, Capt Bob Schoultz, Virginia O. Rubel, Dr. Brad Johnson, Dr. Dave Garren, Lcdr. Clyde Haig, Ms. Kim Rawson, Dr. George Lucas, Jr.

"What the Hell Just Happened?"

Written by Chaplain Tom Webber, USN, CHC
Edited by Captain Rick Rubel

In the early hours of OPERATION Iraqi Freedom (OIF), a rifle company came face to face with their first "suicide bomber," or so they believed.

This company was part of the same Battalion and Regiment that had just gone through An Nasiriyah in the middle of the night after Jessica Lynch was captured. Tensions were high as every officer and Staff NCO informed their troops that the loyalists to Saddam Hussein were using car bombs and suicide bombers to slow the Coalition Forces in reaching Baghdad.

The Marine units of this regiment all witnessed or experienced the suicide car bombers seeking to run through the Marine check-points. The death and destruction was all over the roads. The Marines saw, smelled and heard death all around them. They reaffirmed, to a man, their essential training ethos, "God, Country, Corps!" It was a solemn duty to protect each other.

As this company moved into a town closer to Baghdad, their vehicles maneuvered to create a picket on one side of the road as other units from the regiment drove through their positions. The picket was set up on either the left or right side of the road, allowing the Marines to shoot only in the direction of the enemy as they traveled past their fellow Marines. This technique secured both sides of the road as units moved through these small towns and villages.

On one occasion, shortly after seeing the aftermath of a failed suicide car bomb attempt, a rifle platoon in two armored vehicles dismounted and picketed one side of the street. There was sporadic small arms fire coming from down the street.

Then they saw a woman come out of a building carrying something heavy in her arms. The Marines could not see what she was carrying, as she was wearing a full Burkha. They yelled in Arabic for her to stop, but she kept walking. As she slowly makes her way closer to the marine checkpoint, Sergeant Rob Sarra, who was in charge, figures that if they can't stop her, she will approach the vehicles and blow herself up. He is not alone in his thoughts, nearly every Marine of his platoon is wondering what they should do. Sergeant Sarra has her in the cross-hairs. She has not stopped and is still approaching the vehicles. The Sergeant decides in his mind, "This suicide bomber is not going to take us out." He pulls the trigger. As soon as he does, the rest of the platoon fires as well with 12–14 weapons. She falls to the ground dead.

The Marines go up to see what she is carrying. She is clearly dead, but she was not carrying a bomb. She was carrying dishes. The Sergeant immediately says, *"What the hell just happened?* This woman got killed by my actions." He was crying, hysterically. When he wrote in his journal that night, he wrote that he wasn't going to tell anyone about this, including his mother. No one has to know that he killed innocent women. But little did he know it would work itself back up to the surface when he came home.

The rest of the story: For the next few days Sergeant Sarra became despondent and is not engaged with his men. He felt that he has violated the Rules of Armed Conflict, as well as violating his own moral conscious by killing a woman. After a short time, the Marine Corps had to pull him off the line, then out of the war. He is receiving counseling for post-traumatic stress and emotional problems due to this incident.

Questions for Discussion

1. Did the Sergeant do the right thing?
   a. How do we resolve the fact that he did the right thing, but he is no longer able to be a combat Marine?
   b. Did the leadership have the right ROE?
   c. Should he have been prepared better?
   d. What could the leadership have done to better prepare him?

Incident at a Roadblock[1]

(author anonymous)
Edited by Dr. Shannon E. French,
U.S. Naval Academy

We parachuted into the capital of a small country in the dark of night. Resistance to our arrival was substantial and events throughout the following day were somewhat confused and threatening. As evening approached, the entire country was under an absolute curfew, requiring all vehicles and persons to be off public roads by 8:00 PM.

My unit was conducting a movement through the city in order to deliver one of our companies to an outpost on the opposite side of the city limits. We had to cross many thoroughfares to arrive at the outpost. At all crossing sites we placed security units and temporary roadblocks. At the point where we crossed the city's main boulevard we were careful to place out obvious roadblocks to warn anyone violating the curfew to stay clear. There were signs in the native language as well as a loudspeaker team with native speakers. If these were missed, there was the obvious presence of two tanks in plain view to convince anyone that this was not the place to venture near.

Just prior to midnight, one of our security teams alerted their fellow soldiers of a VW bus approaching at a high rate of speed. The vehicle did not alter its speed or course despite repeated broadcasts over the loudspeaker and warning shots being fired over the vehicle.

During these activities I was at the foot-mobile operations center team around the corner and out of view. With the sound of the broadcasts and warning shots I started running toward the crossing site. However, by the time I had arrived the vehicle had already barreled through the roadblock, entered the fields of fire of the security unit, been engaged by our soldiers and come to a stop at the side of the road. When I came forward to investigate with other leaders of the unit, we found to our dismay that the occupants were all young adults, apparently out 'joy riding'. They were, however, dressed in the typical garb worn by the hostile forces we had already come in contact with, i.e. blue jeans and white T-shirts. There were weapons in the vehicle and our soldiers reported that they had heard and observed shots coming from the vehicle.

I approached the driver of the vehicle, the only one left alive. I asked an interpreter nearby to ask him why they did not stop. Didn't they understand to stay away or risk being engaged by our forces? The driver replied, 'We just wanted to see if you would really do it.' I was amazed at his response and watched as the attempts of our medical team failed to save even this man's life.

The thoughts that haunted me after the mission were varied. In the daylight the previous evening's occurrences seemed surreal. I was enraged at the driver having put the lives of the passengers at risk. I was chilled by the thought that soldiers narrowly escaped death from being struck by the vehicle or shot. I was angry at the 'policy' that caused our fine young soldiers to be placed in such a position. This was not the way war was supposed to be.

---

[1] The following is a case study from the *Journal of Military Ethics*, 2, no. 1 (2003).

War Is Big Business:
Blackwater Worldwide Operations in Iraq[1]

Lt Matt Courtney, USN

Lt Sean Maloney, USN

LCDR William Pugh, USN

LCDR Andrew J. McFarland, USN

Mr. Joseph Prisella, DOD/USN,

Patuxent River Naval Air Station, MD

In the first Gulf War the ratio of military to civilian contractor was 60 to1, with most of the contractors providing logistical and support activities. In the second Gulf War and subsequent rebuilding of Iraq, the ratio is nearly 1 to 1. There are currently at least 180,000 private contractors operating in Iraq, more than the total number of U.S. troops. Today's contractor no longer just cooks, cleans or drives supply trucks; they have jumped into an armed quasi-military role. It is estimated that there are over 170 separate companies operating within Iraq with over 20,000 armed personnel, more than all non-U.S. coalition forces combined. These companies provide personnel protection security for the U.S. State Department, the U.S. Military, the Iraqi government, Iraqi private citizens, independent institutions, and Non-Governmental Organizations (NGOs).

One of the largest and highest profile personnel security firms is Blackwater Worldwide (Blackwater). Blackwater was founded in 1997 by former U.S. Navy SEAL Erik Prince and is based in Moyock, NC. According to their website, Blackwater is not simply a private security firm, but a "professional, military, law enforcement, security, peacekeeping, and stability operations firm who provides turnkey solutions." In 2000, the company had $204,000 in U.S. Government Contracts; by 2007 Blackwater had rapidly exceeded $1 billion in U.S. Government Contracts.

Blackwater's capabilities far exceed the notion that they are just a personnel security company. On their website, Blackwater proudly expounds upon its capabilities and the multitude of services they can and have provided. These capabilities include:

- Trained international militaries and organizations "in combating terrorism, maritime security, interdiction of terror activity, and interdiction of weapons of mass destruction."
- Offered advanced weapons and tactics training to law enforcement agencies from around the world.

[1] This case study was written for Naval Postgraduate School Executive Master's in Business Administration Program, GE 3109 "Business Ethics" (Professor George R. Lucas, Jr.) December 11, 2007.

- An aviation division that has over 26 types of aircraft, including airship UAV's, armed helicopters, a Boeing 767, and aircraft that support U.S. Special Operations Command.

- One of the largest tactical driving areas in the country for training with multiple types of vehicles for on and off road operations.

- 7000 acre training area that can be designed to create "complex real world scenarios."

- A Research and Development team creating the "Grizzly," their own version of an armored personnel carrier.

- The "McArthur," a 183ft maritime vessel outfitted with state of the art navigation and communications equipment to support multiple types of maritime operations.

Blackwater and other security companies operate with the U.S. State Department under the Worldwide Personal Protective Services Contract (WPPS), which dictates the minimum personnel requirements. WPPS guidelines include: personnel experience requirements one must have to be hired, the training they must undergo, medical background, and required security clearance checks. The individual company is responsible for recruiting, vetting, hiring and training its personnel to meet the obligations of the contract.

By 2007, Blackwater had 1,000 personnel working in Iraq participating in Personnel Security Detail (PSD) missions for the U.S. State Department. The war in Iraq is not the first time the U.S. State Department has contracted private security companies. U.S. State Department personnel in Haiti, Afghanistan, Bosnia, Israel and many other countries have benefited from the services of private security companies. The primary service provided by these companies is defensive security for Diplomats and U.S. State Department personnel while they are outside of secure areas, thus allowing them to interface with local government officials, agencies, and civilians. While Blackwater is responsible for training and recruiting, the U.S. State Department has operational control over Blackwater personnel once they arrive in country. All WPPS contracts are approved by the U.S. State Department and State Department personnel often observe the training of Backwater's employees.

As violence in Iraq drastically increased following the 2003 invasion, the undermanned U.S. military was unable to provide and maintain the required security throughout the country. The Coalition Provisional Authority (CPA), the first U.S. provisional government in Iraq, sought the help of private security companies to fill the U.S. Military gaps. Under CPA order 17, U.S. contractors were granted immunity from Iraqi government prosecution and guidelines were set for use of force allowing necessary force for self-defense. Even though the CPA no longer exists, no changes were made to these edicts and they currently still apply to private security companies. The Iraqi government has contested the continued application of this order, but because of restraints that inhibit the Iraqi government from changing or revoking CPA orders, Order 17 technically still has legal force in Iraq.

In general, no agency or organization exists to regulate the operations of private security companies. However, the Private Security Company Association of Iraq (PSCAI), a non-profit organization formed and maintained to discuss and address matters of mutual interest and concern to the industry conducting operations in Iraq, seeks to work closely with the Iraqi Government and foster a relationship of trust and understanding. According to Lawrence T. Peter (the Director of PSCAI) during a statement to the Washington Post, Blackwater is a member of the association and has a registered license to operate in Iraq. The PSCAI website further states that their members are "fully aware of the Rules for Use of Force and pride themselves on abiding by those rules." There is conflicting evidence that Blackwater has not attained a license from PSCAI and continues to operate outside of their rules as well. Furthermore, the U.S. State Department is only responsible for investigating incidents for its security companies under contract who discharge their weapons in Iraq, but not their day-to-day operations or how operations are carried out.

Blackwater and its founder, Eric Prince, deny they are mercenaries for hire. Webster's defines a mercenary as "one that serves merely for wages; especially a soldier hired into Foreign Service." Prince argues that his personnel are Americans hired by the American Government to provide security for fellow Americans. They provide security for U.S. State Department personnel heading into the most dangerous areas of the country and are often forced to take the same route time and again due to the location of the meetings, which increases the risk of attack.[2]

Since first putting its employees on the ground in Iraq, Blackwater has conducted over 16,500 PSD missions for the U.S. State Department, of which less than 1% have resulted in their employees discharging their weapons. Yet, in the execution of its duties Blackwater has gained the reputation of being very heavy-handed. This was also the case on September 16, 2007, when Blackwater guards shot and killed 17 Iraqi civilians in Nisour Square, Baghdad. The shootings occurred while Blackwater guards were escorting a convoy of U.S. State Department vehicles to a meeting in western Baghdad with United States Agency for International Development officials. It is believed by many of its own clients that Blackwater's mission seems to counter that of the U.S. Government, which is to "win over the hearts and minds of the Iraqis." Additionally, some other government officials say that Blackwater's corporate culture seems to encourage excessive behavior. Another source asks, "Is it the operating environment or something specific about Blackwater?"

Prince defends his company, stating the reason Blackwater has earned the reputation of being "more aggressive" than some of the other companies operating in Iraq is because his personnel are under contract for the hardest and most dangerous missions. He also affirms that Blackwater's responsibility is to protect the "principle"; it is not their job to be soldiers or diplomats. Blackwater personnel have worked in some extremely dangerous areas and were involved in the infamous Fallujah uprising in 2004. In addition, Blackwater has done an excellent job at protecting "the principle" (i.e., their clients). During the Iraq war, no U.S. State Department personnel have been injured or killed while under the care and protection of Blackwater. However, as of 2008, twenty-seven Blackwater employees have been killed in Iraq, three more have died in Afghanistan, and over 100 have been wounded. Blackwater's argument regarding the justification of its actions in Iraq is the U.S. State Department itself. If the U.S. State Department, its client, was not happy with Blackwater's performance, then why have they continued to provide contracts totaling $678 million to Blackwater since 2003?

The Nisour Square incident provoked widespread controversy and a full-scale review of the increased reliance of allied militaries on private contractors (PMCs). In the U.S., the 2007 Defense Reauthorization act sought to clarify the legal status of PMCs. Those working for the Department of Defense were subsumed under the Uniform Code of Military Justice. In 2009, a new "Status of Forces Agreement" with the Iraqi government subsumed all civilian contractors working in Iraq under Iraqi law. The five Blackwater security guards implicated in the Nisour Square shootings, for their part, have been indicted for manslaughter under the Military Extraterritorial Jurisdiction Act (MEJA), that holds U.S. citizens otherwise living, working, or traveling in foreign nations to the standards of U.S. domestic law. In March, 2009, Erik Prince resigned as CEO of Blackwater, and the company changed its name to escape what it termed the "negative publicity" surrounding its security operations in Iraq. The new company, "Xe," will focus more on providing maritime security and on training military and security personnel at its North Carolina facility.

---

[2] Instructor's note: This is an interesting point in ethics and the history of warfare. Mercenaries have long been condemned in the "just war" tradition. Morally, the concern was that paid mercenaries would not care about the limitations on use of force—the very issue that has Blackwater in "hot water." However, there was also a strong prejudice against people who "fought merely for money" rather than for moral ideals or for defense of their homeland. Since individuals' motives for joining the military vary widely, however, the notion of "guns for hire" seems less morally relevant than the first point, which pertains to fundamental notions of professional military bearing and behavior, including restraint in the use of force. See Sarah Percy, *Mercenaries: the History of a Norm in International Relations* (Oxford: Oxford University Press, 2007).

Question for Discussion

1. Do you think it appropriate for the U.S., or for the military forces of other allied nations, to rely for support on private contractors? Does it matter whether such support is confined purely to provision of logistical services (such as dining and lodging, or equipment maintenance)? Is there a role for privately employed, armed security contractors in a combat zone? If so, how should that role be defined or restricted?

Terror and Retaliation—Who Is Right?[1]
Captain Rick Rubel

Case I:

The young Palestinian man straps an explosive to his body and begins to walk down the street to the city center. He has grown up in a refugee camp and has been taught that if he dies while killing a large number of Jews, he will have eternal happiness in many ways. The importance to him is to ensure that his death results in the killing of his "enemy."

Since he does not own any rifles or handguns, his weapon must be a bomb strapped to his body. He goes into a crowded café, says a short prayer to Allah, and detonates the bomb, killing himself and 14 men, 6 women, and 4 children who were dining in the cafe.

Case II:

In retaliation, the Israeli Army orders a helicopter gunship to immediately fly to a Hammas training building. This is a well-known target, which ground intelligence confirms contains a terrorist bomb-maker inside. The helo fires a rocket into the building killing one terrorist inside the building. The rocket also kills 14 men, 6 women, and 4 children who were sitting at picnic tables behind the building having lunch. The helo pilot did not see the civilians behind the building.

1. Is there a moral difference between the two acts?
2. What is the moral difference between the two acts?
3. How would a terrorist answer question #2?
4. Does the fact that the exact same number of people were killed in both cases affect your evaluation?

---

[1] This is a composite case of many similar incidents.

Intervention in Rwanda
Dr. George R. Lucas, Jr.

"When one lives through an experience like the one in Rwanda, on a human level you can't leave. You have to stay, you have to help in whatever way you can. But we were asked to leave and to let everything just explode around us."

> —Colonel Luc Marchal, commander of the Belgian army troops deployed in Rwanda, and deputy commander, United Nations Assistance Mission in Rwanda (UNAMIR)

"Evil triumphs when good men do nothing." – Edmund Burke

On the night of April 11, 1994, Luc Lemaire, a Captain in the Belgian army, watched tensely from inside the Don Bosco school compound in Rwanda. Inside the walls of the compound, over two thousand men, women and children—all members of the principal ethnic minority population of Rwanda—huddled in fear under his protection while militant fellow citizens from that nation's majority ethnic group, armed with guns, clubs, and machetes, taunted and threatened them from outside the walls. Captain Lemaire's company of some ninety Belgian soldiers were all that stood between the asylum seekers and their angry adversaries, who seemed clearly intent upon massacre. And, on this night, Lemaire had received a communiqué from his commanding officer, Col. Luc Marchal, to withdraw his men at once from the compound in order to assist in the evacuation of remaining European nationals from the Kigali airport.

* * * * * * *

Belgium had a long history in Rwanda, and its policies under colonial rule had done much to foster the ethnic hatred that now boiled into violent conflict around Lemaire's tenuous outpost. In the Treaty of Versailles in 1918, Belgium had been granted exclusive authority over a region of East Central Africa known as Rwanda-Urundi. Belgium had administered the region for nearly half a century through a system of rigid apartheid and ethnic separatism, allying the colonial government with the minority Tutsi population, which encompassed a majority of the region's educated professionals and civil servants. The majority Hutu population, an agricultural people with little formal education, was thus largely excluded from the political and economic elite.

Beginning in the 1950s, Belgium instituted reforms designed to lead to self-governance and an end to colonial occupation. The longstanding ethnic rivalries cultivated during the colonial period, however, helped to force a division of the region into two autonomous, neighboring states: Rwanda and Burundi. Hutu seized power in the former, instituting reverse discrimination against the Tutsi who remained, and often fomenting violence against them. Tutsi fled to Burundi and into neighboring Uganda, where the exiles established an armed militia, the Rwandan Protective Force (RPF), for the purpose of regaining political dominance in the region.

On October 1, 1990, the RPF attacked Rwanda from Uganda. Rwandan President Juvénal Habyarimana, a Hutu, responded by appealing even more strongly to ethnic loyalties, and by fanning the old hatreds to muster support for his own regime and to persecute any Rwandans who might side with the Tutsi militia. Habyarimana's administration founded an armed "civilian defense force" and an armed Hutu youth militia, the "Interahamwe." This ethnic militia was armed at first with firearms, and when this proved too costly, with machetes. A special broadcast station, the Radio Television Libre des Mille Collines (RTLMC) was created for the sole purpose of relentless dissemination of hate propaganda directed against Tutsis. The government then enlisted these various forces and factions in a campaign of terror and assassination directed against both ethnic Tutsis and Hutu political opposition leaders.

The United Nations intervened to ameliorate these tensions beginning in June, 1993. In early August, a peace agreement calling for democratic elections was negotiated between the Rwandan government and the RPF, brokered by U. N. observers and the President of Burundi. The so-called Arusha Accords, "gave the surface appearance of fulfilling all the conditions required for a potentially successful transition from a civil war to a multiethnic democracy."[1] On October 5, 1993, the United Nations Assistance Mission for Rwanda (UNAMIR) was established as a multinational peace-keeping force under the command of Major General Romeo Dallaire of the Canadian Army. Reporter and author Samantha Powers later described him:

> "If ever there was a peacekeeper who believed wholeheartedly in the promise of humanitarian action, it was Dallaire. A broad-shouldered French-Canadian with deep-set blue eyes, Dallaire has the thick, calloused hands of one brought up in a culture that prizes soldiering, service, and sacrifice. He saw the United Nations as the embodiment of all three."[2]

His second-in-command was Colonel Luc Marchal of the Belgian army. Belgium, in tacit recognition of its historical ties and responsibilities in the region, provided the largest and by far the best trained and equipped contingent of military troops for the U.N. peacekeeping mission in Rwanda. In all, however, Dallaire commanded a mere 2,548 U.N. personnel, including civilian police and unarmed military observers, while he estimated that a country such as Rwanda would need at least 4,500 peacekeepers. The majority of these forces were from developing nations; some of the troops were badly equipped and poorly trained, and required food, medical care, and proper armaments themselves. Dallaire noted that "they did not have a kitchen and prepared their food on the ground under a canvas . . . Two hundred logisticians or engineers without vehicles, radios and equipment are only 200 mouths to feed."[3]

UNAMIR equipment and intelligence were two additional problems. One commentator on the unfolding tragedy later wrote:

> "Strikingly, UNAMIR was never provided with two things that would have proved useful: a strong intelligence capacity; and defensive equipment, such as armored personnel carriers (APCs). No member state contributed an armed unit, so DPKO found spare equipment from the UN operation in Mozambique, and commercial contractors were contracted. In the end, the APCs that arrived from Mozambique were largely nonfunctional. What intelligence capacity UNAMIR had was provided informally by the Belgian contingent."[4]

Indeed, shortly after his arrival and posting in Rwanda, Col. Marchal met with a secret informant, a Hutu highly placed in the Rwandan government, who warned him that massive acts of violence on the scale of genocide would soon be launched against the Tutsi, and that the Belgian peacekeepers themselves would be systematically targeted in order to drive them out of Rwanda.

By April of 1994, U.N. observers had become alarmed at the slow pace of democratic reform, the rise in hate propaganda, and the failure to form an integrated transitional government as prescribed in the Arusha Accords. On April 5, the Security Council voted to extend the operational date of UNAMIR to the end of July. One day later, a plane carrying President Habyarimana and President Cyprien Ntaryamira of Burundi was shot down, and both leaders were killed. Hard-liners in Habyarimana's administration who had opposed the Arusha Peace Accords seized on this event to order the assassi-

---

[1] Michael Barnett, *Eyewitness to a Genocide* (Ithaca, NY: Cornell University Press, 2002), 13.

[2] Samantha Powers, "Bystanders to Genocide," *The Atlantic Monthly* (September, 2001), 86–87.

[3] Romeo Dallaire, quoted in David Pugliese, "Mission Impossible," *The Citizen's Weekly* (September 22, 2002).

[4] Bruce D. Jine, *Peacemaking in Rwanda*, Lynne Rienner Publishers, Boulder London, 2001, p. 108.

nation of moderate leaders, including Rwanda's Prime Minister, and urged the general population to undertake the mass killing of Tutsi.

On April 7, a small contingent of U.N. peacekeepers arrived at the Prime Minister's compound to provide protection from marauding Hutu death squads. Ten Belgian soldiers were among the contingent. Hutu gunmen in the Presidential Guard surrounded the compound, took the peacekeepers prisoner, and killed Prime Minister Agathe Uwilingiyimana and her family. Taking their U.N. prisoners to a nearby military camp, they released all but the ten Belgians, whom they killed and savagely mutilated. Prior to their brutal execution, the young commander of the ten Belgian peacekeepers, Lieutenant Thierry Lotin was able briefly to establish communication with his headquarters. When he understood that he and all his men were going to be killed he sent off a call. The call for help was discounted; the lieutenant's immediate supervisor, Lieutenant Colonel Joe Dewez even responded: "Don't you think you are exaggerating a bit?" Later in Belgium, Dewez explained his behavior: "I believed in the assurance, the night before, of the command of the Rwandan army that they would help us to assure security and order . . . I was blinded by this logic, paralyzed by it . . . the fact that my men had been taken prisoner by the Rwandan army assured me that they were safe."[5]

Thereafter, any semblance of law and order rapidly evaporated. One of the U.N. senior military leaders, General Henry Kwami Anyidoho, offered a tragic description of the situation.

> "It became apparent that, apart from political assassinations, the Presidential Guards and the notorious militia (Interahamwe) were murdering the Tutsis in cold blood . . . A large number of Rwandese ran for their lives to UNAMIR headquarters, cathedrals, chapels, religious homes of any type, hospitals, hotel orphanages, the CND, UNDP compound and indeed any UN installation that was close to their homes. They took refuge in all these places with the hope that their lives would be spared. In many cases, it was useless. The Interahamwe desecrated the cathedrals and chapels by raiding and killing those seeking refuge there. They even entered UN installations. While the Presidential guards shot and killed, the Interahamwe used machetes, clubs with sharp nails, grenades, knives, spears and any deadly weapon to kill those they considered their opponents. It was mayhem; they ran amok and behaved as if they were possessed by some abominable evil spirit. They went about destroying lives cruelly and gleefully without a twitch of conscience nor trace of human feeling. The city became littered with the dead and people continued to die, stupefied and listless without uttering a sound."[6]

* * * * * * *

All these facts were apparently known to Captain Luc Lemaire and his men as they guarded the cowering refugees in Don Bosco. By now the situation around the compound was sheer chaos: "From the first hours, I knew there was a risk. [We] heard a lot of explosions in the neighborhoods and we realized immediately that they were murdering people all around Don Bosco."[7] It was clear that, in this region, the Don Bosco school compound under Belgian military protection was the last safe haven for those targeted for genocide. Thus, when the terrified villagers learned of the orders to withdraw, they made a horrifying request: they begged Captain Lemaire and his soldiers to turn their machine guns on the refugees, who would rather be shot by their protectors than face death at the hands of their tormentors.[8]

While the order to withdraw was clear, Captain Luc Lemaire still faced a dilemma. He could not bring himself to carry out the horrifying request of the unfortunate victims under his protection. Should he then defy the order to withdraw, and continue to protect these defenseless people from otherwise certain and violent death?

---

[5] Quoted in Linda Melvern, *A People Betrayed*, Zed Books, London, 2000, p. 126.

[6] Ibid., pp. 28–29.

[7] Steve Bradshaw and Ben Loeterman, "The Triumph of Evil," a *PBS Frontline* film documentary (aired January 26, 1999); transcript available online at: www.pbs.org/wgbh/frontline/shows/evil.

[8] *Ibid.*

* * * * * * *

[Sequel: Capt. Luc Lemaire decided reluctantly that he had no choice but to obey the order to withdraw from Don Bosco to the Kigali airport. As a result, the 2000 victims, including 400 children, were all immediately hacked to death. He and Col. Marchal later expressed confusion and regret over the incident. The massive evacuation of Europeans and Americans, and the withdrawal of nearly all foreign peace-keeping troops on the orders of their respective home governments, eviscerated the U.N. mission and command of Maj General Dallaire, who helplessly witnessed the horrifying devastation wrought by the massacre. Dallaire himself was personally ravaged by the memories and subsequently suffered a massive psychological breakdown. His career ruined, he attempted suicide. Years later he wrote of his experiences to fellow Canadians in a letter read aloud to the nation over the air by the Canadian Broadcast Corporation on July 3, 2000. In the letter he commented:

> "There are times when the best medication and therapist simply can't help a soldier suffering from this new generation of peacekeeping injury. The anger, the rage, the hurt and the cold loneliness that separate you from your family, friends, and society's normal daily routine are so powerful that the option of destroying yourself is both real and attractive. . . .
>
> This nation, without any hesitation nor doubt, is capable and even expected by the less fortunate of this globe to lead the developed countries beyond self-interest, strategic advantages, and isolationism, and raise their sights to the realm of the pre-eminence of humanism and freedom . . . Where humanitarianism is being destroyed and the innocent are being literally trampled into the ground . . . the soldiers, sailors, and airpersons . . . supported by fellow countrymen who recognize the cost in human sacrifice and in resources will forge in concert with our politicians . . . a most unique and exemplary place for Canada in the league of nations, united under the United Nations Charter."[9]

Questions for Discussion

1. Should Lemaire have defied orders? What should he have done then? Should he have considered granting the Tutsi villagers' bizarre request?

2. Ought there to be specific rules or principles that guide nations in deciding to become involved in such actions, and that might clarify for their military and political leaders the expectations placed upon them if they do?

---

[9] Quoted in Powers, *Bystanders to Genocide*, p. 108.

Massacre in Srebrenica
Dr. Paolo Tripodi, Marine Corps University (Quantico)

It was just a few minutes after 5 a.m. on July 6, 1995. Dutch Privates First Class Marc Klaver and Raviv van Renssen were deployed in Observation Post Foxtrot (UN OP) around Srebrenica. They were startled suddenly by a loud detonation. Looking into each other's eyes, the two young peacekeepers silently wondered what was going on, and, more than anything else, what they were supposed to do. Had this explosion been the beginning of a long-feared Serbian attack?

Their thoughts were abruptly interrupted by a second explosion. Bosnian Serbs were indeed shelling the Muslim position around UN OP. Muslim soldiers responded with their AK 47s. After two hours, Klaver climbed up on the OP tower. Three Serbian T 34 tanks had taken up positions about 1600 yards east of the observation post. In a scene that reminded Klaver more of World War II than modern warfare, a Serbian T34 shot at the OP any time the Serbian crew could spot the bright blue color of the Dutch paratroopers' helmets.

Although Klaver and van Renssen realized how serious their own situation had become, they could not imagine that in the next few days Srebrenica itself would become infamous as the name for the most tragic massacre since the end of the Second World War. Private First Class van Renssen, however, would not live to witness it. He would shortly be killed by shrapnel from a hand grenade thrown at his APC by a group of Muslim soldiers—the very same people he was supposed to protect—who had promised they would target any peacekeeper who attempted to abandon strategic observation posts around Srebrenica.

Background

The city of Srebrenica is located west of the Drina River in eastern Bosnia, close to the border with Serbia. Its history, as many other Balkan cities, is complex and fascinating. During the time of the Roman empire, the city had been named "Argentaria" (from the Latin: argentums, *silver*) in reference to the city's importance as a silver mining center. This mining tradition continued after the Romans left; the name *Srebrenica* comes from the Serbo-Croatian word for silver, *srebro*.

Of the 37,000 people resident in the municipality in 1991, 73 percent were Muslims, 25 percent Serbs, and the remaining 2 percent described themselves either as "Yugoslavians" or as belonging to other ethnic groups. The quality of life of people living in Srebrenica in the early 1990s, in author David Rohde's words, "rivaled that of the United States and Western Europe."[1] A large and growing number of households had modern appliances such as TV's, VCR's and washing machines, while a number of supermarkets and movie theaters had opened in the city area.

The Serbian "ethnic cleansing" campaign in Bosnia began on or around March 27, 1992, a few weeks after President Alija Itzebegović declared Bosnia-Herzegovina a sovereign and independent state. It was immediately clear that Srebrenica's geographical location would be a serious concern. In April, Srebrenica was surrounded by Serbian paramilitary forces. On April 18, the infamous Arkan's

---

[1] David Rohde, *Endgame*, Farrar, Straus and Giroux, New York, 1997, p. xiv.

Tigers militia occupied the city briefly, but was unable to gain full control. Within two days, Muslim troops engaged the Serbian militias and by May 8 they regained control of Srebrenica. The Serbs took revenge for this defeat, killing a number of Muslim men who had been detained as prisoners in Bratunac.[2] Thus, Srebrenica was in the hands of Muslim militias, but remained an isolated enclave within Serbian-controlled territory.

The violence of the conflict in the former Yugoslavia and the targeting of civilians as part of a strategy known as "ethnic cleansing" finally compelled the international community to intervene. On February 21 the U.N. Security Council approved resolution 743 with which the United Nations Protection Force, UNPROFOR, was established. Shortly thousands of peacekeepers began deploying. UNPROFOR's initial commitment was mainly focused on Croatia, as its main task was to ensure that three United Nations Protected Areas (UNPAs) were demilitarized and that the people living in them would be protected.

In the complex ethnic tapestry with which the U.N. had to deal, Muslim enclaves in Bosnian-Serb–held territory represented a great challenge. Initially, the U.N. mandate contained no specific directives for managing these territories. As the systematic killing and forced emigration and "resettlement" of Muslims in the Serbian-held areas gained momentum, however, the number of refugees arriving in the Muslim enclaves increased beyond the local villages' capacities to accommodate them.

On January 7, 1993, Nasir Oric, the young Muslim military leader of Srebrenica, organized a successful attack against Kravica, a city close to the enclave. On this occasion, atrocities against Serbian civilians were committed, resulting in the deaths of more than 40 children and women. Serb forces waited until March to launch a strong offensive, then took the villages of Konjević Polje and Cerska. Their populations were pushed towards the area of Srebrenica, whose inhabitants by then numbered between 50,000 and 60,000. During these hostilities, the town of Žepa was separated from Srebrenica, becoming another enclave on its own in Bosnian Serb territory.[3]

As a consequence of the Serbian offensive, the humanitarian situation inside the enclaves deteriorated significantly.[4] In the area of Srebrenica, food became a major problem and, as road convoys were not allowed to reach the enclave, the only option became humanitarian airdrops. More than 1,900 tons of food and medicine were dropped in the area of Srebrenica over a period of four months early in 1993.[5]

The U.N. decision to declare Srebrenica—and later on the enclaves of Gorazde, Tuzla, Bihac and Žepa—"safe areas" came about as a result of French General Philippe Morillon, then serving as Commander-in-Chief of UNPROFOR. His concern was that the Muslim population inside the enclaves was in great danger.[6] With permission from Serbian authorities, on March 11, 1993, General Morillon traveled to Srebrenica to meet with local authorities and explore the possibility of declaring Srebrenica a demilitarized zone. This would permit him to negotiate with the Serbians on the creation of a safe corridor through which to allow humanitarian convoys to reach the besieged city.

The most visible consequence of Morillon's presence in Srebrenica was the immediate ending of Serbian shelling of the city. As long as Morillon was in Srebrenica, Serbian artillery refrained from targeting the enclave. When Morillon finally decided that it was time for him to return to his own headquarters, however, he was prevented to do so by a large number of civilians. Under these unusual circumstances, he attempted to calm the inhabitants by stating publicly, "You are now under the protection of the UN forces . . . I will never abandon you."[7]

---

[2] According to the Indictment of the International Criminal Tribunal for the Former Yugoslavia against Slobodan Milosevic on May 9, 1992 approximately 65 Bosnian Muslim and Bosnian Croat civilians were killed by members of the JNA, acting together with Serb paramilitary forces. Available online at http://www.un.org/icty/indictment/english/mil-ii011122e.htm

[3] Smail Čević, Muharem Kreso, Bećir Macić, *Genocide in Srebrenica, United Nations "Safe Area", in July 1995,* Institute for the Research Crime Against Humanity and International Law, Sarajevo, 2001, p. 42.

[4] René André and François Lamy, *Srebrenica: rapport sur un massacre,* Tome I, Assemblée Nationale, Paris, 2001, pp. 16–17.

[5] Jan Willem Honig, Norbert Both, *Srebrenica. Record of a War Crime,* Penguin Books, New York, 1997, p. 82.

[6] General Morillon Audition 25 January 2001, French Commission of Inquiry, in René André and François Lamy, *Srebrenica: rapport sur un massacre,* Tome II, Assemblée Nationale, Paris, 2001, pp, 138–154.

In the following days, however, Gen. Morillon was obliged to leave Srebrenica. A few weeks later, on April 16, the United Nations Security Council passed resolution 819. This resolution asked for "all parties and others concerned treat Srebrenica and its surrounding as a safe area which should be free from any armed attack or any other hostile act. . . . The immediate cessation of armed attacks by Bosnian Serb paramilitary units against Srebrenica and their immediate withdrawal from the areas surrounding Srebrenica."[8]

The following day, 140 Canadian peacekeepers established the first U.N. deployment in Srebrenica. This deployment was not impressive, either in terms of numbers of troops or of weapons. The severely under-supplied Canadian contingent could rely upon a small number of 50-calibre machine guns. Due to the complex situation of the enclave, Canadian troops immediately realized that their task was more than humanitarian and that, were the political conditions suddenly to change, they would find themselves unable to face a serious military threat. The Canadian government immediately asked for a larger contingent of international troops. Specifically, Ottawa asked for French and British reinforcements, but obtained only the unilateral commitment of London to give air support should the Canadians in Srebrenica at any time come under attack from the Serbs.[9]

While the humanitarian emergency in Bosnia remained a serious concern, the violence generated by the "ethnic cleansing" and by the many punishing and retaliatory actions launched against each other by the Serb and Muslim paramilitary militia offered serious evidence that, from a tactical point of view, the larger military situation was extremely unstable. What was extremely clear, particularly in the Serbian camp, was that the willingness to cooperate with the United Nations, or to permit any serious peacekeeping military deployment, was feeble at best. The half-hearted and somewhat isolated deployment of peacekeeping troops offered the potential of becoming part of a greater problem, rather than a factor contributing to a process of stabilization.

It was in this unstable context that the Dutch government, following a request from the U.N. Secretary General, decided to deploy a contingent of peace-keeping troops to Srebrenica. In the Netherlands, the decision to send Dutch peacekeepers to the Muslim town was not an easy one. As Chris Klep explains:

> Initially both the Ministry of Defense and the Army Staff had strong reservations about the risks and usefulness of deploying a combat unit to a country still caught up in a major civil war. Also, the Netherlands Armed Forces were in the process of large-scale reductions and reorganizations following the 1993 'Defense Priority Review'. However, these objections were put aside by parliament, press and public opinion, all of whom demanded quick and decisive humanitarian intervention in the Bosnian war.[10]

The Netherlands offered a unit of battalion size from its newly-established 11th Airmobile Brigade.[11] The Dutch commitment was for an eighteen-month period, and was to occur in three, six-month "semesters" or stages. The Dutch battalion in Srebrenica would be in charge of 150 square kilometers of rough terrain. In the area there were approximately 40,000 people whose conditions were very precarious. The deployment of Dutch forces began with some difficulties. In December 1993 the Serbs delayed Dutch reconnaissance elements from visiting Srebrenica to arrange the battalion deployment. Only after NATO made clear to the Serbs that it was ready to use force in the form of air strikes did the Serbian position soften.

In late January, some elements of the Dutch battalion (or "Dutchbat") were in Srebrenica, although officially the replacement of the 140 Canadian peacekeepers began early in March. Yet the Serbs continued to delay Dutchbat deployment by imposing interminably long "border checks" of convoys, and

---

[7] Quoted in *Ibid.*, p. 86.

[8] S/RES/819 (1993), 16 April 1993.

[9] Jan Willem Honig, Norbert Both, op. cit., 107.

[10] Chris Klep and Donna Winslow, 'Learning Lessons the Hard Way: Somalia and Srebrenica Compared' in Erwin A. Scmidl (ed.), *Peace Operations Between War and Peace*, Frank Cass, London, 2000, p. 96.

[11] http://www.korpscommandotroepen.nl/english/commandostichting/history/1990heden.html

sometimes turning them back. Following the initial Dutchbat deployment, the Serbs felt increasingly confident that they could act more aggressively to cut off humanitarian supply lines to Srebrenica. This was in part because Dutchbat never achieved its full deployment capacity of troops, and also it began to run low on ammunitions, weapons, spare parts and other logistic items, all of which had to pass through Serbian lines. By the time the third stage of deployment ("Dutchbat III") got underway in January, 1995, the Serbs would no longer allow Dutch soldiers who had gone on leave to return to the unit.[12]

For Dutchbat III, a few months into the deployment in mid-1995, fresh food, running water, and communication with home all became serious problems. Jan Willem Honig and Norbert Both offer an accurate description of what the situation was like in the May-July 1995 period among Dutchbat soldiers:

> Morale, which had been decreasing steadily almost from the beginning, now began to hit new lows. The primitive living conditions, the uncertainty of leave, no more mail coming in from home, were completely new and unusual experiences for many soldiers. They felt abandoned by their government and began to wonder what they were doing in Srebrenica. The prospects of adventure and extra pay that had motivated many to sign up for duty in Bosnia began to wear off in the face of the hardship and the loss of faith in their mission.[13]

The Report produced by the Netherlands Institute for War Documentation in 2002 reinforces this description. It stated that "The Dutch blue helmets in the Srebrenica enclave had to contend with motivation as a consequence of the lack of meaning given to the mission and the related 'working and living conditions'."[14]

The Attack on Srebrenica

Thus, by the beginning of July, 1995, just days before the Serbian paramilitary launched its attack against Srebrenica, Dutchbat III was a unit consisting of 429 demoralized and poorly-equipped soldiers, whose main task was to man thirteen indefensible[15] "observation positions" (Ops) within a perimeter of fifty kilometers. On July 6, the Serbian artillery began targeting the enclave and some of the key OPs. The reaction from the Dutch soldiers was extremely confused.

Dutchbat CO, Lieutenant Colonel Ton Karremans thought that, under those conditions, the only possible course of action to stop the Serbian occupation of Srebrenica was calling for NATO Close Air Support (CSA). In a testimony at the Yugoslavia war crime tribunal Karremans stressed that the lightly-armed Dutch soldiers were running dangerously low of food and fuel. He stated, "We had no medicines. We had no spare parts. We had no engineering equipment and no food except our combat rations, and we lived on combat rations for a long time."[16] The overall conditions had convinced Lt. Col. Karrenmans that CSA was the only course of action, and that putting up any type of resistance to stop the Serbian would have resulted in Dutchbat forces being wiped out.

A short report he wrote on July 12 for his chain of command, following a series of meetings with the Serbian paramilitary leader, General Mladic, reveals both the existing state of confusion and, to a certain extent, the emotional impact that the negative conditions had on him. Karrenmans wrote (para. 5) "there are more than 15,000 people within one square kilometer, including the battalion, in an extreme vulnerable position: the sitting duck position, not able to defend these people at all. In direct line and above the compound he [Mladic] deployed two guns, three MLRS and one Anti-aircraft gun, all in direct sight. At this moment I am responsible for these people." The following paragraph stated: "I am

---

[12] Jan Willem Honig, Norbert Both, op. cit., pp. 125–129.

[13] Jan Willem Honig, Norbert Both, op. cit., p. 135.

[14] The NIWD report is available in English at http://www.riod.nl/engels/english.html

[15] The Ops were considered indefensible as they were built to be highly visible from both Muslims and Serbians. This was more in line with a UN Monitoring mission than warfighting.

[16] Dutch commander says U.N., NATO abandoned peacekeepers, CNN, July 4 1996 available at: http://www.cnn.com/WORLD/9607/04/yugo.war.crimes/

not able: a. to defend these people; b. to defend my own battalion; c. to find suitable representative among the civilians because the official authorities are for certain reasons not available; d. to find representative among the military authorities because they are trying to fight for a corridor to the Tuzla-area, and will not show up anyway because of purely personal reasons; e. manage to force AHIB troops to handover their weapons."[17]

The overall situation got worse for Dutchbat when, on July 9, Serb troops took thirty of the Dutch peacekeepers hostage. General Mladic was fully aware that his forces could do very little if the NATO F16s had seriously attacked them. The Dutch hostages thus became an important factor that the Serbian General could use to pressurize the U.N. not to resort to CAS. Even so, Lieutenant Colonel Karremans called for CAS, but General Bernard Janvier, by now serving as Commander of United Nations forces in the former Yugoslavia, was more than hesitant in approving the request. General Janvier finally gave in on the night of July 10, but postponed air strikes until the following morning. On July 11, when the Serbs were dangerously close to the town, Karremans was informed that his request for CAS was submitted on the wrong form and therefore—despite the fact that the situation was extremely critical—he would be obliged to resubmit his request.

By the time the new request reached General Janvier, NATO aircraft already airborne and in place for the proposed air strike, had to refuel. They headed back to their base in Italy. This absurd situation had major tactical implications. As Serbian radar could track NATO aircraft, Serb forces around Srebrenica realized that CAS was not a threat for at least several more hours, during which they could attack the city with impunity. It was indeed many hours later, at 1440 local time, when two NATO F16s dropped two bombs on a Serbian position. At this point, as expected, Serbian Gen. Mladic threatened the lives of the Dutch hostages. Further CAS was abandoned. In only a few more hours Serb troops controlled the U.N. "safe area" of Srebrenica, and, as the Dutch peace-keepers abandoned their positions, the massacre of Muslim inhabitants began.

Sequel

In the weeks after the fall of Srebrenica, more than 7,000 Muslim men were killed in the mountains around the enclave. In the following months, news of the massacre became public as U.S. reconnaissance satellites identified the first mass graves. The Dutch government appointed the Netherlands Institute for War Documentation to investigate responsibilities in the massacre. The NIWD report released on 10 April 2002 concluded that the Dutch Government and senior military leaders were to be blamed for the massacre. Dutch Prime minister Vim Kok resigned the following week. In 1993 at the time when the deployment was decided he had been vice premier. By July of 1995, he was Prime Minister. Years later Lt. Col. Karremans testified: "The air strikes should have been massive, without regard for possible victims in the Dutch battalion or civilians, then we could have turned the tables. These chances were just thrown away."[18]

Karremans' testimony made clear that he felt he was in no position to offer an effective opposition to the Serbian attack. He did not intend to risk the life of his men. John Keegan explained that the tragedy of Srebrenica might have been avoided "had Dutchbat been made larger, given heavier equipment and guaranteed air support and, above all, instructed to fight in prosecution of its mission."[19] From a tactical point of view apparently there was not much more Dutchbat could have done. British General Rupert Smith, however, offered an interesting interpretation at a Dutch parliamentary enquiry into the Srebrenica massacre. According to the retired General, it was clear to him that Dutch authorities had signaled that the Netherlands would not sacrifice its soldiers simply in order to protect the enclave.[20]

---

[17] Dutchbat CO Report to Force Commander Lgen Janvier, 12 July 1995. Copy in René André and François Lamy, *Srebrenica: rapport sur un massacre*, Tome I, Assemblée Nationale, Paris, 2001.

[18] Marin Brower, 'Dutch Colonel: "Our hans were tied at Srebrenica', *Radio Natherlands Wereldomroep*, 19 November 2002.

[19] John Keegan, "'Deterrence by Presence' is not Deterrence at All," *Daily Telegraph*, 17 April 2002.

[20] Geraldine Coughlan, 'Dutch felt Srebrenica 'not worth sacrifice', *BBC*, 6 December 2002 available at http://news.bbc .co.uk/2/low/europe/2550801.stm

A number of interesting doubts have been raised in their book by Smail Čević, Muharem Kreso, Bećir Macić. Although they acknowledged the enormous difficulties that Dutchbat faced against the Serbs, they wrote: "The Dutch UNPROFOR troops in Srebrenica never fired at the attacking Serbs . . . Had they engaged the attacking Serbs directly it is possible that events would have unfolded differently. . . . Perhaps they [Dutchbat] should have allowed everyone into the compound and then offered themselves as human shields to protect them. This may have slowed down the Serbs and bought time for higher level negotiations to take effect. At the same time it is possible that the Serb forces would have then shelled the compound, killing thousands in the process, as they threatened to do."[21]

Questions for Discussion

1. Should the Dutch have resisted, even if some or all would be wounded or killed? Should foreign nationals take casualties to save lives in a country in which they have no personal or political involvement or interest?

2. Likewise, do humanitarian uses of military force require their own unique rules of engagement or laws of combat, that would clarify responsibilities and expectations in ways that might have avoided Dutchbat's dilemma?

3. The Dutch soldiers were court-martialed for dereliction of duty. Is it appropriate to try soldiers in an international court for alleged failures of responsibility or errors of judgment that might arise in humanitarian missions? Does this liability, or the particular kinds of challenges faced in these missions, argue for a special force, specially trained, rather than for the use of the armed forces of miscellaneous nations?

4. Obedience and Dissent: In the preceding case (Rwanda), the national chain of command ordered the soldiers to withdraw, and they obeyed, although they and subsequent critics of this decision think that the Belgians should have refused to obey this lawful order. In Case II (Srebrenica), just the opposite occurs: the immediate U.N. chain of command ordered the Dutch soldiers to defend their positions and protect the city of Srebrenica. They disobeyed this order, and were court-martialed. Was (or would) obedience to lawful orders have been the right decision in both cases? If not, upon whom would the responsibility for disobeying orders likely fall?

---

[21] Smail Čević, Muharem Kreso, Bećir Macić, op. cit., pp. 254–255.

Acting on Conscience:
Captain Lawrence Rockwood in Haiti
Dr. Stephen Wrage, U.S. Naval Academy

Port-au-Prince, Haiti
Barracks compound, Tenth Mountain Division
30 September 1994
1920 hours

Captain Lawrence Rockwood, counterintelligence officer[1] with the U.S. Army's Tenth Mountain Division, crouched by his pallet on the concrete barracks floor and thought back through what had happened over the past seven days.

Six days ago, on his second day in-country, a report from the Belair jail in Port-au-Prince described a mutilated Haitian torture victim spirited out at night. A report two days later traced a beheaded body found in a swamp outside the city back to the Omega jail. All the prison reports featured emaciated and abused prisoners, not criminals in most cases—simply enemies of the regime that the American forces were there to replace.[2]

A report he had received two days before on the 28th said that American forces had entered a prison in the southwestern town of Les Cayes. They found "over 30 men were crammed into a cell no larger than 15 feet square. They were so malnourished that—as with concentration camp victims of World War II—their food intake had to be increased gradually to avoid harming them. When the American

Reprinted by permission of the author.

This case was produced by the Center for the Study of Professional Military Ethics, U.S. Naval Academy. Support was provided by Newport News Shipbuilding.

[1]As a counterintelligence officer, Rockwood's duties were to read intelligence reports and debrief intelligence operatives, both American and Haitian, to discover potential threats to the security of U.S. forces in Haiti. In this role he had unusual access to information, freedom of movement, contact with Haitians and opportunity to exercise initiative.

[2]A Central Intelligence Agency report that Rockwood had requested before he set out for Haiti said "85% of the 300 to 500 people incarcerated [in the National Penitentiary in Port-au-Prince] have not been charged" with a crime. The report found they were political prisoners of the Cedras regime, supporters of the democratically elected Aristide government that the intervention was intended to restore to power. See Meg Laughlin, 'The Rockwood Files," *Miami Herald*, October 1, 1995, Tropic section, page 6.

soldiers removed one invalid from the prison, they discovered that he had lain for so long in one position that some of his skin had fallen off."[3]

"At least we could get food into those places," Rockwood thought. He had seen the pallet-loads of MRE's—Meals Ready to Eat—unloaded from American ships onto the docks in Port-au-Prince. He had even told one prison official he could probably get two per day delivered for each of his prisoners. The official was against it: too great a security risk, he said. "What's the risk?" Rockwood had asked him. "It's the starving prisoners who will riot, isn't it?" No, he was told. The starving ones just lie there. The security risk would come from outside the prison: from all the people who would break in to get at that food.[4]

An Unusual Soldier

Rockwood had arrived in Haiti seven days earlier on September 23, four days after the first American troops were deployed to the island. He had prepared for this mission with eager anticipation. Rescuing the helpless and opposing the tyrannous is precisely what a military is for, he thought.

Rockwood was the son, grandson, and great-grandson of military men, but he didn't fit any traditional mold. He had grown up on military bases—both his parents served in the Air Force—so by the time he went to high school he had lived abroad in Turkey, France, and Germany. The event he remembered best from his childhood was when the family was stationed in Germany.

Years before, his father had been among the forces that liberated the Nazi camps. He wanted his son to know what he had seen and learned, so when Rockwood was eight years old he and his father went together to the concentration camp at Dachau. "My father told me that these camps are not the creation of a few evil, brutal men. They're really the creation of cynicism and blind obedience to authority."[5]

Rockwood considered breaking the pattern of three generations by joining the priesthood instead of the military, but after a year in a Catholic seminary he followed suit and enlisted in the Army. He was 19 then, and along his unusual track to being commissioned as an officer he would earn a bachelors in psychology, a masters in history and become a licensed practical nurse. He would also convert to Tibetan Buddhism. Before his deployment to Haiti he had been treated for depression and at the time of the deployment he was taking the anti-depression drug, Prozac.

In the Army he rose fast and received outstanding evaluations.[6] He chose his models carefully and worked hard to mold himself in their pattern. In his cubicle back at Fort Drum he kept pictures of three men he admired: General George Picard, a counterintelligence officer in the French army during the

---

[3]The prison had been visited by special forces operating independently in the countryside under the command of Lieutenant Colonel Michael Jones. In an interview with Bob Shacochis, author of *The Immaculate Invasion* (New York: Viking, 1999) Jones says, "We found some photographs, pretty damning photographs. People being pulled apart with chains, people being beaten." (Shacochis, p. 150.) Jones later recalled "a pile of live bodies crammed into a cell in which there was neither room to stand nor room to lie down. When soldiers, who apparently did not realize initially that the men were still alive, began pulling one of the men off the pile, his skin simply ripped off his back, exposing his spinal cord to view." Quoted in transcript of U.S. v. Rockwood, no. 261–2–6597 at 1604–5. See also Ian Katz, "Depressed or Just Decent," *The Guardian,* (London) May 30, 1995, at T4 and Peter Slevin, "36 Inmates, One Cell: Haitian Jails in Squalor," *Miami Herald,* October 10, 1994, at 1 A. The horrible conditions in Les Cayes were not unique. General James T. Hill, deputy commander of the 25th Infantry Division deployed to Haiti in 1996, told reporter Anna Husarska in an unpublished interview, "everybody found it in every one of the jails. There is no doubt about it. I've been to almost every one of the jails." Interview with Husarska dated March 2, 1995. See Robert O. Weiner and Fionnuala Ni Aolian, "Beyond the Laws of War: Peacekeeping in Search of a Legal Framework," *Columbia Human Rights Law Review,* Winter, 1996 at note #21.

[4]See testimony of Paul J. Browne, Vice President, The Investigative Group, in United States House of Representatives, 104th Congress, First Session, *Human Rights Violations at the Port-au-Prince Penitentiary,* Hearings before the Subcommittee on the Western Hemisphere, Committee on International Relations, May 3, 1995.

[5]Quoted in Associated Press, "Court-martial Looms for Officer Who Probed Haiti Rights Abuses," *Asheville Citizen-Times,* Asheville, NC, at 3A.

[6]Officer fitness evaluations of Captain Rockwood between 1987 and 1993 characterized his performance as "superb" or "excellent" and recommended he be promoted "ahead of his contemporaries." Transcript at Defendant's Exhibit U, United States v. Rockwood, no. 261–29–6597 (M.J. 1995).

Dreyfus Affair who went to prison to protest Dreyfus' innocence,[7] Colonel Count von Stauffenberg of the German army who gave his life in an attempt to assassinate Hitler, and Chief Warrant Officer Hugh C. Thompson, the helicopter pilot who saw the My Lai massacre in progress, lowered his helicopter into the middle of it, and ordered his door gunner to train his machine gun on American troops who were killing unarmed civilians.

Rockwood's Concern

Well before he left for Haiti, Rockwood was worried about human rights abuses there, and he focused on Haiti's prisons as the likeliest sites of torture, murder, and abuse. On the 10th of August he requested a special classified report from the C.I.A. about Haitian prisons, and later he would point out that the Civil-Military Operations Handbook for the 10th Mountain Division includes a checklist enumerating the information the division staff should obtain about each site where prisoners were confined, including "name, address, grid coordinate, telephone number, type of facility, maximum capacity, present capacity, number of guards, capacity of kitchens, name of warden, overall condition of facility and inmates."[8]

Rockwood was confirmed in his commitment to human rights in Haiti when he heard President Clinton say in his September 15 address to the nation that a primary objective of Operation Uphold Democracy was "to stop the brutal atrocities."[9] He was proud to be part of the team when his unit began to deploy to Haiti on the 19th. He arrived in Haiti four days later.

The Background

For over a year Captain Rockwood had watched the situation in Haiti unfold.[10] As an Army counter-intelligence officer stationed at the headquarters of the 10th Mountain Division in Fort Drum, New York, he had monitored the long play of threats and defiance pass between the Clinton Administration and the Cedras regime.

Three years earlier, in September 1991, General Raoul Cedras had overthrown the only democratically elected government in Haiti's history when he drove Jean-Bertrand Aristide into exile only seven months into his term.

---

[7]"In 1894 Captain Alfred Dreyfus (1859–1935), a French officer, was convicted of treason by court martial, sentenced to life imprisonment, and sent to Devil's Island. The case had arisen with the discovery in the German embassy of a handwritten list of secret French documents. The French army was at the time permeated with anti-Semitism, and suspicion fell on Dreyfus, an Alsatian Jew. . . . In 1898 it was learned that much of the evidence against Dreyfus had been forged by army intelligence officers." *The Concise Columbia Encyclopedia*, (New York: Columbia University Press, 1983) page 242.

[8]Civil Military Operations Handbook of the 10th Mountain Division, Entry #9, "Law Enforcement Agency Checklist." See also the Civil Affairs Operations manual of the U.S. Army (FM 41–10) at Chapter IX (Public Safety) under heading "c."

[9]President Clinton's words: "Our reasons are clear: to stop the horrible atrocities; to affirm our determination that we keep our commitments and we expect others to keep their commitments to us; to avert the flow of thousands more refugees and to secure our borders; to preserve the stability of democracy in our hemisphere." *Foreign Policy Bulletin*, November/December 1994, page 18.

[10]Haiti is a mountainous country of about 11,000 square miles and 9,000,000 people, almost all of African descent. It trails every country in the western hemisphere in such measures of development as literacy, income per capita, doctors per thousand people and miles of roads. 85% of the population is illiterate; 60% are unemployed or underemployed. Less than 40% of the urban population and less than 5% of the rural population have access to piped water. Infant mortality is over 110 per thousand (compared to 40 per thousand in the United States.) Brian Weinstein, *Haiti: The Failure of Politics*, New York: Praeger, 1992, pp. 4–5.

Before 1790, Haiti was France's richest colony, accounting for almost half of France's foreign trade and producing 50% of the world's sugar and 40% of the world's coffee. A series of bloody revolutions in the next twenty years and a brutal but inefficient feudal system throughout the 19th century entrenched Haiti in misery. The country was occupied and governed by U.S. troops from 1915–1934. Since then a succession of dictatorships protected the interests of a wealthy, Europeanized elite at the expense of the mass of the population.

Two years after that, in October 1993, a noisy crowd encouraged by Cedras had blocked the docks in Port-au-Prince when the U.S.S. Harlan County with U.S. and Canadian troops, engineers and trainers aboard, had tried to land. Rather than face the prospect of even minor violence, the Clinton administration pulled back the Harlan County. They may have been unwilling to open a new front in the peacekeeping struggles, since the week before that, 18 American soldiers had been killed by Mohammed Aideed's gunmen in Mogadishu. American enthusiasm for nation building was at a low point and the Harlan County steamed back to the United States.

By spring of 1994, however, the Clinton Administration was facing strong pressure to act. The Congressional Black Caucus had publicized torture and murder in Haiti; Randall Robinson of TransAfrica had begun a hunger strike in sympathy with the victims of the Cedras regime; Clinton's chief advisor on Haiti had resigned and been replaced with a former head of the Black Caucus; midterm elections were six months away and desperate Haitian refugees were appearing on the beaches of Florida.

In July 1994 President Clinton sent the 24th Marine Expeditionary Unit to float in the waters off Haiti and threaten imminent force, and in early September Clinton sent forces aboard the carriers "Eisenhower" and "America" to join them, but Cedras remained adamantly in power. On September 15 Clinton at last said "there is no point in going any further with the present policy"[11] and airborne Special Operations units boarded their planes at Fort Bragg. Rockwood monitored the cable traffic and CNN, expecting see what the military calls a "non-permissive entry."

The paratroopers were already in the air when an emergency mission led by former President Jimmy Carter, Senator Sam Nunn and General Colin Powell induced Cedras and his top circle to leave Haiti. American troops led a multi-national force into the country unopposed, but they entered a strange setting. Aristide was not scheduled to return to Haiti for another month. Until then governance was to be shared by the American-led, U.N.-sponsored forces and the remains of the Cedras regime which had proven itself corrupt, brutal, and frequently murderous. The prisons, for example, remained under local control.

Force Protection

"As I assumed my duties in Haiti on September 23 I was informed that 'force protection' was to be the focus of our efforts," Rockwood later reported.[12] This troubled Rockwood and others but seemed entirely appropriate to many members of the mission. Assuring "force protection," avoiding "combatant status" and resisting "mission creep" were the lessons learned from the previous October's disaster in Somalia. Joint Task Force Commander Lieutenant General David C. Meade and his staff officers were determined that American troops in Haiti would not cross "the Mogadishu Line."[13]

When troops landed on September 19, their rules of engagement had required them to stand by or look the other way as thugs from the Cedras regime beat Aristide supporters who had gathered at the port to hail the Americans' arrival. Americans were to use force only when they were themselves threatened with violence; Haitian-on-Haitian violence was not to be resisted. American troops were to stay for the most part behind barbed wire and sand bag emplacements and were forbidden to leave the barracks compounds unaccompanied. Most troops could move about only in convoys of at least two vehicles with at least two persons in each vehicle.

---

[11]See *Foreign Policy Bulletin,* November/December 1994, page 18.

[12]Interview with the author, August 18, 1999. Rockwood was not alone in that assessment. See also the testimony of Lieutenant Colonel Frank Bragg, Assistant Chief of Staff for intelligence, 10th Mountain Division and Director of Intelligence for the Multilateral Force in Haiti: "Question: Would it be fair to say that actually your whole priority was force protection at that time? Answer: It is fair to say that there was no doubt, that was my number one priority and I had every intelligence asset I could muster focused primarily on that one thing." Transcript of U.S. v. Rockwood, no. 261–29–6597 at 1372.

[13]On "mission creep," see Adam B. Siegel, *The Intervasion of Haiti, Professional Paper* 539, August 1996, Center for Naval Analyses, page 27.

Even though Meade's multinational force had arrived in overwhelming strength——20,000 troops plus heavy equipment"[14]——there were many challenges to its authority. Besides the thugs on the docks who beat the pro-democracy demonstrators, there were a number of tense confrontations with unruly crowds. Violent incidents, however, were few. One American soldier was shot by a Haitian he had arrested, and on September 24, when a patrol of Marines were fired on in Cap-Haitien, they returned fire and ten Haitians were killed.

Rockwood's Odyssey

Rockwood was convinced that Haitians, not Americans, were in the greatest danger. "The main content of the reports that reached me centered on human rights violations against Haitian slum residents rather than any threats directed against our forces," he later said.[15] As soon as he arrived, Rockwood embarked on what he called "my week long odyssey . . . to awake interest of the commander and staff of the Multinational Forces in human rights violations."[16]

On the evening that he arrived in-country, September 24, Rockwood called on Lieutenant Colonel Karl Warner, chief legal officer of the 10th Mountain Division and the man responsible for monitoring human rights violations. Since Colonel Warner was not in, Rockwood left a message requesting authorization to look into the National Penitentiary in Port-au-Prince, which he believed to be the site of atrocities.

The next morning Rockwood met with the command's chaplain to speak of the deteriorating human rights situation in Port-au-Prince slums and the particular problem of the prisons. Rockwood reports that the chaplain said he did not want to get involved in a "political" problem.[17] Rockwood remonstrated with him and later made a formal complaint regarding the chaplain's attitude in a letter to the head of the chaplaincy corps.

That same day, September 25, Rockwood went to the staff Judge Advocate's office and asked for the Laws of War manual, the 1977 Protocol to the Geneva Convention or the report on the U.N. High Commission for Human Rights Conference held in Vienna in 1993. He was determined to prove that the Joint Task Force had an obligation under international law to protect human rights in Haiti. He was disappointed to find the only available reading material was an Army field manual compiled in 1954.

Rockwood's sense of urgency was heightened that day as he received the report from Belair jail mentioned above. Late in the day he took that report to his commanding officer, Lieutenant Colonel Frank Bragg, who had been "something of a mentor to Rockwood. Bragg was sympathetic, but said prison inspections weren't a realistic goal. He told Rockwood to focus on protecting U.S. forces, not Haitian civilians."[18]

Rockwood returned the next evening, September 26, to the Judge Advocate's office to protest the lack of action on human rights violations. Rockwood's sense of desperation was growing as he was convinced that the Cedras regime was using its last few days in control of the prisons to eliminate its enemies—political opponents who had been victims and witnesses to crimes of torture and murder.

On September 27 Rockwood called at the Civil-Military Operations Center hoping to spur a survey of the penitentiaries. He was told that the operations center was not collecting current information

---

[14]Of those 20,000 troops, about half were in logistical, communications, intelligence, or other support roles. The troops of the Joint Task Froce were primarily concentrated in Port-au-Prince and housed in a converted industrial park on the edge of the city. Small units of special forces operated independently in the countryside.

[15]Interview with the author, August 18, 1999.

[16]Interview with the author, August 18, 1999.

[17]"He said he didn't want to get involved in a political issue. He said he was concerned about morale. . . . It was the most categorical response that I got from any officer." Rockwood to Pinsky in a telephone interview. See Mark I. Pinsky, "Changing Role of Armed Forces Complicates Military Clergy's Task," *The Orlando Sentinel,* 1 December 1996 at G-1.

[18]Interview with the author, August 18, 1999. Quotation is from Meg Laughlin, "The Rockwood Files," *Miami Herald,* October 1, 1995, Tropic section, page 8.

on the prisons because the Joint Task Force had no jurisdiction there. He offered the reports he had received on the Belair and Omega jails.

That evening he attempted to organize an intelligence team to visit several prisons but was told he would need a military police escort. The military police refused him an escort, saying their orders were to monitor Haitian police stations and police patrols but not prisons.

Rockwood argued to anyone who would listen that a primary principle of intelligence work is to protect your sources, and warned that the people he talked to during the day were disappearing—apparently being arrested or killed overnight. He needed to go to the prisons to see if they were there. He was told to be patient. It would be some time before troops could be spared for such missions. On the morning of the 29th a liaison officer from Special Operations Forces called on Rockwood to tell him that Rockwood's unit was to take no destabilizing action, and in particular that they were not to inspect a prison without full military support.

Convinced that innocent people were dying and feeling responsible for their fate, Rockwood grew desperate. Late on September 29 he went to the Inspector General and lodged a complaint alleging that the Joint Task Force command was failing to protect the human rights of people in the territory it occupied and controlled. He named eight officers in his chain of command and charged that they had subverted President Clinton's primary mission intent concerning human rights as announced in the September 15 address to the nation. Under "Action Requested" he wrote, "Inform the commanding general as soon as possible of facts that may lend the appearance that the Joint Task Force is indifferent to probably ongoing human rights violations in the [Port-au-Prince] penitentiary."[19] The Inspector General discouraged Rockwood from approaching the command's Chief of Staff on this matter, but he also told Rockwood that his complaint would not be brought to the attention of General Meade for at least a week.

Rockwood did not go to the Chief of Staff. Instead that evening he again confronted his commanding officer, Lt. Col. Frank B. Bragg, and detailed his concerns. He reportedly compared General Meade to General Yamashita, the commander of Japanese forces in the Philippines in 1945.[20] Yamashita was sentenced to death by a war crimes tribunal for his failure to protect American prisoners, even though he neither ordered nor knew of their execution by his soldiers. General Meade, Rockwood argued, had direct and specific knowledge of human rights abuses in the Haitian penitentiaries, and was doing nothing to stop them. Lt. Col. Bragg had no sympathy with these arguments.

The Decision

Now, several hours after that confrontation, late in that long day of the 30th of September, seven packed days after his arrival in-country, Rockwood got up off the floor in the barracks in Port-au-Prince. He knew what he would do next.

---

[19]This series of events is described in Rockwood's testimony before Congressman Dan Burton's Subcommittee on The Western Hemisphere of the House Committee on International Relations. See United States House of Representatives, 104th Congress, First Session, *Human Rights Violations at the Port-au-Prince Penitentiary*, Hearings before the Subcommittee on the Western Hemisphere, Committee on International Relations, May 3, 1995.

[20]Interview with the author, August 18, 1999.

Hiroshima: The First Use
of Nuclear Weapons*
Dr. Manuel Velasquez
and Dr. Cynthia Rostonkowski

In Hiroshima, Japan, the morning of August 6, 1945, was a clear one. Shortly after eight o'clock, people on their way to work heard an airplane flying overhead and many paused to watch it. These people later said they saw something drop from the aircraft. What they saw was an atomic bomb, which exploded over Hiroshima a few seconds later. Seventy thousand people died instantly; fifty thousand others were later killed by the firestorms that raged through the city and by the radiation that rained down on them. The survivors left gruesome accounts of that terrible day:

> As I looked up at the sky from the backyard of my house, I heard the faint buzzing of a B-29 but the plane was not visible. The sun was glaring in the cloudless summer sky. Suddenly, I saw a strange thing. There was a fireball like a baseball growing larger . . . and then something fell on my head. I was 14 years old. How many seconds or minutes had passed, I could not tell, but regaining consciousness I found myself lying on the ground covered with pieces of wood. When I stood up in a frantic effort to look around there was darkness. Terribly frightened, I thought I was alone in a world of death. . . . When the darkness began to fade I found that there was nothing around me. My house, the next-door neighbor's house, and the next had all vanished. . . . I found my mother . . . and my mother began to shout madly for my sister. . . . Children were calling their parents' names, and parents were calling the names of their children. Suddenly mother cried. . . . Four or five meters away my sister's head was sticking out. . . . She was crushed under the collapsed house. . . . Mother and I . . . pulled her out. . . . Night came and I could hear many voices crying and groaning with pain and begging for water. Someone cried, "Damn it! War tortures so many people who are innocent!" The sky was red with flames. . . .[1]

> A girl was standing in the middle of the road staring vacantly. . . . She was eight years old. The wound on her head looked like a cracked pomegranate. Silently I carried her on my back. . . . Then I heard a girl's voice clearly from behind a tree, "Help me,

*From: *Ethics: Theory & Practice*, Eds. Manuel Velasquez & Cynthia Rostonkowski (Englewood Cliffs, NJ: Prentice-Hall, 1985), 169–171. Reprinted by permission of Prentice-Hall, Inc.

[1] From *Unforgettable Fire: Pictures Drawn by Atomic Bomb Survivors*, edited by the Japan Broadcasting Association (New York: Pantheon Books, 1977), pp. 43–44. Copyright © 1977 by NHK. Reprinted by permission of Pantheon Books, a division of Random House, Inc.

[2] Ibid., p. 13.

[3] Ibid., p. 69.

please." Her back was completely burned and the skin peeled off and was hanging down from her hips. . . .[2]

Most of the A-bomb survivors were burned all over their bodies. They were not only naked, but also their skin came off. Suffering from the severe pain of the burns, they were wandering around looking for their parents, husbands, wives, and children.[3]

I was walking along the Hijiyama Bridge. . . . A woman, who looked like an expectant mother, was dead. At her side, a girl of about three years of age brought some water in an empty can she had found. She was trying to let her mother drink from it. . . .[4]

A high school student asked me to give him some water. I heard that if people who had been exposed to the A-bomb drank water, they would die. So I would not give him water. The next day when I passed by the place, he was lying on the ground dead. I wished then that I had let him drink some water, even if he would have died sooner. . . .[5]

We were walking along the streetcar line. Wherever we went we saw dead horses and bodies. . . . When I crossed Miyuki Bridge I saw Professor Takenaka standing at the foot of the bridge. He was almost naked, wearing nothing but shorts and he had a rice ball in his right hand. Beyond, the northern area was covered by red fire burning against the sky. Far away, Ote-machi was also a sea of fire. That day Professor Takenaka had not gone to Hiroshima University and the A-bomb exploded when he was at home. He tried to rescue his wife who was trapped under a roofbeam but all his efforts were in vain. The fire was threatening him also. His wife pleaded, "Run away, dear!" He was forced to desert his wife and escape from the fire. So he was now at the foot of Miyuki Bridge. But I wonder how he came to hold that rice ball in his hand? His naked figure, standing there before the flames with that rice ball looked to me as a symbol of the modest hope of human beings.[6]

The decision to drop the bomb on the people of Hiroshima was made while the United States was at war with Japan. Henry L. Stimson, the American secretary of war, later wrote:

The ultimate responsibility for the recommendation to the President [concerning the A-bomb] rested upon me, and I have no desire to veil it. . . . I felt that to extract a genuine surrender from the [Japanese] Emperor and his military advisers, they must be administered a tremendous shock which would carry convincing proof of our power to destroy the Empire. Such an effective shock would save many times the number of lives, both American and Japanese, that it would cost. . . . Our enemy, Japan, commanded forces of somewhat over 5,000,000 armed men. Men of these armies had already inflicted upon us . . . over 300,000 battle casualties. [They] . . . had the strength to cost us a million more. . . . Additional large losses might be expected among our allies and . . . enemy casualties would be much larger than our own. . . . My chief purpose was to end the war in victory with the least possible cost in lives. . . . The face of war is the face of death; death is an inevitable part of every order that a wartime leader gives. The decision to use the atomic bomb was a decision that brought death to over a hundred thousand Japanese . . . But this deliberate, premeditated destruction was our least abhorrent choice.*

---

[4] Ibid., p. 75.

[5] Ibid., p. 68.

[6] Ibid., p. 46.

*Henry L. Stimson, "The Decision to Use the Atomic Bomb," *Harper's Magazine*, vol. 194, no. 1161 (February 1947), pp. 101, 102, 106, 107.

Tomahawk Target: Collateral Damage
Captain Rick Rubel

In the Command Information Center (CIC) on your Aegis Cruiser, you are loading the targeting data of a "high value" target into the Tomahawk Launch Console in CIC for a missile launch in 12 minutes. According to procedures, you double check the GPS coordinates with the digital chart. When you "zoom" in on the target coordinates, you see that your target, an enemy ammo depot, is right next to a church and a boarding school. The programmed "time on target" is 0950 local, on a Tuesday.

With only a short time before launch, you wonder, "Did the staff that assigned your ship this target know about the church and the boarding school? They must know about this stuff and they probably have a JAG lawyer look at it too." You consider, "Should I bring this to the attention of the CIC officer or the Captain? If I don't say something, then it's on my head that we will kill these civilians and children."

You now have only nine minutes to launch.

As your mind whirls through the images of the warhead detonating, you think, "Look, we need to hit this ammo depot. This is ammo the enemy will use against us and our troops. It just isn't avoidable. And it's not like we mean to hurt the civilians. They're just in the wrong place at the wrong time. And I guess using a Tomahawk Land Attack Cruise Missile we are trying to be as accurate as we can be. Maybe I'm Ok with the launch."

You now have 3 three minutes to launch.

Questions for Discussion

1. Do you have a moral responsibility to say something?

2. Do you bring this to the attention of the skipper, or CIC officer? Or do you assume that the staff that provides the target data has considered the proximity of the school and church?

3. If you tell the CIC officer (a Lieutenant) and he does not pass the information up to the captain, are you morally absolved of responsibility for killing the children?

4. If you launch the missile and find out it destroyed the collateral building, how do you morally defend your actions?

5. How do you resolve your moral conscience?

You now have 1 minute to launch.

Military Means, and Military Ends

Five Short Cases

Captain Rick Rubel

I. Medical Triage: A Fair Battlefield Process?

Over the years, it has been shown that the best process to use in a mass casualty situation in which there are not enough medical workers to take care of all of the injured, is "Medical Triage." Historically, the Triage System goes back at least as far as a French surgeon in Napoleon's army named Baron Dominique Jean Larrey, who determined that by quickly checking the wounded in battle, a doctor could sort the injured into three categories. The surgeon would direct those who cannot be saved due to the extent of their injury to tent #1. Those who do not need immediate medical attention will be sent to tent #2. And those who may be saved with medical attention will be sent to tent #3. The best use of the resources, then is to have the doctors in tent #3. The Chaplains would mostly be in tent #1.

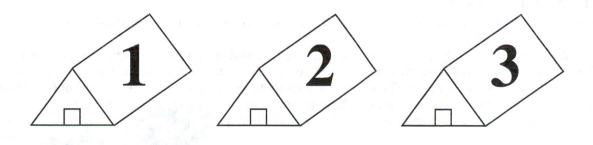

**Expect to die
without extraordinary
measures**

**Will live
—don't treat now**

**Might save if they
get medical attention**

Questions for Discussion

1. Is Triage a "fair" concept?
2. How do we morally justify letting people die without medical attention? Shouldn't we be trying to save every human life?
3. How would you feel if you woke up in tent #1?
4. How do we morally explain to patient in tent #1 they will not see a doctor?

II. Closing the Hatch

In Naval Warfare, when a ship takes a direct hit by a torpedo or a bomb, the interior of the ship will begin to take on water. As the ship progressively floods, the water can begin to enter the large engineering compartments. Ships are designed and built to sustain a certain amount of flooding, but often when the major engineering compartments begin to fill up with water, the large water-tight hatch must be closed quickly or the ship will sink with all hands aboard. This has been an unfortunate occurrence for hundreds of years, since ships have gone to sea to fight naval battles.

In the fictional scene in "Crimson Tide", the engineering compartment is quickly flooding, and the ship will be lost if the hatch is not closed. As the submarine approaches "crush depth" the Chief of the Boat (COB) tells the (acting) Commanding Officer, "If we don't close the hatch the ship will go down." The (acting) Commanding Officer gives the order to "close the hatch" with the three men inside the compartment who try unsuccessfully to stop the flooding. By closing the hatch, the three men will die within a minute.

Questions for Discussion

1. What would you do if you were C.O. of the submarine in the scene?
2. What type of moral reasoning did you use?
3. Does the decision to close the hatch pass the following Moral theories:
   - Utilitarianism?
   - Kant's Categorical Imperative?
   - Doctrine of Double Effect?
4. If you were the C.O. how would you deal with your moral conscience? (You just killed three of your men)

III. Shoot the POW

You are the USMC Battalion Commander in a war in which you find that your 1000 men unit is severely out-numbered by 10,000 of the enemy.

Your troops have advanced far into enemy territory and are essentially cut off from your own forces. The problem is, the weather is poor and your reconnaissance cannot locate the enemy position, and you cannot get air support. The weather is forecast to remain poor for at least four more days. If they find your Battalion, you will certainly be wiped out, or you will have to surrender. Your current mission is to avoid being located.

You capture two enemy soldiers who know where their own forces are, but they are not talking. Your Sergeant tells you that he is certain (assume certainty) that if you shoot one of the prisoners in the head, the remaining one will talk.

For the purpose of this case, assume that these are the only two options:

A. Shoot one POW and find the location of the enemy from the other POW

B. Not shoot the POW, and take a chance of being eventually detected, wiped out, or captured (by randomly picking North, East, West, South)

1. Offer a moral argument for shooting the POW (using utilitarian reasoning)
2. Offer an argument against shooting the prisoner (using any view point you wish)

IV. Torture the Terrorist?

The Special Forces capture a Terrorist in Iraq who you are certain (assume certainty) is a member of Al Qaeda. The Special Forces are also quite certain he knows where several bomb makers and bomb-making facilities are located. He is a hardened terrorist who will endure minor harassment, sleep depravation, and threats. The CIA interrogators say if they get permission to inflict non-life-threatening pain and psychological disorientation, he will certainly talk after a short time.

1. Make a moral argument why it is wrong to torture this terrorist.
2. Make a moral argument why it is right to torture this terrorist.
3. Which argument do you think is the stronger?

V. Live or Let Die?

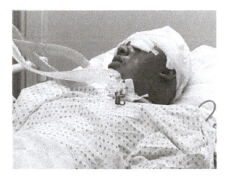

You are a battlefield Commander during a battle. When you walk into the surgical tent to see how the medical triage is going, the Chief Surgeon quickly comes up to you and explains to you that one of the wounded soldiers has been in a coma for several days, and the doctors believe he has severe brain damage and is not certain he will recover. (Their best medical opinion, without an EEG, is that he will probably die of head injuries within a week, but right now he is still breathing on his own).

He explains that a new group of badly wounded soldiers just arrived in need of immediate surgery. They all have shrapnel wounds and he has determined that they need four different organs to live, and there are four surgeons standing by for your decision.

If you take the four organs from the comatose soldier, you can save four people, but you have to start the 4 operations in the next 5 minutes or all four will die. (Assume the surgeries will be successful.)

Questions for Discussion

1. What moral principles are involved with this decision?
2. What virtues of character are involved with this decision?
3. Do you give permission to the surgeon to transplant the 4 organs from the comatose soldier?
4. What is your primary reason for your decision?

The Road to Basra*
Dr. Martin L. Cook and
Major Phillip A. Hamann, USAF

1. The Facts

On Monday, 25 February (the second day of the ground war), American intelligence agencies passed reports from the Kuwaiti Resistance inside Kuwait City to the military command center in Riyadh that the Iraqi occupation forces were preparing to leave the city. Kuwaiti Resistance reported that members of the Iraqi secret police, the Mukhabarat, were attempting to destroy evidence of war crimes (killing all tortured Kuwaitis for example) and pillaging as much property as possible.[1] The Resistance also boasted of mounting a small offensive against the panic-stricken Iraqis. This offensive did not really amount to much—the resistance movement was known to exaggerate at times. But the resistance movement never suggested that the convoy that was preparing to leave Kuwait City contained kidnapped Kuwaiti citizens. (Most of the kidnapped Kuwaiti citizens had already been sent to Basra and other locations weeks prior to this incident.)[2] Air Force intelligence therefore surmised with high confidence that the convoy consisted exclusively of panicked stragglers from the decimated front line divisions (the Iraqi III Corps) and the Iraqi secret police.

In addition, at the start of the ground campaign, American intelligence agencies intercepted an uncoded telephone message from a general officer of the Iraqi Republican Guard.[3] The officer appeared to issue a general order of retreat to Republican Guard units in Kuwait and to order the setting up of a screening or blocking maneuver to allow the Republican Guard to get out of the Kuwait Theater of Operation and into Basra. Hence, American intelligence was aware of preparation for a sudden and massive exodus of Iraqis from Kuwait.

The Mukhabarat secret police is a paramilitary organization with little access to heavy military armor. Its members frequently do not wear uniforms. Therefore, the fact that some individuals on the road were not uniformed was consistent with their identity as Iraqi secret police.

The evening of the same day, a JSTARS aircraft (a recently modified Boeing 707, with discriminating air-to-ground radar tasked to report where and how enemy traffic was moving) detected the large

---

*"The Road to Basra" is reprinted from *Annual of the Society for Christian Ethics.* Copyright © 1994 Society for Christian Ethics. Used by permission. pp. 213–228.

[1] Hamann, interviews with LtCol Charles D. Robertson (August 1991) and Col Christopher Christen. (May 1992) USAF CENTAF Intelligence.

[2] This fact has been confirmed by the National Security Agency and Colonel Christen, the Air Force's chief intelligence officer who was in the air planning office next to Gen. Charles Homer when the information arrived.

[3] Atkinson, *Crusade,* 438–439. Also, *Desert Victory,* 402.

Reprinted by permission of the author.

number of vehicles massing in Kuwait City.[4] There are conflicting reports, even within the military sources, here. One Defense Department document claims that there were up to 200 tanks in this convoy.[5] This is inconsistent with post-battle inventories, which show few military vehicles in the convoy. Although we are not certain, the best explanations of this Defense Department report are either that it confused the Mutlah Ridge convoy with another farther north or that the Arab forces, which were allowed on the highway first to perform Islamic burials of the dead, took advantage of the opportunity to "recover" as much military hardware as possible for their own use. The latter is a quite real possibility in the case of the Soviet built tanks, in particular, since they would have provided spare parts for the same kinds of tanks in the inventories of most Arab armies.

In a ground survey conducted several days after the attack, the Department of Defense confirmed that only 28 of the vehicles destroyed or left abandoned in the convoy were military.[6] The character of the vehicles is ultimately of less moral importance than the question of the *identity of the convoy drivers and passengers and the nature of the convoy's activities.*

The tactical thinking of American military commanders was heavily influenced by close study of the eight-year war with Iran that Iraq fought before its invasion of Kuwait. Iraqi tactics during the Iran-Iraq war were a source of considerable concern regarding this convoy from Kuwait city, and focused the minds of the planners on two major issues. First, the Iraqis demonstrated their will to use their superiority in armor wherever the terrain allowed for it. The Iraqi army favored a "defense-in-depth" strategy. Such a strategy required two to three layers of front line troops. These troops were used both to slow the on-coming Iranian offensive, and as "intelligence fodder" to announce what avenues of attack the Iranians were attempting to exploit. If the Iranian offensive was slowed or stalled by these forces, the rear Iraqi echelons (consisting of the highly mobile Republican Guard armor divisions) quickly crushed the offensive. The success of this type of tactic depends on both the initiative and the ability to maneuver—precisely what a retreating convoy would be attempting to gain.

The second major lesson, and the one that concerned the American commanders most, was the Iraqis' use of chemical munitions. If the situation did not allow the use of rear echelon armored divisions, then the Iraqis on several occasions retreated as quickly as possible in order to leave an open no-man's land between their forces and those of the Iranians. This area was then saturated with artillery shells containing chemical and nerve agents. The results were devastating and militarily effective. In fact, this type of attack accounted for the overwhelming success of the Iraqis in securing Iranian territory in 1988 and forcing a cease-fire.

In light of this history, planners in Riyadh considered it very possible that the Iraqi convoy at Mutlah Ridge was not running *from the Coalition forces but instead from an artillery attack by Iraqi chemical and biological weapons* they had every reason to expect would soon be launched.[7]

That night, after the JSTARS confirmation of the resistance reports, General Schwarzkopf decided not to attack the convoy right away because it was still in the city. This decision reduced the collateral damage to Kuwaiti citizens. In fact, Kuwait City was off-limits to any aerial bombardment. For obvi-

---

[4] James P. Coyne, *Airpower in the Gulf* (Arlington, VA: Aerospace Education Foundation, 1992), 169.

[5] Department of Defense, *Conduct of the Persian Gulf War* (Washington, DC: Office of the Secretary of Defense, April 1992), 631.

[6] Keaney and Cohen, *GWAPS,* 113.

[7] During one of his Riyadh televised press briefings, when asked about the shift of emphasis of the air campaign from strategic targets to battlefield preparation, General Schwarzkopf expressed concern about the chemical threat by referring to it as "the nightmare scenario." The worst-case scenario was a principal war planning assumption and was integral to the working definition of military necessity. Reprisal chemical attacks were even considered as optional strike packages as early as August 1990. The credibility of such a threat was heightened by Saddam Hussein's public warnings. See Lawrence Freedman and Efraim Karsh, *The Gulf Conflict 1990–1991: Diplomacy and War in the New World Order* (Princeton: Princeton University Press, 1993), 363. Paul Christopher, in his recent book, *The Ethics of War and Peace,* correctly identified the mystique that chemical weapons possess: "It is certain that chemical weapons presently cause special psychological effects that conventional weapons do not. In conversations with numerous American soldiers prior to their deployment to Saudi Arabia, I found them to be universally obsessed with the possibility of facing chemical weapons." (Englewood Cliffs, NJ: Prentice Hall, 1994), 211. The news media seemed equally obsessed.

ous reasons, Coalition planners were politically sensitive to postwar criticisms of having "destroyed the city in order to save it."

The convoy managed to leave the city that night, move through the small town of Al-Jahra, and in the early morning hours of the 26th (still dark) was headed north to Basra near a ridge line known as Mutlah Ridge.

Now that the convoy was out in the open, the problem was no longer *whether* to attack the convoy, but *how to attack it.* The tactical difficulty was that it was dark and the weather was bad. The visibility was low and the ceiling had dropped below eight-thousand feet. Most attack aircraft had been ordered to stay above that altitude to avoid Iraqi antiaircraft fire. There was also the so-called "petroleum overcast" resulting from Iraqis setting alight Kuwaiti oilwells. These conditions required the use of the F-15E Strike Eagles. These night and all-weather air-to-ground fighters were ordered to hit the front and back of the convoy at certain choke points along the highway, immobilizing it along the road. They accomplished this mission quite successfully, and the convoy was brought to a halt by bottlenecking it at Mutlah Ridge.

The next morning, in daylight and with better weather, the "kill box" method of air interdiction was employed to funnel attacking aircraft into the Mutlah Ridge area. In this method, latitude and longitude demarcations were given that designated a thirty-mile by thirty-mile area. In this region were large numbers of mobile targets and aircraft were authorized to acquire targets and fire at will. Safe separation of aircraft was maintained by airborne command posts, which gave individual aircraft time on target commands and monitored the numbers and types of aircraft in the box at any given moment. Throughout the rest of the day, a large number of Air Force, Marine, and Navy aircraft of different types attacked and strafed this now "target-rich environment" of two to four miles length. Many pilots described the result as a "feeding frenzy" or a "turkey shoot."

There were some points of contention and bureaucratic compromise between the Air Force and the Navy concerning the command and control of aircraft. One such compromise was the Navy aircraft were not controlled by the much touted ATO from Central Command (CENTCOM) in Riyadh.[8] This central planning of the air campaign had worked well for the first three days of the air war and had maintained a single authority for targeting. According to the official Gulf War Air Power Survey, however, by this point in the war, the ATO had become a mere general outline of attacks desired, with the details filled in by local commanders.

Because of this general immunity of the Navy from the daily ATO, lines of command and control were drawn up to separate Navy and Air Force areas of responsibility for air operations. In other words, in order to insure that there were no collisions or "friendly fire" episodes between Air Force and Navy aircraft, they were given discrete geographical areas within which to operate, surrounded by buffers that, de facto, were immune to attack. The Mutlah Ridge kill box happened to be drawn right on top of this Air Force-Navy "demarcation line." (This arrangement inadvertently provided a corridor through which, on an earlier day, several Iraqi aircraft had managed to fly unhindered into Iran.) The effect of this quirk of command demarcation in the immediate vicinity of Mutlah Ridge was predictable—there was no real command and control of aircraft in and around the box. Reports and interviews with provisional wing commanders verified that several pilots failed to adhere to command and control guidelines in an effort to participate in the "turkey shoot."[9] So eager were they to join the battle that they violated standard procedures of checking in with Forward Air Controllers before entering the kill box.

Another significant aspect of this attack involved the actions of those being attacked. Several reports indicated that the Iraqis were waving white flags along the highway. But this fact must be coupled with an event that occurred two days earlier. An Iraqi unit in southern Kuwait had used the white flag as an illegitimate ruse to expose a Saudi regiment during the initial stages of the Coalition attack.[10] Iraqi

[8] Keaney and Cohen, GWAPS, 153-54; Friedman, *Desert Victory* 173-179; Freedman and Karsh, *The Gulf Conflict,* 318.

[9] Major Hamann, telephone interview with LtCol. Robert E. Duncan, USAF, 3. Feb.1993. Lieutenant Colonel Duncan was Director of Combat Plans, Tactical Air Control Center, Riyadh, Saudi Arabia, during the Gulf War.

[10] Department of Defense, *Conduct of the Persian Gulf War,* 621.

forces had engaged in other such illegal tactics such as parking combat aircraft by mosques and archeological sites. Such acts of illegal perfidy by the Iraqis posed tough challenges on the commanders in the field.

As a result of these previous episodes, as well as the immediate circumstances of this attack, white flags on the highway were generally ignored (although some pilots did express reservations about this to their commanders). Even though some white flags were present, civilian vehicles in the same convoy were directing anti-aircraft fire at the attacking aircraft. Several pilots reported that the anti-aircraft fire was apparently coordinated with respect to the variable cloud ceilings throughout the day. This suggests that elements of the convoy retained at least some capability to communicate with each other and that elements, at least were still under effective command and control—*i.e.*, that they were still organized military units. In other words, despite the initial appearance of an enemy force withdrawing in chaos, the convoy, according to pilots, continued to show signs of organized retreat and command and control.

The attacks were aimed specifically at the vehicles on the highway. The goal of the air campaign throughout the theater of operations at this time was the attrition of Iraqi military hardware. This fit well with the stated U.S. national security objective of restoring security and stability to the Gulf region, which translated operationally into the destruction of the Republican Guard units of the Iraqi army.

The convoy in the area around Mutlah Ridge was the only one of several convoys throughout the Kuwaiti theater area that included a large number of civilian vehicles. It was also the only convoy that received media attention because the others were too far north inside of Iraq for press pool coverage. These convoy attacks continued into the next day (the 27th) at several other locations throughout northern Kuwait and southeastern Iraq, primarily against military vehicles, and were terminated only with the cease-fire at midnight.

2. Moral Questions Raised by Basra Road

In this section we will focus on three moral themes: 1) noncombatant immunity and the question of surrender, 2) military necessity and proportionality, and 3) observations regarding the psychology of combat and the possibilities of right intent in combatants.

First, regarding noncombatant immunity and surrender. As we saw above, popular concern that large numbers of civilian hostages were in the Basra convoy was unwarranted. Convoy participants were almost exclusively Iraqi soldiers and un-uniformed paramilitary Iraqis—and were reasonably believed to be so at the time. Although not morally decisive, they were, in fact many of the perpetrators of the worst horrors of the occupation of Kuwait City. Many military officers interviewed did appeal to the language of reprisals as justification for this attack.[11] We are not suggesting that their destruction on the road to Basra was a kind of morally justified "rough justice" for war crimes. But these facts show, at least that the objects of the attack were not innocents, either in the technical legal sense or in the more general moral sense.

There is, therefore, no question that the Iraqis on the road to Basra were not *hors de combat*. Although many in the press failed to make this distinction, it is crucial to note that they were and remained combatants. Mere armed retreat does not and should not be constructed as tantamount to surrender. Participation in such a retreat does not entitle one to any of the rights of immunity from attack granted to civilians or to surrendered military personnel. Whether we view this convoy as retreating or withdrawing, given the stated military objectives of this campaign and the imminence of the chemical threat retreat and withdrawal were synonymous and in all likelihood will continue to be viewed as such in future conflicts. Prior to any surrender or cease-fire agreement both are military maneuvers, and therefore subject to legitimate attack.

---

[11] These same officers were unaware of the additional legal requirements that various American service pamphlets specify in detail (such as the requirement that reprisals be announced to the enemy and that such actions must be authorized by national command authorities at the highest political level). Both of these conditions for a reprisal were absent here. In the absence of such constraints, this reasoning amounts to no more than an attitude of revenge or punishment which is prohibited by the laws of war.

There is, however, a legitimate and important question about surrender. As we indicated above, some Iraqi troops apparently did display tokens of surrender and, in the normal case, such tokens should be accepted. But in the case at hand, the failure of the American air forces to accept these tokens seems warranted. The previous perfidious use of white flags and other indicia of surrender, the fact that flags were interspersed with elements of the convoy still engaged in coordinated hostile fire against American aircraft, and the lack of ground or even helicopter-borne troops in the area to accept the surrender and provide benevolent quarantine all justify dismissing these displays.

Perfidious use of the white flag is governed explicitly by the Annex to the Hague Conventions, summarized in the United States Army's *The Law of Land Warfare,* as follows: "Flags of truce must not be used surreptitiously to obtain military information or to obtain time to effect a retreat or secure reinforcements or to feign a surrender in order to surprise an enemy."[12] Perfidious acts are prohibited for a variety of reasons. Such acts reduce the mutual respect for the laws of war and the humanitarian principles they attempt to express. Such acts also promote the unnecessary escalation of the conflict and impede the restoration of peace. Although there does not appear to have been any centrally directed Iraqi policy to carry out acts of perfidy, actions during the Iran-Iraq conflict and several isolated incidents during Desert Storm did, in fact color the Coalition's perceptions of Iraqi attempts to offer surrender. Good faith efforts are required, insofar as they do not involve unreasonable risks to one's own troops, to determine the legitimacy of each and every white flag. In this case, it was readily apparent that surrender was not being offered on the part of entire units and that the white flags in question were the result of uncoordinated actions of individuals.[13] In light of these facts, we do not judge there to have been any moral requirement that the attack be ended because of these flags.

There is a larger in-principle question here, and one that deserves further thought and elaboration in the laws of war. There are actually no well understood conditions with respect to the concept of surrender. In fact, in the field the opposite is the case and presents yet another challenge to individual commanders and the just war tradition alike. An enemy who wishes to surrender must manifest an unconditional and unambiguous intent to surrender by way of customary indicia. Traditionally these include laying down of arms and no longer demonstrating a willingness to resist.

Unfortunately, there is no recognized universal procedure for conveying this message. One might expect and hope for a clearer description of the means of conveying this message. Yet even the current U.S. Army field manual on the law of land warfare does not delineate acceptable methods of indicating an intention to surrender. The onus at present falls on the would-be prisoner to communicate the will to surrender unambiguously.[14]

Also, even if we leave aside the perfidy question, there is a difficulty with determining whether the white flag represents the desire of the individual soldier to surrender, or that of the entire unit. The U.S. Army Field Manual, *The Law of Land Warfare,* includes the following instruction: "[The] white flag, when used by troops, indicates a desire to communicate with the enemy. The hoisting of a white flag has no other signification in international law. . . . If hoisted in action by an individual soldier or a small party, it may signify merely the surrender of that soldier or party. It is essential, therefore, to determine with reasonable certainty that the flag is shown by actual authority of the enemy commander before basing important action on that assumption. The enemy is not required to cease firing when a white flag is raised."[15] This regulation incorporates an important moral point. There is a

---

[12] Department of the Army, Field Manual 27-, *The Law of Land Warfare* (Washington, D.C.: Office of the Secretary of the Army, 1956), par. 53.

[13] For a full discussion of this question in another episode of the Gulf War, see Horace B. Robertson, Jr., Rear Admiral, Retired, "The Obligation to Accept Surrender," *Naval War College Review* 46, no. 2, sequence 342 (Spring 1993): 3-115. In this case, white flags were displayed by individuals on oil platforms. These platforms were subsequently attacked and Iraqi soldiers killed. An investigation was conducted which determined that there was no obligation to accept these "surrenders" on grounds that it was not clear these individuals had control or command over the units on the platforms. But it was additionally found that the display of flags should have been reported to higher headquarters, in case additional information was available that would have altered the perceived situation.

[14] See Robertson, "The Obligation to Accept Surrender," 3–115.

[15] Department of the Army, *Law of Land Warfare,* par 458.

tradeoff between allowing for the return of combatants to non-combatant status, on the one hand, and the practical constraint that although individuals may, in the face of attack, be quite prepared to quit their combatant status, surrender is normally the action of military units. Certainly, when it is practical to allow individual surrender, individuals should be granted such rights. And if, indeed, pilots deliberately targeted individual soldiers who manifested an apparent intent to surrender as *individuals* (something which we do not, in fact, know occurred) then a moral and, at least arguably, legal violation occurred. But individuals flying a white flag in the midst of an organized and armed military unit engaged in hostilities with aircraft are rarely going to find themselves in a position for surrender, nor is it practically realistic or morally requisite that the laws of war attempt to incorporate such a possibility.

On the other hand, had the facts been slightly different and entire units or even the whole column wished to surrender, there is no provision in current law or regulation that clearly indicates applicable and unambiguous indicia for such an air-to-ground engagement. Nor is it clear in such engagements what the practical implications of surrender would be, since obviously air forces can neither gain practical control over ground forces nor provide them with the benevolent quarantine required by the laws governing surrender. Hence, law and moral thought are at a conceptual limit here, and further thought needs to be given about the moral meaning of conflict and surrender during such engagements.

The second set of considerations concerns military necessity and proportionality. Was it *necessary* in military terms, to attack this convoy, or could it have been allowed safely to withdraw from Kuwait (thereby fulfilling the announced goal of the war)?

In light of the historical patterns of Iraqi tactics, and the fact that these units included some of the most elite of the Iraqi army, the attack seems well justified. As we noted above, the Coalition air commanders had every reason to fear that this withdrawal was the precursor to renewed attack or even to artillery attack using gas or biological warheads (warheads which we now know were in fact deployed and available for use with Iraqi troops).[16] General Schwarzkopf's intention was to keep such pressure on troops engaged in armed retreat that they would not be given the opportunity to regroup for attack or to set up artillery emplacements necessary to execute this tactic. Therefore, attacking the column seems well warranted indeed, and militarily desirable and necessary.

But even if necessary, was it proportionate? Probably not, at least not in the full scope of the attack. Certainly bottling up the column was warranted. The intention to destroy the armor and artillery in the column, and perhaps even the other vehicles, seems likewise warranted. But there seems little question that gratuitous destruction was wreaked upon individual soldiers and groups far off the road and well away from the vehicles and weapons. If reports of the use of cluster bombs against soldiers on foot are true, there seems to be little justification indeed.[17]

On the other hand, determinations of proportionality require specification of both sides of the balance. In this case, much depends on what one thinks is the military and political goal of this attack. The real goal and hope in the minds of the planners went considerably farther than the destruction of this unit. Indeed, the hope was the long term crippling of the Iraqi Republican Guard, that is, rendering it incapable of inflicting further damage on the Shiites of the south and the Kurds of the north. But even

---

[16] Friedman, *Desert Victory* 233.

[17] "Rumors of gratuitous violence posted several years after the fact are admittedly difficult to discern as either evidence of criminal fact or misplaced accolades. But certainly boasts of firing antitank missiles at infantry troops coupled with the official disclosure that 57% of the pilots assigned to the Tactical Air Command used medical stimulants and sedatives during the war is disconcerting." Keaney and Cohen, GWAPS, 178.

this intention was in careful balance with the recognition that Iraq should not be left defenseless in the face of Iran at the end of the war.[18]

The third and last topic we wish to explore here is, we think, too rarely seriously entertained by academic discussions of military ethics. This is the psychological effect of modern combat on the soldiers and airmen who fight the battles. From St. Augustine's letter to Boniface to the present day, the Christian just war tradition has always had an emphasis on the proper mental and intentional state of the warrior. Boniface, Augustine counseled, was to go to war "mournfully"—without hate or rancor, letting "necessity" and not his will do the killing.[19]

Similarly, much of the "moral armor" of the military professional consists in the belief that the destruction they bring on others is not personally or emotionally motivated, but is instead simply an instance of professionalism in conduct.

Yet much in the human dimension of the Basra Road engagement raises questions about the limits of human ability to retain such attitudes in the heat of battle. Major Hamann's interviews with many veterans of Basra Road reveal a fairly wide range of intense emotional reactions to this situation.

On the one hand, there was clearly a kind of overwhelming excitement in the minds of many pilots. Some disregarded even considerations of personal safety, neglecting to check in with and receive clearance from forward air controllers, which suggests eagerness to join in the "turkey shoot" some pilots themselves called a "feeding frenzy." Perhaps precisely because these were units directly from Kuwait City widely reported to have committed outrages against the civilians of Kuwait, the motive of revenge seems to have joined with the technical thrill of videogame-like opportunities to fire on multiple targets at will. On the other hand, some pilots felt revulsion at what they were doing and requested permission *not* to return to the scene of battle following refueling and rearming.

Besides the previously mentioned reservations about the Iraqi attempts to surrender and admissions that some pilots disregarded command and control in this engagement (aberrations in the context of the entire air campaign), the attacks on the roads to Basra revealed some startling yet persistent behaviors that can be classified into three general areas.

---

[18] The true objectives of the war remain contentious. The UN Resolutions never explicitly mentioned the destruction of the Iraqi Republican Guards. But by the time those resolutions were translated into specific military goals by way of the American national security objectives, destroying these divisions in the name of "regional stability" became a clear targeting priority. "There was no doubting the ultimate objective of forcing Iraq to leave Kuwait but there were questions with regard to the relationship of particular targets to this objective. As so often in the past an opportunity to mount a strategic air campaign was seen by the USAF as a key test of airpower doctrine. . . . The campaign had objectives independent of the expulsion of Iraqi forces from Kuwait: reducing the long-term ability to exert a regional military influence and weakening the regime's hold on power" (Friedman, *Desert Victory*, 314). As a result of the failure to close off the escape routes to Basra and the decision by President Bush to halt the air attacks on the retreating Iraqi convoys, it has been estimated that over four Republican Guard divisions successfully retreated into Iraq. These seventy or eighty thousand troops took with them roughly eight hundred tanks, fourteen hundred armored personnel carriers, and hundreds of artillery pieces (Atkinson, *Crusade*, 476). "If any confirmation of the Guard's role was needed, it was provided in the uprising in Basra immediately after the war: the Republican Guard fought the Iraqi Army. It can even be argued that the course of the war strengthened Saddam's hand, in that the regular Iraqi Army was badly punished, whereas the Guard divisions were partly saved by the timing (which some would now call premature) of the cease-fire. Thus the immediate postwar balance between the strength of the Guard and the strength of the regular army was actually tilted in the direction of the Guard." (Friedman, *Desert Victory*, 22). These issues invite investigation of the *ad bellum* issues of the war and of the connection between the announced and actual war aims and the strategies and tactics employed *in bello*. But such discussions lie beyond the scope of this essay.

[19] Augustine, "Letter to Count Boniface," in *War and Christian Ethics* (Grand Rapids, MI: Baker Book House, 1975), 61–63. "Of the multiple determinants of combat motivation, one of the least discussed and studied is hate. . . . Likewise, a review of the social-psychological literature on combat behavior found very little written about hate, especially in comparison to other aspects of combat behavior, such as fear and stress." John A. Balland and Alecia J. McDowell. "Hate and Combat Behavior" *Armed Forces & Society,* 17, no. 2 (Winter 1991): 229–41.

First some pilots delighted in the amount of destruction they could wreak on the convoy. They expressed an odd sense of pleasure in shooting a large number of live targets after weeks of destroying only hardened stationary targets. This sometimes resulted in the expenditure of a large number of antitank rounds into civilian vehicles and regret only at having wasted extra rounds of ammunition.[20] But the general delight in destruction is also a well documented psychological phenomenon of war. To quote a classic passage from Glenn Gray's *The Warriors:*

> Men who have lived in the zone of combat long enough to be veterans are sometimes possessed by a fury that makes them capable of anything. Blinded by the rage to destroy and supremely careless of the consequences . . . it is as if they are seized by a demon, or are no longer in control of themselves. From the Homeric account of the sacking of Troy to the conquest of Dienbienphu, Western literature is filled with descriptions of soldiers as berserkers and mad destroyers.[21]

This phenomenon of battle is a constant, a constant which the technological evolution of modern weapons probably will never eliminate.

Second, several pilots expressed a certain satisfaction in demonstrating the full capabilities of their aircraft on the convoys retreating into Basra. Pilots have always developed an attachment for their flying machines, even to the point where the machine seems to take on a personality of its own. This devotion varies from one type of aircraft to another, and frequently evolves into a competition amongst pilots of different weapons systems. The attacks on the roads to Basra are an illustration of this competition. Fast fighter pilots (F-15 and F-16 pilots) tend to look with disdain on the close air support mission and the aircraft that fly that mission.

The American Air Force purchased several hundred A-10 Thunderbolt II close air support aircraft in the 1970s. The pilots of those aircraft affectionately called it the "warthog" because of its ungainly appearance. Despite its appearance, the A-10 has proven to be a highly effective weapon on the modern battlefield. In fact, this aircraft was the first to be literally built around the gun it was designed to employ. The gun, a Gatling-type, which is almost twenty feet long and weighs over two tons, can fire its 30mm rounds at the incredible rate of seventy per second. It can loiter over a target area for up to one hour and is capable of destroying a significant number of tanks, armored personnel carriers, and infantry.[22]

Before Desert Storm and throughout the air campaign preceding the ground war, the A-10 had been assigned several secondary, low-priority, and low-visibility missions. While the fighters were either striking downtown Baghdad or searching for the glorious and elusive air-to-air dogfight, the results of which were guaranteed to be replayed on CNN, the A-10 was tasked for missions (search and rescue, SCUD hunts, and even battle damage reconnaissance) that it was not designed to do and its pilots were

---

[20] Two additional points can be made here. First, some military historians have noted that easy killing does seem to generate in humans symptoms of vindictiveness and even pleasure. See John Keegan, *The Face of Battle* (New York: Vintage Books, 1976), 278. Second, some psychologists have discovered evidence that shows quite clearly that the farther the initiator of aggression is from the outcome or results of his acts, the more aggressively he will act. See Ben Shalit, *The Psychology of Conflict and Combat* (New York: Praeger Publishers, 1988), 51. Modern warfare (especially air warfare) can be characterized as the ability to inflict severe damage at great distances. Distort that distance further with the layers of technology inherent in modern weapon systems, and the alienation can actually escalate the violent nature of such acts. With enough distance and time, crimes become misdemeanors.

[21] Glenn Gray, *The Warriors* (New York: Harper and Row, 1959), 51.

[22] The A-10 was responsible for over half of the reported and confirmed battle damage assessments in the Kuwaiti theater, even though it flew only thirty percent of the total number of Coalition sorties. See William L. Smallwood, *Warthog* (New York: Brassey's US, 1993), 206. Smallwood also reports that according to the debriefings of Iraqi prisoners of war, the A-10 was the single most recognizable and feared aircraft by the Iraqis (203).

never trained to fly. Although the aircraft and crews performed those missions with distinction, the retreating convoys on the road to Basra provided them a real opportunity to demonstrate to the Air Force chain of command (primarily consisting of fast fighter pilots) the capabilities of A-10 aircraft. Several pilots boasted to Major Hamann that it was gratifying after so many years of frustration to show those idiots in command post "how much killing an A-10 could really do!"[23] A certain amount of enthusiasm is sometimes warranted and even desirable in terms of the motivation needed to face combat. But the indulgent exhibition of machines—machines with unprecedented lethality—comes precariously close to excessive violence and threatens to ignore the just war tradition's plea for restraint and virtuous conduct on the part of soldiers, even in war.

The mystique regarding soldiers' attachment to their weapons has received very little attention in the study of war. "The fear engendered by these weapons—a backdrop of unimaginable horror lying just beneath the surface—has led to a sort of paralysis of inquiry. . . . By virtue of an odd sort of consensus of opposites, weapons are generally perceived as matter-of-fact objects, mechanisms with little more symbolic and cultural significance than a pair of pliers."[24] But to understand weapons in this way is to misunderstand them.

Of Arms and Men by Robert O'Connell, a military intelligence officer and historian, explores this complex relationship between soldiers and their weapons. In his review of military history from the perspective of the evolution of weapons, O'Connell distinguishes between predatory and intraspecific aggression.

Intraspecific conflicts are characterized by ritual and ceremonial restraint, he claims. Weapons are symmetrical in size and lethality and are employed with much posturing. The virtues of the military hero in this type of conflict are coupled with an aesthetic valuing of the weapons, almost to the point where actual killing becomes a secondary objective.

In predatory conflict killing is no longer an art form. Instead, it is a mechanical process governed by an objective scientific pattern of thinking. The enemy is hunted down with casual ruthlessness, is shown no sympathy, and is not the object of feelings of shared humanity. It is here that we find language that dehumanizes the enemy.

A third observation regarding the psychology of combat was this: in Major Hamann's interviews, all of the pilots who expressed both their love of their machines and a delight in destruction also referred to the Iraqis in animal or subhuman terms. John Keegan, a noted military historian, has commented that the impersonalization of battle is one of the indices of divergence between the facts of everyday morality and battlefield morality.[25] Reflexive comments by participants on the roads into Basra are a manifestation of this index. Several pilots even went as far as to describe the enemy as a creature of indeterminate qualities—an eerie coping strategy reminiscent of the testimonials of veterans of World War II and Vietnam.[26]

There are several possible explanations for this particular psychological mechanism for coping with combat stress. All of these can be generalized as attempts to perceive as simple what is in reality very complex and, therefore, frustrating to the individual decision maker. A compartmentalized, prejudiced environment is much easier to deal with. "It must be counted as one of the particular cruelties of modern warfare that, by inducing even in the fit and willing soldier a sense of his unimportance it encouraged his treating the lives of disarmed and demoralized opponents as equally unimportant."[27]

---

[23] Hamann, personal interviews with pilots, summer 1992.

[24] Robert L. O'Connell, *Of Arms and Men* (New York: Oxford University Press, 1989), 5.

[25] Keegan, *Face of Battle*, 320.

[26] Whereas American veterans often times regarded the Japanese as vermin or insects, and the Viet Cong as the beast in the jungle, Major Hamann was taken aback when veterans of the Gulf War made reference to "the monster." Here individual enemy soldiers are collectively viewed not as a corruption or privation of good, but as an embodiment of evil. Whatever the motivations, the retreating Iraqis actually acquired the status in their minds of evil incarnate. Facing this "monster" was part of a rite of passage—a sort of personal trial that separated those who had tasted the horrors of battle and survived from those who had not. This vocabulary is hauntingly familiar to the well-known hero myth in which overcoming the monster is a condition of elevation.

[27] Keegan, *Face of Battle*, 322.

This observation brings us back to one of the most obscure of all battlefield transactions—how soldiers get their offer of surrender communicated and accepted. Insofar as these psychological dynamics are at play, clearly this too complicates that transaction.[28]

Religious and cultural differences also contributed to the common language for this dehumanization. What they were destroying were not individual persons whose plight one could sympathize with, but "camel jockeys," "rag heads," and other labels of segregation. Clearly O'Connell is right when he notes that aversion to weapons and to tactics that are deemed less than honorable is sharply reduced when the enemy is seen as fundamentally alien.

---

[28] Although not as extensive as some other officers, Major Hamann's personal training and experience with military war games and simulations has highlighted a shared characteristic: the lack of clarity on how to end a conflict. For example, most NATO or European simulations (which were relied upon in the initial planning of the Gulf War air campaign) either end with escalation to tactical nuclear weapons, or are left open-ended for civilian national command authorities to resolve.

The People or the Mission?*
Submitted by Dr. Deane-Peter Baker

Your Marine infantry platoon has been on patrolling operations for five days in the former Republic of Zavajistan, as part of Operation Just Peace, a multinational peace enforcement operation. Your Marines are bone-tired after running contacts with irregular Zava and Kroa combatant forces and long nights of half-on, half-off duty. In three days your platoon will move to landing zones about three miles to the south for helicopter extraction.

That afternoon you encounter the local official in charge of Red Cross relief operations in the nearest town. He informs you that he is sheltering a group of Zava civilians, about 30 older men and women with a few children. The civilians are fleeing the battle area to an enclave some distance to the west. They have no food or supplies of any kind and are physically spent and in bad shape. Several of them need medical attention for wounds.

You discuss the situation with your platoon NCOs. One suggests collecting the rations that were airdropped yesterday and giving them to the group of civilians, and also giving medical attention to those most in need. One of your section commanders argues that the platoon needs to keep its food, because it's possible that your orders could change, in which case you could be out for several more days. He is especially concerned about the suggestion about using the medical supplies. The few supplies available were those deemed strictly essential. Fighting is on the increase, and the chance of soldiers getting wounded is high, and the operational environment makes resupply and evacuations of casualties problematic. You also recall the commanding officer cautioned you strongly against giving supplies to civilians. Such actions have, in the past, resulted in charges that U.S. forces have favored one side over the others, which caused considerable political and operational difficulties.

Just then, the Red Cross official returns, carrying a limp child in his arms, and begs you to help. Behind them, you see a CNN camera crew setting up, and the reporter is approaching, microphone in hand. What should you do? [Assume that you cannot get instructions from the chain of command for the time being. Broad-band jamming by the belligerents has rendered your radio useless.]

Questions for Discussion

1. What are the moral principles involved with this decision?
2. What are the virtues of character involved with this decision?
3. What is the primary consideration involved with this decision?
4. What would you do if you were the Platoon Commander?

*Adapted and edited version of a scenario by Maj Rock Hau, Canadian Forces: http://www.dep-ped.forces.gc.ca/publications/hau-eng.aspx

III

Ethics Within the Military Profession: Upholding a Higher Standard?

Chief Warrant Officer Hugh W. Thompson at My Lai

Edited by Dr. George R. Lucas, Jr.[1]

Historical Background: The "War in Vietnam"

In 1954, following a protracted civil war, a peace settlement between French military forces in the former French colony of Indochina resulted in a partitioning of the territory known as Vietnam into the Republic of South Vietnam (located south of a line of demarcation at the 17th parallel) with its capital in Saigon, and the People's Democratic Republic of Vietnam, or "North Vietnam" (the territory from north of the line of demarcation to the southernmost border of China). The north, under the leadership of the communist insurgent leader, Ho Chi Min, maintained its capital in the city of Hanoi, and continued to provide assistance to communist insurgents in the south, known as the "National Liberation Front" or Viet Cong. The latter ("northern" sympathizers who lived south of the line of demarcation) defied the original French armistice and sought to re-unify the entire country under Ho Chi Min's rule.

Beginning in the early 1960s, Presidents John F. Kennedy and Lyndon B. Johnson ordered a steadily-increasing American military deployment to the region in an effort both to stem the spread of communism in the wider area of southeast Asia, and to support the established regime and the Army of the Republic of Vietnam (ARVN) in their efforts to resist the Viet Cong guerrillas. This gradual troop buildup and the ensuing, extensive American military intervention in the ongoing hostilities between north and south in Vietnam, lasted until 1973.

The My Lai Massacre

My Lai is a small village located close to the seacoast in the Quang Ngai province, the narrow northern neck of South Vietnam. My Lai (also known as Son My) lay about 100 miles south of the line of demarcation, and was thus in the northernmost part of South Vietnam. The allegiance of a great many of the villagers and local peasant farmers in the province lay with the regime in Hanoi, and the Viet Cong operated extensively in the area with local support. Skirmishes between Viet Cong revolutionaries and American and South Vietnamese troops took place frequently in this region, especially after the "Tet Offensive" of January, 1968. Many villages in the surrounding area were destroyed in this fighting, but My Lai's 700 inhabitants largely escaped any extensive damage from, or involvement in, these skirmishes.

Early on the morning of March 16, 1968, the three platoons of ground forces comprising Charlie Company, from "Task Force Barker" of the U.S. Army 11th Brigade (under the command of LtCol Frank

---

[1] *Editor's note:* The following account is drawn from an article by reporter Nell Boyce, published in *U.S. News and World Report* (20 August, 2001), from a "60 Minutes" television interview by CBS reporter Mike Wallace of Hugh Thompson and Larry Colburn upon their return, 30 years later, to My Lai, and from a legal brief by retired General and Judge Adjutant Telford Taylor, "War Crimes: Son My," in *From Nuremberg to My Lai*, ed. Jay W. Baird (Lexington, MA: D.C. Heath & Co, 1972). I have amplified these sources with the *viva voce* reminiscences of CWO Thompson himself, drawn from several visits and lectures at the U.S. Naval Academy.—grl

A. Barker, Jr.), were ordered to enter the area around the village of My Lai. Charlie Company was to engage the enemy, while the remaining two companies, Alpha and Bravo, would be set down by helicopter north and east of the village, in order to cut off Viet Cong escape routes. There was considerable confusion at the time, however, over whether the Viet Cong were actually in the hamlet of My Lai, or located in the nearby hamlet of My Khe. In any event, when his forces failed to encounter the expected enemy resistance in the target area, Captain Ernest Medina, CO of Charlie Company, ordered the First Platoon, under the command of Lieutenant William L. Calley, to enter the nearby village and "secure it." One account of the incident reads as follows:

> By 0800, Calley's platoon had crossed the plaza on the town's southern edge and entered the village. They encountered families cooking rice in front of their homes. The men began their usual search-and-destroy task of pulling people from homes, interrogating them, and searching for VC. Soon the killing began. The first victim was a man stabbed in the back with a bayonet. Then a middle-aged man was picked up, thrown down a well, and a grenade lobbed in after him. A group of fifteen to twenty mostly older women were gathered around a temple, kneeling and praying. They were all executed with shots to the back of their heads. Eighty or so villagers were taken from their homes and herded to the plaza area. As many cried "No VC! No VC!", Calley told soldier Paul Meadlo, "You know what I want you to do with them." When Calley returned ten minutes later and found the Vietnamese still gathered in the plaza he reportedly said to Meadlo, "Haven't you got rid of them yet? I want them dead. Waste them." Meadlo and Calley began firing into the group from a distance of ten to fifteen feet. The few that survived did so because they were covered by the bodies of those less fortunate.[2]

Calley's own account of his actions and the backdrop for them provide a grim portrait of the degraded morale of American troops and of their leadership, engaged for the first time in a large-scale "insurgency" or guerilla war.[3] Virtually all that conflicting accounts agree on about the context of this action is that, two days before the massacre, a small squad from Charlie Company had run into a booby-trap. A popular sergeant leading the squad was killed, another GI blinded, and many others wounded. At the sergeant's memorial service a day later, Captain Medina, a popular CO, had given his men a "pep talk" in preparation for the My Lai operation. His words suggested, at least, that "revenge" for these casualties was not inappropriate. The villages in the target sector were to have been "cleared of enemy civilians" from preparatory gunship air attacks. By the time the soldiers on the ground arrived at My Lai, Medina informed them, they could expect that none but VC would remain. They were then to "explode brick homes, set fire to thatch homes, shoot livestock, poison wells, and destroy the enemy."

CWO Hugh Thompson

As these events unfolded below, 24-year old Chief Warrant Officer Hugh Thompson, U.S. Army, was flying a small reconnaissance helicopter low over the treetops near My Lai. Accompanied by Glenn Andreotta and Lawrence "Larry" Colburn, his mission was to draw fire from Viet Cong strongholds below, so that two gunships flying higher above could locate and destroy the rebel forces.

On the morning of March 16, however, no one was shooting at them. As he passed over the village of My Lai at approximately 0900, Thompson reports that he and his crew had a clear view of the ground below. Despite an absence of hostile fire or evidence of enemy troops in the area, they saw bodies everywhere. Flying down for a closer look, Thompson hovered a few feet over a paddy field, and watched as a group of Americans approach a wounded young woman lying on the ground. Their leader nudged her with his foot, then shot her.

---

[2] "An Introduction to the My Lai Courts-Martial," Doug Linder, University of Missouri (Kansas City) Law Center: http://www.law.umkc.edu/faculty/projects/ftrials/mylai/Myl_intro.html.

[3] *Lieutenant Calley: His Own Story*, as told to John Sack (NY: Viking Press, 1971).

Thompson reports that he was flabbergasted by what he saw. He flew over the eastern side of the village and saw dozens more bodies of Vietnamese, including elderly and children, piled in an irrigation ditch. Soldiers were standing nearby, smoking cigarettes. Thompson set his helicopter down near the irrigation ditch, and asked a sergeant on the ground if the soldiers nearby could render medical aid to the civilians, some of whom were still moving. The sergeant, Thompson recalls, suggested that his men should simply "put them out of their misery." Thompson reports that he then encountered the platoon leader, Lt. Calley, and asked him to order the men to assist the wounded and dying. Calley (Thompson recalls) told him to "mind his own business." In stunned disbelief, Thompson returned to his helicopter and prepared to lift off. At that moment, however, crewmate Glenn Andreotta called out in horror that the soldiers had begun firing at the wounded lying in the ditch!

Thompson flew above the carnage for several minutes, outraged, dumb-founded, and wondered what, if anything, he could or should do. Suddenly he saw several elderly adults and children running towards a crude bunker, being chased by American soldiers. In that critical moment, Thompson decided to land his helicopter between the troops and the shelter. He jumped out and confronted the soldiers leading the chase. He requested assistance in escorting the civilians safely out of the bunker and out of the line of fire. One soldier, according to Thompson, replied that "he'd get them out with a hand grenade."

Furious, Thompson announced that he himself was going to escort these civilians to safety. He called back to Colburn and Andreotta in the helicopter and ordered them to fire their weapons at their fellow American soldiers if any of them should attempt to interfere with the rescue, or try to shoot any more of the Vietnamese civilians. Thompson's two crew-members received these orders in disbelief. Colburn later admitted that he never actually pointed his gun at an American soldier, but allowed that, had Thompson been attacked, he would then have surely fired on his fellow soldiers. Both Colburn and Thompson described the stand-off as intense and surreal. No one knew what to expect next.

The soldiers in Lt. Calley's platoon, however, did not pursue their quarry any further or provoke a confrontation. Instead, they stood by sullenly and watched while CWO Thompson coaxed the Vietnamese out of the shelter with hand gestures. As the terrified and sobbing villagers hesitantly began to follow Thompson toward his three-man helicopter; he realized he had nowhere to put them. Quickly, Thompson got on the radio and begged the gunships accompanying him on his original mission, and still in formation above, to land and fly the four adults and five children to safety. They complied.

Once this evacuation was completed, Thompson then reports that he prepared to return to base, when suddenly the entire helicopter crew saw something moving in the irrigation ditch. It was a child, a boy about 4 years old. Andreotta waded through piles of dead bodies in the ditch in order to pull him out. Thompson, who had a son of his own, was overcome by emotion. He flew the child to a nearby hospital.

Thompson at last returned to base, whereupon (he reports) he sat on the edge of his cot, trembling with rage, trying to understand what had just happened. He remembers that his tent mates said that he was screaming quite loudly. "I remember that I was hopping mad. I told my commanding officer what had happened. I threatened never to fly again," he recalls. "I didn't want to be a part of that. It wasn't war."

His CO promised to report the incident. An investigation followed, and Thompson recalls telling Army investigators his entire story, carefully and thoroughly. He heard nothing further. A month later, Glenn Andreotta died in combat. Thompson himself was shot down, injured, and subsequently sent back to the States to teach helicopter piloting. Larry Colburn served out his tour of duty and left the military. Both assumed that the soldiers from First Platoon, Charlie Company who had been involved in the killing had been court-martialed. In fact, however, nothing came of that preliminary investigation. Rumors of a "massacre" by American GIs at My Lai persisted, and, in 1969, these rumors, supported by letters sent from other witnesses to government officials, led to a full investigation of the incident.

Hugh Thompson identified Calley in a police line-up as the lieutenant in charge of the platoon at My Lai. Captain Medina was charged with murder as the commanding officer of the unit in question, and for dereliction of duty in participating in a subsequent attempt to suppress the investigation.

Defended at trial by the prominent defense attorney, F. Lee Bailey, however, Medina was eventually found not guilty by reason of insufficient evidence. Only Lt. Calley was formally indicted, court-martialed, and after lengthy deliberations, convicted of murder and sentenced to life at hard labor, suspension from the service, and loss of all pay and benefits. After several appeals and a growing public sentiment that he had been made a "scapegoat" for the military's actions in Vietnam, he served a minimum sentence and was paroled in 1974.

Courtesy of AP/Wide World

Tiananmen Square
Captain Rick Rubel

Background

The spring of 1989 was a time of extraordinary upheaval in the People's Republic of China. For a number of reasons, there was an unprecedented series of pro-democracy protests by university students in Beijing. The large gatherings started with the mourning of the death of Hu Yoabang, former General Secretary of the Communist Party. Over 100,000 students took advantage of this event to gather outside the Great Hall and demand to meet with Party leaders to discuss freedom of the press and other democratic reforms. The leaders refused. In late April, the demonstrations escalated and moved to other cities in China. Members of the Party leadership genuinely feared leadership that this might lead to full scale chaos and eventually to rebellion.[1]

Inside the Politburo, the new General Secretary, Li Peng called a meeting to decide what to do about the growing insurrection. He concluded that the students' aim was to overthrow him and the Communist Party. The Chinese Government issued a statement that the "The Party has thus far been tolerant and restrained, but the time has come for action. They must explain to the whole Party and nation that they are facing a most serious political struggle . . . and they have to be explicit and clear in opposing this turmoil."

The statement set off more demonstrations, and now, as many as 10% of all working Beijing citizens were involved in the protest.

---

[1] From Wikipedia, the free encyclopedia

As Mikhail Gorbachev arrived in Beijing for the first Sino-Soviet summit since 1959, the Chinese government was embarrassed by student hunger strikes and more rioting in Tiananmen Square during his visit.

On May 17, the government declared martial law in the city, but that proclamation was met by an increase of 1.2 million protestors. The People's Liberation Army was marshaled from their posts in outlying provinces. The Army formed up outside the city for briefings by General Chi, the operational commander of the 350,000 army troops that had been called together to stop the protestors. The Chinese army is known for intense training, strict discipline, with serious consequences for insubordination. But just to ensure that his troops would fire on the Chinese people, General Chi took two crucial actions. First, he kept his troops on the outskirts of the city for 10 days for intense political indoctrination. The young, peasant soldiers were told over and over they were being sent in to protect the city from "hoodlums." They knew nothing of the demonstrations for democracy in Tiananmen Square. Second, Gen. Chi used the 27th Group Army as his spearhead. He had spent many years with the 27th, ultimately rising to be their senior political officer. He knew they were loyal to the party and they would not let him down.[2]

In the early morning hours of June 3rd, the Army's assault on Tiananmen Square began. The Army was ordered to clear the square of protestors by 6:00 AM. As the protestors threw rocks and bottles at the Army, incredibly, the soldiers started firing machine guns into the crowd. As dozens of people fell, the others ran away and retreated. Then, over and over again, the people in the crowd regained their nerve and came back to the corner of the square to yell and throw more objects. Each surge of the crowd was met by another round of machine-gun fire. Many protestors were run over by tanks or injured by the brutal Chinese army soldiers and their bayonets.[3]

By June 5th, the army was in complete control and an eerie silence came over an empty Tiananmen Square. But the silence came only after 2,600 civilians had been killed and 7,000-10,000 had been injured in the previous two days.[4]

At this time, with resistance broken, the rest of the Army tanks and troops were able to easily enter the city from all four corners and join up at Tiananmen Square.

The Tank

On the morning of June 5th, Corporal Wen Zhang, of the Peoples Liberation Army sat in the driver's seat of his T-69 tank on the front left side looking out of his small, bullet-proof viewing window.[5] The viewing window was continuously fogging up from the humid air of this Beijing morning in June. He would continuously wipe off the condensation with a rag, and then wipe off his own forehead below his helmet. Since his tank was not carrying any 105mm ammunition for the main gun, there was room for him to move both arms around his small seat area. They were carrying, however, three times the normal load of ammo for the 7.62 mm co-axial machine gun and 12.7 mm smaller machine gun.[6] Wen had been in the Army for over two years, and was proud to serve his Republic. He had quickly worked his way up to Tank Driver 3rd Merit and was respected among the other Tank Drivers for his achievements in their qualification training in the hills of Ding Xian. Since there were many more tank drivers than tanks, there was a certain prestige in actually being assigned to a tank. Wen grew up on farm near Shijiazhuang and had never been to a big city—and now he found himself driving his tank down Chang'an Boulevard toward Tiananmen Square in Beijing. He had heard over the radio in the tank the past night that the Army soldiers had successfully put down a threat to the capital by "valiantly" killing the "hoodlums" that opposed his government.

---

[2] When China's General Chi comes to call, William Triplett II, The Washington Times, 4 December, 1996

[3] The Tank Man (Tiananmen Square Anniversary) PBS Frontline, April 14, 2006 (transcript)

[4] The Tank Man (Tiananmen Square Anniversary) PBS Frontline, April 14, 2006 (transcript)

[5] The name of the tank driver is fictionalized. Extensive searches have not been able to identify the name of the tank driver. In order to personalize the case study, the writer has taken some liberty in describing the actual scene inside the tank.

[6] Global Security. Org : *http://www.globalsecurity.org/military/library/report/2004/04fisher/9armysystems.htm*

As Wen's tank traveled down Chang'an Boulevard, his tank commander took the lead of a small column of eight tanks. There were another 60 tanks that were preparing to reposition, after his column had completed their move. As Wen wiped the condensation off his viewing sight he saw a man standing in front of his tank, wearing a white shirt and carrying two shopping bags, one in each hand. Wen slammed on the hydraulic brakes of his T-69 Tank and the 83,000-pound tank jerked as it came to a stop.

Wen watched the man for a few seconds, not knowing what to do. Neither Wen nor the man moved for over 30 seconds. As the other tanks jerked to halt behind Wen's tank, the radio speakers began to screech, "What is happening? Proceed! Proceed!" On the intercom inside his tank, his tank commander echoed the order, "Proceed! Proceed!" Wen disengaged the brakes and turned his tank to the right to miss the man in the white shirt. Incredibly, the man moved to his left and blocked the tank again. Wen stopped. Then he tried to go to the left, and the man moved to his right to block them again.

By this time, several minutes had passed, and the Armor Battalion Commander was now angrily yelling in the radio, "Proceed! Proceed!" Wen was completely confused. He had never seen anything like this in his training command or even in political army school. As he furiously once again wiped the condensation off the viewing port and his forehead, he reached over and turned off the huge V-12, 730hp engine to cool off the tank during this impasse. When he turned off his engine, the tanks behind him did the same. There sat Corporal Wen Zhang, of the Peoples Liberation Army, inside his tank in the quiet humid darkness of Tiananmen Square–wondering, "What has just happened?"

Aftermath

The man in the white shirt was quickly grabbed by some other anonymous citizens and taken away to safety. The Western press has been unable to determine who this man was. Nevertheless, the photographic image of this one man, shortly after such a horrible massacre, standing in front of a column of tanks in Tiananmen Square, reverberated around the world. After these events, China significantly changed their economic policies and gave their people more individual and civil rights. Before the Berlin Wall came down later that same year, the East Berliners were heard to be chanting, "If one man can stop the Chinese Army, we can tear down the Iron Curtain." In 1998, Time Magazine listed the man in the white shirt as one of the top 100 "Most influential people of the 20th century."[7]

But what about the tank driver in that T-69 tank that stopped?

Why did he stop?

Questions for Discussion

1. With the entire People's Liberation Army behind him, why do we think that tank driver stopped?

2. Would you attribute the virtue of moral courage to him?

3. How does his moral courage differ from the man in the white shirt?

4. How would you compare the ethics of the actions of the tank driver and the man in the white shirt? Are the actions of one of the two men more morally praiseworthy than the actions of the other? Explain.

5. If the tank driver had not stopped, how differently would history have viewed this incident?

6. Which action do you think it would take more character to perform—to stand in front of the tank, or to stop the tank (disregarding direct orders, despite all of your training and the strict discipline of your service)? Do you think you could do either?

---

[7] The writer would like to acknowledge Dr. Al Pierce for his assistance with this case.

7. What factors other than a tank driver's character could make it more or less likely that he would stop his tank in such a situation? Generally, what factors affect obedience under authority? (*Note: the famous Milgram experiments addressed this question.*)

8. Do we want our troops to be morally responsible, or do we want them to do as they are told?

Major Knight and Cambodia

Dr. Stephen Wrage

Date: March 17, 1969

Time: 2130

Place: Bien Hoa Air Force Base, South Vietnam

In 1969 Air Force Major Hal Knight commanded a "Skyspot" radar center, providing close-in ground control for B-52 raids launched from Guam, Okinawa, and Thailand. Bombing missions were designed and approved in Washington and the target lists were cabled to Knight's commanding officer, Lt. Colonel David Patterson at Bien Hoa Air Base. Patterson passed them on to Knight, or to one of three other Skyspot radar centers in Vietnam.

Knight's duty was to compute the particulars of each bombing run and communicate them to the planes' crews as they entered the war zone. He and three controllers he supervised matched the position, altitude, and airspeed of the planes to the ballistics of the bomb load and the coordinates of the drop site.

As the B-52's entered the war zone sometime between nightfall and dawn, Knight and his men picked up each plane and established radio contact, gave the navigators the coordinates for their missions, tracked the planes as they proceeded to their target zones, and laid down a narrow radar beam to guide the planes precisely over the targets. The controllers watched on their screens as the planes formed up into cells of three for the bombing run, then counted down for the bombardiers to give the precise instant to release the bombs.

When the mission was complete, Knight filled out a post-strike report form and entered the coordinates of the bombed sites into the computer system of the Strategic Air Command, and thus into the official record system of the Pentagon and the official history of the war.

By March of 1969 the Air Force had been conducting "continuous limited air strikes" for four years and one month. The North Vietnamese had long before moved their main supply line, the Ho Chi Minh Trail, west across the border into Cambodia. Although Cambodia was nominally neutral, Prince Sihanouk, the Cambodian head of state, had long ago yielded to a mix of bribes and threats and looked the other way when they brought in supplies through the port of Sihanoukville and set up permanent base camps in Cambodia's eastern fringes.

In 1967 and 1968, Americans and South Vietnamese had conducted numerous reconnaissance missions across the Cambodian borders, some of which Sihanouk had protested and others he had ignored. In January of 1968, the North Vietnamese launched the Tet Offensive, and in November Richard Nixon was elected on a platform promising to shift the burden of the war from American to Vietnamese troops. It was widely speculated that increased bombing coupled with action against sanctuaries in Cambodia would buy time for what came to be called "Vietnamization."

Stephen Wrage is a professor of political science at the U.S. Naval Academy. This case was produced by the Center for the Study of Professional Military Ethics at the U.S. Naval Academy. Support was provided by Newport News Shipbuilding. Reprinted by permission of the author.

Hal Knight was aware of all this, and he had spoken to veterans of the Long Range Patrols or "Daniel Boone" crews—special forces teams who had crossed into Cambodia and come back with reports of underground hospitals, weapons and supply caches, and regiment-sized concentrations of troops.

On the evening of March 16, Major Knight was called into Lt. Colonel Patterson's office and informed of a change in procedure. The next day at 1500, he was to be at the edge of the runway to meet a special courier plane which would bear a sealed envelope for him. He was to guard the envelope carefully, to open it at 2100, and to follow the instructions it contained.

At 2100 on the 17th, Knight opened the envelope and discovered a set of target coordinates which he recognized as being along the far side of the border with Cambodia. He was instructed to calculate bombing runs for those coordinates and have his controllers direct the B-52s to those sites for the predawn raids on the 18th. Other coordinates would be cabled from Washington as usual, but that target list was to be set aside. His controllers were to say nothing of the change in procedures that night.

When the bombing mission was complete, Knight was to gather up every scrap of paper and tape with which the bombing runs were plotted and lock them up until daytime. All computer files used in the calculation were to be erased. In the daylight, when there would be no danger of dropping a piece of paper, he was to shred and incinerate every record of the mission. Finally, he was to refer back to the set of coordinates that had been cabled in the usual manner from Washington, and he was to enter that set in the Strategic Air Command computer system, designating them as having been bombed that night.

When Lt. Colonel Patterson gave Major Knight the envelope earlier that day he had said firmly and finally, "Follow the instructions it contains."

It's 2130 on March 17, 1969. The bombers will shortly be overhead. Put yourself in Major Knight's position. What would you do?

Questions for Discussion

1. What would you do if you were Major Knight?
2. What questions would you want to ask if you could?

The Death of a Marine
Colonel Paul E. Roush

Case Study

Having completed basic training, LCpl Jason J. Rother reported to Battalion Landing Team 3/2 (BLT) and was assigned to the First Squad, Second Platoon, Company E, on 10 July 1988.

The BLT was preparing for training in the desert and on 8 August, Company E received a class on the "introduction to desert survival." The purpose of the class was to acquaint the individual marine with desert survival techniques. The first general point made was the requirement for personnel accountability.

The training commenced on 29 August, at the Marine Corps Air Ground Combat Center in 29 Palms CA. On day two of the exercise, the BLT received an order to use the cover of darkness to reposition forces for an attack to the northwest. The order required the BLT to conduct a 21 mile unilluminated motor march while maintaining light and noise discipline. Emplacement of route guides and quartering parties (advanced parties) was permitted before dark.

1stLt Allen V. Lawson, the Heavy Machine Gun Platoon Commander, was tasked with conducting motor march route reconnaissance, and simultaneous guide emplacement. Standard operating procedures (SOP) required two route guides per station. Lawson would get two to four marines from each of the five companies within the battalion. A total of fourteen men would make up his route guide detail.

Captain Edwards, the Battalion Logistics Officer, was tasked with picking up check point route guides with the last vehicles in the logistics train. Earlier that day he asked 1stLt Lawson to provide him with a by-name roster of those marines he would be picking up at the check points.

1stLt Lawson had filled only eight of the 14 route guide billets as the required departure time elapsed. Darkness was approaching and Major Holm, the Battalion XO, was concerned at the possible delay to the operation. At this point Maj Holm confronted 1stLt Lawson saying, "It's almost dark; what are you still doing here?"

There are conflicting stories as to whether or not Lawson made it clear to Maj Holm that he did not have a complete route guide detail. Maj Holm then said words to the effect, "If you don't leave now, you'll get as lost as we will without road guards." Shortly thereafter, Lawson departed 6 billets unmanned failing to provide Capt Edwards with a head count or roster of the Marines that he would be responsible for picking up after the night motor march was completed.

At Check Point #1, LCpl Rother and LCpl Key dismounted the vehicle. 1stLt Lawson directed LCpl Key to board the vehicle, explaining that each post would have only one marine. Another passenger, LCpl Adamson, reminded 1stLt Lawson that the XO had specifically directed the marines to be posted in pairs. First Lt Lawson replied "I'm the Lieutenant and you're the Lance Corporal." LCpl Adamson ceased protest, and LCpl Key boarded. Without any further posting guidance or pick up directions, LCpl Rother was posted alone and the vehicle drove away.

While conducting a reconnaissance, the CO designated a different route, which resulted in the BLT and an artillery battalion taking the same route. This resulted in the combination of guides from both units sharing the same road. The marine designated to drive the pick-up vehicle for BLT 3/2 understood that he was to pick up pairs of route guides identified by chemlites. The duty driver did not know the exact number of personnel to pick up, or their precise locations.

Many of the drivers were operating at high speeds in order to maintain close positioning in the formation. These high speeds created a great deal of dust that restricted visibility. One road guide said that just before he was picked up that he could see Rother's chemlite, but the Platoon Sergeant said that he did not see it. LCpl Key boarded the recovery vehicle alone, and did not indicate to anyone that the road guard with whom he was supposed to be paired, LCpl Rother, was not among them. The assumption among them was that Rother was aboard another vehicle. The last vehicle in the convoy headed for home, thus leaving LCpl Rother in the desert alone, with minimal survival gear.

The motor march concluded early in the morning of the 31st of August. 1stLt Lawson questioned a sergeant from the recovery vehicle in the assembly area regarding the number of road guides picked up. Later that morning, his concern for the number of route guides that were picked up resurfaces when he asks Maj Holms if any companies had reported missing Marines.

LCpl Rother's absence from camp was questioned by his Platoon Commander 1stLt Christopher E. Johnson, but the Platoon Sergeant, Sgt Christopher P. Clyde, had said that LCpl Rother was still on route guide detail. He and Sgt Turnell, Rother's squad leader, knew Rother did not return with his four-man fire team and believed he was assigned to another detail and that accounted for his absence. Turnell left camp on liberty without actually accounting for Rother.

On the morning of 1 September, Sgt Clyde, the Platoon Sergeant, submitted an "all present" platoon report. That evening, the acting squad leader mentioned to the platoon Sergeant that LCpl Rother had not been seen all day. The Company Gunnery Sergeant was informed of the problem and notified the rest of the chain-of-command. A search was underway within an hour.

Hundreds of marines combed the desert for days on foot and in the air. The search found only Rother's pack and some rocks positioned in the shape of an arrow. The Marine Corps' initial report to Rother's parents was that their son could have taken unauthorized leave from duty.

At the Rothers' request, another search was conducted on November 4–6, this time involving civilian search and rescue experts. No further trace was found. On 4 December the remains of LCpl Jason J. Rother were discovered about 17 miles from where he had been posted.

The following excerpt is an opinion on the circumstances surrounding the death of LCpl Rother by an NIS agent. It is based on the available evidence, the behavior of other people in similar situations, and the experience of search and rescue personnel.

> "It will never be known exactly why he was missed when the vehicle went through which was supposed to pick him up. It is possible he was asleep, but this is only conjecture on my part.
>
> "He began his attempt to walk out fairly early in the day. He managed to cover nearly 20 ground miles. The direction arrow at the position last seen aimed to the east was left by LCpl Rother, and he in fact went in that direction. The lone set of foot prints I tracked north up the sandy dry wash in early November to the vicinity of Bench Mark 18 were in fact left by LCpl Rother. I would speculate that he returned to Bench Mark 18 in the hope that some element of his unit was still located in that area.
>
> "Upon discovering that there was nobody left at Bench Mark 18, LCpl Rother decided to attempt to walk out to the highway which was clearly visible to the north of Bench Mark 18. The distance to the highway from the point where I lost the tracks was approximately five miles straight line distance.
>
> "He was attempting to conserve his water, as evidenced by the fact that there was a small amount remaining in one canteen. I would guess that at the spot where he stopped (less than one mile from the highway) he was considerably dehydrated and close to exhaustion and simply wanted to rest. He made a serious mistake by pitching his poncho liner lean-to with the large area of the poncho liner facing west. I estimate it was mid-afternoon at this time and the heat that poncho liner soaked up must have been incredible. He took off his web gear and laid it with his rifle at the south end of the lean-to, and crawled in to rest.
>
> "For whatever reason, he came awake one last time, but totally delirious. He came out of his lean-to and ripped it loose in the process, which accounts for it being found fifty yards away. It was probably blown to that location by the winds. He ripped off all of his clothing at this time (which accounts for the anomaly of finding all the dis-

carded clothing in one area as opposed to being scattered along the trail), but for some unknown reason took his military identification card and one empty canteen and started walking southeast, barefoot and dressed only in his t-shirt and underwear. The canteen was discarded almost immediately. After 50 yards, he ripped off his t-shirt, which does fit the pattern of discarded clothing. Shortly thereafter, he dropped the ID card.

"Only 15 yards further, LCpl Rother dropped to the ground for the last time. He died in that location. He was still wearing his shorts, as evidenced by their soiled condition. After his body decomposed, the coyotes found it and scattered it to the locations where the search recovered the various parts. In this period, the coyotes tore off his shorts.

"I doubt seriously if he was alive 36 hours after being missed by the vehicle which was supposed to pick him up. It seems probable that he did not even make it 24 hours. Based on the evidence available to me, I find it inconceivable that LCpl Rother was attempting to go UA. The path he took indicates his best attempt to survive and nothing else. I am impressed that he made it as far as he did and it is a shame he came so close and did not survive."

Iran-Contra

Colonel Paul E. Roush
Edited by Dr. George R. Lucas, Jr.

Background

In the 1970s, Anastosio Somoza Debayle's rule over Nicaragua had become increasingly corrupt. Because of his policies a civil war had erupted with a resistance group called the Sandinistas. In carrying out the civil war, Somoza and his National Guardsmen were accused of terrible atrocities and human rights violations. In protest to the conduct of the Somoza regime, U.S. aid to Nicaragua was scaled back and eventually stopped. By July of 1979 the Sandinistas had gained enough support to overthrow Somoza.

The U.S. saw the Sandinista victory as progress and immediately sent 39 million dollars in emergency food assistance and 75 million in economic assistance. Unfortunately, the promised liberation of Nicaragua did not come to fruition as the Sandinista leadership refused to institute the personal freedoms it had fought for, and instead formed ties with Cuba, Eastern Europe, and the Soviet Union. In the fall of 1979, President Carter authorized covert assistance to democratic elements in Nicaragua that were opposed to the communist leanings of the Sandinistas. Before he left office in January of 1981, President Carter suspended all aid to the Sandinista government.

President Reagan followed up on President Carter's policy by holding up the last 15 million of approved aid to the Sandinistas. As was feared, in early 1981 the Sandinista government began assisting the leftist rebels in neighboring El Salvador by providing arms, ammunition, and money. The Nicaraguan involvement in El Salvador increased to the point that President Reagan signed National Security Decision Directive 17 in December of 1981. The directive provided for up to 20 million dollars to build a 500 man force of Central Americans to conduct operations in Nicaragua. The administration's publicized goal was to interdict the arms flow to El Salvador. Many in Congress questioned the U.S. involvement in Nicaragua but could not stop it because the law requires only that the President inform Congress of his intentions since it was within the 50 million dollars in contingency funds that he has at his disposal.

In February 1982, the U.S. backed resistance was ready to begin operations. Negative press reports attacked the operation throughout the year claiming that a large proportion of the Contras were former National Guardsmen for Somoza and that Contras were saying that their real intention was to overthrow the Sandinista government. In December 1982 when the CIA briefed Congress that the Contra force had grown to 4000, the negative press came to a head. Fearing that U.S. involvement in Nicaragua might be growing increasingly contrary to international law, Congress passed the first Boland Amendment. The amendment outlawed the use of CIA or Defense Department funds for the purpose of overthrowing the government of Nicaragua. The law did not prevent aid to the Contras, it only attempted to hold the Administration to its word that the purpose of aid was only to interdict arms going into El Salvador.

Through early 1983 the number of Contras increased to several thousand. Negative press, growing fears of another "Vietnam," and Congressional uncertainty of U.S. policy in Nicaragua prompted

All quoted excerpts in this case are from *Under Fire: An American Story,* by Oliver L. North. Copyright 1991, Oliver L. North.

Congress to begin taking action to reduce U.S. involvement. In May of 1983 the House Intelligence Committee voted 9–5 to cut off further funding to the Contras. A compromise was reached with the Administration, whereby funding would continue for 5 months, and an additional 19 million dollars would be funded the next year if the President would sign a broader finding that presented a clearer picture of what his policy in Nicaragua was.

Meanwhile, half a world away, in November of 1979 an arms embargo was placed on Iran by the U.S. Government in protest for taking American hostages. In December of 1983 the administration launched Operation "Staunch" in an attempt to cutoff arms shipments to Iran from other countries in order to shorten the Iran-Iraq war. In January of 1984, after a wave of terrorist acts, the Secretary of State declared Iran a sponsor of terrorism. Israel had been selling arms to Iran for several years but stopped after the declaration of the Secretary and his plea for world-wide support.

Oliver North

Major Oliver North was assigned to duty at the National Security Council in early 1981. He worked on various low-level staff duties until mid 1982 when his competence and abilities started to bring larger assignments. Major North was tasked with preparing a military perspective on Central America. The quality of his report earned him a seat at the Saturday morning study groups on Central America held at the CIA by Director Casey. An area that the Administration wanted to expand was the attention given to improving the public opinion of the Contras. The Outreach Working Group was formed to present the Administration's policy in Central America in a more positive light than it was getting in the press. North briefed many groups over the next several years on the danger of communism in Central America. In the summer of 1983, Major North was assigned as the NSC's representative to the Restricted Interagency Group (RIG) which was a committee composed of representatives from the various intelligence gathering agencies in the executive branch. North was also appointed to a Presidential commission on Central America headed by Henry Kissinger. The commission traveled to several Central American countries and reported that the communist threat was real and proposed increasing U.S. support of democracies and would-be democracies in the region. In September of 1983 the Congress approved an expanded finding on Nicaragua by the President. The new finding authorized support and guidance for the resistance which would be increased to 12–15,000 men and declared the U.S. intention to induce the Sandinistas to negotiate with their neighbors and stop supplying the Salvadoran rebels.

In October 1983 the Grenada invasion took place and Major North had an active and important role in facilitating the liaison between the military and intelligence communities. A month after the operation, Major North was promoted to lieutenant colonel.

In December 1983 LtCol North again traveled to Central America as the NSC representative on a trip to El Salvador by Vice-President Bush. That same month a Congressional declaration that no more than 24 million dollars could be spent by the CIA or the Defense Department or any other entity or agency of the U.S. Government involved in intelligence activities to support military operations in Nicaragua during the next fiscal year went into effect. In early 1984, the CIA assisted the Contras in mining Nicaraguan harbors. Another barrage of negative press and congressional hearings followed the news of the mining. The 24 million dollars was beginning to run out and the atmosphere in Congress was such that asking for additional funds was not advisable. In May of 1984, National Security Advisor McFarlane convinced Saudi Arabia to give 1 million dollars per month to the Contras. LtCol North had his Contra contacts follow instructions he claims to have received from CIA Director Casey to set up an off-shore account to keep the transaction secret. The deal was kept from the full cabinet and when the possibility of seeking foreign assistance was brought up at a cabinet planning session the next month some of the members were adamantly opposed to it because they felt the 24 million dollar cap was on *all* assistance, not just U.S. assistance. That late spring and summer, press accounts began to speculate that the U.S. was bypassing Congress by seeking Contra funding from its allies. Congress asked for an explanation and were assured by the administration and CIA Director Casey in particular that the reports were false.

Congressional dissatisfaction with the White House policy on Nicaragua along with press reports that the administration was circumventing funding restrictions resulted in the passing of Boland II.

The second amendment specified that no appropriations or funds made available to the CIA, Defense Department, or any other agency or entity of the United States involved in intelligence activities could be spent to support directly or indirectly military or paramilitary operations in Nicaragua by any nation, group, organization, movement or individual during the next fiscal year. A provision was included to appropriate 14 million dollars after 28 February 1985 if the White House could persuade Congress to ease the restrictions. With the CIA and the vast network it had set up out of the picture the only remaining link to the Contras was LtCol North at the NSC. Admiral Poindexter, the Deputy National Security Advisor, and LtCol North agreed that the Boland restrictions did not apply to the NSC. None of the CIA facilities could be used so North had to create his own network to channel assistance. One person could not run such a vast operation so many civilians and former military and intelligence personnel were hired to perform the necessary functions. Retired Air Force General Secord was the primary executor of the operation aside from North. Together, over the next two years, they built a complex network that included a small air force of transport planes, logistics support, corporate and individual fundraising, and congressional lobbying. The majority of the financial transactions were controlled by Secord. North claims that advice and technical assistance was also supplied by Director Casey. By the end of 1984, LtCol North saw the need to have more control over the distribution of the resistance's money. He received travelers checks and cash from Secord and his Contra contacts that he kept in his office. A total of over $100,000 passed through his covert account and he claims all transactions were recorded in a ledger. The funds were used to distribute to various resistance groups, travel, and other operational expenses.

In 1985 various sources contributed to the Contra accounts. In February Saudi Arabia pledged another $24 million in covert funding. In the fall Taiwan provided $2 million in covert funding. The Congress extended their restrictions on U.S. assistance to the next fiscal year but did appropriate $27 million for the Contras for humanitarian assistance. Contributions from private sources came to over $10 million total during 1985 and 1986. Through the spring and summer of 1985 press reports continually reported that the NSC and specifically LtCol North was providing intelligence and assistance to the Contras.

In August 1985 Congressmen sent letters to the NSC pressing for inquiries. National Security Advisor McFarlane assured Congress that there was no direct or indirect involvement by the NSC.

Elsewhere around the world, terrorism and numerous abductions of foreigners in Lebanon had grabbed center stage. Another of LtCol North's specialties was in the tracking of terrorism. In August and September of 1985 Israel engaged in a sale of U.S. TOW missiles from its arsenal to Iran in exchange for Iranian assistance in freeing hostages in Lebanon. The intermediary was an Iranian named Ghorbanifar. McFarlane ordered North to monitor the transaction. Shortly after the transfer of over 500 TOW missiles one hostage was released from Beirut.

In September and October of 1985 the Intelligence Oversight Board, a White House organization, conducted a cursory review of the NSC and LtCol North in view of the Congressional inquiries. The investigator was given only selected documents and was told by LtCol North that he was in no way involved in the Nicaraguan resistance. The investigator and the Congress accepted the denials of the NSC. In October the Achille Lauro hijacking took place. LtCol North was instrumental in the planning and liaison with Israel that was necessary to capture the hijackers.

On November 17, 1985, LtCol North received a phone call from Israeli Defense Minister Rabin asking that he help Israel get a shipment of U.S. HAWK missiles that were stuck in Portugal to Iran. Moments later McFarlane called North authorizing the assistance. North asked Secord to go overseas and make the arrangements. Through a series of complex maneuvers the 80 HAWK missiles arrived in Iran by the end of November. The Iranians were angered because they were lead to believe the missiles would be long-range high-altitude instead of the low-altitude relatively close-in anti-aircraft missiles that they were. In December the President signed a finding authorizing the transaction in clear "arms for hostages terminology." LtCol North and others advocated cutting out the Israelis from future transactions. Also in December of 1985, McFarlane resigned as the National Security Advisor and Admiral Poindexter succeeded him.

In January of 1986 the President signed a finding authorizing direct transactions with Iran. In a meeting to discuss another arms for hostages transaction in January of 1986, Ghorbanifar, after having his offer of a bribe rebuffed by LtCol North, suggested that if the deal was a success some of the residuals could go to the Nicaraguan resistance. In February 1000 TOW missiles were sold to Iran, with no hostages released in return. In April LtCol North drafted a memo to Admiral Poindexter that detailed how the Israeli arsenal would be replenished and that 12 million dollars of the profits would be used for the resistance. In April 1986, the finding of evidence that linked Libya to terrorism against the U.S. resulted in the U.S. attack against select installations in Libya. LtCol North was actively involved in the intelligence planning and military liaison conducted before and during the operation. The Palestinian terrorist Abu Nidal issued a list of Americans his organization would retaliate against; LtCol North was on the list. Concern for his family prompted North to seek protection for his home. The FBI and Defense Department were unable to assist him. Secord suggested using a friend of his who owned a security company. The contact resulted in a security system being installed without payment. That same month North proceeded with McFarlane to Tehran for another meeting about hostages. The trip lasted three days but ended in disappointment as no agreement could be reached. North returned with the HAWK spare parts he took with him. In June 1986 Congress approved $100 million for the Nicaraguan resistance.

In July of 1986 a Congressman introduced a resolution of inquiry into the dealings of LtCol North. That same month a hostage was released. In early August North met informally with 11 members of the House Intelligence Committee and assured them that he was in no way involved in the Nicaraguan resistance. In October 1986 one of the resistance transport planes was shot down and the lone survivor, an American claiming to be working for the government, was captured by the Sandinistas. The White House denied any involvement. In late October 500 more TOW missiles were sent to Iran. In early November another hostage was released. The news was dampened by the fact that two more American hostages were abducted. Shortly after the hostage release details of the U.S. arms for hostages deal was published in Lebanese newspapers. North destroyed as much of the documentation as he could, including the ledgers concerning the Contra funds he administered. Not all of the documents were destroyed and the discovery by the Attorney General of North's memo detailing the diversion resulted in the November press conference in which LtCol North was relieved of his duties at the NSC and reassigned to Headquarters, U.S. Marine Corps. A month later, remembering that he had not paid for the security system, LtCol North sent for back dated copies of the bill and falsified letters responding to each of the bills.

Subsequently, LtCol North provided testimony to Congress under immunity concerning the extent of the deception of the operations that he had conducted. This deception included, he freely admitted, lying to members of the House Intelligence Committee, destroying key documents, and falsifying chronologies of events for the President and Congress.

North argued that the Finding signed by the President in December of 1985 had clearly authorized trading arms for hostages. The subsequent Finding, signed in January, 1986, however, was worded much more carefully and established the mission as much broader than simply "arms for hostages" negotiations.

Admiral Poindexter and LtCol North believed that if the first Finding was ever revealed, the President himself would be politically embarrassed. Accordingly, the Admiral destroyed the original copy of the 1985 Finding. North himself wrote:

> "... In changing the chronology and in destroying the superseded Finding, Bud [MacFarlane] and the Admiral had taken steps to preserve lives and to protect the President."

LtCol North expressed concern that the release of information regarding the people and countries involved would endanger their lives and unravel the Nicaraguan resistance. Again, he wrote:

> "... I look back on that meeting [with the Congressmen] today knowing that what I did was wrong. I didn't give straight answers to the questions I was asked ... I know the difference between right and wrong, and I can tell good from bad. But I also know that the more difficult decisions come when we have to choose between good and better. The toughest of all are those we have to make between bad and worse. That was the choice I was faced with August 6 in the Sit[uation] Room ... Looking back on it today, it's clear to me that the best thing I could have done was not to have gone to

that meeting at all. I should have said, 'Admiral, I can't do it. You and I both know what these guys are going to ask, and we also know that I can't answer those questions without destroying the [Nicaraguan] resistance . . .' "

North surmises that maybe the reason he was not convicted for lying to Congress was because, ". . . until special prosecutors came along, these kinds of informal, unsworn exchanges between the Executive and the Congress had always been treated as part of the political process. Regardless of whether it was morally right or wrong—and I knew it was wrong—I certainly never imagined that anything I was doing was a crime . . ."

The sequence of events known widely as "Iran-Contra" became the subject of inquiries conducted by a special commission led by former U. S. Senator and Secretary of Defense, John Tower, as well as of special hearings by the U.S. Senate and House of Representatives. Granted immunity for his testimony, LtCol North was able to bring to light many of the details of the linked covert operations in Iran and in Nicaragua. In 1990, a coalition of resistance groups managed to defeat the Sandinistas in a general election. By 1992, all of the surviving American hostages held in Lebanon had been released.

Questions for Discussion

1. How do you characterize the fundamental conflict or dilemma that LtCol North appeared to face in this instance? How would you, faced with such a conflict, proceed to resolve it? To whom or to what would you be loyal, above all?

2. LtCol North frequently notes that his superiors knew what he was doing. How does that assertion, if true, affect the rightness or wrongness of his own actions?

3. How would you resolve the conflict, as LtCol North portrays it in this instance, between "lives and lies?"

Aviano EA-6B Gondola Mishap
LtCol Gary Slyman, USMC

Introduction

On 3 February 1998, a Marine EA-6B, a four-seat electronic warfare aircraft, sliced through aerial cables supporting a ski gondola in the Dolomite Mountains of Calvalese, Italy, killing twenty people onboard the gondola. On 12 March 1998, a Command Investigation Board, headed by a Marine Corps major general, concluded that aircrew error was the cause of the mishap. The four aircrew members were charged with 20 counts of negligent homicide and several lesser offenses. Two Article 32 Investigations[1] were held—one for the two back-seat crew members in May 1998, and one for the two front-seat crew members in June 1998. Charges were dropped against the back-seat aircrew. The front-seat crewmembers were brought to a General Court Martial. The Commanding Officer, Executive Officer, Operations Officer, and Director of Safety and Standardization were subjected to a Nonjudicial Punishment hearing in August 1998 for systemic errors in the squadron. On 6 August 1998, the Commanding Officer was relieved of command.

Approximately one week after the Commanding Officer was relieved, it came to light that a videotape of portions of the flight existed and had been destroyed by the front-right seater. The revelation came from one of the back-seaters when he was granted immunity and ordered to testify. Consequently, additional charges of conduct unbecoming an officer were brought against the two front-seaters to be handled at two separate courts martial.

In February 1999, the General Court Martial for negligent homicide commenced against the pilot. He was found not guilty of all charges. The charges of negligent homicide were subsequently dropped against the right-seater. In March 1999, the General Court Martial for conduct unbecoming an officer was convened against the right-seater for the destruction of the videotape. He pleaded guilty. His sentence was dismissal from the Marine Corps. At the time of this writing, the case is in appeal.

The trial for the pilot followed shortly thereafter. He pleaded not guilty to conduct unbecoming an officer. He was found guilty and sentenced to six months in confinement and dismissed from the Marine Corps.

The narrative that follows is the story of the right front-seater, Captain Joe Schweitzer, and the events leading up his court martial for the charges of conduct unbecoming an officer.

Tragedy in the Dolomites

Marine Tactical Electronic Warfare Squadron-2 (VMAQ-2), a Marine EA-6B squadron, was deployed in support of Operation DELIBERATE GUARD, flying missions over Bosnia-Herzegovina. The squadron had just over a week left before it headed home from this six-month deployment. On 3 February 1998, a crew of four Marine captains took off from Aviano, Italy in an EA-6B for a low-level training mission. On the last leg of the low-level route, the pilot spotted a cable in front of him and saw a yellow flash to his right. The pilot went full-stick forward, negative G, and heard and felt a loud thud.

Reprinted by permission of the author. With support from the Center for the Study of Professional Military Ethics.

[1] An Article 32 Investigation is a pretrial investigation to determine whether a case should be recommended for forwarding to a general court-martial. It is similar to a grand jury investigation in civil law.

This was immediately followed by the right-seater's command, "climb, climb, climb!"[2] The two back-seaters immediately put themselves in a good ejection position, expecting the worst. After some tense moments, the crew determined the aircraft was badly damaged but still flyable. Two cables supporting a ski gondola had sliced into the right wing, creating two large holes and taking off a portion of the vertical stabilizer. When the cables snapped, the gondola fell 370 feet to the ground killing 20 people.

The Aircrew

Captain Richard "Trash" Ashby from Mission Viejo, California was the pilot on this mission; he was on his second deployment to Aviano. His first deployment was with the same squadron from March to September 1997, enforcing the no-fly zone over Bosnia-Herzegovina during operation DECISIVE ENDEAVOR. This deployment would be his last as a Prowler pilot since he was recently selected to transition to F/A-18 Hornets. Although he had fewer than 500 hours in the Prowler, Captain Ashby had a reputation as a talented pilot. The rest of his crew consisted of three electronic countermeasures officers (ECMO's). ECMO-1 sits to the pilot's right, and has the duties of a copilot and navigator. ECMO-2 and 3 sit in the back, and operate the aircraft's weapon systems—the radar jamming pods hung under the wings, managed through the onboard computer system.

ECMO-1 was Captain Joe "Guiseppe" Schweitzer, a 1989 Naval Academy graduate, a well-respected officer and aviator who would break 1000 hours in the Prowler on his next hop. As the squadron logistics officer, he was the only captain department head, a job normally held by a major. Captain Schweitzer was an experienced ECMO and officer, having completed three deployments in his previous assignments. He had been assigned to the squadron two months prior to this deployment, after returning from a one-year forward air controller tour with a Marine tank battalion. He had plans to leave the Marine Corps and go to business school. The day before the incident, ECMO-2, Bill "Rainman" Raney, had been promoted to captain. He was the only married officer on this flight and was just completing his first deployment. ECMO-3 was Chandler P. "CP" Seagraves, a second-generation Marine aviator from Indiana. He was part of the "advance party" from VMAQ-4, the Marine EA-6B squadron scheduled to relieve VMAQ-2. He was added on to the schedule the night before, and he was not introduced to the rest of the crew until mission brief. There was an open seat, and the operations officer notified him he would be flying in order to familiarize him with the local area and their course rules.

The Flight on 3 February 1998

The crew met around 1200, completed its planning, and briefed the flight at 1230 in the ready room. The ready room was a portable trailer about 20x30 feet, which all Marine EA-6B squadrons had used since 1996. The crew dressed in their flight gear and took the "breadtruck" to the aircraft. A lance corporal drove them on the mile-and-a-half ride around the runway to where the squadron's aircraft were parked. The preflight was uneventful, but the aircrew were temporarily delayed while they waited for the lance corporal to return with something left in the ready room. The driver arrived back at the aircraft with two 8mm videotapes. He had willingly retrieved the tapes when the crew mentioned they left them behind. Captain Schweitzer had wanted to tape portions of the route as a personal memento using Captain Ashby's camera. After final checks, the crew taxied on time.

Safely airborne, enroute to the low-level entry point, Schweitzer was having difficulty operating the video camera. After several minutes, Ashby asked him to put the camera away because the entry point was approaching, which he did. Unknown to the back-seaters, Schweitzer began to film again at some point during the first leg. After several minutes of filming in the low-level environment, while maneuvering and pulling G's, including an inverted ridgeline crossing, he decided that filming was a nuisance and put the camera away again. The next time he took the camera out was at 5000 feet above Lake Garda while flying wings-level. He was never sure if he was operating the camera correctly. At one point he turned the camera toward his face and filmed himself smiling in the cockpit.[3]

---

[2] Wilkinson, Peter. "Easy 01 has an Emergency." *Rolling Stone*, Dec 10, 1998: 77.

[3] Record of Trial (ROT) *US versus Captain Joseph P. Schweitzer* General Court-Martial, pp. 2752–52753, 3432–3436, 3456.

The weather was a little hazy, but fine for the low-level flight. They were on the sixth and final leg of the low-level route, and the final turnpoint, a mountain peak, was in sight when they hit the cable. After the cable impact and the aggressive climb to achieve separation from the ground, the pilot slowed the aircraft. Luckily, they were only sixty miles from the airfield. As they neared Aviano, the pilot placed the landing gear handle into the down position, and all three wheels indicated down and locked. With a badly damaged wing, the aircrew elected not to attempt to lower the flaps and slats. (It didn't matter, because the combined hydraulic system failed when the pilot lowered the gear, making lowering the flaps impossible).

Establishing radio contact with the Aviano airbase, the crew declared an emergency and requested an arrested landing.[4] They continued enroute to Aviano, completing the damaged aircraft checklist, and slow-flighted the airplane to see how controllable it would be at landing airspeeds. The aircrew determined they were committed to a no-flap, no-slat, no-speedbrakes approach at about 200 knots. Without the combined hydraulic system, they would not have normal brakes to stop with upon touchdown. The weather was clear, allowing them to fly a visual approach all the way to touchdown. They entered the downwind, flew a left-hand pattern, and touched down at about 190 knots. A sharp tug let them know they had successfully caught the arresting gear.

After shutting down the engines, the crew climbed out of the aircraft. The two back-seaters got out as rapidly as possible by jumping off the back of the wings. Raney was in such a rush that he landed awkwardly, breaking a bone in his heel. About 75 yards in front of the aircraft, the back-seaters gathered and turned to wait for the front-seat crew, who were still in the cockpit. While shutting down all of his systems, Schweitzer looked at the video camera in front of him sitting on the radar boot and said, "Let's take the tape."[5] He then handed the pilot a blank tape to swap with the tape in the camera. After several seconds, they egressed and rejoined the back-seaters, while the Air Force Crash Fire and Rescue crew took control of the aircraft. Squadron maintenance Marines joined the crew and waited to tow the aircraft off the runway. No one said anything about the tape.[6] The flight was over, with the aircraft safely on deck and the crew still alive. But their lives had changed forever.

Immediate Aftermath

The aircraft had struck the cables of a ski gondola support system at time 1512, and was safely recovered around 1535. Following the landing, the crew were transported to the squadron's operations spaces. The front-seat crew followed the commanding officer to his office to debrief him while still dressed in their flight gear. They told him they thought they hit a wire and where they thought it was on their chart. They changed out of their flight gear and were transported to the Air Force hospital for a flight physical, accompanied by the squadron flight surgeon. (The physical is required after all major mishaps and becomes part of an aircraft mishap investigation.) The crew still did not know the extent of the accident. The squadron was just beginning to get reports on the severity of the mishap. The crew acknowledged they saw a yellow flash prior to the thud, but said they did not know it was a gondola.

The four aircrew were ushered into a hospital waiting room, while the civilians waiting for appointments were shuffled to another room. An Air Force captain, a psychologist, arrived, and an orderly shut the television off. The crew pressed the flight surgeon to let them know what was going on. He didn't say anything. Around 1830, the squadron commanding officer entered and told them that fourteen people were killed in a gondola after it crashed to the ground. Stunned, one member went off by himself to pray. Another put his head in his hands. All were shocked.[7]

Back at the airfield the aircraft was towed from the runway to a normal parking spot and roped off. The aircraft's damaged tail could be seen from the main road outside the base, and local news media and photographers had already gathered to take pictures. However, nightfall limited their

---

[4] An arrested landing is when an aircraft uses its tailhook, which is attached to the rear of the aircraft, to catch a cable strung across the runway to stop the aircraft.

[5] ROT p. 3442.

[6] ROT p. 3442.

[7] ROT p. 3445.

opportunity. The local carabinieri, the Italian paramilitary police, claimed jurisdiction over the aircraft, as it was now considered evidence for a crime committed in Italy. When VMAQ-2's maintenance Marines attempted to tow the aircraft to a hangar to remove it from public view, the Italian base commander ordered that it remain where it was.

Finished with most of their physicals, the crew returned to their quarters and waited to be called by the squadron safety officer. Starting around 2100, each aircrew member gave a taped statement to the squadron safety officer. The statements were privileged information, for use only in the safety investigation. Only the individual aircrew and the safety officer were present as the statements were provided.

Aviano: 4–8 February

After a sleepless night for the crew, the next morning brought the confirmation of twenty deaths—nine women, ten men, and one child, from Germany, Hungary, Poland, and Italy. There was a second gondola that had been left dangling from the cable. Its one passenger, the operator, was rescued.

The aircrew continued with their flight physicals. The four traveled to the hospital via a back gate, in civilian clothes, in order to avoid protestors gathered at the main gate. To get to the hospital, they had to travel off base through a portion of the town of Aviano. The Air Force psychologist they had met the previous evening accompanied them. Midmorning, during their physicals, they were called to return to 31st Fighter Wing Headquarters in their flight suits to talk to the Italian magistrate (equivalent to an American prosecutor). In the Wing Headquarters building, the aircrew met with Italian defense attorneys (provided by the 31st Fighter Wing to defend them in Italian court.) At this meeting they learned there was the possibility they might go to Italian jail. They then traveled across the base with their lawyers to the Italian headquarters building to be interviewed by the Italian magistrate from Trento.[8]

They sat in a small waiting room in the headquarters building, shocked, scared, sleep deprived, and not really sure what was going on. One by one they were called to tell their story to the Magistrate. Accompanied by their Italian lawyers, they gave what they thought were confidential statements to the magistrate. Only other Italians and carabinieri, and no other Americans, were in the room. When they finished making their statements, they signed what they believed was a charge sheet for involuntary manslaughter. They then proceeded upstairs to sign for the death certificates of all of the victims, which brought it home to them. Captain Schweitzer said this was a very "humanizing" event for him— to see the names, ages, and hometowns of the deceased: "... it was almost like seeing a picture of somebody . . . and that was a difficult thing to see."[9] Now extremely frightened, the crew walked out of building and found no one waiting for them. They called the squadron to get a ride back to the squadron area.[10]

Their four military defense attorneys also arrived in Aviano from Naples, Italy, late the evening of 4 February—a Marine captain as senior defense counsel, two Navy lieutenants, and one lieutenant junior grade.

The squadron Aircraft Mishap Board[11] had been convened the night of the mishap, but one day later, it was clear that a much higher-profile investigation would take place without any members of the squadron on the investigation team. The squadron board members were limited to gathering evidence to hand over to a team of investigators traveling to Aviano. The squadron gave the aircrew a separate 20x30 foot trailer to work in with their lawyers.

The day following the interviews with the Italian magistrate, the Italian and American press carried many quotes from their sessions with the magistrate. There were also many stories characterizing the aircrew as "Rambos," "murderers," and "cowboys." President Clinton spoke with the Italian prime

---

[8] ROT pp. 3306, 3348.

[9] ROT p. 3450.

[10] ROT pp. 3307, 3348–3349.

[11] An Aircraft Mishap Board (AMB) is a standing panel of officers within the squadron appointed to investigate an aircraft mishap and determine its causes.

minister, expressing his condolences for the loss of life, and promising a full investigation. The smashed gondola in the valley, with the blood still in the snow, was a frequent scene on CNN.

On 5 February, the USMC advance party for the Command Investigation Board (CIB), consisting of three colonels, three majors, and a captain, arrived in Aviano around 0300. Three investigations were to be conducted simultaneously to determine the cause of the mishap. The Marine Corps conducted a CIB; the Italian magistrate a criminal investigation; and the Italian Air Force a privileged safety investigation. Because of the seriousness of the mishap and the requirement for complete openness, Commander, US Marine Corps Forces, Atlantic, determined that the normal privileged safety investigation, called an Aviation Mishap Board (AMB), would be delayed or satisfied by the Command Investigation Board. The purpose of an AMB is to determine the cause of a mishap and to disseminate the lessons learned to the fleet aviators to prevent future mishaps.

In a press conference that same day in Aviano, a Marine Corps brigadier general stated that the aircraft hit the cable on an authorized low-level within the route structure, which contradicted a previous statement by the Italian defense minister.[12] The general left Aviano, and the following day, the 31st Fighter Wing issued an apology for the statement.[13]

Within several days of the mishap, the aircrew wrote a letter to the victims' families to convey their sympathy. They presented the letter to the Marine public affairs officer, who had traveled to Aviano to support the investigation. He refused, saying he worked for the Marine Corps and not the aircrew, so they had to go to their Italian defense counsel to get the letter released to the families of the victims.[14]

Within a few days, the media were pressing the Marine Corps for the names of the aircrew. The crew had decided not to give permission to release their names because they wanted to protect their families. A senior officer in their squadron told the aircrew to notify their families about their involvement in the mishap, or run the risk that their families would find out by watching CNN. They all acquiesced, and the names were released on 6 February.[15]

The crew also learned that the Magistrate had now filed criminal charges against the commanding officer and another squadron pilot. The commanding officer was charged with the same offenses as his aircrew. The charges against the squadron pilot originated from his non-cooperative conduct in the interview with the magistrate.[16]

In the days immediately following the mishap, the crew had someone with them at all times to ensure they did not attempt suicide. By the third day, the flight surgeon was giving them medication to help them sleep. They had support, but felt distanced from the squadron, describing themselves as a leper colony.[17]

Cherry Point, North Carolina: 4–8 February

The mishap in Italy touched off a series of events at VMAQ-2's home station, Marine Corps Air Station, Cherry Point, North Carolina. Cherry Point is home to all four USMC Prowler squadrons that fall under the 2nd Marine Aircraft Wing. Emails and telephone traffic reported events as they unfolded.

When VMAQ-2 deployed to Aviano, it relieved its sister squadron, VMAQ-3, from a six-month deployment. During VMAQ-3's deployment, they also had flown several low-level training flights. On one flight the VMAQ-3 aircrew videotaped the same low-level route that the VMAQ-2 mishap occurred on, including the cockpit audio. Copies of that tape were made and distributed to members of VMAQ-3. The day following the gondola mishap, VMAQ-3's squadron commander called an All-Officer Meeting to discuss the gondola mishap. During this meeting he brought up VMAQ-3's videotape. He stated

---

[12] "US pilot on first flight over Dolomites when hit ski-lift," *Agence France Presse* (5 February 1998) online. Internet.

[13] ROT pp. 3451–3453.

[14] ROT pp. 3447–3448.

[15] ROT p. 3452.

[16] ROT p. 3453

[17] ROT pp. 2765, 3458.

words to the effect that if anyone had one of the videotapes he needed to make it "disappear."[18] After the meeting, one of the VMAQ-3 officers approached the commanding officer and let him know that his comments sounded like obstruction of justice. The commanding officer reconvened his officers and stated that the videotapes were to go through him to higher authorities. One of VMAQ-3's officers reported his remarks to the Wing.

On 5 February, after hearing the initial reports from Italy and learning about the VMAQ-3 videotape, the commanding general of the 2nd Marine Aircraft Wing addressed all the officers of the EA-6B community at Cherry Point. He acknowledged that he could possibly be the convening authority (the person with legal jurisdiction) over the Aviano incident, and thus probably should not discuss the case. He then read headlines about the incident and implied that the mishap was caused by aircrew errors. He accused the community as a whole of violating flight rules on low-level flights, and stated that if the Marine Corps found any aircrew violating flight rules, they would be punished. On that same day he began an investigation at Cherry Point to determine trends in adherence to flight rules in the EA-6B community. As part of the investigation, all EA-6B aircrew were read their legal rights and interviewed by a military lawyer and the assistant wing commander, a brigadier general. The results of this investigation were ultimately provided to the Aviano Command Investigation Board.

On 6 February the commanding general relieved the VMAQ-3 commanding officer.[19] The VMAQ-3 videotape showed the squadron had violated flight rules with the commanding officer in the aircraft. Over the next few days, the commanding general addressed all the aircrew in his wing emphasizing strict adherence to flight rules.

The Decision to Destroy the Tape

Back in Aviano, on 3 February, prior to egressing the aircraft, the two front-seaters (Ashby and Schweitzer) took the tape from the cockpit and left a blank tape in the camera. The pilot, Ashby, had possession of the first tape and hid it in his room. He neither viewed the tape, nor talked about it for several days. Both the front-seaters knew the tape would be a subject of the impending investigations, which by the second day included an Italian criminal investigation. Schweitzer thought that his commanding officer would have been upset by the use of the video camera, even though there was no specific prohibition on using it. Prior to the investigation team's inventory of the cockpit, he approached his commanding officer and one other senior officer in the squadron, and mentioned that there was a video camera in the front cockpit, leaving them with the impression it was not used during the flight.

On or about 6 February, the two front-seaters approached Seagraves (ECMO-3) and told him they had removed the tape from the cockpit. They then asked him what they should do with it. He asked, "Well what's on it?" After they said they didn't know, he responded, "I would get rid of it if I were you," and then walked away.[20]

Schweitzer asked Ashby for the tape. Ashby protested because he wanted to view it. Schweitzer persisted. They discussed the possibility that the tape showed the "flaperon roll" they had made on their inverted ridgeline crossing. They knew the maneuver was authorized, but thought the Italians would misinterpret it. Schweitzer added: ". . . the Italians will eat you alive." Hearing that, Ashby gave up the tape. Schweitzer took the tape, hid it in his room, and never viewed it. Several days after taking the tape from Ashby, Schweitzer destroyed it in a bonfire.[21]

The tape was not mentioned again until approximately four months after the mishap, back in Cherry Point, when Schweitzer and Seagraves had a conversation in their office spaces. Seagraves said that if the question of the videotape came up, he was going to tell the truth. Schweitzer responded that

---

[18] Court Order and essential findings on remaining phase 1 motions, Captain Richard Ashby USMCR and Captain Joseph P. Schweitzer USMC 8 January 1999.

[19] ROT Vol 46/51 AE LXXX p. 4 of 69.

[20] ROT p. 3457.

[21] ROT p. 3458, Volume 42/51 PE 22 Stipulations of Fact pp. 1–8.

that was what he expected him to do.[22] In Seagraves' testimony, he admitted to advising Schweitzer and Ashby to get rid of the tape.[23]

The existence of the videotape became publicly known in mid-August, more than six months after the mishap. Seagraves was granted immunity and ordered to testify. His statements to investigators after the grant of immunity revealed the existence of the tape. Prior to this time, only Ashby, Schweitzer, and Seagraves (and their defense attorneys) knew of the tape. Raney never knew the tape was taken from the cockpit. The only reason Seagraves knew anything about it was that Ashby and Schweitzer asked him for advice on what to do with it.

At a general court martial in March 1999, Captain Schweitzer pleaded guilty to conduct unbecoming of an officer, for conspiracy to obstruct justice in the destruction of the videotape.

---

[22]ROT Vol 49/51 AECLII p. 37.
[23]ROT pp. 3324.3342.

Loyalty vs. Honor
Submitted by LtCol Joe Dauplaise, USMC (Retired)
Edited by Captain Rick Rubel

You are the division officer for the airframes branch of the Maintenance Department of an EA-6B Marine Squadron. You are a pilot, but your collateral duty has you responsible for about 50 Marines.

Background: The squadron is currently flying combat missions over enemy country and the first flight was scheduled for a take off at 0800. You were in the first of two aircraft.

Lance Corporal Barns called Corporal Coover this morning to tell him he was going to be late and would not be at the 0600 muster and turnover. He did not give Corporal Coover a specific reason for this, and hung up quickly. Lance Corporal Barns and Corporal Coover were close friends and had known each other since "A" school, so when Lance Corporal Barns called and asked him to "cover" for him, he reported him "present" on the 0600 report to the Maintenance Chief.

The time was 0700 and the aircraft were getting ready to start up. After engine start, the plane captain (PC) noticed hydraulic fluid coming out of engine bay door and upon his investigation noticed a hydraulic pump fitting needed to be replaced. It was a quick 10-minute fix—no problem. The plane captain could help and the hydraulics man on the flight line was ready with the part. Once the part was replaced, all it needed was a CDI(Collateral Duty Inspector) to sign off the work and the plane is "up for flight".

(CDI is the final Quality Assurance checker in the maintenance department—there is one for each subsystem on the aircraft. "Safety of Flight" requires sign offs to ensure procedures have been followed to avoid aircraft accidents, injury or death.)

When the PC radioed back into the hydraulic shop for the CDI—Corporal Coover started to worry—he hadn't see Lance Corporal Barns and thought he had already arrived and was out at the airplane observing the launch. Time was then 0715. Corporal Coover couldn't find Lance Corporal Barns, so he called back to the tents where the Marines are staying and had the duty NCO look for Lance Corporal Barns in his tent. The duty NCO called back at 0725 and said he wasn't there.

The EA-6B that was currently "down" for a hydraulic leak was the 2nd of two aircraft scheduled to take off at 0800. As you were in the first aircraft, you knew that it was critical to your mission this morning that two EA-6B's get airborne with the strike package. As a matter of fact, you know the Strike commander briefed the General that without two EA-6B's airborne, the mission would be scrubbed. (Corporal Coover probably didn't know this)

Corporal Coover was frantic. He needed a CDI to verify the maintenance procedure. At 0740, Lance Corporal Barns still hadn't shown up. The plane captain was calling maintenance control looking for his CDI. The Master Sergeant in maintenance control was calling Corporal Coover for the CDI. The aircrew in the down aircraft were frantic because they had only 10 minutes to get down to the end of the runway to arm missiles and prepare to takeoff on time with the strike group. The operations officer was livid and was calling the maintenance control and asking questions. He said," The CO is going to be told in 5 minutes that the EA-6B is down (can't fly) and they are going to have to make the call to the strike commander (General) that the mission is going to be scrubbed. He's not going to be happy!"

Five minutes passed, and the strike mission was scrubbed.

Truth vs. Loyalty: The Case of the Missing Flashlight

Midshipman Zachary D. Thrasher,
Class of 2011[1]

The night shift on an aircraft carrier is one of the most dangerous jobs a person can have. Even during the day, dodging and weaving through the maze of chains, aircraft, equipment, spinning propeller blades and live ordinance can be a difficult task. At night, the pitch black flight deck and the "dimming cones" we affix to our flashlights make the job that much harder.

Every night, those of us assigned the night shift would meet at 1800, just as the sun was setting. We would look over the flight schedule, plan what needed to be done, and then set out to relieve the day shift.

We literally saw ourselves as a "band of brothers." We watched over each other carefully, so that, on each of the 100+ nights we would have to work a flight schedule, none of us would get killed or seriously injured. We also checked each other's work meticulously in order to make sure that there was never a problem with an aircraft that was going to fly that night. I myself could never imagine the horror I would experience if ever "my plane" were to take off from the carrier deck, and suddenly lose power and nose-dive into the ocean, just because I had forgotten to check a gauge, or had carelessly left a tool inside some vital interior area of the plane. That was why we were such a tight-knit group, loyal ultimately to each other. We realized we were especially prone to accidents under these stringent night-watch conditions, and so we took extra care to make sure the man next to us never lost any of his tools in the jet and always did a proper job.

Navy tool control procedures are very specific: a lost wrench, floating around the flight deck, for example, is one of the worst things that can happen. Every tool that a shop is assigned is etched with the squadron, shop, and toolbox from which it came. When a sailor needs a tool he signs it out specifically under his name. The Lead Petty Officer, or the night shift supervisor, will sign out the tool along with the individual sailor, in order to verify that the sailor did, in fact, take the tool from the box. When the shifts switch over, all tools are accounted for in the entire shop and signed over to the next shift. In accordance with this strict Navy tool control procedure: should a sailor ever find a tool on the flight deck unaccounted for, that individual is required to bring the errant tool down to the Senior Chief or Master Chief in charge of maintenance control for each squadron. The person who lost the tool is then due, *at very least*, for a very serious "chewing out"; more likely, that individual will probably face a Captain's Mast. Likewise, if a workshop has to report a tool as lost, then the entire flight deck operation will be suspended and everyone on the flight deck will search for the tool. It isn't a trivial thing to have all flight ops cease in order to look for a screwdriver. Hence, if the person who lost a tool signed for it in the shop tool log, and if the LPO or supervisor also signed for it, then both sailors are in serious trouble.

---

[1] This case is based on a second-prize essay in the annual VADM William Lawrence Ethics Essay Award competition, sponsored by the U.S. Naval Academy Class of 1981. The incident is based on events that transpired aboard the aircraft carrier U.S.S. Theodore Roosevelt, where the author served as an enlisted Airmen prior to his admission to the Naval Academy. Names of principals have been altered to protect their privacy. This essay was nominated by USNA ethics instructor, Captain Willim DeFillippo, USN (retired).

So it was that I was working on my aircraft one evening, when I saw a wrench left in the wheel well. I looked at the etching and noticed it was from the AD shop. I checked around and saw no one. At that instant, I was faced with a choice: I could follow procedure and run down to Maintenance Control, inform the Senior Chief of my discovery, and watch all my buddies get in trouble. Or I could run the tool down to the AD shop, toss it to the LPO and say "watch your stuff man," then run back on deck and give my "bird" a close look-over to make sure nothing else was wrong. I chose the latter course of action in this case. I didn't want my friends to get in trouble, and I certainly wouldn't want someone to turn in a tool to Maintenance Control that I had somehow forgotten, should this ever happen to me. (And, on other occasions, I *had* been the guilty party). This was our unspoken rule. I think all of us, at one point or another, lost something for a time, and had one of our buddies return it for us.

So this was how our shift ran for four months, until one evening in January. It was around 1700 when I stepped onto the flight deck. I waited topside with my chains and necessary gear to recover and inspect a returning jet. Scout 706 hit the deck and taxied to the fantail of the boat. I ran down aft and chained her down. Everything was normal through shutdown. The pilots spoke with us for a minute about normal S-3B problems, after which I set about completing my usual turnaround inspection. As I came around to the number 2 engine and opened up the cowling, however, staring me in the face was a flashlight. A flashlight!!! A *flashlight,* still turned on, hot as hell, apparently left there from the night shift before. This flashlight rode for almost 12 hours inside the engine. Who knows what sort of catastrophe it could have caused? I stood frozen in place, staring at this flashlight as my mind raced. I could have just grabbed the flashlight and put it in my tool pouch, quietly returned it to the shop it belonged to, and nothing would have happened. Or I could have given it to Maintenance Control in accordance with proper procedure, and stirred up a serious storm around the squadron.

That night in January I was faced with what I perceived to be a very serious moral dilemma. I held in my hands the careers of the sailors who had left that tool in the engine. I would later find out that these Sailors were AD2 Smith, AD3 Jones and AD1 Jenkins. I knew all three of these men very well. Jones was not only my good friend and liberty buddy, he was also the guy who had taught me everything I knew about my job. Earlier on cruise, AD2 Smith had once pulled me away from spinning propeller blades, barely three feet away, that I was in danger of walking through. How could I send them to Captain's Mast by turning in the flashlight? How could I betray the loyalty that they had shown to me? I had no idea what to do, or what I *would* do.

Only the thought of loyalty to my friends was running through my mind as I stood there in front of the flashlight. I reached in and took it from the airplane, but as I held it in my hand, my Chief, ADC Grenski, came around the plane and saw the tool in my hand. He walked up, took it from me, looked at the etching on the side, hung his head in disappointment, and then quickly walked off the flight deck with the light in his hand. Chief loved the three men that were responsible for this light. He was one of those Chiefs that would stick his neck out for any one of us. As our leader, he placed great faith and trust in his subordinates. This time, however, Chief marched the light straight to Maintenance Control, and the storm that I had mentioned proceeded to hit us all very hard. The three AD's had signed for the flashlight on three separate occasions, saying on paper that it was safe in its tool box. This mistake was so heinous that every shop was inspected, tool logs scrutinized, everything checked then rechecked. The three AD's, who were otherwise among the best and most consistent performers in VS-24, nonetheless went straight to Captain's Mast where, reluctantly but forcefully, they were punished by the CO.

I hated seeing my friends, these outstanding enlisted sailors, get reduced in rank. For a long while after, I hated Chief, as I imagined him some day turning in a mistake that I had made, getting me in trouble, and sending me to Mast. A large portion of the squadron felt the same way about his decision.

I came at last to realize, however, that Chief had literally saved our squadron. He saved all of our careers, including the three that went to Mast, and he saved the lives of whatever two pilots might otherwise have ended up as the unlucky flight crew aboard one of our aircraft harboring a serious and unnoticed discrepancy. Chief made his decision the way he did, because he understood the true meaning of what it is to be truthful and loyal at the same time. All of the previous mistakes that we had covered up were essentially lies—little deceptions we had practiced upon ourselves, reassuring ourselves that everything was running smoothly, when in fact this was simply not true. These deceptions brought about a bias in our squadron that the *perception* of the quality of our maintenance was more important than the actual quality of our work. Sissella Bok put it best when she observed:

> "*Bias* causes liars often to ignore [a] second type of harm [that they do]. For even if they make the effort to estimate the consequences to individuals [to whom they lie], they often fail to consider the many ways in which deception can spread and give rise to practices very damaging to human communities . . ."[2]

There is, finally, no debate between "truth" and "loyalty," because loyalty is telling the truth *to* those, and *about* those, to whom you are loyal. In my opinion, Chief Grenski was ultimately loyal to all of us by recognizing and adhering to this difficult truth.

---

[2] Sissela Bok. *Lying* (1979); as cited in *Ethics and the Military Profession*, revised edition. Eds. George R. Lucas, Jr. and Rick Rubel. (New York: Pearson/Longman, 2008) p. 421.

The Obligations of Officership: The SENTINEL* Case[1]

Colonel Paul E. Roush

For Lieutenant Junior Grade (LTJG) Annette Ramey life had a positive aura. She had recently graduated from college with a bachelor's degree in chemistry, she was happily married, and she was about to embark on what she assumed would be a wonderful professional career. Her passion in life was to be a successful naval officer. She regarded the naval profession as her calling, and she brought all her energy to bear in whatever she thought would further that goal. Not all fields were open to women officers when she entered the navy in the mid-1980s, but she wanted to be where the action was. She was athletic—physical fitness was a high priority for her—and wanted to be a diver. She graduated from the Basic Diving and Salvage Officer Course at the Naval Diving and Salvage Training Center in June 1985. She was not a quick learner, but a classmate described her as the best student in the class because of her intense desire to understand the principles behind the material in the curriculum. He also regarded her as the safest diver in the class because of her commitment to the physical training aspects of diving and underwater techniques. She completed Basic Surface Warfare Officer's School in December 1985, and she reported to USS SENTINEL (ARS 50) on December 31, 1985. Capable of manned diving operations to depths in excess of 300 feet, SENTINEL was the first of a new class of ship designed to operate in towing, salvage and rescue operations. LTJG Ramey reported while the ship was still in a training period, in which its capabilities would be evaluated under operational conditions.

The ship was commanded by LCDR Chace, a former enlisted sailor who had come up through the ranks and who had a reputation as a very capable mariner. Unfortunately, the relationship between the captain[2] and LTJG Ramey got off to a rough start. Two issues in particular set her teeth on edge. The first was that, on reporting aboard, she was told by the commanding officer (CO) that she would be berthed in senior enlisted quarters, even though she was a commissioned officer. Specifically she was told to share a living space occupied by a female chief petty officer (CPO). A stateroom had been set aside for women officers, but it was occupied by a male warrant officer who did not want to move to

*This case was produced by the Center for the Study of Professional Military Ethics, U.S. Naval Academy. Support was provided by Newport News Shipbuilding. This case recounts actual events documented by the author's research; the names of the principal ship featured in the case and of the individuals have been changed.

[1] Author's note: the material in the case study was obtained from five sources. First was a JAG Manual Investigation (INVESTIGATION TO INQUIRE INTO THE ALLEGATIONS OF MISCONDUCT COMMITTED BY COMMANDING OFFICER USS SENTINEL (ARS 50). Second was a Naval Inspector General's Hotline Complaint Report (HOTLINE COMPLAINT #88045; ALLEGED CONTINUED HARASSMENT ONBOARD USS SENTINEL (ARS 50)). The above sources were obtained under the provisions of the Freedom of Information Act. Third was an interview that the author conducted with the person who was director of the Defense Advisory Committee on Women in the Services when the events of the case study took place. Fourth was a series of interviews conducted by the author with current and former officers having personal or professional knowledge of the facts of the case. Fifth was a case study prepared at the Kennedy School of Government at Harvard (WOMEN IN THE NAVY(C16-88-853.0).

[2] By naval custom, the commanding officer of any ship is referred to as its captain, regardless of his or her rank.

a double stateroom in which a lone male officer was living. Apparently the captain had made an agreement with the warrant officer to be berthed alone as a precondition for his presence on the ship. LTJG Ramey found the arrangement demeaning, and she petitioned both the executive officer (XO) and the captain on several occasions to be allowed to berth in the officer stateroom. It was only after another officer left the ship at the end of February that she was permitted to occupy an officer's stateroom.

The second point of contention was also something of a status question. She believed she was deprived of the opportunity to work in operational assignments, which would enhance her professional competence. When she reported aboard as the first woman officer to be assigned to USS SENTINEL she was scheduled to be communications officer (a position previously held as a collateral duty by the leading radioman—an enlisted petty officer). When the ship's supply officer was relieved for incompetence, she was tasked to be his replacement, but was not given any opportunity for schooling to prepare her for the task. Nevertheless she threw herself into learning what was required. Her fitness report for this period was highly laudatory of her successful efforts to improve the status of the supply department. When another officer, an ensign, reported aboard, he was named as the interim supply officer, and LTJG Ramey was assigned as repair officer, a position that had been a collateral duty of the chief engineer. When a trained supply officer reported aboard, the interim supply officer became the repair officer and LTJG Ramey became the equivalent of the "odd jobs officer." She repeatedly went directly to the XO and CO to protest what she saw as inequitable treatment.

To her dismay, her complaints to the chain of command were having minimal success. She was not satisfied with the answers she was getting from the XO and CO, and so she sought help beyond the ship. She talked to the squadron chaplain on at least three occasions, beginning in January 1986, when she had been aboard for less than a month. She went to see him because she was deeply offended: In her mind, no male officer would have been treated so cavalierly. She specifically asked the chaplain not to report their conversations to anyone. She was simply looking for help in dealing with her personal disappointment and frustration. Toward that end, she also talked with a psychologist at the Pearl Harbor Family Services Center, with Human Relations Council officers in Pearl Harbor, and with the chief staff officer of Service Squadron (SERVRON) 5, all during her first year on USS SENTINEL. Each time she was told that the circumstances that so upset her were not all that different from what junior officers sometimes encounter.

Her situation was made more difficult because she was easily rattled by LCDR Chace's leadership style, which included significant shouting, cursing, and denigrating language directed toward junior officers under his supervision on the bridge.[3] When he treated her this way, she became confused and unable to perform adequately, which probably led other officers to view her as less than competent. LCDR Chace had a habit of physically putting his hands on LTJG Ramey and moving her roughly about the bridge which was apparently his way of communicating that she was not capable of knowing where to go on the bridge or how to get there even if she knew. On the other hand, there were a number of enlisted personnel who believed that LTJG Ramey was an excellent officer whose performance was superior to her male junior officer counterparts. At any rate, she seemed not to know how to cope and among some of her officer peers this disorientation was seen as a lack of initiative.

She found particularly galling an incident in April 1986 in Kailua-Kona, Hawaii. In her capacity as ship's Public Affairs Officer (one of her collateral duties), she was told by the CO to dive with a civilian woman. LCDR Chace had authorized the civilian, a representative of the Hawaii Navy League, to dive from the ship using the Navy diving equipment on board. His motivations were twofold: he wanted to gain favorable publicity for the ship, and he wanted to thank the woman for a social event she hosted for the entire crew, on behalf of the Navy League. LTJG Ramey protested being ordered to accompany the civilian woman, arguing that it was not only illegal but also wrong to be forced to put herself at risk in such a situation. LCDR Chace was adamant in his decision, and she ultimately obeyed, even though both of them knew that the action was in violation of Navy Regulations. But LTJG Ramey did not then press the issue any further.

At the conclusion of its training period USS SENTINEL sailed from Pearl Harbor to the Western Pacific on January 16, 1987 with twenty enlisted women and the two women officers on board. LTJG Ramey hoped to become Operations Officer after this deployment. Those hopes were dashed, how-

---

[3] The bridge is a platform above the deck of a ship, from which the ship is controlled.

ever, when a second woman officer, Lieutenant LT Susan Parker, arrived just prior to deployment. It was she, rather than LTJG Ramey, who was assigned as Operations Officer. The two women officers shared a stateroom, a second bunk having been added in the interim. Though they lived together, they were worlds apart in terms of their assimilation into the ship's culture and their responses to that culture.

LT Parker had several alcohol-related incidents while serving on USS SENTINEL, including one shortly after reporting aboard. On January 29, 1987, LT Parker participated in a "hail and farewell" party in Guam. After the party she was driving an official vehicle carrying the CO, XO, and several enlisted persons to various clubs. After being stopped by a military policeman, she failed a sobriety test. Later in the evening, this time while a passenger in the same vehicle, she was charged by local, civilian police, along with the captain, for consuming alcohol in a moving vehicle. The enlisted persons in the vehicle later said she had allowed the CO to kiss her several times as the entourage bar-hopped throughout the night. On another occasion she became so inebriated at a party for single officers held at the XO's house that she had to sleep there overnight. As a result she failed to show up to relieve LTJG Ramey of her watchstanding duties, an act for which LT Parker received administrative punishment.

On one occasion several enlisted women crew members approached LT Parker about sexual harassment problems they were experiencing. These women were entering a formerly all-male world. Many of the men did not welcome their presence in that world and a number of the men wanted to make sure the message was not missed. One obvious way the men could demonstrate both their disapproval of the women's presence and their power over the women was to maintain a sexually intimidating environment. The women crew members desperately needed role models to teach them two survival skills they were unlikely to bring on their own to this strange, new world—first, how to decide which behaviors they need not tolerate, and second, what actions they could take when intolerable behaviors occurred. After hearing the women sailors out, LT Parker merely told them to file their complaints up the chain of command. She later said that she felt no obligation to intervene in any way on behalf of these enlisted women.

Unfortunately, the one point of agreement between LT Parker and LTJG Ramey was in the maintenance of a "hands-off" approach in precisely these areas. The following paragraphs provide a small sampling of the kinds of situations to which the women crew members were exposed on a daily basis.

The women crew members had experienced degradation and humiliation in a variety of ways. One was language: they were routinely referred to and directly addressed as "bitch," "cunt," and "whore." Verbal sexual overtures were the norms on a daily basis. For example, LCDR Chace routinely propositioned for sexual favors a female seaman assigned to his wardroom. The woman petitioned her supervisor for a transfer elsewhere on the ship, but when LCDR Chace learned of it, he canceled the reassignment, required her to continue in the wardroom, and continued to make verbal sexual advances including inappropriate touching with sexual overtones toward her.

In addition he required her to accompany him, on at least one occasion, on a visit to a Korean ship. En route to the ship he told her that the commanding officer of the Korean ship wanted to sleep with her and said that it would be a favor to him (LCDR Chace) if she were to do so. The Korean officer assumed, wrongly, that the female sailor was in agreement with LCDR Chace's offer and made physical advances toward her. This was not an isolated incident, but one of several times LCDR Chace urged women crew members to sleep with officers in the Korean Navy.

The CO and the XO took pleasure in staging events calculated to embarrass the SENTINEL women. At one social gathering in Sasebo, Japan attended by male and female crew members, three male sailors dropped their trousers and exposed their bare buttocks as part of a "hairy ass" contest, at which time LCDR Chace assigned three women crew members to serve as judges. He then asked the women to follow suit and bare their buttocks, an action that the women managed to avoid. On another occasion, LCDR Chace, in the presence of all—men and women, officers and enlisted—stretched out horizontally on the floor of a night club while a nude Filipino female squatted above him and lowered her genitalia to his face. The command master chief, BMCM David Torrance, then followed suit with the same Filipino woman.

At Chism-Do Island in Korea a number of the male crew members and one officer decided to swim nude in the presence of women crew members who were working in the vicinity. LCDR Chace watched this but chose not to stop it. Instead he filmed the event with his personal camcorder. Once, while at sea and alongside a Soviet intelligence ship, LCDR Chace, using the ship's public address system (the

1MC) ordered the women to appear on deck in bikini swim suits. On other occasions he would have the XO announce over the 1MC that the women would stage a wet T-shirt contest on the fantail, although no such contest ever took place.

Unplanned pregnancy was a particularly vexing problem, which was complicated by arbitrary and changing policy decisions by the CO. During a thirty-month period from January 1985 through June 1987, six women assigned to USS SENTINEL became pregnant and had to be transferred. LCDR Chace told the female crew members that he considered unplanned pregnancies to be irresponsible behavior, which would result in low performance evaluations for those who became pregnant. He said that intimate (i.e., sexual) relationships on or off the ship would be treated as fraternization, and would be punished under provisions of the Uniform Code of Military Justice. He later changed his policy to say that only intimate relations *on board* the ship would be treated as fraternization. Then he changed it back to the original policy. He said, however, that if an existing intimate relationship were reported to him by a certain date, there would be no action other than to transfer one of the parties. A male chief and a female sailor were intimate off the ship. The chief reported this to the captain. LCDR Chace said he would not allow it to occur on or in the vicinity of the ship, but no other action was taken. On the other hand, he lowered the performance mark of a female sailor who became pregnant off the ship by a male sailor, and then the captain brought formal charges against him.

LTJG Ramey herself was rarely the target of harassing behavior that was overtly sexual in nature. On the other hand, she was very aware of LCDR Chace's sexual harassment proclivities toward the enlisted crew. Sometimes she was present when such behavior occurred. For example, she overheard LCDR Chace telling the master of USNS MISPILION that SENTINEL had some pretty women on board and he would be glad to swap them for a ten pound bag of shit, which is all, in his opinion, they were worth. The remarks were made in the immediate presence of an enlisted female helmsman who approached LTJG Ramey with a comment about what the Captain had said, obviously hoping for intervention on her behalf. LTJG Ramey simply walked away.

LTJG Ramey heard and observed many such incidents and knew the details of much of LCDR Chace's lewd behavior. She never asked him to stop this behavior, although it unambiguously constituted sexual harassment under any objective reading of pertinent Navy Regulations. She reserved her protests for those incidents in which she believed LCDR Chace was unfair to *her* professionally. Likewise, all her reports of discrimination to the chaplain and other complaints dealt solely with what she perceived to be lack of equity in his treatment of her as a professional naval officer. They did not include any references to his frequent and blatant episodes of sexual harassment and other forms of sexual misconduct directed primarily toward the enlisted female crew. Her focus was on her own personal professional survival. Toward that end she was apparently willing to tolerate a climate in which the women of the crew were routinely demeaned, degraded, and humiliated.

In March 1987 in Shibushi, Japan, one of the ship's male officers came into a hotel room occupied by a female enlisted crew member from USS SENTINEL, undressed, got in her bed, and attempted to have sex with her against her will. The incident was reported to LCDR Chace, who assigned LT Parker to conduct a Judge Advocate General Manual (JAGMAN) investigation. He gave her two and a half days to complete it. Her investigation concluded that the male officer was drunk and that sexual advances were made. LCDR Chace then counseled the offending officer and issued him a nonpunitive letter of caution. The CO did not discuss the incident in any manner with the enlisted woman that had been sexually assaulted. Further, he decided not to report the incident up the chain of command and not to forward the JAGMAN investigation for review—in violation of Navy Regulations. LTJG Ramey learned of this cover-up from her roommate, LT Parker.

Once, while the captain and LTJG Ramey were returning to SENTINEL on a liberty boat, he got her in a headlock and refused to release her until she was eventually able to free herself after very strenuous exertion. On yet another occasion while she was on liberty and having a meal at a restaurant with the captain and several other officers, including a Korean naval officer, the Executive Officer decided to perform a mock marriage ceremony in which he "married" LTJG Ramey to the Korean officer. LCDR Chace then proceeded to grab their heads and pushed them together in an attempt to force them to kiss. She did not officially report this or any of the above incidents when they happened.

The ship returned to Pearl Harbor on July 4, 1987. Thirty-two days later, the director of the Defense Advisory Committee on Women in the Services (DACOWITS) and several of the committee's members were in Pearl Harbor on the first stop of a tour in the Pacific. The DACOWITS was established in 1951 to assist the Department of Defense in the recruitment and retention of Servicewomen. In the intervening, years it has advised the Secretary of Defense on policies relating to women in the services. It has no legal power to impose its recommendations, but it has considerable moral authority and can focus high-level attention on particular problems. Accordingly the committee is usually treated with some deference when it visits military installations.

When the delegation requested that it be allowed to visit military women who had been deployed on a ship, Navy officials were happy to comply. Because of its excellent reputation, USS SENTINEL was selected. The women were assembled on the fantail and given the opportunity to interact with members of the DACOWITS away from the presence of the ship's chain of command. The women crew members told a story that was utterly at odds with the expectations of those who had recommended USS SENTINEL for the visit. After months of having to tolerate abuse, seemingly with no means for alleviating their plight, the women portrayed LCDR Chace as nothing less than a sexual predator. The same characterization, in lesser degree, was applied to much of the senior leadership on board, as well.

Upon conclusion of the meeting with the women, the DACOWITS members reported what they had learned. Rear Admiral Michael Payne, Commander, Naval Surface Group MIDPAC, ordered a JAG-MAN investigation and administratively relieved LCDR Chace of his command, pending its completion. The investigating officer and his assistants interviewed all the officers, nearly all the women crew, and many of the male crew in an effort to sort out the facts of the case. The statements from the crew members provided a mass of detail confirming the unlawful behavior of LCDR Chace and some of the senior leadership. In contrast, the officers, except for LTJG Ramey, were reluctant witnesses. They volunteered nothing and provided only minimal information, and that only in response to direct and specific questioning by the investigating officers. On the other hand, LTJG Ramey came forward with extensive detail concerning all the incidents about which she had personal knowledge.

The director of DACOWITS wrote the report on its visit to the Western Pacific. She included a lengthy segment that described the abuse of power on SENTINEL. She pointed out that most of the women on board had accused LCDR Chace of sexual harassment and his officers and senior enlisted leadership of complicity and cover-up. She went much further, however, adding that she believed the problem was not merely about specific actions on a specific ship, but was related to the institutional climate with respect to women that was part of the Navy culture everywhere the DACOWITS had gone.

The JAGMAN investigation was completed in approximately one month. After reviewing the completed investigation, Rear Admiral Payne charged LCDR Chace with numerous violations of the Uniform Code of Military Justice (UCMJ). They included several instances of violation of lawful regulations, dereliction in the performance of duties, conduct unbecoming an officer, fraternization, failure to report misconduct, submitting a false report, mistreatment of a subordinate, and assault.

The officers and crew of SENTINEL were keenly aware that the material submitted to the JAG-MAN investigating officers by LTJG Ramey was instrumental in the case against LCDR Chace. She was relieved of all duties except Communication Material Systems Custodian. Three times, subsequent to LCDR Chace's relief, she appeared before a board of the same five officers from USS SENTINEL in an effort to pass the oral examination for her surface warfare qualification. On each occasion she was found not qualified. All five board members had received non-judicial punishment, administrative actions, or counseling for their various acts or omissions in the performance of their duties. One of the board members, the Chief Engineer, was overheard by an enlisted crew member to say that LTJG Ramey would never qualify so long as he was around. On the other hand, she was also examined by a board of officers not from USS SENTINEL, with the same results (though it is highly unlikely that they were ignorant of the circumstances on SENTINEL).

On the home front, things were no better for LTJG Ramey. She began receiving obscene and threatening phone calls. In one phone call, her husband was told that if his wife kept talking she would be killed. On several occasions garbage was dropped on her lawn and once gasoline was drained from her motor scooter. The two daughters of the command master chief were heard yelling obscene names at LTJG Ramey and her husband from a passing car. The Naval Investigative Service (NIS) declined to investigate these incidents, and her command did not support her in requiring NIS to pursue the investigation. NIS did, however, investigate her, based on an allegation of lesbianism, a charge that subsequently could not be substantiated.

LTJG Ramey's final fitness report from LCDR Chace and two she received subsequent to his departure were extremely negative. She was not promoted to lieutenant in 1987, and she was initially prevented from being assigned to another ship because of her bad fitness reports, her failure of selection to Lieutenant, and the ongoing investigation by NIS. In the face of all these setbacks, LTJG Ramey refused to "go gently into that dark night." She initiated a request to the Board for Correction of Naval Records (BCNR) seeking to have expunged from her records all her SENTINEL fitness reports. Additionally she wrote several letters to the Naval Inspector General in which she outlined the retaliatory actions taken against her by her shipmates. Finally, she initiated a hotline complaint alleging continued harassment in retaliation for her exposure of lawlessness and abuse of power by her commanding officer and the senior leadership on the ship.

The Naval Inspector General's endorsement on the subsequent investigation of LTJG Ramey's hotline complaint included the following statement: "The investigation largely substantiated the allegations of LTJG Ramey that she was the victim of sexual harassment, discrimination, and retaliation for her complaints against her previous CO, LCDR Chace. . . ." He added that after LCDR Chace was relieved, LTJG Ramey was also subjected to "general isolation by the SENTINEL wardroom and crew."

Falsification of MV-22 Readiness Records[1]
LtCol Gary E. Slyman, USMC,
Patricia Jacubec, and Jonathan Cox

Introduction

Nineteen Marines were killed on April 8, 2000, when their MV-22 Osprey crashed in Arizona. Four more were killed only eight months later on December 11, 2000, when a second MV-22 crashed in North Carolina.[2] These accidents, which closely preceded the following incident, may have contributed to closer scrutiny of maintenance readiness reporting of the MV-22 aircraft. The pressures perceived by officers to get the Osprey program into production and the two MV-22 mishaps probably provided the impetus for increased awareness of the training squadron's readiness reports. In short, the accidents helped set in motion a series of events in which some senior officers were caught manipulating MV-22 data to show false aircraft readiness.[3]

Marine Corps leadership still considers the MV-22, which has been in development since 1981, a vital component in the transformation and modernization of the Marine Corps' warfighting capabilities. All recent USMC Commandants have testified before Congress on the importance of the Osprey to the Corps. For various reasons, MV-22 funding has been in jeopardy more than once over the long course of its procurement history.

On January 10, 2001, the Commander of Naval Air Systems Command, the command responsible for the acquisition, development, and support of all navy aircraft, received an anonymous letter alleging that the Commanding Officer (CO) of Fixed Wing Marine Medium Tiltrotor Training Squadron 204 (VMMT-204) directed his subordinates "to lie" about MV-22 maintenance and readiness data.[4] The anonymous package also contained Aircraft Status reports purportedly showing falsified data, several photographs of the squadron's aircraft status display board, and an audiotape of the squadron CO during a meeting with all hands.

Background

The MV-22 Osprey is a medium fixed wing, tilt-rotor aircraft. It is designed for vertical-lift in order to replace aging helicopters (specifically, the CH-46 and the CH-53) used by the Marine Corps for combat and support.[5] Essentially, the MV-22 is a propeller airplane that can take off and land like a helicopter.

This case is sponsored by the Center for the Study of Military Ethics

[1] "Report on the Investigation Concerning the Falsification of MV-22 Osprey Maintenance Readiness Records," (Office of the Inspector General, Department of Defense, December 11, 2001), 2.

[2] The above paragraph contains opinions derived from an investigation by the Inspector General of the Department of Defense.

[3] "Report on the Investigation Concerning the Falsification of MV-22 Osprey Maintenance Readiness Records," (Office of the Inspector General, Department of Defense, December 11, 2001), 1–2.

[4] Ibid, 3.

[5] Ibid, 3.

MV-22 Program Overview: The Office of the Secretary of Defense and the Navy separately tested the MV-22. The Navy's testing, which was completed in July 2000, concluded that the MV-22 had several major deficiencies, including a low mission-capable/fully mission-capable (MC/FMC) rate (also called the "readiness rate"), but also that the aircraft was operationally effective and suitable in a land-based environment.[6] The Office of the Secretary of Defense disagreed that the Osprey was operationally suitable. A decision to proceed with the next phase of the program—full rate production (FRP) with aircraft delivered to the Marine Corps—was planned for December 2000.[7]

From October to December 2000 senior Department of the Navy and Marine Corps officials repeatedly expressed concern in e-mails to each other about the MV-22's readiness. They believed that low MV-22 readiness rates would adversely affect the decision to proceed with full rate production.[8]

Chain of Command: The mission of VMMT-204 was to train all MV-22 aircrew and maintenance personnel. In June 1999, LtCol Odin F. Leberman, Jr. assumed command of the squadron, which was one of thirteen aviation squadrons subordinate to Marine Air Group-26 (MAG-26), commanded by Col James Schleining. Marine Air Logistics Squadron-26 (MALS-26), another squadron within MAG-26, provided supplies and maintenance support to aircraft in MAG-26 (including those in VMMT-204). MAG-26 was subordinate to Second Marine Aircraft Wing (2nd MAW), commanded by MajGen Dennis Krupp, who took command in June 2000.[9]

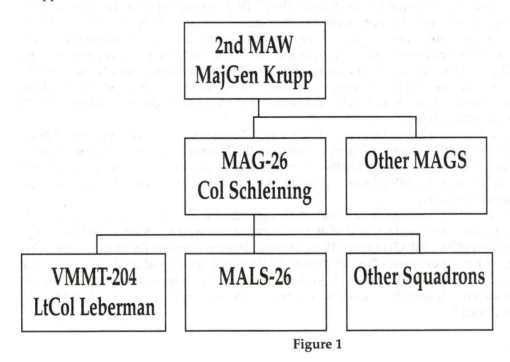

Figure 1

Maintenance Reporting 101

For reporting purposes a squadron's aircraft are either "in" or "out " of reporting status. Aircraft that are "out of reporting status" do not count against a squadron's readiness rate. Going through a modification* is a typical reason for an aircraft to be "out of reporting status." An "in reporting status" aircraft counts against the squadron's readiness rate. In general any aircraft that a squadron has possession of and is maintaining counts against its rates.

---

[6] Ibid, 3–4.

[7] Ibid, 7.

[8] Ibid, 2.

[9] Ibid, 6.

*A modification is when an aircraft is having major work performed by contractors or other personnel outside of the squadron maintenance department. Modifications are done to make a major repair or upgrade to an aircraft.

Problems with an aircraft are called aircraft discrepancies, which are reported on a work order. Work orders are entered into a computerized, automated system called the Naval Aviation Logistics Command Management Information System (NALCOMIS), which allows tracking of all data associated with repairing that particular discrepancy to include automatically ordering parts through the supply system. The nature of the discrepancy determines the status of the aircraft: "up" (mission capable, i.e. the aircraft is safe to fly with the discrepancy); or "down" (not mission capable, i.e. the aircraft is unsafe to fly with the discrepancy). Readiness rates are calculated as the percentage of a squadron's aircraft that are "up."

When VMMT-204 took delivery of the first Osprey, the squadron also switched over to an improved logistics information system. The newer system was designed to increase data accuracy and to prevent technicians from manipulating the information.

The squadron generates two different readiness reports: a daily Aircraft Material Readiness Report (AMRR) submitted each morning, and a monthly summary. Using data from the logistics information system and other squadron documents, the morning report provides a snapshot of the squadron's readiness level ("up" and "down" aircraft) at the start of the day. The monthly summary is a historic document from the logistics information system detailing the overall readiness (up, down) percentages of all aircraft on a 24 hours per day, seven days per week basis.

The Maintenance Control Division, one of five or six divisions in the Maintenance Department and manned with senior enlisted marines with significant experience on maintaining aircraft, generates both reports. The officer in charge of maintenance control, the Maintenance and Material Control Officer, is trained in maintenance procedures and reporting.

A 2nd MAW Wing Order directs unit commanding officers to "take direct and continuing action to ensure aircraft are properly classified" as being mission capable or not. Another 2nd MAW Wing Order directs that MAG COs are responsible for ensuring that daily reports are accurate and submitted on time.[10]

Situation

Shortly after MajGen Krupp assumed command of 2nd MAW in June 2000 he made clear to Leberman and Schleining that he was disappointed with the low readiness rate of the Osprey. On September 25, 2000, Schleining emailed the month's readiness rates to MajGen Krupp—23% mission capable and 77% not mission capable—and predicted an improvement in readiness rates in the coming weeks.[11] Krupp directed Schleining to "keep the heat on" to improve readiness rates.[12]

In October 2000, high-level Navy, Office of the Secretary of Defense, and contractor officials involved in the MV-22 acquisition effort indicated they were unimpressed with the Osprey squadron's readiness rates. There were some personnel in the Program Office—the Navy's organization responsible for the acquisition of the Osprey—who strongly believed that Leberman was not always considering readiness in his decision-making and that he needed a strong counseling session to get him focused. Leberman felt the pressure for improved readiness. He was witnessed commenting to squadron personnel that his seniors questioned his ability to command the squadron and that he might lose his job. During that same month, Krupp warned Schleining that the low readiness figures had high visibility and that they needed to reach 75% before he would back off his oversight and scrutiny (75% was the figure the squadron told Krupp was necessary to accomplish the required training of pilots and enlisted).[13]

While the readiness results from the first two weeks of November were making their way up the chain of command through e-mail, senior Marine Corps officials at Headquarters Marine Corps noted that the readiness figures were "bad news" and not helpful for the production decision. Senior officials also felt that reported readiness rates would have been higher under the old computer tracking system

---

[10] Ibid, B-1.

[11] Ibid, B-2.

[12] Ibid, B-3.

[13] Ibid, B-4.

because "you can't cheat on" the new version of NALCOMIS.[14] Krupp cautioned against confusing the old and new reporting systems and said that "we must be very careful" about what was entered on work orders. "This is not cheating, but simply understanding how the system works." Schleining forwarded the e-mail exchanges containing the senior officials' concerns and comments to Leberman. Krupp instructed Schleining to "see if we can put a positive spin on" the data. Schleining advised Leberman and others that guidance from Krupp directed them to "put a positive spin on what we are really doing at this end." Marine headquarters "needs some help on the [Osprey production] decision in December."[15]

Krupp's e-mail requesting a "positive spin" on the November readiness figures was forwarded the VMMT-204 Assistant Aircraft Maintenance Officer, Captain Christopher Ramsey.[16] Ramsey decided that to reduce the amount of "down" time, the maintenance personnel initiating work orders for aircraft would annotate the aircraft status as "up" in the status code field, a block not used to by the system to record aircraft status. Therefore, the computer system would recognize the aircraft as "up" when it was really "down." As a result, the "down" clock would not be ticking. Maintenance Control personnel would later review the work order and only then assign a job code, which would, in turn, start the "down" clock for that aircraft. The aircraft would accumulate less down time, thereby improving readiness rates.[17]

On December 5, 2000, the Department of the Navy postponed the decision on full rate production until April 2001 and requested more information on the most critical issues of MV-22's rapidly declining reliability rate.[18]

On December 19, 2000, VMMT-204's quality assurance division conducted training for all its personnel. Several attendees at that meeting related that Capt Ramsey directed them to write all work orders as "up"—meaning the aircraft was capable of flying a mission. Some recall this was done to improve "down" time by having the system track the aircraft as "up" in the computer system instead of down. Attendees collectively decided to write "*D*" in the "System Reason" block of the work orders for an aircraft with a downing discrepancy. The asterisks denoted the aircraft was falsely entered in the computer as being "up." This was done to ensure that down aircraft would be recognized internally as unable to fly even though all computerized work orders were showing them as "up." The investigation by Defense Criminal Investigative Service (DCIS) determined that personnel under Capt Ramsey initiated 26 of these false work orders.[19]

The Maintenance Material Control Officer, Chief Warrant Officer 2 (CWO2) Smith, had been on temporary duty away from the squadron investigating the second Osprey mishap from December 11, 2000 until December 22, 2000. Upon Smith's return from leave, Capt Ramsey notified him that VMMT-204 had put into effect "a new way of reporting readiness" and that all aircraft would be reported "up" and readiness would be reported at 100 percent on the daily reports.[20] Smith disagreed with this implementation and went to Leberman to discuss his concerns. Leberman said he understood Smith's concerns, but that "Wing" had directed it. Leberman subsequently told Smith to come up with a way to internally keep track of inoperable aircraft, but to still report them in the computer system as mission capable. This would prevent "unsafe" Ospreys from being flown.[21]

Smith returned to Maintenance Control to review the measures that were instituted in his absence, including the *D* annotation and other measures of noting that an aircraft coded as "up" in the reporting system was, in fact, "down."[22]

---

[14] Ibid, B-4 & B-5.

[15] Ibid, B-5.

[16] Ibid, B-5.

[17] Ibid, B-6.

[18] Ibid, 9 & B-7.

[19] Ibid, B-11.

[20] Ibid, B-11 & B-12.

[21] Ibid, B-12.

[22] Ibid, B-8.

On December 28, 2000, Schleining called a meeting with Leberman, Ramsey, Smith and the commanding officer and aircraft maintenance officer from MALS-26. Schleining told them he wanted to ensure the squadron was flying safe aircraft and reporting accurately. He also told them that maintenance control was no longer authorized to "down" aircraft. Later that day in an e-mail to Krupp, Schleining said he was "changing the way 204 does business."[23] MALS-26 would begin to order parts "off-line" and then initiate the work order afterward, thus avoiding having to put an aircraft in a down status. Ordering parts "off line"—meaning not through automated channels—would hide from the computer system that an aircraft needed repairs, because the necessary parts would not be tracked in the system. Krupp acknowledged receiving Schleining's message: ". . . I believe this is ethical, will save [down] time and will not cause the system to say we are forging documents or cutting corners."[24] Schleining emailed Leberman saying, "we need to explore options before we down an aircraft."[25] Leberman instructed Capt Ramsey to bring all downing discrepancies to him and he would take them to Schleining for approval. Schleining was now making the decisions normally made by a maintenance controller, a senior enlisted marine with significant maintenance experience.[26]

On December 29, 2000, Leberman advised Schleining that the readiness rate would be 100% or "very close" on the next daily status report.[27] The next morning report did state 100%, although two out of seven aircraft were actually down. Replacement parts for the two down aircraft were ordered, but the order said the parts were for an "out of reporting status" aircraft, thereby avoiding accumulating down time against the "in reporting status" aircraft. In theory, to reduce "down" time, the parts could have been cannibalized (removed) from the out of status aircraft to get the two down aircraft operational.[28] Later Capt Ramsey rationalized his actions stating he ordered spare parts against the "out of reporting status" aircraft for the two downed aircraft to save time. Rather then the maintenance crew cannibalizing parts from the "out of reporting status aircraft" and putting them into the two downed aircraft, and then later installing the newly ordered parts in the two repaired aircraft and returning the cannibalized parts to the "out of status" aircraft, the newly ordered parts would be put directly into the downed aircraft. Ramsey said he briefed this plan to Leberman, who approved.[29]

On December 29, 2000, Leberman held an all-hands meeting. His remarks on readiness included Krupp's concern about accumulating "down" time for an aircraft that was downed over the Christmas holidays. Here is some of what he said: "What you've been doing all week is trying to stop the SCIR (down) clock. . . . Why is that important? We all know [the new and improved automated system] is put into place to keep us from lying. . . . In the past, we were able to screw with the data a little bit in the [older version]. And we were able to show readiness in, much greater than what it really was—which was a lie. . . . The problem is we have it here and we need to lie. And the reason we need to lie or manipulate the data, however you want to call it is that until . . . a full rate production decision [is made] this program is in jeopardy. Everyone says readiness is bad. . . . Everybody is hinging on that particular bit of information . . . So what we have to do is . . . try to reduce the [down] time as best we can until that [MV-22 full production] decision is made. . . ."[30]

After the all-hands meeting, LtCol Leberman met with the senior non-commissioned officers (NCOs) and told them that they were going to hear some "off the wall things come out of upstairs here and down to you guys this week to stop the [down] clock. It's that important. . . . I don't want you to

[23] Ibid, B-8.

[24] Ibid, B-8.

[25] Ibid, B-8.

[26] Ibid, B-9.

[27] Upon investigation, it was discovered that the replacement parts were ordered on December 28 and that replacement parts had been ordered against the "out of reporting status" aircraft twice previously.

[28] "Report on the Investigation Concerning the Falsification of MV-22 Osprey Maintenance Readiness Records," (Office of the Inspector General, Department of Defense, December 11, 2001), B-9 & B-10.

[29] Ibid, B-10 & B-11.

[30] NCOs are enlisted members in positions of leadership throughout a command who work under the commissioned officers.

do anything dishonest, totally, I want you to be creative" in trying to gain 100% readiness.[31] After Leberman ended the meeting, Capt Ramsey and the NCOs continued the debate about the maintenance process. Ramsey told them to find new ideas for improving the maintenance process: ". . . safety is paramount . . . [but] we need to explore ways to try to meet both objectives."[32]

On January 3, 2001, the e-mailed morning report to Schleining, Leberman, and others reflected seven aircraft at 100% mission capable and one out of reporting status. The report also showed nine parts ordered against the single out of status aircraft. Investigations after the fact revealed that, in fact, three of the seven up aircraft were down and unable to fly on that date.[33]

In a January 9, 2001 meeting that included Schleining, Leberman, and the commanding officer of MALS-26, Leberman commented that data was being manipulated at VMMT-204 to show 100% readiness on daily reports. This was the first time the commanding officer of MALS-26 had heard this alarming information. After the meeting, the MALS-26 CO discussed Leberman's remarks with Schleining, who said he would take care of it.[34]

On January 10, 2001, Leberman met with the Maintenance Department to discuss how maintenance was being performed, including using a new code to obtain parts faster without accumulating down time. Some at the meeting recall that he seemed unaware that maintainers were already using the *D* codes on work orders.[35]

The next day, the commanding officer of MALS-26 reported to Schleining that VMMT-204 was still reporting 100% readiness. That afternoon, Schleining met with Leberman, Ramsey, Smith, and officers from MALS-26 to discuss the squadron's maintenance reporting. Schleining told officers that his intention was not for the squadron to report 100% readiness if it was not accurate, nor did he want anyone to go outside the procedures of the Naval Aviation Maintenance Program. The result of the meeting was that VMMT-204 returned to normal reporting.[36]

On January 12, 2001, Leberman held an all-hands meeting, where he informed them that he believed he had been misunderstood in the December 29, 2000 meeting. He directed squadron personnel to no longer change or manipulate data and instructed them to "return to doing business as usual."[37]

The events described above resulted in the initiation of the DCIS investigation, which was conducted from January 26 to July 9, 2001. The investigation focused on the criminal charges brought against Marine Corps personnel who acted in this affair.

---

[31] "Report on the Investigation Concerning the Falsification of MV-22 Osprey Maintenance Readiness Records," (Office of the Inspector General, Department of Defense, December 11, 2001), B-11.

[32] Ibid, B-12.

[33] Ibid, B-14.

[34] Ibid, B-14.

[35] Ibid, B-14 & B-15.

[36] Ibid, B-15.

Pass the Inspection
Captain Rick Rubel

You are a division officer on a Cruiser, and you have a big inspection on Monday when the Squadron Commodore and his staff will review your maintenance boards and Administration. (Note: the Commodore is the officer that writes the FITREP of your skipper).

On the Friday before the Monday inspection, your Chief Petty Officer comes to you and says, "Sir, to get ready for the inspection on Monday, I was looking at our maintenance board for the division. There are five maintenance jobs that were not completed this week as scheduled on the board. Three of the men who were scheduled to perform the maintenance were at school this week. Just so that we don't get hammered by the Captain and the Commodore on Monday, I went ahead and marked them off the as complete."

You reply to your CPO, "Chief do you think that's a good idea? What if the Squadron material officer checks and the jobs are not complete."

The Chief says, "Sir, first of all they never check the jobs. Secondly, I promise you the jobs will get done next week. There is no way we will run this equipment over the weekend. And third, sir, we do this all the time. I've been doing this for 18 years. The work will get done, I promise. You have to trust me, sir. We don't want to be hanging out for the big inspection. That would look real bad to the old man."

Questions for Discussion

1. What would you do? (Are you willing to take on your chief over this?)
2. What kind of reasoning did you use to choose your action?
3. What is your "mission"?
4. What do you think your commanding officer would want you to do in your situation?
5. What is the primary consideration here when trying to decide what to do?

The Tailhook Scandal—
Her Story: Paula Coughlin*

Tom Philpott

Washington—Ten days after Lt. Paula Coughlin was sexually molested by a group of Navy and Marine Corps aviators in the hallway of a Las Vegas hotel last September, she still wasn't sure what she would do about it.

Coughlin already had raised the incident several times with her boss, Rear Adm. Jack Snyder, telling him she had almost been gang raped by a horde of jet pilots, describing how she had to "kick and bite and fight my way off the floor and out of that hallway."

Snyder's response had always been the same: " 'That's what you get when you go on the third deck full of drunk aviators,' " Coughlin recalled.

Now, a week and a half later, someone had stopped by Coughlin's desk outside the admiral's office at Patuxent River Naval Air Test Center to ask about Tailhook.

"I said, 'It stunk. These guys are a bunch of animals.' " Walking by, overhearing the conversation, Snyder turned and let loose with a now-familiar bromide, but this time it would spark the largest sexual harassment case in Navy history and ultimately lead to the resignation of Secretary of the Navy H. Lawrence Garrett III.

"He said, 'That's what you get. I told ya.' "

Paula Coughlin, 30,—helicopter pilot, naval officer, loyal aide—"blew a fuse."

"I said to myself, 'That's NOT what I get!' " She stuck a finger in her boss's face and said loud and slow, "You'd better watch what you say, now!"

Mouths fell open and the office fell silent at the sight of an aide yelling at her admiral, Coughlin recalled. Snyder had a plane waiting. She declined to escort him out this time. Instead, she walked into the office of the deputy commander, Capt. Bob Parkinson, and resigned.

"I said, That guy told me 'That's what I get.' And that's not what I get. That guy doesn't give two hoots about me. I'm here living, breathing and working 14 hours a day as his aide and he doesn't care enough to say, 'Are you all right?' I'm not working for him.' "

Parkinson, who before that day had heard nothing about the attack on Coughlin, asked her to give him the details. "That's the first time I recounted, blow by blow, what happened. . . . It was the first time even I remembered what had gone down because it was so bad I decided not to think about it.

"This is a really ugly story," Coughlin said. But "there are so many people who don't know what these guys did to one of their fellow aviators, don't understand what the big deal's about. Yet they'd be horrified if it had happened to their sister, or their wife or their cousin or their friend. But it happened to me and that's the big stink."

Exposure to Tailhook

Tailhook '91 was Coughlin's second trip to the annual symposium. In 1985, while still in flight training, she accompanied a group of Navy and Marine instructors there. Her group that year even visited the now-infamous third floor of the Hilton where jet squadrons rent suites and host late-night drinking parties. Of her squadron, Coughlin said, "They all stayed as a group, they all drank beer, they all had a good time, they all kept their clothes on, and they all made it through the passageways safely without being touched."

What Coughlin remembered most vividly from Tailhook '85 was the flag panel, where the Navy's most senior aviators stood before the assembly and got bombarded with tough, irreverent questions.

"I was impressed. These guys, standing up in civilian clothes, yelling at admirals. . . . They were so devoted to their community."

Coughlin saw no misconduct, although she did hear later that the Tailhook Association lost a $50,000 bond they had put down to pay any damage to the hotel. "That's all I heard . . . It was just a big wild party and nobody was hurt."

Last September Coughlin went back to Tailhook, this time on orders as Snyder's aide. Weeks before she left, Coughlin said, she had asked friends who were jet pilots if she would see them there. At least one of them said, "No, it's too out of control. It's just a drunkEX [drunken exercise]."

"Nobody said, 'Don't go, Paula. You'll get attacked.' "

During her first two days, Sept. 5 and 6, Coughlin only attended the afternoon symposium. "I didn't go anywhere near the third floor. I didn't even go to the Hilton on Thursday night or Friday night."

Saturday evening, Sept. 7, was the climax of the formal schedule, with Garrett giving the keynote banquet address. Afterwards, about 10 p.m. after the banquet broke up, Garrett's aide, Lt. Michael "Trusty" Steed introduced Coughlin to the secretary. Then Steed, Coughlin and several other "loops," or admirals' aides, said they would go back to their own hotels, change into casual clothes and meet back on the third floor patio.

Coughlin said it was after 11 p.m. when she returned to the Hilton, wearing a tank top and jean skirt. She got off the elevator on the third floor and walked to the patio looking for the other aides.

The Attack

"It was a mob scene. It was a big, huge cocktail party. . . . Loud music, a lot of people standing around with cocktails and beers."

Not finding anyone she knew on the patio, Coughlin said she went back toward the elevator, looked down the hall and, 40 feet away, saw "a group of naval and Marine officers talking. Some of them had beer in their hands. . . . I thought it was just overflow from the suites. So I thought, well, I'll go down there, check it out and see who's there."

"I've been in the Navy a long time," Coughlin said. "I know how to maneuver around a group of guys. I said, 'Excuse me.' And a big, tall guy just kind of kicked it off. He bumped me real hard to throw me off balance a little bit. I said. 'Excuse me!' "

After Coughlin passed him, the man "just grabbed my behind and lifted me off the floor." Shocked, Coughlin turned. "I said, "What the 'blank' do you think you're doing?' It's been my experience, even with the drunkest of drunk sailors, if you call them on the carpet like that, they go, 'Whoa. She doesn't like that.' Some little light bulb goes on and that stops."

But as Coughlin yelled at the one officer, another grabbed her from behind. "I turned around and gave him the same question, 'What the 'blank' do you think you're doin'!' "

Then Coughlin said another young officer, whom she later learned had the informal title of "master of ceremonies," yelled "Admiral's aide! Admiral's aide!" "I had no idea why this guy was yelling that," she said. The same officer, Coughlin later learned from the Naval Investigative Service report, was responsible for calling "wave offs." The term refers to the decision on an aircraft carrier to abort a landing. In this case, the MC used it to abort attacks on women.

"This person would call 'Wave off' when [the approaching woman was] a senior officer's wife or an older women or an unattractive woman that they didn't want to mess with. The wave off would allow that person to pass with minimal harassment. . . . It was an organized sport, without a doubt."

When the second man grabbed Coughlin, the first tall one "pressed his chest to my back. I mean I felt his breath on my neck. He was pushing me down the hallway with his body . . . That's when the potshots started. People start grabbing at my shirt, grabbing at my skirt. Then the guy behind me's hands went over my shoulders and down . . . into my tanktop, into my bra, had both breasts. It was just an over-the-shoulder assault."

To break off the attack, Coughlin said she crouched down, "but he followed me down. I went down to the floor in a squatted position and he bent over with me. So I bit him. I bit him absolutely as hard as I could and his left hand came out. I bit his right hand on the thumb and he finally released. But while I was down there, another guy reached up between my legs, under my skirt, and tried to pull my panties off.

"Then guys tried to reach up the sides of my skirt. I kind of got a kick in on one guy . . . At this point I'm starting to think, 'I'm in serious trouble.' I honestly thought, 'I'm strong as shit. I can do 100 pushups without stopping, and I can't get this guy off me.' "

Coughlin kicked and fought to get to her feet and rushed for an open door in front of her. But "two guys jumped in front of the door, with their arms crossed, and said, 'Uh, uh,' just smiling and giggling. Someone grabbed me from behind again. I knew I was in serious trouble. At this point I really figured I was going to get gang raped."

The crowd began "pulling up my clothes, which was more unsettling than anything else. I moved up the hallway a few more feet, trying to get out of there. I saw a man leaning up against the wall, with one foot up, like a stork. He took his foot off the wall as if to leave. Had his back to me. I reached out for him, hit him back on his Levis tag and was saying 'Please . . . Let me get in front of you, please. Let me get in front of you to get out of here. Help me. Help me.'

"He turned around grabbed both breasts."

At times during the attack, Coughlin was incredulous that "these guys are naval officers and they know I'm a naval officer . . . And they know I'm an admiral's aide [but somehow] this works out much better for them."

Coughlin said she finally broke free and ran into a near-empty hotel room where she sat in a dark corner. "I decided, 'That didn't just happen to me. I cannot believe that just happened to me.' "

Another officer Coughlin knew found her there and said, "Paula, you didn't just go down that hallway did ya? You didn't go through the gauntlet?"

" 'The gauntlet? What is the gauntlet?' I said. "Do you know what those guys are doing out there? Do you understand?"

"He said, "Oh, yeah. You shouldn't have gone down that hallway."

"He walked on," Coughlin said. "And I still sat there in dumb shock."

Garrett's Aide

Coughlin walked onto the patio looking for a friendly face but saw no one she knew. She returned to the elevator. Two other women jumped in behind her.

"One was crying and the other one was just fuming mad," Coughlin recalled. When the door closed, the angry one turned to Coughlin and asked if she had gone down the hallway. "These guys are supposed to be naval officers? Did they do that to you?," Coughlin recalled the woman asking.

"I was still trying not to believe it happened. I said, "Yeah, they did that to me, too. And I'm a naval aviator."

These women, Coughlin said, "weren't hookers. They weren't sluts. They weren't anything but young women who had been invited to the hotel."

When the trio reached the bottom floor, Coughlin said the two women hurried away. Coughlin didn't want to be walking around by herself. She returned to the third floor patio, this time finding Steed.

"That's pretty much when I fell apart," Coughlin said. The two officers sat on the grass beside the patio. Coughlin, between sobs, kept repeating, "I can't believe what those guys did to me." Steed escorted her back down the hallway toward the elevator to leave the hotel. On the way, Coughlin passed another helicopter pilot who mouthed the words "Are you all right."

"But he didn't say the words because he didn't want his buds to know he had seen what had happened. . . . He didn't have the courage to step forward."

Coughlin said she later read this colleague's statement to the NIS which confirmed he had seen the attack. "He talked about it freely. 'I saw the crowd falling on her and I heard them yelling, 'Admiral's Aide.' I saw her go to the ground. Then I turned and got a drink.' That's the only thing that made me cry in all that crap I read in the NIS file."

Steed and Coughlin went to a casino restaurant for coffee where they continued to discuss the attack. But Coughlin said she never described the specifics to Steed.

Did he then tell Garrett about the incident? Coughlin said she never asked, and doesn't know. As aide to the SecNav, Steed probably wasn't as close to Garrett as she was to Snyder, she said. "We didn't have an [executive assistant], we didn't have Marines, we didn't have schedulers. I was a one-man show."

But later, to encourage Snyder to do something about the attack, Coughlin would remind him that Garrett's aide knew of the incident, that he escorted her out of the hotel that night. "I said, 'I don't know whether [Garrett] knows or not but I think we should act like the Secretary of the Navy is waiting to hear from you.' That was my ploy to instill a little action."

After coffee, Coughlin returned alone to her hotel but didn't sleep well. The next morning she called Snyder. Still acting in the role of aide she had checked on separate flights for them that morning. Then Snyder asked, "How was the third deck last night?"

"I said, 'It stunk. I was practically gang-banged by a group of fucking F-18 pilots.'

"He said, 'I know. It's so out of control. That's why I go there, have one drink and that's it.' I said, 'I'll tell you about it at breakfast because they were way out of line.' "

At breakfast Coughlin said she told Snyder, "Those guys were completely out of control. They knew I was an admiral's aide. They were so out of line I can't tell you how out of control. I mean I kicked and bit and fought my way out of that hallway.'

"He said, 'That's what you get when you go on the third deck full of drunk aviators.' "

With that statement, Coughlin figured Snyder didn't want to know the details. But she said her words clearly indicated she had been attacked.

"Everybody kind of hopes their boss is going to stick up for them," she said. "He just didn't see it like I did.

"There was another admiral's aide sitting at the table with us. And he said, 'Admiral Snyder, I just can't believe that happened. If I had been there I would have nailed one of those guys. I probably would have been pummeled but I'd just like to get my hands on one of them.'

"The admiral said, 'Those folks are just out of control, they're too rowdy, too rambunctious.' " Coughlin recalled.

Coughlin left that day for San Diego for simulator training where she met a friend, a Navy SEAL, and told him about the attack. "He was mortified. And I hadn't even gone into blow-by-blow with him. . . . He said, 'I can't believe naval officers behave like that.' He said, 'Paula, time is of the essence. You need to report this right away. You need to get your boss hot on that right away.' "

She returned to Pax River. When Snyder got back a few days later, Coughlin brought the subject up "a couple different times, in different ways. And it got shot down both times."

Once she said, "You know, admiral, I don't want a witch hunt. Wait a minute! I want a goddamn witch hunt! I'm going to find those guys and hang them. Those cretins should not be naval officers."

According to Coughlin, Snyder responded: "You can't go off like a Roman candle and leave those people with burns on their hands that say, 'Paula Coughlin.' "

Days later, Coughlin described the attack to Parkinson in detail. Her deputy commander, she said, told Snyder when he returned the next day that "there was a huge, ugly incident that needed to be handled, now."

"So I sat down with Admiral Snyder . . . I said, 'All right, this is what happened to me. Since you haven't asked I'm telling you.' "

On Oct. 10, the Naval Investigative Service began its Tailhook Investigation. On Nov. 4, Adm. Frank Kelso, Chief of Naval Operations, removed Snyder from command of Pax River, "for lack of timely action" in handling Coughlin's complaint. Now assigned to the Naval Air Systems Command, Snyder refused to comment for this report.

Coughlin said she was able to identify her first attacker, the tall one, to NIS agents. He was a Marine pilot, she said. But Coughlin said it's too early to say whether she is satisfied with the investigation.

Why Go Public?

For the past nine months, Coughlin said, a lot of people, particularly in the aviation community, have been sending her the same message Snyder did: That's what you get. "This is important to understanding why I came forward now," Coughlin said. Two days before this interview, Coughlin sat down with a reporter from the *Washington Post* and ABC news anchorman Peter Jennings.

"Throughout this investigation I had so many people tell me, 'You don't want to talk about this. You don't want to open yourself up to the scrutiny of your peers, because they're going to speculate why it took so long.'

"But not speaking about the incident—thinking, 'That's what I get,' that's a crime right there. That's a crime that should never be committed. That's why I'm speaking out.

"We're not talking about a group of gangsters or a street gang that attacked me. It was . . . part of my extended family. Aviators. And every single day when I had to face that, it made me not want to be a part of that group anymore," Coughlin said.

"I came forward because I started to feel like a criminal. Too many people thought it was my fault. Too many people who were not aware of how bad it was [and] were projecting their own opinions of how and why this Tailhook investigation has been blown into something so large.

"I was the wicked witch of the West who got Tailhook canceled and her boss fired. But if they had just said, 'God, if that had happened to my wife' . . ."

By remaining anonymous, Coughlin said, she was sending a bad signal to other women attacked at Tailhook: Keep quiet. "If they felt as bad as I did, it's time to step up and say, 'It wasn't your fault. It's not what you get.' "

Coughlin said it was time to "put a face" on the Tailhook attacks.

"We've got Navy policies, we've got memoranda, we've got directives, we've got instructions. But why? Well, I'm one of the reasons why. I'm a human being. I'm a naval officer . . . and that shouldn't happen."

Her Future

Coughlin graduated from the ROTC program at Old Dominion University in December 1984 and got commissioned that same day by her father, a retired Navy pilot whose career spanned 26½ years.

Asked to describe herself, Coughlin said, "I make this joke—I've inherited my dad's legs and his integrity. Damn his legs." Perhaps the most difficult part of the ordeal was having to share the details with her parents.

"I was mortified when my dad had to read the accounts in the newspapers of what happened . . . reading that the admiral's aide was attacked . . . and all his friends, who know who I am, reading it. It made me feel sick.

"But I thought the more people who understand why this is such a bad thing is key to making it go away," she said.

Coughlin said she still loves the Navy and flying.

She flew H-2 anti-submarine warfare helicopters on a couple of cruises aboard research ships, serving as both maintenance and operations officer of her detachment. She's now in training to fly H-53s.

"I think I'm a great pilot," Coughlin said. "Every pilot thinks they're a great pilot."

Coughlin "absolutely" intends to stay in the Navy even though "thousands of aviators out there hate me.

"The CNO said yesterday he expects me to have a long and happy career. I expect I'll have at least a long career. And I'll be happy in the Navy as long as they let me do my job.

"It's different now because I'm talking to you, and everybody else who understands what happens. I had an obligation as an officer to stop what was going on in that hallway. I have an obligation as a human being to let everyone know you have to come forward when something bad like that happens."

"People I don't even know have called and said, 'You did the right thing.' The people in favor of airing a problem and understanding it and rectifying it support me. But there are a lot of guys out there who still don't get it."

And what has her coming forward done to her service career?

"I feel the Navy is going to come out of this better. I really do. . . . The key is understanding. Understanding it's a very, very harmful atmosphere that tolerates that kind of abuse."

As a woman in the Navy, Coughlin said she has felt sexual harassment before, "everything from being called 'Admiral Snyder's girl' to some really out-of-line propositions. . . . [But now] the Navy has got a task and at least now it's defined."

"I want to tell this story once. I want everyone to hear it, understand it and then let's move on. That's it," she said. "Hear it, learn from it and move on."

Concepts of Honor
and of Intellectual Property
Dr. George R. Lucas, Jr.

Case Background

Midshipman 3/C Heather Smith was extremely well liked by the vast majority of her shipmates at the U.S. Naval Academy. Despite a continued prevailing attitude of suspicion toward women in service academies, even skeptics felt that her personality was positive, perky, and "can do." Her classmates, both male and female, viewed Smith as a pleasant person, who was fully competent and qualified, both academically and physically, for admission to the Academy, and believed that she would one day serve with distinction in the fleet.

A few of her closest acquaintances in the Brigade, however, harbored suspicions that Smith was not above using her good reputation on occasion to try to "cut corners" on academic assignments, or to lobby for special treatment or waivers of standard requirements. For the most part, her chain of command dismissed these rumors as stemming from jealousy or from the normal kinds of personality conflicts that inevitably arise among competitive individuals within a large organization. Her Company Officer, Maj. Henry Jones, USMC, was aware of these concerns, which worried him, but his honest hope was that they were groundless and that Smith was shaping up as just the kind of officer the Navy hoped to recruit and retain.

The Event

CAPT Anthony "Tony" Capalleti was a popular battalion officer, well liked by the midshipmen under his command. He had a habit of "hanging out" with random gatherings of midshipmen in various company wardrooms under his command, where he would spin out fascinating and entertaining sea stories. Many of his stories were classics among 1/C members of the Brigade.

Midshipman Smith often joined these sessions, and admired Capalleti's personality and charisma, and expressed keen interest in his various experiences. Hearing one of Capalleti's most poignant stories of command at sea during one of these sessions, she approached the Captain afterwards to ask permission to share it with others. "My English class is discussing the narrative structure of sea stories," she declared. "Might I have permission to tell your story to the members of my class? I know they'd enjoy it and learn from it." Capalleti granted his permission for this particular story to be retold by the midshipman. "However," he cautioned, "I would want to remain anonymous. The events are real, some are a bit 'juicy,' and some of the personnel described are still on active duty. I'd prefer, Miss Smith, that you fictionalize the names and places, and leave my name out of it." In fact, Capalleti himself had written a slightly fictionalized transcript of the story in question (which he had been asked to repeat many times before) and offered to share this draft essay with Midshipman Smith to assist in her presentation, *"as long,"* he continued to caution, *"as the true author remained anonymous."*

Soon thereafter, Capalleti himself retired from active duty and left the Academy.

The Problem

About eighteen months later, Maj. Jones learned that Midshipman 1/C Smith had submitted the story in question as an assignment for a senior English class. The story (with her name listed as author, and no other attribution) had been so well-liked that it was about to be published in *The Trident*, the Academy's weekly newspaper. Jones remembered the so-called "Capalleti story" well. He knew that some of the other senior officers on the Yard who had been present during Capalleti's tour of duty there were bound to recognize it as well. Indeed, he obtained a copy of the English assignment and showed it to some of the older company officers in his own battalion, who readily identified this as "the Capalleti story."

Concerned, Jones contacted the *Trident* staff to suggest that they had made an error, and that they should simply insert Capalleti's name as the true author. Knowing nothing of Capalleti's draft essay, Major Jones simply assumed that Smith had transcribed a written version of a widely known oral case and had then proceeded herself to fictionalize some of the details. This, he thought, certainly qualified as her as the story's "co-author" in some reasonable sense. This seemed, accordingly, like an amicable way of settling a potentially dicey matter.

The *Trident* editorial staff informed Midshipmen Smith of Major Jones' request. To everyone's astonishment, she reacted angrily: "I was given permission to use this story and charged to keep Capalleti's name anonymous," she retorted. "Besides, I consulted others and did considerable work to transcribe and to modify the story." She *demanded* that the story be published as written, with her name alone as the author.

Recalling the concerns raised by some of her closest shipmates, however, Major Jones thought it wise to confirm her account of the story's origins. He located the now-retired Captain Capalleti, who dropped by to review the text.

Capalleti was deeply puzzled. "I think I gave her permission to share my story with her classmates in 'Youngster' (i.e., 3/C) English," he said. "But, apart from a couple of name changes, this is verbatim the printed copy of my own written version that I gave her almost two years ago, asking her simply not to use my name. There is simply no evidence of any further research or writing on her part. I don't think I gave her permission to replace my name with her own, or to claim sole authorship—not that I really care. I just didn't realize the 'use' to which she would put this would involve credit to herself for a course assignment, let alone a publication with a by-line."

Sequel

Faced with this sequence of revelations, Major Jones referred the case to the Brigade Honor Council. In her initial deposition before the Council, Midshipman Smith claimed that the entire matter was a misunderstanding, and that Major Jones had always "had it in for her." "He should have come to talk to me first!" she fumed. "But he seems determined to expose and misconstrue all my actions. I think he wants me dismissed."

Questions

1. What word or concept comes most readily to your mind to describe, in brief, what Midshipman Smith has done? Do you consider the act you have labeled an honor offense? Why/why not?

2. Does CAPT Capalleti's final account justify Midshipman Smith's earlier actions? Does it excuse them? Do you find her own account of the sequence of events truthful?

3. According to your understanding of the Honor Concept, what would be the normal expectation of response to an action of the sort perpetrated by Midshipman Smith? Is she guilty of any wrongdoing? Is the nature of the wrongdoing minor, or serious? Give reasons/explain your position with reference to the Honor Concept.

4. Is Midshipman Smith's response to Major Jones's interrogation in any way relevant to this case? In what way? Do her Commanding Officer's actions in tracking down the details vindicate Midshipman Smith's claim that he is out to persecute her? Should he have come to talk to her first, before conducting such an inquiry?

Mini-cases of Ethical Leadership

1. You are told by your boss to change a few readiness numbers in the computer to make the aircraft look better to the "Washingtonians" who are looking at the program. If the readiness figures look better, he says, we will get more funds, to make the aircraft better— so we are in fact helping the aircraft readiness in the long term. So you just change a few numbers to comply with his orders.
   - Are you right or wrong?
   - Why?

2. As a Division Officer, one of your men has a history of abusing the "special request chit" system. Your boss, the Department head, has told you (clearly) he does not want to ever see another request chit from this guy. The sailor then submits a chit for to take his wife to the doctor for a routine pre-natal check because the wife cannot drive. You tell the sailor, "Sorry, the Department Head said he doesn't want to see anymore chits from you."
   - Are you right or wrong?
   - Why?

3. The CO of a ship is having problems with his crew with respect to fraternization. To get control of this problem he meets with all women officers and enlisted separately and then with the men to explain the policy.
   - Is the C.O. right or wrong in his approach to the problem?
   - Why?

4. You are told to by your boss to nominate a minority for a force-wide award to help improve the image of the minorities. He explains by doing this, it will help all members of that minority to give them "role models."
   - Is the boss right or wrong?
   - Why?

5. You are senior watch officer and have to fill out the duty assignments for the holidays. You assign all the bachelors duty on the holidays since they don't have families.
   - Is this right or wrong?
   - Why?

6. You tell your platoon that if they did well on the upcoming exercise they will all get the weekend off. They do better than you expected, but the Company Officer cancels liberty for the whole company because the company didn't do as well compared to other companies. You do not talk to the Company Officer, but tell your troops, "Company Officer says No Liberty."
   - Are you right or wrong in how you handled this?
   - Why?

7. You notice in your most recent Leave and Earnings statement that you were significantly overpaid for the past pay period. You do not say anything because they may not catch it.
   - Are you right or wrong?
   - Why?

8. The Captain stops you in a passageway and congratulates you on something he thinks you accomplished. Although he has you confused with someone else, you do not correct him, because you don't want to embarrass him.
   - Are you right or wrong?
   - Why?

9. As C.O., one of your male sailors grabs a female sailor and tries to kiss her in a small closet. After this is reported to you by her division officer, the female begs you (in tears) not to press charges on the male. To honor her request and to keep from having a messy Captains Mast, you allow the issue to go quietly away.
    – Are you right or wrong?
    – Why?

10. You are a Platoon Commander in a battle for an Iraqi town. You receive an order from your boss to shell a quadrant of the town that is known to have enemy forces you're your artillery. You can see with your binoculars that there are civilians present in the free fire zone. You ignore the order.
    – Are you right or wrong?
    – Why?

Loyalty and Promotion
Captain Rick Rubel

You are Commanding Officer of the unit and it's time to write Fitness reports on your 0–4s. You have a clear breakout of quality and are considering how to rank them. You know that the words are important, but the real promotion opportunity is seen in how you rank your junior officers, numerically. You can only give one "Must Promote" and then two "Promotes" and the 4th will be given a less favorable rating.

By far your top 0–4 is LCDR Jerrod. He is probably the best officer you have seen in your entire 26 year career, and has done an excellent job in everything you have asked him to do. But he has had his separation papers in for approval for over 6 months and is planning on leaving the service in two months. He already has a civilian job lined up and has indicted that he is not considering transiting to the reserves.

Your next highest officer is LCDR Lee. He is hard working, career-minded, but not nearly the caliber of LCDR Jarrod. His achievements during the performance period have been very good, and he always gets the job done with hard work and "brute force." He works late at night, comes in on the weekend to make sure his area of responsibility is covered—he is extremely conscientious. His work ethic will serve him well as a future XO and CO.

The next two 0–4s are clearly below the performance level of LCDRs Jarrod and Lee.

So you are thinking about to whom to give your top rating. This rating will likely determine who gets promoted and who doesn't. You think, "Do I want to waste this top rating on a guy who is getting out and seems to have less loyalty to the service than LCDR Lee?" On the other hand, "LCDR Jarrod is clearly the better officer."

Questions

1. To whom do you give your top rating?
2. How did you make that determination?
3. What is the "fair" thing to do?
4. What is the "right" thing to do?

IV

Religion and the Military:
Respecting Belief

A Sailor's Request for Abortion[1]
Captain Rick Rubel, USN (Ret)
Edited by Commander Lisa Franchetti, USN

I. Background

Regulations on Emergency Leave

Navy regulations state that emergency leave is at the discretion of the Commanding Officer.

Emergency Leave while forward deployed will only be given in "emergency situations." The emergency usually must require the emergency presence of the service member for their immediate family (spouse, children, mother, father, sisters, brothers).

Naval Regulations mandate that no matter how close the person was to a friend or non-immediate family member, that their illness or death is not considered to meet emergency leave considerations.

If the emergency involves the medical condition of an immediate family member, it is necessary to get the doctor to specify the nature of the problem in some detail, as well as a prognosis and whether the service member's presence is required.

Even in the most valid emergency leave situation, the Commanding Officer sometimes may not grant emergency leave or must delay granting emergency leave, due to operational commitments.

When emergency leave is given to deployed/oversees service members, the logistics often make travel back to the United States a difficult and lengthy process, since transportation to the United States is funded by Emergency Leave orders.

U.S. Law Regarding Abortion

Although the U.S. Supreme court has ruled that abortions in the U.S. are permitted, current law is that U.S. military doctors are not required or permitted to perform elective abortions.

In 1973, the Supreme Court legalized a woman's right to an abortion through decisions in *Roe v. Wade and Doe v. Bolton.* Since that time, states have set forth their own laws, regulating the provisions for when/how a woman can obtain an abortion. Although laws are different in each state, an abortion is normally performed as early in the pregnancy as possible. States with requirements generally limit abortions to the first and second trimesters, up until about 20-24 weeks, except in specific cases.

Regulations on Pregnancy at Remote/Forward Deployed Shore Installations

The Secretary of the Navy recognizes that pregnancy is a natural condition and not a medical emergency. The Navy estimates 5% of women on ships are pregnant at any given time. Navy pilots are grounded during pregnancy due to unknown risks to the fetus.

Pregnant servicewomen can be assigned to "an Overseas Duty Station/Geographically Isolated Duty Station if they have not reached their 20th week of pregnancy, and if sufficient Military medical facilities with obstetrical capabilities can provide care as required." (OPNAVINST 6000.1B)

---

[1] This case has been slightly modified to avoid attribution to any service member in the case.

II. Forward Deployed Isolated Duty Station and Pregnant

The command was a small island in the middle of the Indian Ocean. The command supports over 1500 military and 1200 contractors and provides direct support to transiting ships, houses B-2 Bombers for the Air Force, and serves as a primary communications facility for the south-eastern hemisphere. There are no children allowed on the island, and there are approximately 47 women assigned and the command has adequate medical care facilities for pregnant women as long as there are no complications. The policy has been that women who are pregnant, or who become pregnant on the island can remain on duty until their 20th week, unless medical complications arise.

The Commanding Officer of the command is well liked and respected by his officers and enlisted for being tough, but fair. He is a deeply religious man, who prays at least twice a day. He has a strong personal relationship with his Command Chaplain, and the Captain has a daily devotional with his Chaplain every morning at 0830 in the Captain's Office. The Captain has encouraged and supported the Chaplain to begin many programs, including Base Bible study, adopting a small Catholic school back in the States, and has helped raise money for many charitable causes. As part of his upbringing and religious conviction, he has strong beliefs against abortion, and has deep respect for the sanctity of human life.

Petty Officer Third Class Taylor has been assigned to this remote command for 6 months, and has 6 months remaining on this tour before she is eligible for reassignment. Each member stationed on the base is entitled to 2 weeks of leave, every six months, to go back to the US. She just returned from her CONUS leave one month ago.

She has just determined that she is early in her second month of pregnancy, and that she wants to terminate the pregnancy. She is an unmarried 19-year old. She is currently not having any medical complications, except for some very mild nausea in the morning. She is a 2.9 sailor who does her job, but her division officer says she "lacks motivation to excel". She has been in the Navy for 14 months, and this is her first tour out of "A" school.

Petty Officer Taylor has submitted a Special Request Chit to her Commanding Officer to go on emergency leave to go back to the U.S. to get an abortion. The chain-of-command up to the captain have recommended approved the chit.

The Commanding Officer asks to talk to Petty Officer Taylor.

"Sir, Petty Officer Audrey Taylor reporting as ordered, sir."

"Come on in Petty Officer Taylor, and please leave the door open."

"Yes, sir."

"I have your special request chit here for emergency leave, and I have a few questions. First of all, I'm not sure this meets OPNAV requirement for emergency leave. You appear healthy to me. But I would like to understand more about why you want to have the abortion?"

"Sir, I didn't intend to get pregnant, and I'm not ready to raise a kid . . . by myself. I have two more years in the Navy, and I'm not sure what I'm going to do after that. I may go back to college. I don't know. But I do know I don't need a kid right now."

The Captain pointed out to her that there are adequate medical facilities here to take care of her, and by normal procedures, she should be ready to transfer back to the U.S. in 4 months to have the baby. He also counseled her (in accordance with OPNAVINST 6000.1B) that she was eligible for reduced duty, but would have to stand her watches. He reminded her about the squadron of ships that were arriving shortly as well as a wing of B-2 Bombers that would require her services as a Storekeeper.

The Captain finished his conversation with Petty Officer Taylor, and dismissed her.

He is sitting at his desk, with his ball-point pen in hand, looking at the Request Chit trying to decide whether to approve or disapprove.

III. Timeline for Petty Officer Taylor

Month Of Pregnancy	1	2	3	4	5	6	7	8	9
	ON LEAVE IN US	TIME NOW				ELIGIBLE TO TRANSFER TO US (20 wks)	ELIGIBLE FOR 2 WEEKS LEAVE IN US		BIRTH OF BABY

Questions for Discussion

1. Should the Commanding Officer approve or disapprove the chit?
2. What should be his considerations in this reasoning process (primary consideration, second, 3rd, . . .)
3. Should he take into account his own strong religious beliefs about abortion?
4. What would you do if you were the Captain of this Support Facility?
5. Do your religious beliefs in this area *in any way* effect your decision?
6. Is there anything wrong with allowing our religious beliefs to guide us in our decision making? Don't we want our leaders to follow their moral conscience on moral questions?

Altering the Uniform
Edited by Gerald Gunther

Goldman v. Weinberger
475 U.S. 503 (1986)

JUSTICE REHNQUIST delivered the opinion of the Court.

Petitioner S. Simcha Goldman contends that the Free Exercise Clause of the First Amendment to the United States Constitution permits him to wear a yarmulke while in uniform, notwithstanding an Air Force regulation mandating uniform dress for Air Force personnel. The District Court for the District of Columbia permanently enjoined the Air Force from enforcing its regulation against petitioner and from penalizing him for wearing his yarmulke. The Court of Appeals for the District of Columbia Circuit reversed on the ground that the Air Force's strong interest in discipline justified the strict enforcement of its uniform dress requirements. We granted certiorari because of the importance of the question, and now affirm.

Petitioner Goldman is an Orthodox Jew and ordained rabbi. In 1973, he was accepted into the Armed Forces Health Professions Scholarship Program and placed on inactive reserve status in the Air Force while he studied clinical psychology at Loyola University of Chicago. During his three years in the scholarship program, he received a monthly stipend and an allowance for tuition, books, and fees. After completing his Ph.D. in psychology, petitioner entered active service in the United States Air Force as a commissioned officer, in accordance with a requirement that participants in the scholarship program serve one year of active duty for each year of subsidized education. Petitioner was stationed at March Air Force Base in Riverside, California, and served as a clinical psychologist at the mental health clinic on the base.

Until 1981, petitioner was not prevented from wearing his yarmulke on the base. He avoided controversy by remaining close to his duty station in the health clinic and by wearing his service cap over the yarmulke when out of doors. But in April 1981, after he testified as a defense witness at a court-martial wearing his yarmulke but not his service cap, opposing counsel lodged a complaint with Colonel Joseph Gregory, the Hospital Commander, arguing that petitioner's practice of wearing his yarmulke was a violation of Air Force Regulation (AFR) 35–10. This regulation states in pertinent part that "[h]eadgear will not be worn *** [w]hile indoors except by armed security police in the performance of their duties." *** Petitioner argues that AFR 35–10, as applied to him, prohibits religiously motivated conduct and should therefore be analyzed under the standard enunciated in Sherbert v. Verner, 374 U.S. 398 (1963).***

Our review of military regulations challenged on First Amendment grounds is far more deferential than constitutional review of similar laws or regulations designed for civilian society. The military need not encourage debate or tolerate protest to the extent that such tolerance is required of the civilian state by the First Amendment; to accomplish its mission the military must foster instinctive obedience, unity, commitment, and esprit de corps.***

These aspects of military life do not, of course, render entirely nugatory in the military context the guarantees of the First Amendment. But "within the military community there is simply not the same [individual] autonomy as there is in the larger civilian community." Parker v. Levy, [417 U.S.], at 751.

In the context of the present case, when evaluating whether military needs justify a particular restriction of religiously motivated conduct, courts must give great deference to the professional judgment of military authorities concerning the relative importance of a particular military interest.***

The considered professional judgment of the Air Force is that the traditional outfitting of personnel in standardized uniforms encourages the subordination of personal preferences and identities in favor of the overall group mission. Uniforms encourage a sense of hierarchical unity by tending to eliminate outward individual distinctions except for those of rank. The Air Force considers them as vital during peacetime as during war because its personnel must be ready to provide an effective defense on a moment's notice; the necessary habits of discipline and unity must be developed in advance of trouble. We have acknowledged that "[t]he inescapable demands of military discipline and obedience to orders cannot be taught on battlefields; the habit of immediate compliance with military procedures and orders must be virtually reflex with no time for debate or reflection."***

Petitioner Goldman contends that the Free Exercise Clause of the First Amendment requires the Air Force to make an exception to its uniform dress requirements for religious apparel unless the accoutrements create a "clear danger" of undermining discipline and esprit de corps. He asserts that in general, visible but "unobtrusive" apparel will not create such a danger and must therefore be accommodated. He argues that the Air Force failed to prove that a specific exception for his practice of wearing an unobtrusive yarmulke would threaten discipline. He contends that the Air Force's assertion to the contrary is mere *ipse dixit*, with no support from actual experience or a scientific study in the record, and is contradicted by expert testimony that religious exceptions to AFR 35–10 are in fact desirable and will increase morale by making the Air Force a more humane place.

But whether or not expert witnesses may feel that religious exceptions to AFR 35–10 are desirable is quite beside the point. The desirability of dress regulations in the military is decided by the appropriate military officials, and they are under no constitutional mandate to abandon their considered professional judgment. Quite obviously, to the extent the regulations do not permit the wearing of religious apparel such as a yarmulke, a practice described by petitioner as silent devotion akin to prayer, military life may be more objectionable for petitioner and probably others. But the First Amendment does not require the military to accommodate such practices in the face of its view that they would detract from the uniformity sought by the dress regulations. The Air Force has drawn the line essentially between religious apparel which is visible and that which is not, and we hold that those portions of the regulations challenged here reasonably and evenhandedly regulate dress in the interest of the military's perceived need for uniformity. The First Amendment therefore does not prohibit them from being applied to petitioner even though their effect is to restrict the wearing of the headgear required by his religious beliefs.

The judgment of the Court of Appeals is
Affirmed.

JUSTICE STEVENS, with whom JUSTICE WHITE and JUSTICE POWELL join, concurring.

Captain Goldman presents an especially attractive case for an exception from the uniform regulations that are applicable to all other Air Force personnel. His devotion to his faith is readily apparent. The yarmulke is a familiar and accepted sight. In addition to its religious significance for the wearer, the yarmulke may evoke the deepest respect and admiration—the symbol of a distinguished tradition and an eloquent rebuke to the ugliness of anti-Semitism.[3] Captain Goldman's military duties are performed in a setting in which a modest departure from the uniform regulation creates almost no danger of impairment of the Air Force's military mission. Moreover, on the record before us, there is reason to believe that the policy of strict enforcement against Captain Goldman had a retaliatory motive—he had worn his yarmulke while testifying on behalf of a defendant in a court-martial pro-

---

[3] Cf. N. Belth, A Promise to Keep (1979) (recounting history of anti-Semitism in the United States). The history of intolerance in our own country can be glimpsed by reviewing Justice Story's observation that the purpose of the First Amendment was "not to countenance, much less to advance Mahometanism, or Judaism, or infidelity, by prostrating Christianity; but to exclude all rivalry among Christian sects," 2 J. Story, Commentaries on the Constitution of the United States § 1877, p. 594 (1851)—a view that the Court has, of course, explicitly rejected. See Wallace v. Jaffree, 472 U.S. 38, 52–55 (1985).

ceeding. Nevertheless, as the case has been argued,[5] I believe we must test the validity of the Air Force's rule not merely as it applies to Captain Goldman but also as it applies to all service personnel who have sincere religious beliefs that may conflict with one or more military commands.

JUSTICE BRENNAN is unmoved by the Government's concern "that while a yarmulke might not seem obtrusive to a Jew, neither does a turban to a Sikh, a saffron robe to a Satchadananda Ashram-Integral Yogi, nor do dreadlocks to a Rastafarian." He correctly points out that "turbans, saffron robes, and dreadlocks are not before us in this case," and then suggests that other cases may be fairly decided by reference to a reasonable standard based on "functional utility, health and safety considerations, and the goal of a polished, professional appearance." As the Court has explained, this approach attaches no weight to the separate interest in uniformity itself. Because professionals in the military service attach great importance to that plausible interest, it is one that we must recognize as legitimate and rational even though personal experience or admiration for the performance of the "rag-tag band of soldiers" that won us our freedom in the revolutionary war might persuade us that the Government has exaggerated the importance of that interest.

The interest in uniformity, however, has a dimension that is of still greater importance for me. It is the interest in uniform treatment for the members of all religious faiths. The very strength of Captain Goldman's claim creates the danger that a similar claim on behalf of a Sikh or a Rastafarian might readily be dismissed as "so extreme, so unusual, or so faddish an image that public confidence in his ability to perform his duties will be destroyed." If exceptions from dress code regulations are to be granted on the basis of a multi-factored test such as that proposed by JUSTICE BRENNAN, inevitably the decisionmaker's evaluation of the character and the sincerity of the requestor's faith—as well as the probable reaction of the majority to the favored treatment of a member of that faith—will play a critical part in the decision. For the difference between a turban or a dreadlock on the one hand, and a yarmulke on the other, is not merely a difference in "appearance"—it is also the difference between a Sikh or a Rastafarian, on the one hand, and an Orthodox Jew on the other. The Air Force distinctions between such persons when it is enforcing commands of universal application.

As the Court demonstrates, the rule that is challenged in this case is based on a neutral, completely objective standard—visibility. It was not motivated by hostility against, or any special respect for, any religious faith. An exception for yarmulkes would represent a fundamental departure from the true principle of uniformity that supports that rule. For that reason, I join the Court's opinion and its judgment.

JUSTICE BRENNAN, with whom JUSTICE MARSHALL joins, dissenting.

Simcha Goldman invokes this Court's protection of his First Amendment right to fulfill one of the traditional religious obligations of a male Orthodox Jew—to cover his head before an omnipresent God. ***

***If Dr. Goldman wanted to wear a hat to keep his head warm or to cover a bald spot I would join the majority. Mere personal preferences in dress are not constitutionally protected. The First Amendment, however, restrains the Government's ability to prevent an Orthodox Jewish serviceman from, or punish him for, wearing a yarmulke. ***

***When a military service burdens the free exercise rights of its members in the name of necessity, it must provide, as an initial matter and at a minimum, a credible explanation of how the contested practice is likely to interfere with the proffered military interest.[2] Unabashed *ipse dixit* cannot outweigh a constitutional right. ***

The contention that the discipline of the armed forces will be subverted if Orthodox Jews are allowed to wear yarmulkes with their uniforms surpasses belief. It lacks support in the record of this

---

[5] Captain Goldman has mounted a broad challenge to the prohibition on visible religious wear as it applies to yarmulkes. He has not argued the far narrower ground that, even if the general prohibition is valid, its application in his case was retaliatory and impermissible.***

I continue to believe that Government restraints on First Amendment rights, including limitations placed on military personnel, may be justified only upon showing a compelling state interest which is precisely furthered by a narrowly tailored regulation. See, e.g., Brown v. Glines, 444 U.S. 348, 367 (1980) (BRENNAN, J., dissenting). I think that any special needs of the military can be accommodated in the compelling interest prong of the test. My point here is simply that even under a more deferential test Dr. Goldman should prevail.***

case and the Air Force offers no basis for it as a general proposition. While the perilous slope permits the services arbitrarily to refuse exceptions requested to satisfy mere personal preferences, before the Air Force may burden free exercise rights it must advance, at the *very least*, a rational reason for doing so. Furthermore, the Air Force cannot logically defend the content of its rules by insisting that discipline depends upon absolute adherence to whatever rule is established. If, as General Usher admitted at trial, the dress code codified religious exemptions from the "no-headgear-indoors" regulation, then the wearing of a yarmulke would be sanctioned by the code and could not be considered an unauthorized deviation from the rules.

The Government also argues that the services have an important interest in uniform dress, because such dress establishes the preeminence of group identity, thus fostering esprit de corps and loyalty to the service that transcends individual bonds. In its brief, the Government characterizes the yarmulke as an assertion of individuality and as a badge of religious and ethnic identity, strongly suggesting that, as such, it could drive a wedge of divisiveness between members of the services.***

I find totally implausible the suggestion that the overarching group identity of the Air Force would be threatened if Orthodox Jews were allowed to wear yarmulkes with their uniforms. To the contrary, a yarmulke worn with a United States military uniform is an eloquent reminder that the shared and proud identity of United States serviceman embraces and unites religious and ethnic pluralism.***

The Government dangles before the Court a classic parade of horribles, the specter of a brightly-colored, "rag-tag band of soldiers." Although turbans, saffron robes, and dreadlocks are not before us in this case and must each be evaluated against the reasons a service branch offers for prohibiting personnel from wearing them while in uniform, a reviewing court could legitimately give deference to dress and grooming rules that have a *reasoned* basis in, for example, functional utility, health and safety considerations, and the goal of a polished, professional appearance.[4]***

Furthermore, contrary to its intimations, the Air Force has available to it a familiar standard for determining whether a particular style of yarmulke is consistent with a polished, professional military appearance—the "neat and conservative" standard by which the service judges jewelry. No rational reason exists why yarmulkes cannot be judged by the same criterion. Indeed, at argument Dr. Goldman declared himself willing to wear whatever style and color yarmulke the Air Force believes best comports with its uniform.***

Department of Defense Directive 1300.17 (June 18, 1985) grants commanding officers the discretion to permit service personnel to wear religious items and apparel that are not visible with the uniform, such as crosses, temple garments, and scapulars. JUSTICE STEVENS favors this "visibility test" because he believes that it does not involve the Air Force in drawing distinctions among faiths. He rejects functional utility, health, and safety considerations, and similar grounds as criteria for religious exceptions to the dress code, because he fears that these standards will allow some service-persons to satisfy their religious dress and grooming obligations, while preventing others from fulfilling theirs. But, the visible/not visible standard has that same effect. Furthermore, it restricts the free exercise rights of a larger number of service persons. The visibility test permits only individuals whose outer garments and grooming are indistinguishable from those of mainstream Christians to fulfill their religious duties. In my view, the Constitution requires the selection of criteria that permit the greatest possible number of persons to practice their faiths freely.***

The Court and the military services have presented patriotic Orthodox Jews with a painful dilemma—the choice between fulfilling a religious obligation and serving their country. Should the draft be reinstated, compulsion will replace choice. Although the pain the services inflict on Orthodox Jewish servicemen is clearly the result of insensitivity rather than design, it is unworthy of our military because it is unnecessary. The Court and the military have refused these servicemen their constitutional rights; we must hope that Congress will correct this wrong.

JUSTICE BLACKMUN, dissenting. [Omitted.]

---

[4] For example, the Air Force could no doubt justify regulations ordering troops to wear uniforms, prohibiting garments that could become entangled in machinery, and requiring hair to be worn short so that it may not be grabbed in combat and may be kept louse-free in field conditions.

JUSTICE O'CONNOR, with whom JUSTICE MARSHALL joins, dissenting.

* * *

I believe that the Court should attempt to articulate and apply an appropriate standard for a free exercise claim in the military context, and should examine Goldman's claim in light of that standard.

Like the Court today in this case involving the military, the Court in the past has had some difficulty, even in the civilian context, in articulating a clear standard for evaluating free exercise claims that result from the application of general state laws burdening religious conduct. In Sherbert v. Verner, 374 U.S. 398 (1963) and Thomas v. Review Board, 450 U.S. 707 (1981), the Court required the States to demonstrate that their challenged policies were "the least restrictive means of achieving some compelling state interest" in order to deprive claimants of unemployment benefits when the refusal to work was based on sincere religious beliefs. In Wisconsin v. Yoder, 406 U.S. 205, 215, (1972), the Court noted that "only those interests of the highest order and those not otherwise served can overbalance legitimate claims to the free exercise of religion" in deciding that the Amish were exempt from a State requirement that children attend school through the age of 16.***

These tests, though similar, are not identical. One can, however, glean at least two consistent themes from this Court's precedents. First, when the government attempts to deny a Free Exercise claim, it must show that an unusually important interest is at stake, whether that interest is denominated "compelling," "of the highest order," or "overriding." Second, the government must show that granting the requested exemption will do substantial harm to that interest, whether by showing that the means adopted is the "least restrictive" or "essential," or that the interest will not "otherwise be served." These two requirements are entirely sensible in the context of the assertion of a free exercise claim.***

There is no reason why these general principles should not apply in the military, as well as the civilian, context.***

The first question that the Court should face here, therefore, is whether the interest that the Government asserts against the religiously based claim of the individual is of unusual importance. It is perfectly appropriate at this of the analysis to take account of the special role of the military. The mission of our armed services is to protect our Nation from those who would destroy all our freedoms.*** The need for military discipline and esprit de corps is unquestionably an especially important governmental interest.***

***The second question in the analysis of a Free Exercise claim under this Court's precedents must also be reached here: will granting an exemption of the type requested by the individual do substantial harm to the especially important governmental interest?

I have no doubt that there are many instances in which the unique fragility of military discipline and esprit de corps necessitates rigidity by the Government when similar rigidity to preserve an assertedly analogous interest would not pass constitutional muster in the civilian sphere. Nonetheless, as JUSTICE BRENNAN persuasively argues, the Government can present no sufficiently convincing proof in this case to support an assertion that granting an exemption of the type requested here would do substantial harm to military discipline and esprit de corps.***

First, the Government's asserted need for absolute uniformity is contradicted by the Government's own exceptions to its rule. As JUSTICE BRENNAN notes, an Air Force dress code in force at the time of Captain Goldman's service states:

> "Neither the Air Force nor the public expects absolute uniformity of appearance. Each member has the right, within limits, to express individuality through his or her appearance. However, the image of a disciplined service member who can be relied on to do his or her job excludes the extreme, the unusual, and the fad." AFR 35–10, P 1–12.a.(2) (1978)

Furthermore, the Government does not assert, and could not plausibly argue, that petitioner's decision to wear his yarmulke while indoors at the hospital presents a threat to health or safety. And finally, the District Court found as fact that in this particular case, far from creating discontent or indiscipline in the hospital where Captain Goldman worked, "[from September 1977 to May 7, 1981, *no objection* was raised to Goldman's wearing of his yarmulke while in uniform."

In the rare instances where the military has not consistently or plausibly justified its asserted need for rigidity of enforcement, and where the individual seeking the exemption establishes that the assertion by the military of a threat to discipline or esprit de corps is in his or her case completely unfounded, I would hold that the Government's policy of uniformity must yield to the individual's assertion of the right of free exercise of religion. On the facts of this case, therefore, I would require the Government to accommodate the sincere religious belief of Captain Goldman. Napoleon may have been correct to assert that, in the military sphere, morale is to all other factors as three is to one, but contradicted assertions of necessity by the military do not on the scales of justice bear a similarly disproportionate weight to sincere religious beliefs of the individual.

I respectfully dissent.*

---

* [Ed. Note. In the wake of the *Goldman* decision, Congress enacted a statute providing that a member of the armed forces may wear an item of religious apparel while wearing the uniform of the member's armed force." Pursuant to the new statute, items of religious apparel may be prohibited *only* if they would interfere with the performance of member's military duties" or if they are "not neat and conservative." See 10 U. S. C. § 774 (1988).]

The Christmas Party
Captain Rick Rubel

He was the Commanding Officer of a shore command with several hundred military and civilians who worked for him. Each year, the command had a Christmas party with many of the other organizations that worked with them. They would often have over 400 people attend, with lunch, carols, music, and a Santa who would give out gag gifts. This was an important time of year when they were able to socialize with the other people in the command.

One year, a civilian who worked at the command came to the C.O. three weeks before the Christmas party and said that, since she was a non-Christian, she did not feel comfortable going to this Christmas party. This lady was a good worker and a sincere person.

"Captain, can I speak to you a moment?"

"Certainly, Margaret. Come in. Can I offer you a cup of coffee?"

"No thank you. Sir, I feel awkward bringing this up, but for the past few years, I did not feel I could attend the Command Christmas party. I am not a Christian, and although you have nothing at the party that worships Christ, it is a Christmas party, and that is a problem with my faith. I have not attended the party for the past 5 years for this reason."

"Well, I think I understand, Margaret. But we have over 400 people attend each year and, frankly, its one of the highlights of year for us. It really raises the Command morale. Big Bob plays Santa, and hands out gag gifts. Last year he gave me a 3-foot rubber cell phone to poke fun at me always being on the phone. It's really a lot of fun. If I change the format or cancel the party everyone will be disappointed."

Questions for Discussion

What would you do if you were the C.O.?
- *How do you deal with her religious beliefs?*
  - *Tell her to get over it; it's one versus 400?*
  - *or, change the format or cancel the party?*
- *If you would not change or cancel the party:*
  - *Is that fair to her to dismiss her religious beliefs and imply that she cannot attend her own command office party.*
  - *She is sincere in her beliefs*
  - *What if four people approached you with the same concern?*
  - *What if 10, 25, 50 people approached you? At what point do you consider the problem?*
- *If you believe that you would change the format, or cancel the party, remember:*
  - *There are over 400 people who really enjoy this format each year*
  - *Why change just for one person?*

Flex Deck Ops: The Sea of Japan
Captain Rick Rubel

A U.S. Aircraft Carrier is in a naval exercise off the coast of Korea in the Sea of Japan.

The purpose of the exercise to demonstrate to the North Koreans that we can fly around the clock for three weeks with one carrier. This is done with "Flex Deck Ops": launch the E-2C, launch the A-6 tanker, then the launch the first air cycle. Two hours later, the next cycle is launched, followed immediately by the recovery of the first cycle. This continues, without a break for three weeks. Note: the flight deck crew who launch, recover, refuel, and re-arm the planes have to be on-station continuously—there is no A team and B team—just one team.

After 2 ½ weeks of this ops cycle the some of the crew are complaining to the Chaplains that there is no time on Sunday even to have a worship service. (For some faiths, not attending a worship service or communion is a serious problem.) The Chaplains are trying to get around to the various watch stations, but in this type of cycle ops, the crew are working, eating or sleeping.

1. As Commanding Officer, how do you deal with their religious beliefs?
   Do you tell them to go do their jobs, or do you revise the operation plan to take Sundays off for worship? How do you deal with this conflict of mission and faith?

2. Are the worship concerns of your men and women more important than the show of military power to North Korea? Or should this just be looked at as an exercise?

Missiles: Ready to Fire
Captain Rick Rubel

You are the Missile Officer on a DDG in the Persian Gulf. As Missile Officer you are responsible for the effective training and operation of the Missile system. You have been training your missile team for the past 8 months, and the equipment and missile team are working well. The ship is in a potentially dangerous combat operation in protecting the task force from the air threat, so the ship has been in Condition Three Watch status for 5 weeks. This means that the consoles are manned around the clock, the guns are loaded to the transfer trays, and the missiles are ready to fire.

At 0945 you answer a knock on the door of your stateroom. GMM2 Parks enters your office, and asks to talk to you. Petty Officer Parks is one of the best sailors in your division. You remark to him that you haven't seen him lately, since the ship has been in Condition III watch, and you and he are on a different rotation. You ask him how he is doing on his preparation for the E-6 exam, and he gives you an optimistic response.

GMM2 Parks then says, "Sir, over the past few months, I have been reading the Bible, and attending several bible study groups around the ship. I have come to realize, that for me to be true to my faith, I must take the words of the gospel literally. I read Exodus 20:13 and Deuteronomy 5:17 as 'thou shall not kill.' Therefore, I am telling you now that I cannot pull the firing key on the Missile Launching Console (SMLC). I know I have been through all the training and everything, but now, if I fire a live missile, it will mean killing another person and I cannot do that in keeping with my faith."

As you continue to talk to GMM2 Parks, it seems that he believes sincerely in what he is telling you. The problem is, that through a series of circumstances, he is your only qualified Missile Firing Petty Officer. (One GMM3 flew back to the States for major knee surgery and will not return, and the other resigned from the Navy before the deployment. The Bureau of Naval Personnel will not be sending you another GMM for three months.)

You tell GMM2 Parks to see the Command Chaplain, and he does that. The following day when you talk to the Chaplain, he informs you that he feels that GMM2 Parks is sincere in his beliefs. If you take him off the firing panel, you must tell the Captain that the missile system is not fully functional, and the ship, therefore cannot complete its current mission.

1. What do you do as Missile Officer?
2. What are your primary considerations?
3. Do you consider his religious beliefs, or tell him he has a job to do?

V
The Navy Chaplain
and the Mission

The Chaplain in Haiti
Written by a U.S. Navy Chaplain
Edited by Captain Rick Rubel

The Chaplain was assigned to the United States Support Group Haiti as the Group Chaplain. Haiti was a country in transition following the threat of a United States led invasion which led to the sudden resignation of General Cedras' military dictatorship the year before. The democratically elected government of Haiti's President Preval was struggling to maintain order and rebuild the depleted infrastructure of the poorest country in the Western Hemisphere. The United Nations forces were responsible for security while the U.S. Support Group was charged with rebuilding roads, bridges, schools, and the country's police force. The doctors and nurses assigned to the Group also conducted many mobile clinics in the surrounding areas of Port au Prince, the nation's capitol. The Group Chaplain was responsible for taking care of the spiritual needs of all the troops in the Group and was also assigned to work with numerous charities, missionaries, and various Non-Governmental Organizations (NGOs) located in the area. There were Community Relations Projects (COMRELs) that needed to be done in whatever direction one looked.

After arriving in Haiti on December 29, 1996, the first stop for the Chaplain that day was St. Theresa's hospital, school and orphanage run by the Missionaries of Charity. After a brief greeting, the Sister said, "Chaplain, come with me." Without any other words the chaplain and his RP2 (enlisted assistant) walked up the walkway and steps to the hospital. They were overwhelmed with the more than 100 beds filled with seriously ill, sick and dying children. They were most touched by the 20 or so children who swarmed RP2 and the chaplain with outstretched arms. Because of severe malnourishment, many of these beautiful children of African descent from Haiti's slave history had swollen arms and legs, distended bellies, and orange hair. Some were orphans, and some had parents who simply couldn't afford to take care of them so they had abandoned them on the doorstep of the orphanage. Hungry, sick, and alone, their greatest need was simply to be held, to be loved. With children hanging on both legs and in both arms, the chaplain knew exactly why he was in Haiti.

Over the next three months, the RP2 and the Chaplain made several COMRELs to St. Theresa's Hospital. There was always some painting or construction work that had to be done at the orphanage, hospital or school. There were trucks that need mechanical work and chalkboards or fences that needed paining. Mostly, there were the children and it became apparent that they needed more than to be held and loved. Sister Immaculata was growing more frustrated every day because all combined, the hospitals were losing about seven children a day when only one year ago they were losing only one child a week. Most of the deaths were directly related to malnutrition. Sensing her frustration one Friday afternoon, he asked Sister Immaculata if there was anything he could do to help. She said, "Come back on Monday. I want you to meet someone."

The following Monday the chaplain arrived at St. Theresa's Hospital and met a member of the organization called Bridges America, who described a scenario that was simply unbelievable. He explained that Bridges America had sponsored a shipment of goods that he was coordinating for the local missionaries, including the Sisters and many other NGOs, and that it had been held up at a local shipping yard for more than six months. There were thirty-four, 40 foot CONEX boxes containing over 2,000,000 pounds of food, medicine, medical supplies, school supplies and items that were donated by charities from across the United States, shipped to Haiti on U.S. Merchant Marine vessels, and approved by both the U.S. State Department and Haiti's Interior Ministry. The shipping company and its local foreman were holding up delivery of the shipment from the docks in Port au Prince by insisting that the Haitian Interior Ministry authorize the release of the shipment. He explained that he had contacted several U.S. Congressmen and Senators, and had been working through the U.S. Embassy in Haiti, the military liaison, and the U.S. Support Group trying to obtain the release of the shipment. No one had been successful. He explained that seven of the CONEX boxes were filled with items just for the Missionaries of Charity.

With that bit of information they all piled into the government vehicle and proceeded into downtown Port au Prince to the Interior Ministry. With their translator, they began a daylong journey from one desk to the next seeking proper authorization for release of the shipment. At 1630, and after dozens of signatures and frustrating stops the Chaplain stood outside of the Interior Minister's office. His secretary was insisting that the Minister didn't have time for them, but they insisted otherwise. It was explained that they would not leave until the letter authorizing the release of the shipment was signed. After a few minutes the secretary disappeared into the Minister's office, and emerged with the authorization letter in hand.

The plan was that they would all meet at the shipping yard the next day and present the letter to the foreman. At this point the Chaplain thought that it would be a good idea to let the Commanding Officer of the U.S. Support Group know what he had done. At dinner that night the Chaplain recounted all from the beginning. As he listened, the CO sat there smiling. He finally said, "Chaplain, we've been trying to get that shipment out since before I arrived. The State Department, and several members of Congress have made it a high priority. The Ambassador and his Deputy have tried. Our military liaison has worked the issue and the Group's J-6 Officer has tried. We failed. How did you do it in one day?" He replied, "Sir, I have a very big RP and I am persistent. Besides, I am tired of watching children die. Not succeeding wasn't an option." The CO said, "Chaplain, just don't get thrown into jail. I understand the Haitian prisons aren't very nice." The Colonel offered to assist the Chaplain in any way possible, offering trucks, trailers, drivers and volunteers.

The final obstacle was the Customs officials. After much argument with the officials, the Chaplain proceeded to the shipping yard. After being told by the Customs officials that it would take a long time to clear the shipment, the Chaplain looked him square in the eye, smiled, and said "I'll be back tomorrow, and those CONEX boxes are leaving!"

While waiting for customs, they visited St. Theresa's and talked with Sister Immaculata. When they explained to the Sister the situation, she shared these words: "I called Calcutta last night, and I spoke with Mother Theresa. I told her what you were doing for the children and she said that she would pray for you." The Chaplin replied, "Well Sister, that isn't very fair. It's not like we can back out now."

The first four CONEX boxes rolled out at 1600 the next day.

Over the next six days, more than 150 volunteers, including the Colonel himself, worked through the days and long into the nights unloading the CONEX boxes at the warehouse. It took four weeks for all the charities to come and collect all the donated materials. After the Missionaries of Charity picked up their food and medicine, he asked Sister Immaculata how long this would help their children. There was enough food in their portion of the CONEX boxes to feed all of the children in each of their nine hospitals in Haiti for seven months or more. Perhaps as many as 1,300 children would be saved for at least that short seven months.

The Ambassador was thrilled that the shipment got out, but his Deputy complained that the Chaplain had "stepped all over the sovereignty of Haiti."

The Coast Guard Commander, who was the military liaison to Haiti, told the Chaplain that the NGO, Bridges America had used him, but the Chaplain I replied respectfully, "Sir, I know for a fact that they lost money on the shipment, but if saving starving children is getting used, then I don't mind getting used in that way at all."

Questions for Discussion

1. Did the Chaplain do the right thing in this case?
2. Did he violate the sovereignty of the government of Haiti?
3. What character strengths and virtues did the Chaplain demonstrate?
4. Do you possess these strengths and virtues shown by the Chaplain to do what he did?
5. Do we want our officers to take matters in their own hands like this, or do we want them to follow established procedures?

"By My Presence . . ."
Captain Rick Rubel

As the Iraq war of 2003 was beginning, the Chaplain was sent to the Marine unit to ensure that they were spiritually cared for at the dawn of combat operations.

Shortly after attaching to the battalion, the unit entered into heavy combat operations. While in An Nasiriyah, his CO called the Chaplain to the front lines. The CO felt this was where the Chaplain needed to spend his time, because of the number of casualties being incurred, as well as the rapidly deteriorating situation with the local population. The Chaplain agreed wholeheartedly with the CO's assessment. It was in this capacity that the Chaplain was able to ensure that his men were being cared for, as well as allow the Chaplain to began working with the locals. He did this by talking with the local populace's appointed leaders, ensuring that civilians were properly buried (before sundown), and attempting to convince the indigenous population through word and deed, that the U.S. Marines were not there to conquer, but to liberate. As a result of these actions, he was very effective in dealing with Iraqi locals. Interestingly enough, the Chaplain consistently wore his cross on his flack jacket, even in dealing with the predominantly Muslim population.

At this early point in the war, most detainees were being held in makeshift facilities close to the front lines, in hopes that valuable intelligence could be gathered and directly used by those in direct combat action in helping to rescue captured American POWs, as well as save lives of those on the front lines. The pressure on the Intelligence guys was great, understanding they didn't have much time to extract such information from the prisoners. At this point in the conflict, the CO asked the Chaplain if he would stay at the makeshift prison each night with the Marine guards. The Chaplain complied and spent the nights at the prison, walking around talking to the guards. When asked at a later date why he was assigned to spend the nights at the prison, the Chaplain explained that this seemed to produce a calming and moral atmosphere in the chaos of the makeshift prison that may not have been there otherwise. When asked how he did that, he replied simply, "By my presence. . . ."

Questions for Discussion

1. Is it the job of a Chaplain to ensure that detainee guards act in an appropriate manner?
2. How does the Chaplain weigh any possible discomfort placed on the detainees during interrogation versus the valuable information the Intel guys can extract?
3. How would a Chaplain know where the "lines" are for this sort of interrogation?
4. What would he do if "his presence" wasn't enough and he had to speak up?
5. Could he find himself going up against the mission of intelligence gathering?

Can't Phone Home

Captain Rick Rubel
Based on a true story of a Navy Chaplain

She was a Navy Chaplain assigned to the Medical Battalion preparing to go from Kuwait into the War in Iraq. After arriving in Kuwait from Camp Lejeune, her augmentation unit met up with the rest of the unit from Camp Pendleton. After the long trip to the Middle East, along with the uncertainty of upcoming combat, the officers in the unit wanted to call home to notify their families they had arrived safely. The Commanding Officer of the Battalion announced that the members from the Lejeune unit would not be allowed to use the phones, but could correspond "the old fashion way; by using a letter." For some reason, however, this did not seem to be true for the Pendleton officers. This glaring inconsistency was just one of the many decisions of favoritism between the units, and apparently stemmed from years of prior disputes between the C.O. of the Battalion and the Augmentation Unit Commander.

As tensions of war mounted, the letters from families were not received and in fact, the outgoing letters of reassurance were returned without receipt. After six weeks of no communication, there was great deal of emotion and anxiety from the service members, as they had no way to contact their loved ones. Even the Red Cross began to inquire into the well-being of these service members.

During a staff meeting with all the chaplains in the area, the Chief of Staff of the Marine Expeditionary Force paid a visit. After making a short presentation to the gathered chaplains he looked directly at the Chaplain and asked, "So, Chaplain, how are things going?" The Chaplain thought to herself in this brief moment that she could say that all was fine, or she could expose this problem of inconsistencies and the CO's refusal to let them call their families. Knowing that the CO was a very autocratic man who would, no doubt, take retribution on her, it would certainly be much easier to say nothing. "Why should I have to take the lumps for this?" she thought to herself. "If I get caught in the middle of the personal feud between the two senior officers, I will just become a casualty, along with my career. I have to think about my own career, don't I? I should stick to my job of ministry, and let the staff worry about satellite communications." As she went down this thought path, she then realized that the worst case would be that she tell the Chief of Staff, put her CO on report, draw his anger, and then the Chief of Staff do nothing about it! Then she would lose on all counts.

Then, without further hesitation, she said, "Chief of Staff, things are not fine. We have not been able to call our families for six weeks, and morale is at an all-time low. We are receiving incoming Red Cross messages now generated by anxious family members back home who have heard nothing from their service member since they left Camp Lejeune." The Chief of Staff quickly said, "Chaplain, thanks for telling me. I'll take care of this right now." The Chief of Staff left the room, and the other officers that had heard this conversation, immediately turned to the Chaplain and said, "You just put your CO on report. How could you do that?"

Two hours later, they had a bank of satellite phones in their tent, and everyone was allowed to call home for three minutes.

As expected, the CO was cold to the Chaplain, and his own Command Chaplain tried to explain to her that she had made him look bad in front of the General's Chief of Staff.

Although she was concerned about that, she was assured that she had done the right thing and was comforted by the large number of people that came up to her as she crossed the compound to shake her hand, hug her, and thank her for her courage to speak up.

Questions for Discussion

1. Did she do the right thing in this case?
2. Was satellite communications really her business?
3. Doesn't the Navy Chaplain have an obligation to support the Commanding Officer?
4. What is the major consideration in this decision?
5. Should she have done anything differently?
6. How else could she have resolved this conflict?

Part of the Combat Mission
Captain Rick Rubel
Based on the True Story of a Navy Chaplain

The Chaplain was assigned to a Marine unit training for combat in Iraq. During the training phase he found a number ways to support the Commanding Officer and the direct mission of the unit. One of these ways included the Commanding Officer's request for him to train the Marines on Rules of Engagement (ROE). Although the chaplain was a non-combatant, he studied the command doctrine as explained by the unit Commander and began going from squad to squad explaining the ROE for the upcoming deployment to the war. The Chaplain soon realized that he was in a unique position to explain these important rules that shaped the battlefield. Unlike the unit leader who told the Marines who they should kill, the Chaplain operated from a moral high-ground that elevated the significance of the ROE. His tone for the training was clearly one of "who *you do not kill*". In other words, coming from the Chaplain, this became a moral doctrine as well as a combat doctrine. During the training, the Chaplain asked one of the Marines, "What do you do if a civilian non-combatant steals something of yours, such as your Camel-Back (water supply)?" A Marine replied "I kill him, sir, because it's government property." The Chaplain was able to use this illustration to explain that it is just as wrong to kill someone for that, as it would be to kill someone back home in the States for stealing a piece of equipment. The Chaplain explained to his Marines that their actions effect how the world sees our armed forces and their personal actions will win or lose the battle for the hearts and minds of the Iraqi people. The ROE are the beginning of how we affect our U.S. policy during a war.

The official relationship between the C.O. and his Chaplain continued to improve as they entered the war zone.

During the build-up in Kuwait, the Chaplain was able to encouraged Marine leadership to discourage Marines from referring to locals as "Hajjis" The Chaplain believed the nicknames the Marines gave these groups were not only derogatory, but contributed to the "dehumanizing" of the enemy. The chaplain knew that once they started dehumanizing the enemy, they could easily become killers instead of highly trained warriors. Out of concern for the Marines, the Chaplain was not going to let that happen, and the Marines in his unit soon understood and began to correct their behavior.

There were several times when the Chaplain had to set the moral standard for the men in the unit. After taking Baghdad, his unit took the National Soccer Stadium. While clearing the building of enemy combatants, the Marines/Navy Corpsman found some boxes of new Iraqi National soccer jerseys. The Marines started to put several of these in their packs as a great souvenir of the war. The Chaplain immediately stepped in and said, "Hey, guys, put them back. They don't belong to us. That equipment belongs to the Iraqi people." With the help of the SNCOs, the equipment was gathered back up and left in the national stadium.

In looking back at the war and remembering his Chaplain, the C.O. of that unit told his Chaplain, "Chaps, you were part of our combat team. When I looked down the table and saw your face . . . it would remind me of my moral conscience."

Questions for Discussion

1. Should a Chaplain conduct Rules of Engagement training when asked by his C.O.? What are the pros and cons to this argument?

2. Should the Chaplain set higher moral standards for his/her unit? Is it the Chaplain's role to be the "moral policeman"? What if the Chaplain's standards are higher than the C.O.'s standards. Which one should the Chaplain impose?

3. Why was this Chaplain so relevant to his command and their direct mission? Was it just the personality of his CO or was something else involved?

4. Was he shaping the character of his Marines? How was he doing that?

How Do We Honor the Fallen?
Captain Rick Rubel

Case I Based on a True Story of a Navy Chaplain

Case I

The Chaplain was assigned to a Marine Corp unit in Iraq.

A Corporal who was assigned to the counter-intelligence group was suddenly discovered missing. Since his job was covert intelligence, it was not clear for a while what his exact status was. His picture then showed up on Arab TV being threatened with beheading. This video still did not clarify his status, since there were inconsistencies in the video. There was even some concern that he had "gone native" while under-cover.

As the Chaplain discussed the situation with his CO, they determined that the possibilities of his eventual status would be one of: (a) A deserter who was caught by insurgents, (b) a corporal who sided with the insurgents (a traitor), or (c) a corporal who foolishly and naively trusted persons who turned out to be insurgents. If he were killed as his apparent captors threatened, we might never know the true status. The question the CO and the Chaplain had to discuss was; if he was found dead, what kind of memorial service, if any, should be held for him, particularly in light of others from the unit who had been killed leading their Marines in action?

They explored the range from full honors and heroic eulogies to a low key memorial, where much would be left unsaid.

Questions for Discussion

1. What should the Chaplain recommend?
2. Is the memorial service for the living at the service, or the deceased?
3. How should the status of a Marine at the time of death, or the circumstances surrounding that death, affect the kind of memorial to be held?
4. If a Soldier, Sailor or Marine dies as a result of suicide, would that change the type of memorial performed?
5. How would the other Marines respond to the various memorial services? Is their response a consideration?

Case II What Do We Call His Death?
Based on a True Story of a Navy Chaplain

The Lance Corporal was killed in Iraq as a result of an Iraqi civilian vehicle running him over. The circumstances were that he was crossing a road at night as part of a patrol; the driver of the vehicle was probably intoxicated, and may or may not have intended to hit the Lance Corporal with his car.

The question before the CO and the Chaplain was whether or not this was a "Combat Death" or a "non-combat accident."

Note: In the strictest interpretation of the rules, this was probably a non-combat accident. However, there is a big difference for the Marines in his unit in terms of how they deal with the loss and there may be a similar difference for the family. It is easier to accept "My buddy was killed in combat in Iraq" than "My buddy was run over by a drunk in Iraq." It also makes a difference in whether he is (posthumously) awarded the Purple Heart for wounds received in combat.

Questions for Discussion

1. What should the Chaplain recommend to the CO?
2. What are all the considerations of this decision?
3. What is the right thing to do?

Digging Fox-holes with My Marines
Captain Rick Rubel
Based on a True Story of Navy Chaplain

The Senior Chaplain was assigned to a Marine MEU ready to go into Iraq.

When he first met the Lieutenant Colonel in charge of the Battalion Landing Team to report for duty, the Chaplain told the CO, "Sir, before you tell me what my role is in your unit, I'd like to tell you what I think my role is."

The Colonel said, "Fine, go ahead, Chaplain."

The Chaplain continued, "Sir, my job is the *men*. My job is going from fighting-hole to fighting-hole, to be there to talk to them, to comfort them and to pray with them. The best time to talk to these young Marines is while you're working next to them. I may not spend a lot of time in the headquarters tent with you, because I can do more good out there. I need to be there when they want to talk to someone, and pray with someone; and the best way to do that is to gain their respect."

The CO thought for a short time, and said, "Chaps, you're absolutely right."

The Chaplain then did just that. Then when the unit pulled up for the night, he would go out into the field to help the Marines dig their fighting-holes or fill their camelbacks or canteens with water, while he told them what was really going on with the unit with his current information. After the Chaplain spent the evening helping the Marines dig their holes, inevitably the First Sergeant would say, "Hey Chaps, where's your fighting hole? Hey Marines, everybody pitch in and dig the Chaps' hole."

During a tense time, when the unit was expecting a Scud missile attack, the Chaplain, in full MOP gear, went from hole to hole along with this RP to pray with the Marines. "I was scared to death. Everybody was tense and nervous. But it was important that they see me." he said later.

The Chaplain also felt that he had a role in teaching his Marines what was right. In an Iraqi town, while the senior officers and staff NCOs were in a building talking to the local officials about security, two Marines got into a dispute which turned into a fight. As an Iraqi crowd gathered around them, the Chaplain realized he was the only officer around, and there was no SNCO present. He knew he had to impose order himself. So he went over to stand between the two fighting Marines and said, "What are you two doing? Stop this right now." They immediately stopped, and apologized to the Chaplain and to one another.

Questions for Discussion

1. Should the Chaplain have been so brash as to tell the CO what his job was before the CO told the Chaplain his job?

2. Is the Chaplain's job to be in the fighting holes with his Marines or to be with his CO—as his ethical advisor? Can he/she do both?

3. Should the Chaplain have stopped the fight himself, or should he have gone to get a Line officer?

4. Is the combat role of the Chaplain to dig fighting holes and deliver water to his Marines?

5. What is the primary role of the Chaplain in combat?

Why Should We Take the Risk?
Captain Rick Rubel

The Chaplain was assigned to a Marine unit in Afghanistan. The unit's mission was to provide security and stabilization operations for forward operating bases and the presidential election, locate weapon caches, provide humanitarian support to the locals and counter Anti-Coalition Forces (ACF) activity. With these various missions, the Marines were required to be out patrolling constantly, winning the hearts and minds of the people.

Shortly after arriving in Afghanistan, the Marines were informed that if they got into a fire-fight with the ACF, they were not to "shoot through any civilians." Specifically, the order was that even if it meant taking a risk to themselves or their buddies, that "We should take the hit, before we hurt any civilians."

Several of the Marines from one particular element had some personal problems with these "rules of engagement." The Chaplain had sufficient credibility with his Marines that they felt they could come to him to discuss this conflict. Several of the men came to the Chaplain and expressed their concern, "Chaplain, I don't know about this. I'm not going to risk myself or my squad buddies for the sake of some >"&*# Afghan!"

Questions for Discussion

1. What should the Chaplain tell the Marines that came to him with these concerns?
2. How should he/she help them work through this conflict between self and mission?
3. Should he favor the side of the mission (ROE) or favor their real concerns of risk to human life?
4. Should a Chaplain even be discussing rules of engagement?
5. How does a Chaplain build credibility with the Marines and Sailors so they will come to him/her to discuss these conflicts?
6. What is the role of the Chaplain in combat?

VI
Equality, Justice, and the Law

Justice or Mercy:
Captain's Mast–Non-Judicial Punishment
Captain Rick Rubel

In order to quickly deal with infractions with the Uniform Code of Military Justice (UCMJ), and to maintain "good order and discipline," the Captain of a naval ship or unit is given authority to hold a Non-Judicial Proceeding (NJP) called Captain's Mast. In this proceeding the Captain is jury, judge and prosecutor. The maximum punishments given at NJP are less than allowed at a court martial, but once an accused waives his/her right to courts-martial, and accepts NJP, there is little room to appeal.

The Case:

You are Commanding Officer of a Destroyer, and two men come to captain's mast for the same offense. They both got a car ride to the ship from another sailor who works at the Naval Station . On that particular morning they were both late in arriving to the ship and missed ship's movement, when the ship got underway on a scheduled departure at 0800. (They were actually required to be aboard by 0700). The sailor who gave them a ride picked them up late, they were stuck in traffic, and they arrived at the pier 25 minutes after the ship departed. This is a serious offense in the fleet, because a service member cannot join his/her command until either the ship returns, or an arrangement is made to transport the tardy crew workers to the ship by helicopter.

The maximum punishment you can give at NJP is:
45 days restriction
Forfeiture of ½ of one month's pay for 3 months
Reduction in rank one pay grade

The "standard" punishment for missing ships movement:
30 days restriction
Forfeiture of ½ of one months pay for 2 months
Reduction in rank (suspended–unless there is another mast offense in the next 12 months)

Profile of accused:
Petty Officer 3/c Barnaby: A 24 year-old bachelor. Known by all aboard as a "wild man." Has been to NJP two times in the past 3 years (Charges of: Disrespect towards a Superior Petty Officer, and Drunk and Disorderly ashore). He is a 2.0 sailor. His division officer says he does a barely marginal job, and gets in trouble a lot ashore.

Petty Officer Goodman: 29 years old , married with 4 children, ages 1 month to 9 years. He has never been to Captains Mast, and is a 3.8 sailor. His Division Officer says he is extremely responsible and always does his job well. He also volunteers aboard ship tutoring sailors to obtain their High School Equivalent courses (GED), and serves as ships drug abuse counselor. His wife works nights at the 7–11 store.

1. What punishment do you give to each?
   - would you give them the same punishment, or different? Why?
2. What were the considerations in your decision in order of priority?

To: Commanding Officer,	USS Destroyer		Date of Report:	27 Mar 04

I hereby report the following named person for the offense(s) noted:

NAME OF ACCUSED	SERIIAL NO.	SOCIAL SECURITY NO.	RATE/GRADE	BR. & CLASS	DIV/DEPT
PO3 Barnaby		**444-55-6789**	**E-4**	**Deck D-1**	**Deck**

PLACE OF OFFENSE(S)	DATE OF OFFENSE(S)
USS Destroyer (DDG-99)	12 Mar 04

DETAILS OF OFFENSE(S) *(Refer by Article of UCMJ if known. If unauthorized absence, give following info: time and date of commencement, whether over   leave or liberty, time and date of apprehension or surrender and arrival on board, loss of ID card and/or liberty card, etc.):*

Violation UCMJ Art 34, Missing ships movement.
To wit: On 12 Mar 2004, PO3 Barnaby was not present on board while the USS Destroyer got underway.

NAME OF WITNESS	RATE/GRADE	DIV/DEPT		NAME OF WITNESS	RATE/GRADE	DIV/DEPT
QDWO	**ET2**					

(Rate/Grade/Title of person submitting report)	_(Signature of Accuser)_

I have been informed of the nature of the accusation(s) against me. I understand I do not have to answer any questions or make any statement regarding the offense(s) of which I am accused or suspected. However, I understand any statement made or questions answered by me may be used as evidence against me in event of trial by court-martial (Article 31, UCMJ).

Witness: _____

(Signature)	_(Signature of Accused)_

PRE-MAST RESTRAINT	☐ PRE-TRIAL **CONFINEMENT** ☐ NO RESTRICTION	☐	RESTRICTED: You are restricted to the limits of _____ in lieu of arrest by order of the CO. Until your status as a restricted person is terminated by the CO, you may not leave the restricted limits except with the express permission of the CO or XO. You have been informed of the times and places which you are required to muster.

(Signature and title of person imposing restraint)	_(Signature of Accused)_

REPORT AND DISPOSITION OF OFFENSE(S)
NAVPERS 1626/7

INFORMATION CONCERNING ACCUSED

CURRENT ENL. DATE	EXPIRATION CURRENT ENL. DATE	TOTAL ACTIVE NAVAL SERVICE	TOTAL SERVICE ON BOARD	EDUCATION	GCT	AGE
14 Jun 01	14 Jun 2005	4 yrs	2 yrs	10th Grade		24

MARITAL STATUS	NO. DEPENDEN TS	CONTRIBUTION TO FAMILY OR QTRS. ALLOWANCE *(Amount required by law)*		PAY PER MONTH *(Including sea or foreign duty pay, if any)*
Not Married	**0**			**$1950**

PRELIMINARY INQUIRY REPORT

From: Commanding Officer   Date: _____

To: _____

1. Transmitted herewith for preliminary inquiry and report by you, including, if appropriate in the interest of justice and discipline, the preferring of such charges as appeal to you to be sustained by expected evidence.

REMARKS OF DIVISION OFFICER *(Performance of duty, etc.)*

REPORT AND DISPOSITION OF OFFENSE(S)
NAVPERS 1626/7

To: Commanding Officer,	USS Destroyer				Date of Report:	27 Mar 04

I hereby report the following named person for the offense(s) noted:

NAME OF ACCUSED	SERIIAL NO.	SOCIAL SECURITY NO.	RATE/GRADE	BR. & CLASS	DIV/DEPT
PO3 Goodman		**123-44-0321**	**E-5**	**E-2 Div**	**OPS**

PLACE OF OFFENSE(S)	DATE OF OFFENSE(S)
USS Destroyer (DDG-99)	12 Mar 04

DETAILS OF OFFENSE(S) *(Refer by Article of UCMJ if known. If unauthorized absence, give following info: time and date of commencement, whether over   leave or liberty, time and date of apprehension or surrender and arrival on board, loss of ID card and/or liberty card, etc.)*

Violation UCMJ Art 34, missing ships movement.
To wit: On 12 Mar 2004, PO3 Goodman was not presenton board while the USS Destroyer got underway.

NAME OF WITNESS	RATE/GRADE	DIV/DEPT	NAME OF WITNESS	RATE/GRADE	DIV/DEPT
QDWO	**ET2**				

(Rate/Grade/Title of person submitting report)	*(Signature of Accuser)*

I have been informed of the nature of the accusation(s) against me. I understand I do not have to answer any questions or make any statement regarding the offense(s) of which I am accused or suspected. However, I understand any statement made or questions answered by me may be used as evidence against me in event of trial by court-martial (Article 31, UCMJ).
Witness: _____

(Signature)	*(Signature of Accused)*

PRE-MAST RESTRAINT

☐ PRE-TRIAL **CONFINEMENT**

☐ NO RESTRICTION

☐ RESTRICTED: You are restricted to the limits of
_____
_____ in

(Signature and title of person imposing restraint)	(Signature of Accused)

INFORMATION CONCERNING ACCUSED

CURRENT ENL. DATE	EXPIRATION CURRENT ENL. DATE	TOTAL ACTIVE NAVAL SERVICE	TOTAL SERVICE ON BOARD	EDUCATION	GCT	AGE
15 April, 1998	15 Apr 2006	6 yrs	2 yrs	12th Grade		29

MARITAL STATUS	NO. DEPENDENTS	CONTRIBUTION TO FAMILY OR QTRS. ALLOWANCE *(Amount required by law)*	PAY PER MONTH *(Including sea or foreign duty pay, if any)*
Married	4		$1950

RECORD OF PREVIOUS OFFENSE(S) *(Date type action taken etc. Non-judicial punishment incidents are to be included.)*

_____
(Signature of Investigating Officer)

ACTION OF EXECUTIVE OFFICER

			SIGNATURE OF EXECUTIVE OFFICER
☐	DISMISSED	[X] REFER TO CAPTAIN'S MAST	

RIGHT TO DEMAND TRIAL BY COURT-MARTIAL

(Not applicable to persons attached to or embarked in a vessel)

I understand that nonjudicial punishment may not be imposed on me if, before the imposition of such punishment, I demand in lieu thereof trial by court-martial. I therefore (do) (do not) demand trial by court-martial.

WITNESS	SIGNATURE OF ACCUSED

ACTION OF COMMANDING OFFICER

☐ DISMISSED	☐	CONF. ON_____ 1, 2, OR 3 DAYS
☐ DISMISSED WITH WARNING (Not considered NJP)	☐	CORRECTIONAL CUSTODY FOR _____DAYS
☐ ADMONITION: ORAL/IN WRITING	☐	REDUCTION TO NEXT INFERIOR PAY GRADE
☐ REPRIMAND: ORAL/IN WRITING	☐	REDUCTION TO PAY GRADE OF _____
☐ REST. TO_____FOR_____DAYS	☐	EXTRA DUTIES FOR_____DAYS
☐ REST. TO_____FOR_____DAYS WITH SUSP. FROM DUTY	☐	PUNISHMENT SUSPENDED FOR_____
☐ FORFEITURE: TO FORFEIT $_____PAY PER MO. FOR _____MO(S)	☐	REFER TO ART. 32 INVESTIGATION
	☐	RECOMMENDED FOR TRIAL BY GCM

☐ ~~DETENTION: TO HAVE $_____ PAY PER MO. FOR (1, 2, 3) MO(S) DETAINED FOR ____ MO(S)~~	☐ AWARDED SPCM	☐ AWARDED SCM

DATE OF MAST	DATE ACCUSED INFORMED OF ABOVE ACTION	SIGNATURE OF COMMANDING OFFICER
		DATE: _____

Justice at Sea: The Case of "Billy Budd, Sailor"*

Herman Melville

Editors' notes:

The following "case study" is actually an excerpt from the novel Billy Budd, *by the great American novelist, Herman Melville (1819–1891).* It is based upon a true story.*

In Melville's novel, Billy Budd is rated an "able seaman" aboard the British Man 'o War, Bellipotent *("Ready for Battle"). He is a gentle, trusting, and very highly regarded member of the crew, a fact much resented by his superior officer, John Claggart. Jealous of Billy's popularity, the unscrupulous Claggart entices Billy to appear before the ship's commander, Captain Vere, where he accuses the unsuspecting seaman of fomenting mutiny among the crew. Budd suffers from a speech impediment that causes him to stammer unintelligibly when startled or confused. He is thus unable to defend himself verbally from these malicious lies, and in his amazement and frustration, he lashes out, knocking his accuser to the deck. Striking a superior officer itself is a serious offense, tantamount to mutiny; but to make matters worse, the evil Claggart strikes his head while falling, and dies.*

Melville's portrayal of the military tribunal that convenes to consider Billy Budd's punishment is considered a literary masterpiece, a gripping and dramatic portrayal of the gravity of dispensing justice, and of the difficulties encountered in attempting to enforce good order and discipline fairly while at sea. When describing the conclusion of the trial, the narrator of this case makes reference, in the third paragraph from the end, to the true circumstances on which it was based.

In 1842, a surly and disobedient midshipman and two sailors were accused by their commander of fomenting mutiny aboard the U.S. warship, Somers. *Rather than throwing the accused in the brig for court-martial in port, only a few days sail away, the ship's captain chose to execute the accused at high sea, exercising his right of judgment under the "Articles of War." The execution caused a scandal in the United States, aided in part by the fact that the midshipman in question was the son of the sitting Secretary of War, who ordered a thorough investigation of the circumstances. In part as a result of this event, Congress enacted legislation founding the U.S. Naval Academy at nearby Annapolis in 1845, in order to provide a more orderly and professional setting for the training and education of midshipmen preparing to serve as future naval officers.*

---

*Reprinted from *Billy Budd: Sailor,* edited by Harrison Hayford and Martin Sealts (1972), by permission of University of Chicago Press.

Who in the rainbow can draw the line where the violet tint ends and the orange tint begins? Distinctly we see the difference of the colors, but where exactly does the one first blendingly enter into the other? So with sanity and insanity. In pronounced cases there is no question about them. But in some supposed cases, in various degrees supposedly less pronounced, to draw the exact line of demarcation few will undertake, though for a fee becoming considerate some professional experts will. There is nothing namable but that some men will, or undertake to, do it for pay.

Whether Captain Vere, as the surgeon professionally and privately surmised, was really the sudden victim of any degree of aberration, every one must determine for himself by such light as this narrative may afford.

That the unhappy event which has been narrated could not have happened at a worse juncture was but too true. For it was close on the heel of the suppressed insurrections, an aftertime very critical to naval authority, demanding from every English sea commander two qualities not readily interfusable—prudence and rigor. Moreover, there was something crucial in the case.

In the jugglery of circumstances preceding and attending the event on board the *Bellipotent*, and in the light of that martial code whereby it was formally to be judged, innocence and guilt personified in Claggart and Budd in effect changed places. In a legal view the apparent victim of the tragedy was he who had sought to victimize a man blameless; and the indisputable deed of the latter, navally regarded, constituted the most heinous of military crimes. Yet more. The essential right and wrong involved in the matter, the clearer that might be, so much the worse for the responsibility of a loyal sea commander, inasmuch as he was not authorized to determine the matter on that primitive basis.

Small wonder then that the *Bellipotent's* captain, though in general a man of rapid decision, felt that circumspectness not less than promptitude was necessary. Until he could decide upon his course, and in each detail; and not only so, but until the concluding measure was upon the point of being enacted, he deemed it advisable, in view of all the circumstances, to guard as much as possible against publicity. Here he may or may not have erred. Certain it is, however, that subsequently in the confidential talk of more than one or two gun rooms and cabins he was not a little criticized by some officers, a fact imputed by his friends and vehemently by his cousin Jack Denton to professional jealousy of Starry Vere. Some imaginative ground for invidious comment there was. The maintenance of secrecy in the matter, the confining all knowledge of it for a time to the place where the homicide occurred, the quarterdeck cabin; in these particulars lurked some resemblance to the policy adopted in those tragedies of the palace which have occurred more than once in the capital founded by Peter the Barbarian.

The case indeed was such that fain would the *Bellipotent's* captain have deferred taking any action whatever respecting it further than to keep the foretopman a close prisoner till the ship rejoined the squadron and then submitting the matter to the judgment of his admiral.

But a true military officer is in one particular like a true monk. Not with more of self-abnegation will the latter keep his vows of monastic obedience than the former his vows of allegiance to martial duty.

Feeling that unless quick action was taken on it, the deed of the foretopman, so soon as it should be known on the gun decks, would tend to awaken any slumbering embers of the *Nore* among the crew, a sense of the urgency of the case overruled in Captain Vere every other consideration. But though a conscientious disciplinarian, he was no lover of authority for mere authority's sake. Very far was he from embracing opportunities for monopolizing to himself the perils of moral responsibility, none at least that could properly be referred to an official superior or shared with him by his official equals or even subordinates. So thinking, he was glad it would not be at variance with usage to turn the matter over to a summary court of his own officers, reserving to himself, as the one on whom the ultimate accountability would rest, the right of maintaining a supervision of it, or formally or informally interposing at need. Accordingly a drumhead court was summarily convened, he electing the individuals composing it: the first lieutenant, the captain of marines and the sailing master.

In associating an officer of marines with the sea lieutenant and the sailing master in a case having to do with a sailor, the commander perhaps deviated from general custom. He was prompted thereto by the circumstance that he took that soldier to be a judicious person, thoughtful, and not altogether incapable of grappling with a difficult case unprecedented in his prior experience. Yet even as to him he was not without some latent misgiving, for withal he was an extremely good-natured man, an enjoyer of his dinner, a sound sleeper, and inclined to obesity—a man who though he would always maintain his manhood in battle might not prove altogether reliable in a moral dilemma involving aught of the tragic. As to the first lieutenant and the sailing master, Captain Vere could not but be aware that though honest natures, of approved gallantry upon occasion, their intelligence was mostly confined to the matter of active seamanship and the fighting demands of their profession.

The court was held in the same cabin where the unfortunate affair had taken place. This cabin, the commander's, embraced the entire area under the poop deck. Aft, and on either side, was a small state-room, the one now temporarily a jail and the other a dead-house, and a yet smaller compartment, leaving a space between expanding forward into a goodly oblong of length coinciding with the ship's beam. A skylight of moderate dimension was overhead, and at each cut of the oblong space were two sashed porthole windows easily convertible back into embrasures for short carronades.

All being quickly in readiness, Billy Budd was arraigned, Captain Vere necessarily appearing as the sole witness in the case, and as such temporarily sinking his rank, though singularly maintaining it in a matter apparently trivial, namely that he testified from the ship's weather side, with that object having caused the court to sit on the lee side. Concisely he narrated all that had led up to the catastrophe, omitting nothing in Claggart's accusation and deposing as to the manner in which the prisoner had received it. At this testimony the three officers glanced with no little surprise at Billy Budd, the last man they would have suspected either of the mutinous design alleged by Claggart or the undeniable deed he himself had done. The first lieutenant, taking judicial primacy and turning toward the prisoner, said, "Captain Vere has spoken. Is it or is it not as Captain Vere says?"

In response came syllables not so much impeded in the utterance as might have been anticipated. They were these: "Captain Vere tells the truth. It is just as Captain Vere says, but it is not as the master-at-arms said. I have eaten the King's bread and I am true to the King."

"I believe you, my man," said the witness, his voice indicating a suppressed emotion not otherwise betrayed.

"God will bless you for that, your honor!" not without stammering said Billy, and all but broke down. But immediately he was recalled to self-control by another question, to which with the same emotional difficulty of utterance he said, "No, there was no malice between us. I never bore malice against the master-at-arms. I am sorry that he is dead. I did not mean to kill him. Could I have used my tongue I would not have struck him. But he foully lied to my face and in presence of my captain, and I had to say something, and I could only say it with a blow, God help me!"

In the impulsive aboveboard manner of the frank one the court saw confirmed all that was implied in words that just previously had perplexed them, coming as they did from the testifier to the tragedy and promptly following Billy's impassioned disclaimer of mutinous intent—Captain Vere's words, "I believe you, my man."

Next it was asked of him whether he knew of or suspected aught savoring of incipient trouble (meaning mutiny, though the explicit term was avoided) going on in any section of the ship's company.

The reply lingered. This was naturally imputed by the court to the same vocal embarrassment which had retarded or obstructed previous answers. But in main it was otherwise here, the question immediately recalling to Billy's mind the interview with the afterguardsman in the forechains. But an innate repugnance to playing a part at all approaching that of an informer against one's own ship-mates—the same erring sense of uninstructed honor which had stood in the way of his reporting the matter at the time, though as a loyal man-of-war's man it was incumbent on him, and failure so to do, if charged against him and proven, would have subjected him to the heaviest of penalties; this, with the blind feeling now his that nothing really was being hatched, prevailed with him. When the answer came it was a negative.

"One question more," said the officer of marines, now first speaking and with a troubled earnestness. "You tell us that what the master-at-arms said against you was a lie. Now why should he have so lied, so maliciously lied, since you declare there was no malice between you?"

At that question, unintentionally touching on a spiritual sphere wholly obscure to Billy's thoughts, he was nonplused, evincing a confusion indeed that some observers, such as can readily be imagined, would have construed into involuntary evidence of hidden guilt. Nevertheless, he strove some way to answer, but all at once relinquished the vain endeavor, at the same time turning an appealing glance toward Captain Vere as deeming him his best helper and friend. Captain Vere, who had been seated for a time, rose to his feet, addressing the interrogator. "The question you put to him comes naturally enough. But how can he rightly answer it?—or anybody else, unless indeed it be he who lies within there," designating the compartment where lay the corpse. "But the prone one there will not rise to our summons. In effect though, as it seems to me, the point you make is hardly material. Quite aside from any conceivable motive actuating the master-at-arms, and irrespective of the provocation to the blow, a martial court must needs in the present case confine its attention to the blow's consequence, which consequence justly is to be deemed not otherwise than as the striker's deed."

This utterance, the full significance of which it was not at all likely that Billy took in, nevertheless caused him to turn a wistful interrogative look toward the speaker, a look in its dumb expressiveness not unlike that which a dog of generous breed might turn upon his master, seeking in his face some elucidation of a previous gesture ambiguous to the canine intelligence. Nor was the same utterance without marked effect upon the three officers, more especially the soldier. Couched in it seemed to them a meaning unanticipated, involving a prejudgment on the speaker's part. It served to augment a mental disturbance previously evident enough.

The soldier once more spoke, in a tone of suggestive dubiety addressing at once his associates and Captain Vere: "Nobody is present—none of the ship's company, I mean—who might shed lateral light, if any is to be had, upon what remains mysterious in this matter."

"That is thoughtfully put," said Captain Vere; "I see your drift. Ay, there is a mystery; but, to use a scriptural phrase, it is a 'mystery of iniquity,' a matter for psychologic theologians to discuss. But what has a military court to do with it? Not to add that for us any possible investigation of it is cut off by the lasting tongue-tie of him-in-yonder," again designating the mortuary stateroom. "The prisoner's deed—with that alone we have to do."

To this, and particularly the closing reiteration, the marine soldier, knowing not how aptly to reply, sadly abstained from saying aught. The first lieutenant, who at the outset had not unnaturally assumed primacy in the court, now overrulingly instructed by a glance from Captain Vere, a glance more effective than words, resumed that primacy. Turning to the prisoner "Budd," he said, and scarce in equable tones, "Budd, if you have aught further to say for yourself, say it now."

Upon this the young sailor turned another quick glance toward Captain Vere; then, as taking a hint from that aspect, a hint confirming his own instinct that silence was now best, replied to the lieutenant, "I have said all, sir."

The marine—the same who had been the sentinel without the cabin door at the time that the foretopman, followed by the master-at-arms, entered it—he, standing by the sailor throughout these judicial proceedings, was now directed to take him back to the after compartment originally assigned to the prisoner and his custodian. As the twain disappeared from view, the three officers, as partially liberated from some inward constraint associated with Billy's mere presence, simultaneously stirred in their seats. They exchanged looks of troubled indecision, yet feeling that decide they must and without long delay. For Captain Vere, he for the time stood—unconsciously with his back toward them, apparently in one of his absent fits—gazing out from a sashed porthole to windward upon the monotonous blank of the twilight sea. But the court's silence continuing broken only at moments by brief consultations, in low earnest tones this served to arouse him and energize him. Turning, he to-and-fro paced the cabin athwart; in the returning ascent to windward climbing the slant deck in the ship's lee roll, without knowing it symbolizing thus in his action a mind resolute to surmount difficulties even if against primitive instincts strong as the wind and the sea. Presently he came to a stand before the three. After scanning their faces he stood less as mustering his thoughts for expression than as one only deliberating how best to put them to well-meaning men not intellectually mature, men with whom it was necessary to demonstrate certain principles that were axioms to himself. Similar impatience as to talking is perhaps one reason that deters some minds from addressing any popular assemblies.

When speak he did, something, both in the substance of what he said and his manner of saying it, showed the influence of unshared studies modifying and tempering the practical training of an active career. This, along with his phraseology, now and then was suggestive of the grounds whereon rested that imputation of a certain pedantry socially alleged against him by certain naval men of wholly practical cast, captains who nevertheless would frankly concede that His Majesty's navy mustered no more efficient officer of their grade than Starry Vere.

What he said was to this effect: "Hitherto I have been but the witness, little more; and I should hardly think now to take another tone, that of your coadjutor for the time, did I not perceive in you—

at the crisis too—a troubled hesitancy, proceeding, I doubt not, from the clash of military duty with moral scruple—scruple vitalized by compassion. For the compassion, how can I otherwise than share it? But, mindful of paramount obligations, I strive against scruples that may tend to enervate decision. Not, gentlemen, that I hide from myself that the case is an exceptional one. Speculatively regarded, it well might be referred to a jury of casuists. But for us here, acting not as casuists or moralists, it is a case practical, and under martial law practically to be dealt with.

"But your scruples: do they move as in a dusk? Challenge them. Make them advance and declare themselves. Come now; do they import something like this: If, mindless of palliating circumstances, we are bound to regard the death of the master-at-arms as the prisoner's deed, shell does that deed constitute a capital crime whereof the penalty is a mortal one. But in natural justice is nothing but the prisoner's overt act to be considered? How can we adjudge to summary and shameful death a fellow creature innocent before God, and whom we feel to be so?—Does that state it aright? You sign sad assent. Well, I too feel that, the full force of that. It is Nature. But do these buttons that we wear attest that our allegiance is to Nature? No, to the King. Though the ocean, which is inviolate Nature primeval, though this be the element where we move and have our being as sailors, yet as the King's officers lies our duty in a sphere correspondingly natural? So little is that true, that in receiving our commissions we in the most important regards ceased to be natural free agents. When war is declared are we the commissioned fighters previously consulted? We fight at command. If our judgments approve the war, that is but coincidence. So in other particulars. So now. For suppose condemnation to follow these present proceedings. Would it be so much we ourselves that would condemn as it would be martial law operating through us? For that law and the rigor of it, we are not responsible. Our vowed responsibility is in this: That however pitilessly that law may operate in any instances, we nevertheless adhere to it and administer it.

"But the exceptional in the matter moves the hearts within you. Even so too is mine moved. But let not warm hearts betray heads that should be cool. Ashore in a criminal case, will an upright judge allow himself off the bench to be waylaid by some tender kinswoman of the accused seeking to touch him with her tearful plea? Well, the heart here, sometimes the feminine in man, is as that piteous woman, and hard though it be, she must here be ruled out."

He paused, earnestly studying them for a moment; then resumed.

"But something in your aspect seems to urge that it is not solely the heart that moves in you, but also the conscience, the private conscience. But tell me whether or not, occupying the position we do, private conscience should not yield to that imperial one formulated in the mode under which alone we officially proceed?"

Here the three men moved in their seats, less convinced than agitated by the course of an argument troubling but the more the spontaneous conflict within.

Perceiving which, the speaker paused for a moment; then abruptly changing his tone, went on.

"To steady us a bit let us recur to the facts.—In wartime at sea a man-of-war's man strikes his superior in grade, and the blow kills. Apart from its effect the blow itself is, according to the Articles of War, a capital crime, Furthermore—"

"Ay, sir," emotionally broke in the officer of marines, "in one sense it was. But surely Budd purposed neither mutiny nor homicide."

"Surely not, my good man. And before a court less arbitrary and more merciful than a martial one, that plea would largely extenuate. At the Last Assizes it shall acquit. But how here? We proceed under the law of the Mutiny Act. In feature no child can resemble his father more than that Act resembles in spirit the thing from which it derives—War. In His Majesty's service—in this ship, indeed—there are Englishmen forced to fight for the King against their will. Against their conscience, for aught we know. Though as their fellow creatures some of us may appreciate their position, yet as navy officers what reck we of it? Still less recks the enemy. Our impressed men he would fain cut down in the same swath with our volunteers. As regards the enemy's naval conscripts, some of whom may even share our own abhorrence of the regicidal French Directory, it is the same on our side. War looks but to the frontage, the appearance. And the Mutiny Act War's child, takes after the father. Budd's intent or non-intent is nothing to the purpose.

"But while, put to it by those anxieties in you which I cannot but respect, I only repeat myself—while thus strangely we prolong proceedings that should be summary—the enemy may be sighted and an engagement result. We must do; and one of two things must we do—condemn or let go."

"Can we not convict and yet mitigate the penalty?" asked the sailing master, here speaking, and falteringly, for the first.

"Gentlemen, were that clearly lawful for us under the circumstances, consider the consequences of such clemency. The people" (meaning the ship's company) "have native sense; most of them are familiar with our naval usage and tradition; and how would they take it? Even could you explain to them—which our official position forbids—they, long molded by arbitrary discipline, have not that kind of intelligent responsiveness that might qualify them to comprehend and discriminate. No, to the people the foretopman's deed, however it be worded in the announcement will be plain homicide committed in a flagrant act of mutiny. What penalty for that should follow, they know. But it does not follow. *Why?* they will ruminate. You know what sailors are. Will they not revert to the recent outbreak at the *Nore?* Ay. They know the well-founded alarm—the panic it struck throughout England. Your clement sentence they would account pusillanimous. They would think that we flinch, that we are afraid of them—afraid of practicing a lawful rigor singularly demanded at this juncture, lest it should provoke new troubles. What shame to us such a conjecture on their part, and how deadly to discipline. You see then, whither, prompted by duty and the law, I steadfastly drive. But I beseech you, my friends, do not take me amiss. I feel as you do for this unfortunate boy. But did he know our hearts, I take him to be of that generous nature that he would feel even for us on whom this military necessity so heavy a compulsion is laid."

With that, crossing the deck he resumed his place by the sashed porthole, tacitly leaving the three to come to a decision. On the cabin's opposite side the troubled court sat silent. Loyal lieges, plain and practical, though at bottom they dissented from some points Captain Vere had put to them, they were without the faculty, hardly had the inclination, to gainsay one whom they felt to be an earnest man, one too not less their superior in mind than in naval rank. But it is not improbable that even such of his words as were not without influence over them, less came home to them than his closing appeal to their instinct as sea officers: in the forethought he threw out as to the practical consequences to discipline, considering the unconfirmed tone of the fleet at the time, should a mall-of-war's mall's violent killing at sea of a superior in grade be allowed to pass for aught else than a capital crime demanding prompt infliction of the penalty.

Not unlikely they were brought to something more or less akin to that harassed frame of mind which in the year 1842 actuated the commander of the U.S. brig-of-war *Somers* to resolve, under the so-called Articles of War, Articles modeled upon the English Mutiny Act, to resolve upon the execution at sea of a midshipman and two sailors as mutineers designing the seizure of the brig. Which resolution was carried out though in a time of peace and within not many days' sail of home. An act vindicated by a naval court of inquiry subsequently convened ashore. History, and here cited without comment. True, the circumstances on board the *Somers* were different from those on board the *Bellipotent.* But the urgency felt, well-warranted or otherwise, was much the same.

Says a writer whom few know, "Forty years after a battle it is easy for a noncombatant to reason about how it ought to have been fought. It is another thing personally and under fire to have to direct the fighting while involved in the obscuring smoke of it. Much so with respect to other emergencies involving considerations both practical and moral, and when it is imperative promptly to act. The greater the fog the more it imperils the steamer, and speed is put on though at the hazard of running somebody down. Little ween the snug card players in the cabin of the responsibilities of the sleepless man on the bridge."

In brief, Billy Budd was formally convicted and sentenced to be hung at the yardarm in the early morning watch, it being now night. Otherwise, as is customary in such cases, the sentence would forthwith have been carried out. In wartime on the field or in the fleet, a mortal punishment decreed by a drumhead court—on the field sometimes decreed by but a nod from the general—follows without delay on the heel of conviction, without appeal.

Our Values or Theirs?

Captain Rick Rubel

His mission was to sell major weapon systems to the Saudi Arabia Ministry of Defense as Foreign Military Sales (FMS). Selling major weapons systems to the Saudis has three major advantages for the United States. First, the sale would save the United States almost $500 million dollars, because buying more equipment increases production from our factories and saves a significant amount of money. Secondly, by selling weapons systems to our allies, we strengthen our diplomatic, military, and economic ties with them. Thirdly, we will be providing many additional jobs for our manufacturers and workers. The Saudi Navy would like to buy the weapons systems from us, but we have to convince their Ministry of Defense that they should spend the money.

As the Project leader of the team to go over to Saudi Arabia to make a presentation to the Saudi Naval Staff and the Minister of Defense, Captain Bob Jacobs did not have much time to put the team together. He asked the Office of General Counsel to provide their best lawyer who is an expert in Foreign Military Sales (FMS). When the team first assembled at the departure gate at JFK airport, he learned that the lawyer assigned to the team was a female. She was, in fact the best FMS lawyer in the Department.

The Saudi culture will not permit women to engage in a business transaction. In Saudi Arabia, women are not permitted to pay for merchandise in the store—their son or husband must accompany them. Strictly, they are not allowed to drive or even ride in the front seat of a car, must remain covered, and are rarely permitted to speak in public. The Mutwaa or Mutaween (religious police) will hit women with a stick in public if they are not covered by their Abaya, a long black outerwear from head to toe. This is a long-standing part of their culture.

The Project Leader is now at the departure gate at JFK airport and only has 55 minutes until the flight departs for Riyadh. As he considers what to do, he realizes that it is quite possible that by bringing the female lawyer, the Saudis may not deal with the team. Bringing her could actually jeopardize the entire project. He reasons that he cannot just leave her in the hotel in Riyadh, because he will need the lawyer's expertise on Foreign Military Sales to make sure he does not mis-speak at an important point.

As he sits at the departure gate in a chair off to the side, he continues to think about what to do. "What are the considerations that I should think about here?" he wonders.

"Our culture and our treatment of women clearly differ from theirs. What about the values of our country with regard to 'equal opportunity'? Am I going to throw that away just to make the deal? Our country was founded on those ideals. By not taking her on the trip, it is as if I am giving in to *their* cultural practice."

But then he reasons, "Maybe it's not up to me to judge their culture. They have been living like that for thousands of years and I have read that this actually has a basis in their religion. Our country is new on the block compared to theirs, so maybe I cannot even judge them to be wrong in their treatment of women. What makes us morally right? But how would I explain to the female lawyer that she can't go because she's a woman—that doesn't sound right? This would be a real 'feather in her cap' to be part of this big international deal. Well, maybe she'll just have to be told it's for 'the good of the whole.' But it just doesn't sound right to tell her she can't go with us because she's a female."

Questions for Discussion

1. If you were the senior officer in charge of the "team," would you take the female lawyer?
   - Our culture says that women should be given equal opportunity
   - Their culture says they will not deal with women

   What should you do?
2. What is the right thing to do?

- The right thing is to bring the lawyer

We Treat Her Just Like Everyone Else[1]

Captain Rick Rubel
Edited by Lt. Jessica Lockwood, USN

Background

Ensign Sharon Andrews is a hard-charging Naval Officer stationed on an Aegis Cruiser. She graduated from the University of Texas NROTC program with a degree in Psychology. Her father retired from the Navy as a Commander after 20 years of service; and she would tell people proudly that she wanted to "follow in his footsteps." She had been aboard the USS Gettysburg for about 11 months, and was close to obtaining her important Officer of the Deck Qualifications. As the Assistant CIC Officer, she had demonstrated to most everyone during the current deployment that she could hold her own during fleet operations.

The Commanding Officer of the ship was Captain Beau Robinson. With 28 years in the Navy, five years as an enlisted man, he knew ships and he knew the sea. As he approached the end of his career, he made it a priority to 'train the next generation of mariners to take the helm'. His leadership style could be summed up with his common phrase, "I'll tell you once, and you'd better get it right after that." His wife, Abby was the self-proclaimed 'grandmother' of the crew. She had two of her own grandchildren, and enjoyed bringing cookies to the sailors on duty when the ship was in port.

On the Bridge

The ship was at sea preparing for underway replenishment; pulling alongside an auxiliary ship to take on fuel and supplies. Ensign Sharon Andrews, Junior Officer of the Deck, was on the radio with the auxiliary ship exchanging information. In order to train as many officers as possible, Ensign Paul Rogers was assigned as a third watch-stander, Junior Officer of the Watch (JOOW).

The Captain turned to Lt Paul Simmons, Officer of the Deck, and asked, "Paul, have we established comms with the auxiliary ship?" Lt Simmons, unaware that Ens Andrews was already on the phone with them said "No, sir." The Captain showed his immediate displeasure with Lt Simmons and said, "Well get over there and do it now!" When Lt Simmons went over to the Comm panel, Ensign Sharon Andrews reported that she had already completed the communication check.

As the ship prepared to increase speed to come along side, the Captain told the Lt. Simmons to "Give Sharon the Conn to bring the ship alongside." This was fairly common to give the junior officers a chance to gain this experience. Ensign Andrews had conned the ship several times along side during the deployment, but Ens Rogers had not had the chance yet.

"In the Pilot House, This is Ensign Rogers, Ensign Andrews has the conn!" shouted the OOD, so the Quartermaster could enter it into the Ship's Log. Without hesitation, Sharon responded in a loud voice, "This is Ensign Andrews, I have the conn." The helmsman and lee-helm responded in acknowledgment.

---

[1] This case study is a composite case of observed situations but is not an autobiographical account of either the author or the editor.

As the adrenaline started to kick in, she remembered some of the problems she had in the past with this evolution. She also began to wonder why she was given the conn instead of Paul Rogers, who had just graduated from the Naval Academy a few months ago and could use the training. As she took her position on the port bridge wing, the Captain took his standard position right behind the conning officer.

The approach to the Auxiliary ship was fine, but it took a while for Ensign Andrews to find the right combination of course and speed to line up the replenishment stations. At one point the C.O. of the auxiliary ship called on the radio and asked if everything was ok. As Sharon became increasingly frustrated, the Captain gave her advice and even encouragement. As the first lines began to come across to hook up the rigs, she 'lost control of the bow.' The C.O. saw this happening immediately and told her to come right a few degrees. As she hesitated and came right only one degree, the bow continued to close the other ship. The Captain repeated his advice. She thought she had given enough of a correction and was waiting for the correct to take effect. (often a 4-6 second lag time). Things were getting worse as the ships went from a distance of 150 feet, down to 80 feet. Everyone on both ships froze to see what would happen. The Captain repeated his advice to come a few degrees to the right. She gave the order to come right one more degree, but that clearly was not enough. The Captain kept his calm, and turned toward the helmsman and said in a low voice, "Come right to course 103." The helmsman responded, but Sharon now was not sure if he was now giving the commands or was she. The C.O. must have realized this, because he tapped her on the shoulder and calmly said, "Ok you've got it."

As Ensign Andrews steadied out the ship, the other watch standers couldn't believe it! The C.O. had told her three or four times, and she didn't do it, and instead of yelling at her, he gave her back the conn. He was almost fatherly in his approach to this. What happened to the "I'll tell you once . . . you'd better get it right after that." thought Lt Simmons, the Officer of the Deck?

The Wardroom Table

As the Junior Officers were finishing lunch, they stayed at the table for a few minutes to talk. There were 5 Junior Officers sitting together at the "kids table" (a side table where the Junior officers like to sit so they could talk without being overheard by the Department Heads and XO). As Ltjg Greg Thorp pushed his plate away, he said, "I've got to stop eating and start working out so I can get ready for my PRT (Physical readiness test). It really busted my ass last time I took it." There was no comment from the others; Greg Thorp was known to all as a careerist. He wanted to score well on his PRT so he would receive good marks on his Fitness report in that area. He then looked up and asked Ensign Sharon Andrews, "Sharon, how did you do on your PRT last time? Sharon hoped she could side step the question and just said, "I did fine, thanks." He was not going to let her off the hook. "What was your time in the Mile and a half?" She became increasingly uncomfortable because she knew where this was going. But since her time was "satisfactory," she answered the question, "I ran it in 13:59. How about you, Greg?" Greg gave her an arrogant smile and said, "I ran it in 12:32, but that was a "poor" for MEN. Your time would have failed for MEN." The others looked at Ltjg Thorp but said nothing. Sharon's mind whirled trying to decide whether to just get up and leave, argue using the 'I didn't make the rules' approach, or argue that women don't have the same body strengths as men. Before she could think of a come-back, he continued his attack. "We're all competing for the same ranking and jobs, why should your score be average and mine poor, when I can run right up your ass?" Sharon had been through too much for this to bring her to tears or cause her to leave in frustration. But she knew whatever she said at this point would be turned around on her. So she just stared at him; then stared at the other male officers wondering if anyone would call him on this.

Ltjg Thorp then used her silence against her by saying, "You know I'm right." Then came the crushing comment as Ltjg Thorp said, "I couldn't believe the Captain up there with you on the bridge today. Any of us, and he would have had our ass for losing the bow, and almost colliding. But with you, he just bailed you out and patted you on the . . . . head." (The pause contained a suggestive location of another place to pat.) Sharon knew he was right. The skipper had treated her a bit special today. Again, Sharon wanted to yell, "It's not my fault he treats me like that." But she stared at him, red-faced, embarrassed, but refusing to get up and let him talk about her after she left.

After many more awkward seconds, Lt Thorp told another officer that they both needed to go meet with the XO on another subject and they both left. After they departed, one of two remaining junior officers told her, "Sharon, you know Greg. Don't pay attention to that stuff." Sharon just stared back and slowly shook her head at him in silence.

On Liberty

The ship was pulling into a foreign port on the following day. Ensign Sharon Andrews was walking across the helo deck, and she saw the C.O. walking in the opposite direction towards her, looking like he was late for an appointment. When he saw Ensign Andrews, he returned her salute, and then stopped for a second to say, "Hello Sharon. Hey, tomorrow when we pull into port, the embassy is giving me a car and driver, so I was going to get a few officers together to go site-seeing. Would you like to join us?" Before Sharon could answer, he asked, "Have you been here before?" Once she digested the two questions she politely responded, "No sir, I haven't been here before. . . . and, yes sir, I would like to join you." The C.O. smiled, nodded, and continued his walk aft.

Sharon had mixed feeling at this point. She was pleased that he asked her, but once again worried about the appearance of the favoritism to the other junior officers. But then she replayed the conversation in her head and remembered that he was going to invite other officers; so that should make it ok. After the ship pulled into port and 'liberty call' was sounded, she went off the ship in civilian clothes and waited at the foot of the brow on the pier for the CO and the site-seeing trip. As the Captain was 'bonged off' the ship he was with the XO and the Supply Officer, LT. Bethany Parks. As they gathered around the car, Sharon realized that it was just the four of them. At first it seemed like a thoughtful gesture for the CO to include her. Then she thought, "Why did he ask just Bethany and me?" Then she felt this pang in her stomach. It was the same pang she felt the other day when Ltjg Thorp was verbally working her over at the wardroom table. She suddenly felt like she was on a 'double date' with two older men. She tried to forget that thought and participate in the discussion in the car. But she even became self-conscious of the seating arrangement in the car. As a point of protocol and seniority, the CO and XO sat in the back seat, and the next senior officer (Lt Parks) sat in the front seat next to the driver, which meant that Sharon had to sit between the CO and XO. So what started as a nice gesture, in her mind became an awkward, claustrophobic escape scene.

The four spent the day touring in the car, having drinks at several clubs, and then dinner before returning to the ship. The dinner conversation varied from social talk to ship talk. As they returned to ship, the four of them came up the brow together in order of seniority, as they bonged the Captain back aboard. As they passed by Ensign Rogers, the Quarterdeck Watch officer, he gave Sharon a big grin as she passed by last. What had started out as an awkward evening, finished with a big reminder that her peers were watching. She wished she could have been invisible at that moment.

The XO's Stateroom

She knocked on the door just below the brass plate that read 'XO'.

"Come in," said the voice inside the room. Ensign Andrews opened the door and said, "XO, do you have a minute to talk, sir?"

"Sure. Come in, Sharon, and leave the door open please."

Sharon had sort of rehearsed what she was going to say, but still tried hard to get started.

"Sir, I have had a number of situations happen in the past week that I . . . . . need to tell you about . . . . And ask your guidance on what I should do."

"Go ahead", said the XO and he leaned forward showing his complete interest.

"Sir, on Monday when we were going along side the auxiliary ship, the Captain seemed to be . . . . . treating me special . . . different from the others. When I lost the bow to port, instead of yelling at me, he bailed me out, and then gave me the conn back, without even logging it in the ship's log. The other officers clearly picked up on it, and . . . . even brought it up at the wardroom table. There also seems to be a spoken feeling among some of the male officers that having different standards for men and women for the PRT is somehow wrong.

"Then when we pulled into port Friday, the situation with the skipper, you, and Bethany was very awkward."

The XO frowned and asked, "What was so awkward about it?"

She replied, "To be honest with you, it seemed like a double-date. Why would the skipper ask me and Bethany to go along?"

As she continued, the XO looked more and more puzzled, which made Sharon feel that maybe she was just making too big a deal of all this. The XO then responded by saying, "Sharon, I think a lot of this problem might be in your mind. The Skipper treats all the Junior officers the same. And I guess he just thought that you and Bethany might enjoy seeing the sights. Nothing happened that day did it?" Sharon shook her head, as she realized that the XO was just going to protect the command; that was his job. She started to think, "Well maybe I am just making this a mountain." Then the pang that she felt at the wardroom table came back to her, and she interrupted the XO by blurting out, "XO! None of this is my fault but I feel . . . like I've done something wrong. . . . And I haven't!" All of the frustration of the past week came back all at once and she stood up and said a fairly loud voice, "I'm a good officer, and all this is not my fault!" At this point she had to cover her face to make sure he didn't see a tear. The XO also jumped up to close the door, so no one would see this scene. He just stood there, awkwardly waiting for her to compose herself. She wasn't crying, just covering her face from embarrassment. He instinctively went over to her put his arm around her to consol her. He stood there for a while not exactly sure what to do next.

Then the reality of all this hit her, "Here I am in the XO's stateroom, with his arm around me, not because he believes me, but because he thinks I'm losing it. How did I get myself into this situation? What did I do wrong?"

Questions for Discussion

Scene I: On the Bridge
- Is the C.O. wrong in his actions?
- Should she do anything about this?

Scene II: Wardroom table:
- Is Lt Thorp out of line expressing his frustration?
- How should she handle this?
- Should she address this to her Department Head or XO?
- Is it necessary for the Military to have two standards in Physical Fitness tests?

Scene III: Going ashore on liberty
- Since nothing happened out of the ordinary, Is this situation wrong?
- How should she handle this?

Scene IV: In XO's stateroom
- What should the XO have said to her?
- Did she handle the situation properly?
- What could she have said when addressing the problem to her Chain of Command?

Other questions:
- Is it just about appearance and perception? Don't intentions count?
- Did the CO ever "cross the line"?
- Did the XO "cross the line" in Scene IV?
- If we try to treat everyone the same, then why does it matter how it looks?
- Will it ever "look right"?
- When does a leader "cross the line"?
- What is "the line"?
- If men and women are always going to be attracted to one another, then how do we "solve this"?

Appendix A
Case Sequels

Rescuing the Boat People: The Sequel
Captain Rick Rubel

What the Captain did:

The Captain decided to provide provisions to the refugees on the junk. He gave them 300 lbs of fresh fruit, 107 lbs of canned food, 60 pounds of rice (uncooked), 50 gals of fresh water, and navigational charts.

What happened after the ship departed:

- The food only lasted a few days.
- The boat drifted in the current for 19 more days.
- *Thirty more refugees died* before they reached land.
- As people died, their bodies were eaten by the others in order to survive.

In the confusion of the situation, and with poor translation, the following information was not known by the Captain:

- The boat did have a working engine for the first few days of the trip. The translator got this wrong when he reported the boat had no engine.
- He also mis-translated the fact they had actually been adrift for 17 days, not 7 days as the Captain was told.
- Therefore the Captain miscalculated that boat went 250 miles with the sail.
- Therefore the Captain miscalculated on how long it would take them to get to land, and did not give them enough food.
- The Captain was not aware that one of the swimmers who was trying to get to the ship, actually drown away from the ship.
- There were actually almost 80 people on the junk, not 60 as passed to the Captain.

Disposition of Captain:

- He refused Admirals' Mast, and asked for Court Martial instead (his right)
- He was found guilty of "Dereliction of Duty" for failing to give adequate aid, and given a Letter of Reprimand.

Come Right: The Sequel
Captain Rick Rubel

Points to consider:

1. The Captain has given me a legal, direct, and clear order, three times.

2. The Captain is not asking me my opinion on the subject. He has given me a legal, direct, and clear order, three times. And I have told him twice, that I can't follow his order.

3. The Captain has 21 years in the navy and I have 1½ years. Maybe he knows something I don't know? Maybe I should do as I'm told?

4. I am in conflict with all levels of my Constitutional Paradigm:
    * I am about to kill my *shipmates*
    * I am about to break my *ship*
    * I am going to damage my *service*, by having a collision
    * And my *Mission* (my orders) are . . . . to come right

5. What do you do?

What I did:
I was in conflict with all levels of my Constitutional Paradigm (Priorities of Loyalties).
I took off my binoculars (the symbol of OOD) and announced in the a loud voice,

> "In the pilot House. This is LTJG Rubel, the Captain has the deck and the conn."

I was in conflict with the First Principle of the Constitutional Paradigm, priority of loyalties.
I went to the Second Principle, and I could not resolve it. ("Captain, I can't sir.")
So, I went to the Third Principle and "resigned" my watch station. I had no other choice but to take "self" out of the problem.

My advice to the reader; if you are going to refuse an lawful, clear, and direct order from your Captain, YOU HAD BETTER BE RIGHT. You only get to do that once, if you are wrong.

Captain Lawrence Rockwood in Haiti: The Sequel

Dr. Stephen Wrage

After dark on the evening of September 30, Captain Rockwood put on his battle dress utilities, flak jacket and helmet, took his rifle, full ammunition pouch, two canteens, and a first-aid kit, and set out to inspect the National Penitentiary on his own. On his pallet he left a note that said he was doing "what is legal to stop something that is plainly illegal. Action required: All means necessary to implement the intent of the U.N. and U.S. president, intent on human rights." He pinned a small American flag patch to his note and wrote above it: "Take this flag. It is soiled with unnecessary blood. You cowards can court-martial my dead body."[1]

He jumped the wall of the barracks compound in order to avoid having to pass the guards at the gate. Standing orders required troops to travel in convoys of at least two vehicles with at least two soldiers in each vehicle.[2] Although as a counterintelligence officer Rockwood enjoyed unusual freedom of movement, he would have had to lie to the guards to exit through the gate.

Rockwood paid a Haitian truck driver forty dollars to take him to the penitentiary. It took him just over an hour to find the prison, but at its gate he simply knocked and was admitted. At one point he blocked the door with his foot- later he put a round in his rifle. The night warden, Haitian Major Serge Justafor, happened to be a graduate of The School of the Americas at Fort Benning, Georgia and spoke good English. He does not appear to have resisted Rockwood's single-handed "inspection," but told him the main cell block was locked up until morning.

Rockwood made his own way out of Justafor's office and into the infirmary. In the infirmary Rockwood found twenty-six people. Most lay on the concrete floor and "appeared to be suffering from various wasting diseases: tuberculosis, AIDS, acute dysentery, etc. Many were near death."[3] A trench along the wall was full of feces, urine, and flies.

Rockwood demanded to see a list of the prisoners and to inspect the rest of the premises. Told that there could be no entry until morning, he pulled up a chair in the courtyard and sat down to wait. He also requested that the warden inform U.S. authorities of his presence there. He was convinced at this point that his mission had been a success since now the Joint Task Force would have to take responsibility for the prison.

At Rockwood's suggestion, the warden called the embassy. Rockwood was in the prison for several hours when Major Spencer Lane, USA, the U.S. military liaison in Port-au-Prince, arrived. Lane persuaded Rockwood to unchamber the round in his rifle and to accompany him back to the barracks compound. There Rockwood was given two psychiatric evaluations and found mentally sound. On October 2nd he was on a plane back to Fort Drum, New York.

In his brief inspection of the prison Rockwood saw only the infirmary. He did not get to look into the main cell block where about four hundred gravely emaciated prisoners were crammed in one unspeakably filthy cell.

Two days after Rockwood's visit, Colonel Michael Sullivan, commander of the 16t, Military Police Brigade, visited the National Penitentiary. He found what he called "appalling conditions [that] render this facility unsuitable for human habitation and this must be a priority."[4]

The penitentiary would not be visited again by Joint Task Force officials until almost three months had passed. On December 19, 1994, American forces entered the prison and undertook to improve conditions there by providing water and carrying away filth. Reports about violations of human rights in Haitian prisons had ceased as soon as Captain Rockwood was relieved.[5]

Endnotes

1. Rockwood's statement is quoted in Bob Gorman, "The Media and Captain Rockwood," *Watertown Daily Times*, 3 December 1995 at F6–F7.

2. See Mark S. Martins, "'War Crimes' During Operations Other than War: Military Doctrine and Law Fifty Years After Nuremberg—And Beyond," *Military Law Review*, Summer 1995, note #153.

3. Interview with the author, February 18, 1999.

4. See transcript of U.S. v. Rockwood, no. 261–29–6597 at 19–20. International Police Monitors, a group sponsored by the United Nations, also visited the National Penitentiary, though not until February 1995. They described the penitentiary as "the worst prison we have ever seen." One cell, they reported, contained 412 prisoners, with only one square meter per prisoner. "Conditions were inhuman. . . . The smell is unbelievable. Some prisoners had not been out of their cell for 15 days." (Quoted from Transcript of U.S. v. Rockwood, no. 261–29–6597 at 20.)

5. Anna Husarska, "Court Martial for Trying to Stop Abuses in Haiti," *The Guardian*, February 23, 1995, page 24.

Hugh Thompson: The Sequel

Dr. George Lucas, Jr.

The trial of an American soldier for war crimes committed in the line of duty during an increasingly unpopular war created a public backlash. Many Americans believed Calley was simply being sacrificed as a public gesture to cover up the extensive civilian noncombatant casualties that had resulted from the decision, by General William Westmoreland, to pursue a "war of attrition" against the Viet Cong. Even Georgia's governor, Jimmy Carter, urged citizens to "show support for Lt. Calley."

The investigation revealed that not all the soldiers at My Lai had participated in the carnage. Some men had risked court-martial, or even death, by defying Lt. Calley's direct orders to shoot civilians. Others testified that they had participated, reluctantly, but believed the order lawful and believed the civilians in fact to be "Viet Cong or Viet Cong sympathizers."

Thompson's own role in stopping the massacre did not initially receive a great deal of public attention. Gen. Telford Taylor, presiding magistrate at the Nuremberg trials, wrote an account of My Lai at the time in which he mentioned merely "the pilot of an 'observation helicopter'" who had reported the incident and "repeatedly put his helicopter down to rescue women and children."[1] Hugh Thompson sought no publicity, nor did he seek in any way to call attention to, or to profit in any sense, from his actions. His hope at the time was that, once the story had been told, the lessons learned, and the guilty soldiers punished, that everyone would simply leave him alone. He returned to his normal military routine.

Following Calley's court martial and conviction, however, Thompson began to receive nasty letters and death threats. He remembers thinking: "Has everyone gone mad?" He began to wonder whether he himself should fear a court-martial for his own command, at the time, to fire if necessary on U.S. soldiers. He recalls, shortly thereafter, entering the Officers' Club at the base at which he was then stationed as a flight instructor: "Everyone in the Club just stared and me, and turned their backs." He was utterly devastated. It was, he says, as if his fellow officers thought *he* had committed some kind of atrocity.

Gradually the role of Thompson in Calley's court-martial and conviction was forgotten. Colburn and Thompson, who had by then left the military, lived out their respective lives in relative anonymity until a 1989 television documentary on My Lai reclaimed them as forgotten heroes. *U.S. News* reporter Nell Boyce writes that, subsequently, a Clemson University history professor, Dr. David Egan, took a keen interest in Thompson's story. He had served in a French village where Nazis killed scores of innocents in World War II, and was so moved by what Thompson and his two crewmembers had done, that he led a campaign to have all three soldiers awarded the coveted Soldier's Medal.

Almost a decade later–and nearly thirty years after the events in My Lai–following considerable controversy between the Secretary of the Army and Pentagon officials (who feared an award would reopen old wounds), CWO Hugh Thompson, Larry Colburn, and Glenn Andreotta (posthumously) each received the Soldier's Medal in a special ceremony conducted at the Vietnam Veterans Memorial on March 6, 1998. Shortly after, in a speech to midshipmen at the U. S. Naval Academy, CWO Thompson was asked how it was, at that fateful moment, that he found the moral resources within himself to land his helicopter, risk his own life, and stop the killing. A very modest, and plain-spoken man, he was momentarily overcome by the painful memories of that day, and could not answer for several seconds. When he recovered, he replied very simply, on behalf of all who had served, and the many who gave their lives in that war: "what those soldiers were doing in My Lai that day, . . . that was not what we were sent there to do."

---

[1] "War Crimes: Son My," *From Nuremberg to My Lai*, p. 259.

Major Knight and Cambodia: The Sequel

Dr. Stephen Wrage

At 2130 Major Knight chose to follow his orders precisely. He set the official list aside, took up the alternate list of targets, plotted them, and guided the B-52s across the border into Cambodia. He stayed at his desk until dawn, and then disposed of all the evidence of the Cambodia mission in the burn barrel at the edge of the revetment. (He did not save any evidence to defend or exonerate himself if the secrets came to light.) Finally, he entered into the Pentagon computers the false information that the regularly cabled sites in Vietnam had been bombed. He did this that night and on at least a dozen nights thereafter over the following two months.

Knight waited until four years later, after he had been passed over twice for promotion and had left the Air Force, to break his silence. In January of 1973 he wrote to Senator William Proxmire (D-WI) and described the way reports had been falsified to cover the secret bombing. He was moved to speak up by the news that Air Force Lieutenant General John D. LaVelle, commander of the Seventh Air Force in Vietnam, had been dismissed and demoted for similar falsifications.[1] Knight told Proxmire that he wanted the Senate and the American people to know that falsification of mission reports had happened on other occasions, then he outlined the story told in this case.

Hearings were scheduled before the Senate Armed Services Committee with Knight as the principal witness. Knight raised three main points. First, there was the reality of the order. "I had the rules of engagement, [which ruled out strikes on Cambodia] and I had a man who had given me an order. That is one thing. Another thing is the fact that what was being done would seem to be justified." He seemed to conclude that the military utility of the strikes, and the satisfaction it would give him to strike at the enemy's sanctuaries, made the choice to go ahead very attractive.

"In other words, you agreed with bombing those targets?" asked Senator Harold Hughes (D-IA).

"Yes. We have been given intelligence that indicated that there was a lot of supplies and what not stored over there, that was the main storage dump for the North Vietnamese."

Senator Hughes: "Militarily it was the thing to do, to bomb out these supplies and get rid of the enemy, in your opinion?"

Knight: "Yes."

Senator Hughes: "That is why you agreed with it?"

Knight: "Yes. They were shooting those supplies at us, and it is a very disquieting experience to be shot at, and your impulse is to try to shoot back in any way you can. I felt it was justified in that sense, from a military standpoint, trying to knock those supplies out."[2]

Second, Knight was bothered by the false reporting. ". . . I was disturbed about the method by which we were doing it. It seemed to me that this could have been done in another way. I am not referring to the bombing, I am referring to the way we had to report it, that part of the procedure."[3]

Third, he was troubled at the lack of accountability. He explained that he could very likely have started picking targets himself, as long as they were within twenty or thirty kilometers of the secret targets, and have gotten away with sending B-52s to obliterate them.

Later in the hearing, Senator Strom Thurmond of South Carolina, asked Hal Knight, "Who did you think was deceived?" Knight replied, "Frankly, sir, I felt that the Senate Armed Services Committee was deceived." Thurmond asked sharply, "You were in the military channel weren't you?" "Yes, sir," Knight replied. "It was your duty to act within the military channel and to pass on anything to higher headquarters which you felt was improper, wasn't it?" "Yes sir," Hal Knight replied, "but I didn't take an oath to support the military. I took an oath to support and defend the Constitution."[4]

The story of the secret bombing of Cambodia was widely reported at the time of the hearings, but many were surprised to discover it had been broken much earlier. Two months after the bombing began, William Beecher, of *The New York Times*, happened to be near the Cambodian border on the night of one of the cross-border raids. He heard the explosions, felt the concussions, and saw the flashes across the border in Cambodia. He reported the facts on May 9, 1969. The story appeared at the bottom of the front page.

The article drew surprisingly little reaction, except inside the White House. There Henry Kissinger and his deputy, Colonel Alexander Haig, arranged for secret and illegal wiretaps to be placed on the office and home phones of Kissinger's closest aides and protégés, Roger Morris, Anthony Lake, and Morton Halperin. The taps remained on the phones long after all three aides resigned from Kissinger's staff.[5]

The cover-up grew much more complex and more compromising than the initial act. After he retired, Kissinger continued to retain three lawyers full time to fight the suits from people he ordered illegally wiretapped. All three won their suits against Kissinger. Morris and Halperin extracted substantial payments; Lake wanted only one dollar and a one-page letter signed by Kissinger confessing what he had done and apologizing for it. Kissinger fought the issue for several years, but in the end complied. The framed letter later hung on the wall of National Security Advisor Lake's office in the White House—that is, in Kissinger's old office.

By the early 1980s much more was known about the circumstances surrounding the secret bombing of Cambodia. In the first weeks of the Nixon administration, at the urging of General Earle Wheeler, Chairman of the Joint Chiefs, and of General Creighton Abrams, U.S. Commander in Vietnam, Henry Kissinger sought President Nixon's authority to extend the war into Cambodia. Defense Secretary Melvin Laird argued that if this were necessary and prudent, a case should be made for it to the Congress and the people. Kissinger and Nixon disagreed.

Operating in strict secrecy, Kissinger sent Haig in February of 1969 to instruct Colonel Ray Sitton, a planner with the Strategic Air Command stationed at the Pentagon, to create a way to send B-52s over Cambodia without public knowledge. Sitton refused, saying that a prime mission of the Strategic Air Command is to deliver nuclear weapons and accountability must be inviolable.

At this time (late February 1969) Nixon was in Europe on his first presidential trip abroad. Haig ordered up a military jet to fly Sitton to Brussels. When the plane taxied up next to Air Force One, Sitton was taken to the conference room aboard the presidential plane.

There Kissinger and Haig pressured him to create the secret system that Lieutenant Colonel Patterson later briefed to Major Knight. The Commander-in-Chief did not enter the room, but Sitton was told he endorsed the plan. Secretary of State William Rogers, who was also aboard the plane at the time, was not informed.

The bombing program began a few days later. The earliest missions were code-named "Breakfast." Later sets of missions were named "Lunch," "Dinner," "Dessert," "Supper," and "Snack." They were collectively called "MENU" and amounted to 3875 sorties in all, dropping 108,823 tons of bombs.

The MENU series was discontinued after fourteen months, but not because it was a success. At that point ground forces were sent into the area to do what the bombing had been intended to accomplish. The Secretary of the Air Force, the State Department, and the U.S. Congress were not informed of MENU. In 1971, after both the bombing program and the land invasion of Cambodia were complete, military officials told the Senate Armed Services Committee in closed hearings that there "was no B-52 bombing in Cambodia of any kind during the entire year of 1969."

On July 30, 1974, the House Judiciary Committee, which had approved Article I (the Watergate cover-up), Article H (Abuses of Power), and Article III (Contempt of Congress) voted down Article IV of the Articles of Impeachment of Richard Nixon. Article IV charged Nixon with waging a secret war in Cambodia.

Endnotes

1. In November 1971, General LaVelle had ordered air strikes on fuel depots and airfields in North Vietnam at a time when such targets had been placed officially off limits by executive order. A sergeant on LaVelle's staff wrote to Senator Howard Hughes (D-IA) to say that false reports of the strikes had been filed, and that the strikes had been disguised as "protective reaction strikes," (i.e., responses to attacks from the enemy.) LaVelle was relieved of command and demoted by order of President Nixon three weeks after the news of his unauthorized strikes broke. (See Hersh, *The Price of Power*, p. 507.)

2. United States Senate, 93rd Congress, First Session, *Bombing of Cambodia*. Hearings before the Committee on Armed Services, July 16, 23, 25, 26, 30; August 7, 8, 9, 1973, p. 5.

3. Hearings, page 7.

4. Hearings, page 30.

5. See Isaacson, *Kissinger*. pp. 157–183, Hersh, *The Price of Power*. 59–63 and 121–22.

Aviano EA-6B Gondola Mishap: The Sequel

LtCol Gary Slyman

Admission of Guilt

Captain Schweitzer chose to accept the consequences for his actions in destroying the videotape by pleading guilty. Following the advice of his legal counsel to protect his rights, Schweitzer remained silent for over a year and was presumed innocent. The legal system even pressured him to plead not guilty, even though he knew he was guilty. At his sentencing hearing, the Judge gave the following advice to Captain Schweitzer:

> Even if you believe you are guilty, you still have a legal and moral right to enter pleas of not guilty, and to require the government to prove its case against you, if it can, by legal and competent evidence beyond a reasonable doubt. If you were to plead not guilty, then you would be presumed under the law to be innocent; and only by introducing evidence and proving your guilt beyond a reasonable doubt, could the government overcome this presumption of innocence.[1]

Schweitzer pleaded guilty to charges of "Conduct Unbecoming an Officer and a Gentleman" for conspiracy to obstruct justice by the destruction of the tape. With his guilty plea the prosecution did not have the burden of proving his guilt. The jury's only task was to determine the sentence for his actions.

The prosecution's case centered on confirming Captain Schweitzer's guilt. Their approach was to ensure the jury understood he knowingly and willingly destroyed the tape to obstruct the Italian criminal investigation. The primary witness who made the case for the prosecution was Captain Seagraves.

The defense used numerous affidavits and witnesses to attest to the character and integrity of Captain Schweitzer. He also took the stand himself to tell his story. Since the tape was destroyed without anyone viewing it, nobody can say what was on it. According to his testimony, the tape could have contained at most a few minutes of low-level flying, an inverted ridge line crossing, a picture of Schweitzer's smiling face, and some high-level flying. Schweitzer explained his reasons for destroying the tape: "All I could think about was my face superimposed next to the blood in the snow."[2]

When questioned about what he thought of his actions, his response was: "It was the wrong thing. It was terribly wrong. It's not right as a person. It's not right as a Marine Corps Officer. It's not right as Joe Schweitzer. It was wrong."[3] In the face of numerous direct and cross-examination questions, he continually gave similar answers. He took the tape, he deceived those around him and the investigators, and he pleaded guilty, accepting responsibility for his actions as a Marine officer.[4] Ultimately, he realized that this act not only undermined his integrity, but also his case:

> I knew it was a wrong act. It was a stupid thing to do. I wish I still had it because I think it would answer a lot of questions that everybody wants answered, basically my humiliation, that I tried to prevent, is what I'm dealing with right now.[5]

Schweitzer could have received a maximum sentence of forfeiture of all pay and allowances, dismissal from the service, and other punishments as adjudged, such as reprimand, loss of numbers, or restriction.[6,7] On 2 April 1999, Schweitzer was sentenced to dismissal from the service.[8]

Shortly after Captain Schweitzer's sentencing, Captain Ashby went to trial for his actions concerning the videotape. He pleaded not guilty to the charges of "Conduct Unbecoming an Officer and a Gentlemen." He was found guilty and sentenced to six months confinement and a dismissal from the Marine Corps. Captain Ashby served his sentence in the brig at Camp Lejuene, North Carolina. Captains Seagraves and Raney remain on active duty in the Marine Corps.

Endnotes

1. Record of Trial (ROT) *US versus Captain Joseph P. Schweitzer* General Court-Martial p. 2723
2. ROT p. 3457
3. ROT p. 3459
4. ROT pp. 3440–3480
5. ROT pp. 2753
6. ROT Vol 51/51 AE CCXXXIV
7. Loss of numbers refers to demoting officers within their rank. Each rank has its officers on a seniority list from the most senior to the most junior. A loss of numbers would move the officer down the list thus making the officer junior to his peers and delaying his time to be considered promotion.
8. ROT p. 3438

Falsification of MV-22 Readiness Records: The Sequel

LtCol Gary Slyman

The Defense Criminal Investigative Service (DCIS) investigation found that VMMT-204 created false maintenance data and readiness records on the MV-22 Osprey. The criminal investigation determined that LtCol Leberman, feeling pressure from his superiors, directed his squadron to falsify the records in order to "bolster readiness numbers and, thus facilitate a favorable decision by the Department of the Navy to begin full rate production of the MV-22."

Specific Findings of the Investigation

The investigation found that false daily readiness reports were produced, specifically, from December 21, 2000 to January 11, 2001. During interviews, Chief Warrant Officer 2 (CWO2) Smith acknowledged he was responsible for six of the false daily reports. Capt Ramsey admitted to falsifying two of the daily AMRRs. The investigation did not yield a determination as to who falsified the remaining four reports. Therefore, the squadron lied on a total of 12 of the daily AMRRs. In addition, 26 false work orders were found by DCIS within the computer tracking system (NALCOMIS). The falsification of all of this information took place between December 20, 2000 and January 11, 2001. Subsequently, it was determined that none of this false recording contributed to the two MV-22 mishaps occurring on April 8, 2000 and December 11, 2000.

The Senior Officers

The investigation indicated that no Marine Corps officer senior to Leberman directed any of the personnel in VMMT-204 to falsify records, even though Leberman was repeatedly heard by subordinates saying that the "Wing" (2nd MAW, under MajGen Krupp) or the "Group" (MAG-26, commanded by Col Schleining) had ordered it. Concerning their own parts in the actual investigation, upon the advice of legal counsels, Schleining and Leberman invoked the right to remain silent. MajGen Krupp denied any knowledge of false readiness reporting prior to Schleining informing him of the fact.

Uniform Code of Military Justice (UCMJ) Actions

The Commandant of the Marine Corps provided the UCMJ convening authority with the DCIS criminal investigation report. Each of the officers charged accepted non-judicial punishment (NJP) hearings instead of requesting a trail by court-martial. The NJP hearings took place in September 2001, and the results of those hearings are presented below.

LtCol Leberman was charged with the following:

> UCMJ, Article 92(1), Navy Regulation 1137–failure to obey a lawful general order or regulation
>
> UCMJ, Article 133–conduct unbecoming an officer
>
> UCMJ, Article 107–false official statements

Findings and Punishment:
Leberman committed the offenses, Article 92(1) and Article 133. He was given a Letter of Reprimand.
Col Schleining was charged with the following:

> UCMJ, Article 92(1), Navy Regulation 1137–failure to obey a lawful general order or regulation

> UCMJ, Article 92(3)–dereliction of duty

Findings and Punishment:
Schleining committed the offense, Article 92(3). He was awarded a Letter of Reprimand.
Capt Ramsey was charged with:

> UCMJ, Article 92(1), Navy Regulation 1137–failure to obey a lawful general order or regulation

> UCMJ, Article 133–conduct unbecoming an officer

> UCMJ, Article 107–false official statements

Findings and Punishment:
Ramsey was found guilty of the offense, Article 92(1) and he was given Verbal Admonishment.
MajGen Krupp was charged with UCMJ Article 92(3)–dereliction of duty (two specifications). It was found that he did not commit the offense.
And finally,
CWO2 Smith was charged with the following:

> UCMJ, Article 92(3)–dereliction of duty

> UCMJ, Article 107–false official statements

Smith's NJP hearing found that he did not commit the above offenses.[23]

How Do We Honor the Fallen?:
The Sequel
Captain Rick Rubel

In the actual instances:

Case I

We never reached a definitive conclusion other than that we *would* have a memorial service but that it would be differentiated in some manner from those done for Marines killed in action against the enemy. The specifics of that differentiation were still being hashed out when the Marine turned himself in to the U.S. Embassy in Beirut. My proposed solution was to exclude the boots, helmet & dog tags on the upturned rifle from the ceremony, have only the commanders speak (no buddies), use slightly different music and end with *Amazing Grace* rather than *Taps*. This would have reduced the length of the service, avoided the symbols connected with military honors, and still acknowledged the loss.

Case II

Based on the witnesses at the scene, both U.S. and Iraqi, we determined that the driver of the vehicle did in fact *intend* to run down the Marine, though it was likely a "target of opportunity" for him rather than planned. The decision was then made to class it as a combat death, award the Purple Heart, and so inform the family that he was killed in action (as opposed to accident).

Appendix B

Geneva Conventions Summary

The Geneva Conventions for the Protection of War Victims

Table of Contents

The Geneva Conventions for the Protection of War Victims

Chapter One: Common Provisions of the Geneva Conventions

I. Introduction

In the aftermath of World War II, the world's nations recognized that the Geneva Red Cross Convention of 1929, which had been enacted to protect the wounded, sick and prisoners, had numerous shortcomings. In 1949, four new conventions were adopted to protect the victims of war; collectively, these are known as "The Geneva Conventions for the Protection of War Victims." The individual conventions are:

> Geneva Convention for the Amelioration of the Condition of the Wounded and Sick in Armed Forces in the Field (abbreviated GWS).

> Geneva Convention for the Amelioration of the Condition of the Wounded, Sick and Shipwrecked Members of Armed Forces at Sea (abbreviated GWS SEA).

> Geneva Convention Relative to the Treatment of Prisoners of War (abbreviated GPW).

> Geneva Convention Relative to the Protection of Civilian Persons in Time of War (abbreviated GC).

These conventions are the most comprehensive code of that segment of Law of Armed Conflict (LOAC) that deals with war victims, and they are among the most widely accepted of all international laws. As of 1987, 170 nations were UN members and 163 nations were parties to the Geneva Conventions. Included among these parties are the United States and the former Soviet Union.

The four conventions share a common purpose: the protection of war victims and those who aid war victims. The Geneva Conventions were not intended for the direct regulation of hostilities, although there is unquestionably some indirect effect on the conduct of military operations. "War victims" include civilians who are taking no part in the hostilities and those former combatants who are rendered "hors de combat" ("out of the combat") because of sickness, wounds, shipwreck, or being taken prisoner. The primary focus of the conventions is the protection of these war victims while they are in the hands of the enemy, it being presumed that they do not need the protection of international law while they are under the control of their own government. "Persons who aid war victims" include medical personnel, chaplains, and Red Cross or neutral personnel who use their good offices to assist in the care and treatment of war victims.

II. Common Provisions of the Four Geneva Conventions

While dealing with separate subjects, the four conventions share a number of common provisions, the most notable of which are discussed below.

A. *Applicability of the Conventions*

When does the law set forth in the conventions apply? The simple answer is that it applies in all *international armed conflicts*. Identifying which conflicts fall within this category is not so simple. Obviously, a declared war such as World War II is such a conflict, although it is worthwhile to note that a formal declaration of war is *not* necessary to have an international armed conflict. Also included in this category would be any armed conflict, no matter how small or insignificant between two (or more) parties to the conventions, or between a party and another nation not a party if the latter announces it will adhere in actual practice to the terms of the conventions. Clearly, a conflict wholly internal in its nature, such as one involving skirmishes with rebel insurgents, is not within the category. But consider what happens when a rebellion ripens into a full scale revolution, with different factions holding territory and claiming independence from the other (and announcing acceptance of the Geneva Conventions). Now the conflict more closely resembles an international armed conflict than it does an internal rebellion. And what about other conflicts such as "Peace-Keeping Operations" (Beirut, the Sinai); "Humanitarian Rescue Operations" (Grenada, the Iran hostage rescue attempt); and "responses" to international terrorism (the capture of the *Achille Lauro* hijackers, the Israeli strikes against PLO targets)? Government officials are quick to claim publicly that these are not "wars," seemingly removing them from the category of "international armed conflicts." But out in the field an "armed conflict" is undeniably underway. Bottom line: always assume that the conventions apply in any action involving foreign (non-American) forces. Unless and until a specific renunciation of the application of the Geneva conventions to a particular conflict is announced by the U.S. government, consider that the conventions do apply.

B. Article 3. "Mini-Convention"

What about conflicts not of an international character? Do the Geneva Conventions apply? Article 3, in all four conventions, known as the "mini-convention," applies in such conflicts to provide minimal humanitarian protection for the victims of war. This article mandates "humane treatment" for wounded, sick and "non-participants" in the conflict (including members of an armed force who lay down their arms). Article 3 outlaws such acts as murder, torture, hostage taking, and other cruel, humiliating and degrading treatment. While enemy soldiers who are taken prisoner are entitled to humane treatment, it is important to note that under the "mini-convention," they are not vested with POW status. Therefore, unlike POWs, prisoners captured during a non-international conflict may be tried and punished for their acts of warfare. The "mini-convention" seeks to curb abuses in this area by mandating that sentences may be carried out only after a judgment of guilt by a regularly constituted court (no summary punishments, no sham tribunals) at which the prisoner has been afforded "indispensable judicial guarantees." This vague language (which judicial guarantees are "indispensable" among civilized nations?) leaves room for differences among nations, and you might expect that the rights afforded an accused before a court in Iraq or North Korea would differ markedly from those afforded in U.S. courts. This illustrates something encountered frequently throughout the conventions: provisions are not always specific in their drafting nor perfect in their applicability. Of course, this is to be expected when preparing a document to the satisfaction of a community of sovereign nations. Nevertheless, the conventions do represent a considerable achievement in that the world's nations have agreed that victims of any war, whether it be international or non-international in character, do have basic rights which ought to be respected.

C. Special Agreements Altering the Conventions

Parties to a conflict may enter into special agreements, but these may only expand upon rights afforded to protected persons by the conventions. Provisions within the conventions will not be overridden, nor will protection thereunder be restricted or renounced, by any agreement between parties. In addition, individuals may not renounce their rights under *any* circumstances. The absolute nature of the nonrenunciation provision is designed to eliminate instances in which a ruthless captor might torture a prisoner into signing a statement purporting to renounce his or her protection under the conventions.

D. Protecting Powers and Humanitarian Organizations

Neutral nations and humanitarian organizations are interested in adherence to the conventions by warring powers, perhaps for no other reason than the belief that a conflict fought under humane rules stands a better chance of being resolved with a lasting peace than does inhumane, savage war. The parties to a conflict may designate a Protecting Power to act on its behalf, monitoring compliance with the terms of the conventions and reporting its observations to its sponsor nation. Protecting Powers also lend their "good offices" to attempt resolution of disputes involving the parties to the conflict. Any impartial humanitarian organization may undertake relief efforts for war victims, even while not serving as a Protecting Power. It should be noted that such efforts are subject to the consent of the parties to the conflict. Of course, because these efforts further the spirit of the Geneva conventions, they should usually be welcomed.

E. Obligations to Publish and Enforce the Conventions

Signatories to the Geneva conventions are obligated to publish and enforce the provisions of the conventions. For example, in order to prevent violations, nations must educate their citizens in the principles of the conventions. The course you are now taking is one way in which the U.S. seeks to fulfill this treaty obligation. Also, nations are obliged to take such other actions as may be necessary to suppress all violations of the conventions. Chief among these would be to legislate penalties for offenses and establish courts or other tribunals to enforce such legislation; hopefully, the presence of such statutes and courts would deter misconduct. In the case of "grave breaches," which are the most serious violations of the conventions, the use of the phrase "effective penal sanctions" contemplates harsh penalties such as death, life imprisonment, or imprisonment for a significant period of years. U.S. service members who violate the terms of the conventions are subject to prosecution under the Uniform Code of Military Justice (UCMJ) for the specific offending conduct (murder, rape, larceny, destruction of property, etc.).

"Grave breaches" of the conventions are those involving any of the following acts, if committed against protected persons or property: willful killing, torture or inhumane treatment, including biological experiments; willfully causing great suffering or serious injury to body or health: unlawful deportation or transfer or unlawful confinement of a protected person; compelling a protected person to serve in the forces of a hostile Power; willfully depriving a protected person of the right to a fair trial; taking of hostages; and extensive destruction and appropriation of property not justified by military necessity.

Unfortunately, the existence of penal sanctions and the threat of prosecution do not deter all violations. Offenses sometimes occur, and when they do, there is an obligation to take action against the offenders. Alleged violations are to be investigated and, if of a continuing nature, halted immediately. Offenders should be tried and punished as warranted by the circumstances. Special obligations exist in the case of grave breaches. All parties to the conventions have an affirmative duty to search for and bring to trial persons alleged to have ordered or committed these heinous offenses. Because grave breaches have no statute of limitations, these obligations may continue, perhaps for years following the end of the conflict until the offender dies or is brought to trial.

Chapter Two: Protection of Prisoners of War

I.   Introduction

Throughout much of history, members of a military force captured by the enemy had no substantial rights. Prisoners were largely at the mercy of their captors; they were mistreated, tortured, enslaved, held for ransom and killed. Even after it became the custom to keep prisoners alive, the lack of any accepted standard of treatment led to abuses. For example, during the American Revolution thousands of American prisoners died due to poor conditions on British prison ships, some of which were located in Baltimore harbor. This experience led the fledgling United States government to have an intense interest in the rights of prisoners of war. One of our first international agreements, a 1785 treaty with the Kingdom of Prussia, contained detailed rules to improve the treatment of POWs. These rules were later incorporated into other treaties.

General Order No. 100, also known as the "Lieber Code," promulgated during the American Civil War by the Union Army, contained 48 articles dealing with prisoners of war. This was the first attempt at codifying the laws, rules and customs which made up the international law on prisoners of war. The humanitarian principles contained in this document provided a significant basis for the treatment of prisoners of war in Hague Convention IV of 1907, in the 1929 Geneva Convention Relative to the Treatment of Prisoners of War, and in the present source treaty for POW rights, the Geneva Convention of 1949 Relative to the Treatment of Prisoners of War (abbreviated GPW).

There are two practical reasons why, as a member of the armed forces, you should be familiar with the rights and obligations of prisoners of war under the GPW.

First in any combat situation you must be ready to capture and control enemy prisoners until they are sent to permanent POW camps. The GPW provides the basic humanitarian rules for treatment of prisoners. Fear of mistreatment is a significant deterrent to surrender; decent treatment of prisoners may encourage the enemy to surrender.

The second reason is also related to duty, but in a more personal way. If you should ever become a POW, knowing your rights and duties under GPW could help you deal effectively with your captors. Such knowledge could also help you insist on proper treatment for your subordinates in the POW chain of command.

II. Persons Entitled to POW Status

The protected status of being a POW lasts from the time a person is captured until their final release and repatriation.

Article 4 of the GPW defines six categories of persons as being entitled to POW treatment upon capture. These are:

A. Members of Armed Forces

This is the most obvious and the principal group protected under GPW. This category also includes any corps or force incorporated into the armed forces during time of war; but this category does not include military chaplains or military medical personnel. Rather than becoming POWs upon capture, they become "retained persons." This special status is discussed in Chapter Four.

B. Members of Resistance Movements

During World War II, the Allied Commanders in Europe recognized the French Resistance forces as a component of the Allied forces, and demanded POW treatment for its captured members. The Germans, on the other hand, had treated captured members of the French Resistance as unlawful combatants. GPW seeks to clarify the status of resistance forces in a manner that attempts a balance between a humanitarian concern for the plight of captured belligerents and the legitimate concern of operational commanders for the protection of their regular troops from the attacks of irregular forces. First you should note that under GPW, resistance movements are *not* the type of "militia or volunteer corps" which could become incorporated into the regular armed forces during time of war. Second, to obtain the entitlement to POW status upon capture, a resistance movement must meet the following four criteria:

1. The force must have a command structure, with a commander who is responsible for subordinates. This condition is fulfilled if the movement is commanded by a commissioned officer of the armed forces of that nation or by some other person who occupies a similar position of responsibility as evidenced by documents, badges or other identification. It must be clear that individual soldiers are not operating on their own, but rather are accountable for their actions to a superior.

2. Personnel must wear a fixed, distinctive insignia recognizable at a distance. The wearing of a complete uniform is not necessary to satisfy this requirement. The purpose of the requirement is to make the belligerent forces distinguishable from the general civilian population, and any emblem or insignia that accomplishes this purpose is sufficient.

3. Personnel must carry their arms openly. Again, this will distinguish the members of the resistance force from the general civilian population.

4. The force must conduct its operations in accordance with the LOAC. This condition is satisfied if the resistance movement, as a whole, complies with the LOAC. The fact that an individual member has committed a war crime will not strip the entire group of POW status.

Embodied in the four criteria above is a decided concern with the ability to distinguish true civilians from resistance members. Of course, because the openness suggested in these criteria would run counter to the secrecy under which many resistance groups operate, it is possible that they would elect not to abide by these requirements. The choice rests with the commander: any member of a resistance group which does not satisfy the four criteria enjoys no legal right under international law to POW status. Therefore, if captured, he or she may be tried and punished as a criminal for assault, murder, property damage or other acts hostile to the enemy.

C. Members of a Regular Armed Force of a Government Not Recognized by the Detaining Power

During World War II, a debate arose about the correct status of General Charles de Gaulle's forces which were under the authority of the French National Liberation Committee. Were they legitimate belligerents, entitled upon capture to POW status? Or were they unlawful combatants, entitled to be tried and punished for their acts of warfare? The Germans did not recognize the FNLC as a legitimate government, and therefore contended that those forces were not operating under the direct authority of a party to the conflict. Eventually, through the intercession of the International Committee of the Red Cross (ICRC), the Germans granted POW status to captured members of these French forces. Consistent with this action, GPW Article 4 now clarifies that such forces are entitled to POW status.

D. Civilian Personnel Who Accompany the Armed Forces

Civilians such as news correspondents, supply contractors, tech reps, and welfare service personnel (such as Bob Hope's USO show) are entitled to POW status if captured. The enemy may choose to afford better treatment (i.e., release) to these persons and may indeed do so with news correspondents and welfare service personnel for the favorable propaganda value involved.

E. Civilian Aircraft Crews and Merchant Marine Crews

Whether or not directly supporting the war effort, these crews will be entitled to no worse than POW treatment if captured. Again, they may receive better treatment; for example, a civilian aircraft crew may be released and allowed to continue with its flight once the belligerent has determined that the flight is in no way aiding the enemy's war effort.

F. Levee en Masse

This occurs when civilians spontaneously rise up to defend their homeland against the invading force. Undoubtedly, they will not have the organization nor satisfy the "fixed, distinctive sign" requirement necessary to qualify them for POW treatment as a "resistance movement." Nevertheless, they will be entitled to POW status in the event of their capture if they carry their arms openly and generally adhere to the LOAC in their operations. You should note that a *levee en masse* lasts only until the defenders are subdued or their homeland becomes occupied by the invaders. A civilian living in *occupied* territory enjoys no legal right to engage in acts of warfare against the occupying enemy; when captured, such a civilian may be tried and punished for his or her actions.

The determination of who is entitled to POW status is not made by the capturing forces in the field. Rather, in doubtful cases it is made by a tribunal which reviews any relevant evidence which may assist in an accurate resolution of the issue. During the Vietnam war, the U.S. conducted these tribunals on a regular basis; the tribunal consisted of not less than three officers, at least one of whom had to be a judge advocate or a military lawyer familiar with the Geneva Conventions. These tribunals tended to be liberal in granting POW status, even for enemy personnel who did not fit well into any of the six categories found in GPW Article 4. This was done for a political reason rather than for legal reasons: recognizing that U.S. servicemen were being taken prisoner by the enemy, it was hoped that vesting captured enemy personnel with POW status would encourage reciprocal, favorable treatment for captured Americans.

Since the capturing troops are relieved of any responsibility for determining POW status, the task of field personnel is greatly simplified. Any person captured by U.S. troops, even those persons clearly not entitled to POW status, are to be treated humanely. They should be thoroughly searched, secured (blindfolding and handcuffing during transit away from the battle zone is permissible) and removed from the front. Above all, you may not torture or execute any captured persons. All prisoners must be handled with care.

III. Persons Not Entitled to POW Status

A. Persons Not in One of the Six Groups

Any person who commits hostile acts and who is not included in one of the categories above, is not entitled to POW status. In addition, such persons lack the immunity of a soldier for their hostile acts, and may be tried and punished for murder, assault, or destruction of property, as the case may be. Note that resistance fighters whose units cannot meet the four criteria discussed above fall into this category, as do terrorists.

B. Losing POW Status

Persons normally entitled to POW status may lose their right to that status by their actions.

1. *Spies:* Spies are discussed in NWP 9, paragraph 12.8.

2. *Out of Uniform:* Traditionally, the wearing of a uniform was considered a prerequisite to POW status if the prisoner was taken on the battlefield. GPW makes no mention of this exclusion, but it seems to have persisted in practice. Soldiers fighting while not wearing their own nation's uniform are traditionally not entitled to POW status and therefore could be tried as common criminals for their violent acts. There are, however, three situations in which a person not wearing a uniform on capture clearly is entitled to POW status.

   a. Three exceptions

   (1) Away from the battle zone: A person captured far from the battle zone on leave or liberty could hardly be required to be in uniform.

   (2) Evaders: Evading soldiers are entitled to wear any clothing they desire. An "evading" soldier is one who has been cut off from his unit behind enemy lines, and is merely trying to sneak back to his own forces. If he engages in intelligence gathering or sabotage, however, he becomes a spy and forfeits his POW status.

   (3) Escaping POWs: Escaping POWs are entitled to wear any clothing they desire, and will not forfeit their POW status. Again, they are not entitled to engage in intelligence gathering or sabotage without forfeiting their POW status.

IV. Protection of POWs

The overall goal and emphasis of GPW is clearly the humane treatment of prisoners. No power is obliged to (but all warring nations do) hold POWs. The Geneva Conventions are exceedingly clear that if POWs are taken, the international community expects the captor nation to maintain humane standards and bear all of the costs involved.

A. Humane Treatment at All Times

POWs must at all times be humanely treated and are entitled to respect for their persons and their honor. This includes protection from acts of violence, intimidation and public curiosity.

This is absolutely required regardless of the financial costs involved. Also, the killing or mistreatment of POWs is not permitted for any reason, even when their presence retards the captor's movement, diminishes his power of resistance, or endangers his own self-preservation.

This obligation can not be avoided by transferring POWs to another nation. Transferring POWs is permissible, but only if the original capturing state ensures that the receiving state complies fully with GPW. Furthermore, if the receiving state does not comply, then the original capturing state must retake custody of the POWs.

B. Interrogation of POWs

The capturing state is required to report the capture of each individual POW it detains. To facilitate this reporting requirement, every prisoner of war, when questioned on the subject is bound to give his full name, rank, date of birth, and serial number or equivalent information. It is also for this reason that each nation is required to furnish its forces with personal identification cards. These cards are not to be taken by the capturing state. Indeed, if a POW does not have an ID card, the capturing state must issue one to the POW. This is the only information a prisoner is required to furnish.

No physical or mental torture, or any other form of coercion may be inflicted on prisoners of war to secure from them information of any kind whatever. Prisoners of war who refuse to answer may not be threatened, insulted, or abused.

C. Personal Effects

All personal effects (except weapons, military equipment and military documents), shall remain in the possession of prisoners of war. Personal effects and articles used for their clothing or feeding shall remain in their possession, even if such effects and articles are part of their regulation military equipment.

Badges of rank and nationality, decorations, and articles of personal or sentimental value may not be taken from prisoners of war. Money and other valuables carried by prisoners of war may not be taken away from them except by order of an officer, and then only for reasons of security. If taken, a receipt must be given to the POW and the items returned upon repatriation.

D. Evacuation of POWs

POWs must be evacuated, as soon as possible after their capture, to camps located far enough from the combat zone for them to be out of danger. They shall not be unnecessarily exposed to danger during evacuation. They must be transported under conditions no worse than the conditions the capturing power uses in transporting its own troops.

V. Conditions of Internment

A. POW Camp Location

POW camps may only be located on land, and shall be located in an area that is conducive to the health and hygiene of the POW's. POW's shall not be interned in penitentiaries.

No prisoner of war may at any time be sent to or detained in areas where he or she may be exposed to fire, nor may his or her presence be used to "shield" lawful targets from enemy attack.

Whenever military considerations permit, prisoner of war camps shall be marked with the letters "PW" or "PG" so as to be clearly visible from the air. Only prisoner of war camps shall be marked as such.

B. Parole

Parole is a traditional practice of releasing prisoners in return for their promise not to fight again in the current war: however, no POW can be compelled to accept parole. It was taken quite seriously in the past, to the point that the British actually returned one of their officers who violated his parole to the Germans during World War I. Parole is of obvious benefit to the prisoner, but it can also be a great benefit to the detaining power. The purpose of holding prisoners is to keep them from continuing to fight against you. If you can accomplish that end without the expense and difficulty of maintaining POW camps, so much the better. Partially for that reason, and partially because parole is difficult to enforce and subject to abuse by both sides, United States military personnel generally are not allowed to accept parole.

C. Quarters

Prisoners of war shall be quartered under conditions as favorable as those for the forces of the Detaining Power who are billeted in the same area. These conditions shall make allowance for the habits and customs of the prisoners and *shall* in no case be prejudicial to their health. Separate dormitories shall be provided for female POW's.

Note that prisoner housing standards are tied to those of the captor's troops in the area. If the captor's troops are poorly housed, prisoners may be as well, provided the housing is not so poor as to be unhealthy.

D. Food

The GPW states that food must be "sufficient in quantity, quality, and variety" to keep the prisoner in good health. Further, the detaining power must consider the dietary habits of prisoners. Prisoners must have adequate mess halls and kitchens where they can assist in preparing their own food. The captor must also furnish prisoners with sufficient, safe drinking water. Restricting food as a form of mass punishment is forbidden.

E. Clothing

The detaining power must provide outer clothing, underwear, footwear, and work clothing. It must mend or replace these items regularly. If possible, the detaining power supplies clothing from stocks of uniforms captured from the prisoners' own forces.

F. Health and Medical Care

The Conventions include detailed provisions for meeting the health and medical needs of prisoners. They insure at least a minimum standard of health. For example, camps must include adequate heads, showers, and laundry facilities. The captor "shall be bound to take all sanitary measures necessary to insure the cleanliness and healthfulness of camps and to prevent epidemics." And "Every camp shall have an adequate infirmary." Here, prisoners should receive treatment, preferably by medical personnel from their own captured forces. Sick call occurs regularly; medical inspections, at least monthly. Periodic X-ray examinations for tuberculosis and tests for other infectious and contagious diseases should be made. All needed medical care must be furnished and it is free of charge to the POW.

G. Religious and Recreational Activities

Prisoners may attend services of their faith and otherwise practice their religion. The Conventions require provision for physical exercise. This includes outdoor sports and games. Intellectual and educational activities must be encouraged whenever possible.

H. Mail

As soon as possible after capture, prisoners are to be allowed to inform their families of their whereabouts and health. This is to be done within a week after prisoners reach a POW camp. Usually this message is sent on a standard "capture card." The detaining power also forwards a copy of this card to the Central Prisoner of War Information Agency. This is a clearing house operated by the International Committee of the Red Cross in Geneva.

Whenever a prisoner transfers to another camp or hospital, the detaining power must notify this agency. Prisoners have the right to send letters as frequently as the captor's censorship and postal facilities allow. They may also receive letters and relief packages forwarded through neutral agencies.

I.   Camp Information

Every POW camp must have copies of the Geneva Conventions, in the prisoners' own language, posted in places where prisoners can read them. All camp notices, regulations, and orders must be in a language prisoners understand.

VI. POW Labor

GPW does allow the Detaining Power to utilize POW labor, but there are a great number of detailed provisions in GPW concerning POW labor. This resulted because of the abuses on both sides during WWII. For instance, the Nazis used Russian and other POWs as slave labor, often simply working them until they died. On the other hand, the Allies used German POWs to remove mines in areas formerly occupied by the Nazis. As you might expect many were killed in explosions.

General guidelines for POW labor include the following:

- Only POWs who are physically fit may work.
- Commissioned officers may not be compelled to work, but if they volunteer, they may do supervisory work.
- Noncommissioned officers may be required to do supervisory work. Other enlisted personnel may be required to do manual labor.
- POW labor may not be used for military purposes except for work connected with camp administration, installation and maintenance.
- If additional food, clothing, medical care, training, etc., is required in order for the POW to perform his work, this must be furnished by the Detaining Power. Also, the POW must be paid for his labor.
- Working conditions can be no worse for the POWs than that enjoyed by the citizens of the Detaining Power employed in similar work.
- Unless a volunteer, no POW may be tasked to perform labor which is unhealthy or dangerous (such as clearing mines).

VII. Prisoner Discipline

A. Disciplinary Punishment

Disciplinary punishment is intended to punish infractions of camp rules and minor crimes. The procedure for disciplinary punishment is similar to that for nonjudicial punishment under the UCMJ.

A hearing before the POW camp commandant is all that is required prior to implementing the punishment.

The disciplinary punishments applicable to prisoners of war are the following (all have a 30-day maximum):

1. A fine which shall not exceed 50 percent of the advances of pay and working pay which the prisoner of war would otherwise receive.

2. Discontinuance of privileges granted over and above the treatment provided for by the present Convention.

3. Fatigue duties not exceeding two hours daily (cannot be imposed on officers).

Confinement

In no case shall disciplinary punishments be inhuman, brutal or dangerous to the health of prisoners of war. The maximum of thirty days provided above may not be exceeded, even if the prisoner of war is answerable for several acts at the same time when he is awarded punishment, whether such acts are related or not.

B. Judicial Punishment

Judicial punishment refers to potentially severe punishment awarded by a court. It is reserved for serious offenses, which could include war crimes. GPW requires that disciplinary punishment should be used whenever possible.

If judicial punishment is used, then the POW can be sentenced only if the trial court and the procedures used in court are the same as those that would be used for a member of the detaining power's own armed forces. However, in no event may a POW be tried unless the court and procedures used guarantee at least the *minimum* generally recognized standards of independence, impartiality and due process. Minimum due process includes the right to assistance of lawyer counsel; to the assistance of an interpreter and a fellow prisoner; to the calling of witnesses; and, if convicted, the right to appeal.

The use of the death penalty is discouraged, though not prohibited. If a death sentence is pronounced, at least six months must elapse before the sentence can be carried out. This allows for maximum diplomatic efforts to take place to prevent execution, if possible. Considerations of reciprocity have often prevented the execution of POWs.

One of the most extensively debated subjects at the 1949 Geneva Conference was whether a POW who is prosecuted for a precapture crime—in particular, offenses against the laws of war—should enjoy the benefits of POW status. It was determined that "Prisoners of war prosecuted under the laws of the Detaining Power for acts committed prior to capture shall retain, even if convicted, the benefits of the present Convention." According to this article, POW status is retained, regardless of the crime of which the prisoner is convicted. The former Soviet Union and many of its former satellite states made a reservation to this provision. They reserved the right to deny POW status to convicted war criminals. While the United States has rejected this reservation as contrary to international law, the existence of this reservation demonstrates the importance many governments attach to allegations of war crimes.

C. Escape

The GPW recognizes that all POWs have the right to attempt escape. While such attempts may be punished, the disciplinary punishment system must be used, thereby limiting the extent of punishment. In addition, *non-violent* acts committed in aid of an escape attempt are subject to the same limitations. Such non-violent offenses include offenses against public property; theft without intention of self-enrichment; making and using false papers; and the wearing of civilian clothing. *Violent* acts committed during an escape or an escape attempt may be dealt with through judicial punishment. The use of weapons against prisoners of war, especially against those who are escaping or attempting to escape, is an extreme measure, which under the GPW can only be used after appropriate warnings and as a last resort.

The escape of a prisoner of war shall be deemed to have succeeded when he or she has done one of the following:

1. joined his or her own armed forces or those of an allied power;
2. left the territory under the control of the Detaining Power and its allies, *i.e.,* reached neutral territory;
3. joined a ship flying the flag of his or her country or of an allied Power.

Prisoners of war who have successfully escaped and who are subsequently recaptured, shall not be liable to any punishment for their previous escape.

Chapter Three: Protection of Civilians

I. Introduction and Background

During World Wars I and II, civilians caught in the conflict could look to only one international convention for protection: Hague Convention IV Respecting the Laws and Customs of War on Land. To its credit, that convention sought to establish specific protection for civilians who were under military occupation. The enemy was required to respect family lives, rights and property; pillage and collective punishments were forbidden; and enemy civilians could not be compelled to provide military information or swear allegiance to the occupying power. However, the experiences of two world wars highlighted the limitations of that convention. Those few general provisions pertained only in the case of a formal military occupation. Few articles in the convention could be applied to govern the treatment of civilians in situations other than an occupation, and of those, the terms were unclear, ambiguous, incomplete, and, in some cases, not mandatory. Even in occupied territory, there were no established rules for the trial and punishment of civilians, and no procedures detailed for their *internment*. Rather than condemning the Hague Convention for these shortcomings, it is well to recall that it was concluded in 1907 when hostilities were confined to the area close to the front, and when widespread guerilla war was not common. Total war, which exposed the civilian population of whole countries to similar dangers as those faced by the Armed Forces, required more comprehensive treatment than that provided in Hague IV. From this recognition evolved the Geneva Convention of 1949 Relative to the Protection of Civilian Persons in Time of War (hereafter abbreviated GC), the first international convention devoted exclusively to the codification of the rights of civilians during an armed conflict. GC is the longest of the four Geneva Conventions, with 159 articles. In understanding the substantive provisions of this convention, it is useful to visualize GC as containing three distinct sub-agreements: the first is Article 3; the second is general protection for entire populations (Articles 13–26); and the third is "protected persons" (Articles 27-141).

II. Article 3: Protection of Civilians in a Non-International Conflict

Recall that this article (the so-called "mini-convention"), discussed in Chapter One of this handout provides basic humanitarian protection to noncombatants and former combatants who have laid down their arms or otherwise been rendered *hors de combat* due to sickness, wounds, detention or any other cause. The basic rights provided are protection from being used as a hostage, protection from humiliating and degrading treatment protection from all types of torture and violence (including murder), and protection from summary punishment and executions.

Remember: this article is applicable only in conflicts "not of an international character."

III. Articles 13–26: General Protection of Entire Populations Against Certain Consequences of War

While this portion of GC applies broadly (to "the whole of the population"), the actual protections provided are very few and, in some cases, are not mandatory.

A. *Protect and Respect the Civilian Population*

The provisions of GC Articles 13–26 apply to protect the entire populations of the warring opponents from the hardships of war, but the articles do not provide much in the way of specific, binding protection for those populations. Articles 16 and 24 do obligate the parties to "respect and protect" certain civilians: the wounded and sick; the shipwrecked and those otherwise exposed to grave danger; the infirm (usually thought of as invalids and the aged); expectant mothers; and orphaned children (under age 15). The phrase "protect and respect," refers to protection from such outrages as murder, torture, rape, medical or biological experiments, and cruel treatment of a like nature. Children must be cared for ("not left to their own resources") and educated.

Also, those under 12 must be given some type of identity card or badge. After World War II, the problem of orphaned and separated children was immense, and no doubt spurred agreement among nations that specific procedures for safeguarding and identifying children be included in GC.

GC expresses concern for the plight of families, but the only obligation placed on parties to the convention is limited to facilitating personal communication among family members. This obligation serves to help reunite dispersed family members.

B. Civilian Medical Facilities and Personnel

GC Articles 13–26 also address the issue of respect for civilian medical facilities and personnel. The establishment of hospital and safety zones for the benefit of certain civilians (those being the wounded, sick, aged, children under 15, expectant mothers and mothers of children under 7) is *optional* with a party to the conflict; respect for individual civilian hospitals, however, is *mandatory under all circumstances*. Furthermore, civilian medical personnel, hospital administrators and staff, and medical convoys on land or at sea shall likewise be respected and protected from attack. To facilitate identification of these persons and places, they should prominently display the appropriate emblem (usually a red cross or red crescent on a white background).

However, civilian hospitals, medical convoys, and medical personnel may be attacked if they are being used for military (vice humanitarian) purposes. Note that treating military personnel in a civilian hospital does *not* constitute using the hospital for a military purpose. All wounded and sick, whether civilian or military, are entitled to treatment as a basic humanitarian right. With respect to an attack on a hospital which is being used for military purposes, an attack shall not commence until after the enemy has been warned regarding the misuse of the hospital and then been given a reasonable opportunity to cease the offending military activities. This kind of procedure is fine in situations like that encountered by the U.S. when the North Vietnamese were abusing the protected status of the Boch Mai Hospital: after our protests and warnings were ignored, we bombed the SAM launching sites which had been co-located with the hospital. Of course, this incidentally damaged the hospital in the process. You should note that no protection exists for a hospital from which you are taking live fire. You need not convey any protest or warnings nor wait "a reasonable time limit" for the enemy to cease and desist. Your inherent right of self-defense permits you to fire upon the building immediately. It was this situation which existed in Grenada when U.S. troops fired upon the Richmond Hill Institute.

C. Neutralized Zones

Any party to a conflict may propose the establishment, in the regions where fighting is taking place, of neutralized zones intended to shelter from the effects of war both the combatant and non-combatant wounded and sick, plus civilian persons who take no part in hostilities, and who, while they reside in the zones, perform no work of a military character.

When all parties concerned have agreed upon the geographical position, administration, food supply and supervision of the proposed neutralized zone, a written agreement shall be concluded and signed. The agreement shall fix the beginning and the duration of the neutralization of the zone.

D. Siege

GC encourages parties to the conflict to endeavor to conclude local agreements for the removal from besieged or encircled areas, of the wounded, sick, infirm, and aged persons, children and maternity cases, and for the passage of ministers of all religions, medical personnel and medical equipment on their way to such areas.

GC encourages a besieging force to allow the free passage of all consignments of medical and hospital stores and objects necessary for religious worship intended only for civilians, and to allow the free passage of all consignments of essential foodstuffs and clothing intended for children under fifteen, expectant mothers and maternity cases.

The obligation to allow free passage of these consignments is subject to the condition that the besieging force is satisfied that the consignments will not be diverted from their intended, limited destination, and that allowing the consignments will not result in a definite advantage to the military efforts or economy of the enemy.

Note that these provisions do *not* obligate the parties to institute neutralized zones, or to permit the removal of certain persons from besieged areas, or to allow medical and religious supplies, clothing and foodstuffs intended only for civilian use to pass into the hands of the adverse party. These provisions are purely voluntary; they are "urged," not "mandated." As with any voluntary provision, a military commander should carefully evaluate what effect if any, compliance would have on the accomplishment of the assigned military objective. Consider this: if you were a siege commander, how would permitting wounded, sick, infirmed, children and maternity cases to leave the besieged area affect your objective, the capitulation of the enemy force?

IV. Articles 27–141: Protected Persons

To understand GC Articles 27–141 regarding protected persons, it is essential that you first understand who is a "protected person" for purposes of this convention.

A. Persons Entitled to "Protected Persons" Status

The civilians protected by GC Articles 27–141 are those civilians who find themselves in the hands of the enemy or of an occupying power. Also, certain citizens of neutral states are "protected persons" if their state does not have "normal diplomatic relations" with the nation in which that citizen is located. Of course, being members of "the whole of the population," these people would also receive the limited protection of GC Articles 1326. It is vital to note that an enemy civilian living in his own *unoccupied* territory is *not* a "protected person" under GC. It is presumed that such a civilian will be protected by his own government, and will benefit from its own domestic laws. Thus, there is no need for international law to intervene. International law (in the form of GC) is intended to ensure respect and protection for people who may not benefit from domestic laws: i.e., those civilians who find themselves under enemy control. Also, persons protected under one of the other Geneva Conventions are not considered "protected persons" under GC.

B. Humane Treatment Required at All Times

GC Article 27 provides in part, "Protected persons are entitled, in all circumstances, to respect for their persons, their honor, their family rights, their religious convictions and practices, and their manners and customs. They shall at all times be humanely treated, and shall be protected especially against all acts of violence or threats thereof and against insults and public curiosity."

Succinctly stated, GC Article 27 provides that *in all circumstances*, "protected persons" shall be treated humanely. This means they shall be protected from murder, torture, rape, enforced prostitution, insults, public ridicule, and any form of physical or mental coercion. Protection against these heinous crimes is not the only obligation imposed. The detaining power is obligated also to respect "protected persons," their honor, customs, religion and family rights. It should be obvious that these provisions were intended to address many of the crimes perpetrated against civilians in World War II: the "Rape of Manila," in which thousands of captured civilians were murdered, mutilated, raped and tortured; the use of captured civilians for medical experiments; denying civilians the means to earn a living; uprooting, dispersing or relocating families throughout Europe; and, of course, the Holocaust. A liberal application of the general obligations of respect and humane treatment embodied in the first paragraph of Article 27 likely would obviate the need for further treaty provisions, but experience has shown that, in time of war, "literal" vice "liberal" interpretations are likely. Therefore, many specific protections are stated in the succeeding GC articles, including prohibitions against collective penalties, pillage, hostage taking, and reprisals.

C. Collective Penalties. Pillage and Hostages Prohibited

Collective penalties, supposedly outlawed by Hague IV, were utilized during World War II. GC clearly outlaws them by permitting punishment *only* for offenses personally committed and by requiring a trial before the punishment is administered. Pillage is also proscribed. If "protected persons" and their family rights are to be respected, it seems only natural that their property should be respected and not plundered by the conquering invader. Similarly, a proscription against the use of protected civilians as hostages is consistent with the obligation to respect and to protect against torture, cruelty and collective punishments.

D. Reprisals Prohibited

The GC clearly outlaws acts of revenge taken against protected civilians under the care of the detaining power. The history of warfare is unfortunately dotted with instances in which entire populations of villages, or portions thereof, have been tortured and murdered and had their villages razed as vengeance for acts, whether lawful or criminal, committed against the detaining power. These acts of vengeance against a captive civilian populace are indefensible and unquestionably illegal.

Note: The GC's prohibition against reprisal actions involving protected civilians should not be confused with *lawful* reprisals designed to induce the enemy to comply with the LOAC. *See* NWP-9 section 6.2.3.

V. Other Sections of GC

Other protections afforded by the GC include, similar to POWs, that "protected persons" can not be used to shield a legitimate target from attack. It is a law of war violation to attempt to shield a target by surrounding it with protected persons and conversely, the presence of protected persons does not render the target immune from attack.

GC further provides that any party to the conflict into whose hands protected persons may fall, is responsible for the treatment accorded to them by its agents, irrespective of any individual responsibility which may be incurred. You will recall that in 1982 the Israeli occupation forces in Lebanon delegated some security responsibilities to Phalangist Christian Militia (PCM) allied to their cause. In September of that year, the PCM massacred hundreds of Palestinian refugees at the Shatila and Sabra refugee camps, which were located in an area of West Beirut under Israeli occupation. After initial denials, the Israeli government accepted partial responsibility for this brutality. Under the GC, they had no alternative. As the occupying power, Israel had the ultimate responsibility for the proper treatment of "protected persons" under its occupation.

VI. The Common Caveat throughout GC: The Security of the Detaining Power

Throughout GC are provisions which recognize that the detaining or occupying power's ability to maintain control and security must not be compromised. Even Article 27, one of the most powerful articles in the convention with respect to the humane treatment of civilians, states that the parties to the conflict may "take such measures of control and security in regard to protected persons as may be necessary as a result of the war." Although these frequent caveats to GC provisions clearly authorize detaining or occupying powers some latitude in dealing with protected persons (when necessary for security), they must be read in harmony with the bulk of the convention which mandates respect for protected persons in all circumstances. A protected person who engages in activities hostile to the detaining power continues to be a "protected person"; however, he or she may no longer be entitled to *all* of the rights and privileges that normally accrue to one with that status. Rather, rights and privileges *of that individual* are to be affected (recall the stricture against collective punishments). Note also that the withholding or modification should be limited to only so much as is necessary to maintain security; there is no wholesale forfeiture of all rights, and particularly no forfeiture of the rights associated with a fair trial on the offense charged. Finally, note also that full rights and privileges shall be restored at the earliest possible date. In order to avail oneself of the full protection of GC, the protected person owes a duty to the detaining power to be, in essence, a law abiding and nonhostile person. The protected person who violates this obligation can expect to forfeit some, but not all, of his or her protection under GC.

Chapter Four: The Wounded, Sick and Shipwrecked Conventions

I. Introduction and Background

In June, 1859, 39,000 troops were slain at the battle of Solferino in Northern Italy. Moved by the suffering he witnessed there, Henri Dunant wrote the book *Un Souvenir De Solferino* and, as a result of its publication, an International Congress was held at Geneva in 1863 and 1864 to examine the plight of wounded soldiers in the field. The result was the first Geneva Convention, adopted in 1864, to improve the condition of sick and wounded soldiers. The convention was updated in 1906 and again in 1929; and in 1949, two conventions were enacted which are still in force today. They are the Geneva

Convention of 1949 for the Amelioration of the Condition of the Wounded and Sick in Armed Forces in the Field (abbreviated GWS), and the Geneva Convention of 1949 for Amelioration of the Condition of the Wounded, Sick and Shipwrecked Members of Armed Forces at Sea (abbreviated GWS SEA).

Stated generally, these conventions provide protection for armed forces personnel who are rendered *hors de combat* ("out of the combat") owing to sickness, wounds or shipwreck; protection for chaplains and military medical personnel who minister to the needs of those *hors de combat* personnel; and protection for the places where medical care is provided and for medical equipment and supplies. Obviously, GWS deals with situations on land and GWS SEA deals with those peculiar problems of medical care at sea; however, there is a considerable amount of overlap. This chapter will analyze the protection afforded by these conventions.

II. Protection for Certain Persons

A. The Wounded, Sick and Shipwrecked

Not all wounded, sick and shipwrecked persons are protected by these conventions. For example, wounded or sick civilians are not within the scope of these conventions (recall that they are entitled to certain protection under GC). The persons who are protected by GWS and GWS SEA are the same six categories of people who are entitled to POW status under GPW and who are, in addition, wounded, sick, or shipwrecked. Upon capture by the enemy, they are entitled to POW status.

The definitions accorded the terms "wounded" and "sick" are not technical. A wound is any injury, incurred in battle or otherwise, which requires treatment. Sickness is an illness, vice an injury. "Shipwrecked," on the other hand, is a somewhat technical term. It refers to any person who has suffered the loss of his fighting platform and is now helpless and requires assistance to better his lot. Using the definition offered above, consider the case of personnel who are forced into the water from a disabled amphibious landing vehicle. If they continue to advance toward the beach, it cannot be said that they are "helpless" or that they require your assistance to better their lot. They have lost only their means of transport to the beach. Such personnel are not "shipwrecked," and the obligations of respect and protection which are owed to shipwrecked persons are not applicable. Finally, a "shipwrecked" person includes a person from an aircraft downed at sea.

The first duty thrust upon the parties to a conflict under GWS and GWS SEA is to search for and collect the dead, wounded and shipwrecked. In GWS SEA, the duty clearly attaches "after each engagement," and not during the battle itself. On the other hand, under GWS, the duty exists "at all times, and particularly after an engagement." Does this mean there is an obligation under GWS to commit personnel to search and collection operations during the heat of battle? Not at all, if, given the continuing battle, it is impractical or impossible to carry out a search and collection evolution, no violation of GWS has occurred. Even after an engagement, when the obligation surely arises on land or at sea, no violation of the law occurs if it is impossible to discharge this obligation owing to the nature of a unit or its mission. Mere inconvenience, on the other hand, is no excuse for refusing to undertake search and collection efforts after the enemy has disengaged and your unit has the opportunity for reasonably secure movement. Therefore, despite some differing language, the actual obligations under each convention are quite similar. Other measures, such as armistices and local agreements, for the benefit of wounded and sick persons are *not* mandated; they are certainly encouraged, but their implementation is dependent upon the voluntary assent of both sides.

Both GWS and GWS SEA make it clear that protected persons are to be "respected and protected under all circumstances." Once again, that broad, general language has been fleshed out by examples in the paragraphs which follow: no murder, no torture, and no medical experimentation. Also, the detaining power is responsible for providing such medical care as is possible, utilizing available personnel and supplies. Of particular interest is the priority of medical treatment. The GWS and GWS SEA require that all wounded personnel, regardless of nationality, be treated in order of *medical* priority. The common medical procedure which is used to prioritize patients for treatment is called "triage." Roughly stated, this procedure allocates resources first to those who are likely to survive only if immediate medical assistance is provided. Next to receive care are those not in need of immediate attention to survive (i.e., lesser wounds), and last in line are those who are unlikely to survive even with medical care (i.e., the mortal wounds). Nationality is not an element of the triage process.

The practice of treating all Americans first regardless of the severity of their wounds, would be a violation of these conventions.

B. Obligations Regarding Dead Combatants

GWS and GWS SEA require the parties to a conflict to notify the ICRC's Central Information Bureau (CIB) of the death of individual enemy combatants, and to forward the deceased enemy combatants' personal property to the CIB for return to next-of-kin. The parties are also required to provide dead combatants a dignified funeral, burial, or cremation and, if earthen graves are dug, appropriate markings so the graves may later be located. Compliance with these procedures can eliminate the fear and uncertainty associated with a person being listed as "missing in action" for a lengthy period of time.

C. Medical Personnel and Chaplains

If captured, chaplains and military medical personnel (recall that civilian medical personnel are protected under GC) are not POWs. Rather, they are considered "retained" personnel. This status allows all of the rights and benefits which would accrue to a POW, *plus* whatever additional freedom of the camp is necessary to permit the retained person to minister to the medical and spiritual needs of the POWs. It should be noted that the presence of medical personnel of the same nationality as prisoners does not relieve the detaining power of its obligation to ensure appropriate medical care for wounded and sick POWs.

Captured chaplains or medical personnel should be retained only so long as their humanitarian services are required for the benefit of other prisoners. If their services are not needed, they should be repatriated at the earliest practicable opportunity. This rule is designed to advance the overall objective of humanity permeating the conventions: imprisoning these persons without a need for their services diminishes the amount of assistance available to the wounded, sick and shipwrecked, while allowing chaplains and medical personnel to circulate freely increases the amount of care available.

Only full time medical personnel are given the special status of "retained personnel." Members of the armed forces who are part-time medical personnel, such as those specially trained to be orderlies or stretcher bearers if the need arises, but whose full-time duties are not medical duties, are POWs, not "retained personnel." However, they are to be allowed to continue performing medical duties after capture if they were so employed at the time of capture.

D. Loss of Protected Status

Both GWS and GWS SEA impose the general obligations of respect and protection for protected persons "in all circumstances." These general obligations also include a prohibition against intentionally firing on the wounded, sick and shipwrecked, and chaplains and medical personnel. This is a significant exemption from the general rule of warfare that enemy military personnel are lawful targets whenever and wherever they are found. However, if one of these protected persons engages in acts harmful to the enemy, that person has lost his or her protection.

Persons *hors de combat* (wounded, sick and shipwrecked) who fall into enemy hands sacrifice their usual right to engage in acts of war against the enemy in exchange for the protection of GPW and GWS or GWS SEA, as appropriate. If the protected person engages in acts of war, it should be apparent that the detaining power will be allowed to defend itself with appropriate means, which may include firing upon the transgressor.

Medical personnel likewise may not resist capture or engage in other acts harmful to the enemy (caring for the wounded is not an "act harmful to the enemy," it is a "humanitarian" act). Two consequences may result from medical personnel engaging in "military" (vice "humanitarian") activities. First, the individual risks death or injury from being fired upon by the enemy. Second, if captured, the individual risks loss of "retained" status and becomes merely a POW because that person was not "exclusively" engaged in medical activities. A third consequence is also possible: the offending individual would risk prosecution for a war crime if they misused a protected symbol, such as the Red Cross.

III. Protection for Certain Places

A. Hospitals and Other Medical Unit

Military medical facilities, be they hospitals (NRMC Bethesda) or mobile medical units (M*A*S*H 4077), may not be intentionally attacked. To facilitate this immunity and to guard against incidental damage to such facilities, they *should not* be co-located with legitimate targets. This admonition is frequently ignored. Many U.S. military hospitals are located in large military complexes which are themselves valid military objectives. Obviously, if such complexes were attacked, hospitals could expect to be damaged even if the hospital were not intentionally targeted; such "incidental damage" would *not* be a violation of the LOAC.

Military medical facilities are *not* immune from capture. If captured, the humanitarian character of the facility and its personnel should remain unchanged after capture until such time as the capturing power has removed the wounded and sick to another facility.

B. Sickbays on Vessels

Sickbays are treated in much the same way as hospitals and mobile medical units. However, the obligation not to attack the medical area is softened considerably ("shall be . . . spared as far as possible"), in recognition of the necessary co-location of a sickbay aboard a legitimate target.

C. Special Rules: Hospital Ships

Military hospital ships enjoy the same immunity from attack as hospitals and other medical units. However, it is important to note that, unlike other medical facilities, hospital ships *may not be captured!*

Not only may hospitals ships not be captured, but the religious and medical personnel onboard, and the ship's crew, may not be captured. The purpose in this broad protection is to keep hospital ships in circulation for the benefit of *all* the wounded, sick, and shipwrecked. However, this immunity from capture does *not* extend to the actual wounded and sick combatants onboard, who may be taken prisoner by the enemy so long as they are fit to move and so long as the enemy has the facilities available at hand to ensure continued care.

For a ship to receive the protection of being a hospital ship, the enemy must be notified at least 10 days in advance that the ship is being so used, and must be provided a description of the ship including gross tonnage, length, and the number of masts and funnels. In addition, hospital ships must be painted white and marked with several large red crosses or crescents.

Since the enemy is prohibited from destroying or capturing hospital ships, just what rights does the belligerent have over those vessels? Basically, there are two: the right of "visit and search" and the right of "control."

"Visit and search," discussed more fully in NWP 9, involves stopping and boarding a vessel for the purpose of inspecting its true character. If a search of a vessel reveals that it truly is a hospital ship, then the vessel will be permitted to proceed. Of course, if the search reveals that the vessel is engaged in hostile, vice humanitarian activities, such as ferrying troops or ammunition, the vessel will lose its immunity and be subject to capture.

The right of "control" includes the power to order a hospital ship to stand off, to take a certain course and speed, to control certain communications, and even to detain the vessel for a period of up to seven days. For example, a belligerent may wish to employ any of these measures to maintain the secrecy of certain information about ships in company, or formation course and speed, which have been or could be observed by a nearby enemy hospital ship.

There are certain obligations placed upon the nation which operates a hospital ship. Assistance is to be provided to all wounded, sick and shipwrecked, regardless of nationality. Recall that only medical reasons will determine the order of medical care to be given. Hospital ships shall not be put to any "military" (vice "humanitarian") purpose. Violation of this provision by a hospital ship risks loss of the protection described earlier.

D. Loss of Protection for Medical Facilities

Hospitals and mobile medical units remain protected so long as they do not commit outside of their humanitarian activities, acts harmful to the enemy. If acts harmful to the enemy occur, then a hospital or mobile medical unit may be attacked, but only after a *warning* has been given and the hospital or mobile medical unit fails to heed the warning. This warning requirement does not apply if giving a *warning* is impractical, such as when taking live fire from an anti-aircraft battery positioned on the hospital roof.

Some people mistakenly believe that by merely possessing weapons, medical personnel forfeit their protected status. The bearing of sidearms by doctors and nurses for self-defense does not change the humanitarian character of a medical facility or of the medical personnel therein. Neither does the posting of armed sentries at a medical facility. The GWS and GWS SEA recognize that individuals may need to defend themselves or their patients from wartime threats other than the threat of capture by the enemy. So long as weapons are not used to resist capture of the medical facility (which would, of course, be an "act harmful to the enemy"), the facility and its personnel remain protected. One caveat: sentries and medical personnel should carry "defensive" weapons only. The use of tanks, artillery, mortars and .50 caliber machine guns in and around a "medical facility" will cause the enemy much suspicion and will dramatically increase the likelihood of an enemy attack. A medical facility will also not lose its protected status due to the presence of arms and *ammunition* collected from the sick and wounded.

Hospital ships and sickbays of vessels are entitled to all of these same protections. In addition, note that neither the fact that the crews of ships or sickbays are armed for the maintenance of order, for their own defense or the defense of the sick and wounded; nor the presence on board of apparatus exclusively intended to facilitate *navigation* or communications will deprive them of protection. It is important to note that hospital ships may not use secret codes for communicating. The reason for this prohibition is obviously to prevent a hospital ship from being a spy ship.

IV. Protection of Certain Things

A. Medical Supplies

Under the LOAC, captured enemy military property may be put to use by the possessor or it may be destroyed to deny its possible recapture and use by the enemy. However, special rules exist for captured medical supplies. Material from mobile medical units "shall be reserved for the care of wounded and sick." No exceptions are indicated for this rule. A similar, but not identical rule for hospital buildings and hospital supplies requires that they be used for the treatment of wounded and sick after capture. However, this rule does allow their use for other purposes when "urgent military necessity" requires and when other arrangements have been made for the satisfactory care of the wounded and sick. In no case may medical supplies be destroyed in order to deny their use by the enemy.

B. Medical Transports

Medical transports on land shall not be intentionally attacked so long as they are being used for humanitarian purposes, but they may be captured. Captured land transports may be used for non-medical purposes on the condition that any wounded and sick are otherwise first cared for.

Medical transports at sea may be treated similarly to hospital ships. They are subject to visit and search but may not be attacked or captured. However, there is a significant qualifier to obtain this immunity as a medical transport. Notice of the voyage of the medical transport ship must be given to the enemy and the enemy must approve its voyage. These voyages, if they occur at all, likely will occur under the auspices of the ICRC or some neutral nation.

C. Special Rule: Medical Aircraft

Medical aircraft are given very limited protection. They may be fired upon *unless* they are flying at heights, at times, and on routes agreed to *in advance* between the belligerents. Therefore, a helicopter bearing a large Red Cross usually will *not* be protected when it enters a combat zone to pick-up wounded, since it is unlikely that the belligerents have agreed in advance to its appearance. For medical aircraft on agreed upon flights, they shall obey every summons to land. In the event of a landing thus imposed, the aircraft with its occupants may continue its flight after examination, if any. The difference in this special rule for medical aircraft, and the general spirit of respect and protection for medical transports, apparently stems from a deep-rooted mistrust of enemy airborne platforms in the aftermath of World War II, which saw the advent of massive destruction from the skies. In 1949, the world's nations just did not feel comfortable *granting* an across-the-board immunity to aircraft bearing a medical emblem.

U.S. Rule: U.S. forces are required to respect and protect the enemy's medical aircraft, even if the craft is not on an agreed upon flight, if the aircraft can be recognized as an aircraft being used on a legitimate medical mission. See NWP 9, paragraph 8.2.3.

V. Identification of Protected Persons, Places and Things

Under both GWS and GWS SEA, to facilitate identification of medical persons, places and things, a clearly visible red symbol on a white background should be displayed. The only sanctioned symbols are the Red Cross, the Red Crescent (used by Islamic countries), and the red lion and sun (the emblem of the Shah of Iran). Iran now uses the Red Crescent but has reserved the right to use the lion and sun symbol. Israel uses the red Star of David, which, while not sanctioned, was nevertheless respected in recent Israeli conflicts. These emblems are pictured in NWP 9. The purpose of the emblem is ease of identification. Its display is *not* a prerequisite to protection. If you know that a building is a hospital, it deserves respect even though it does not bear red.

The conventions prescribe that medical personnel shall display the emblem on an armlet worn on the left arm. Buildings and transports shall bear the emblem in such a *manner* that it is clearly visible in all directions, including from the air. Hospital ships are to be painted white on all exterior surfaces, and shall display the emblem so it is visible in all directions, including from the air.

The display of the medical emblem is controlled by "competent military authority." Such authority may direct the camouflaging or even the removal of the emblem. While such directives are not violations of the LOAC, the military commander should consider the risks of attack and destruction when these emblems are not used.

Appendix C
U.S. Army/Marine Corps Counterinsurgency Field Manual
Chapter 7

U.S. Army/Marine Corps
Counterinsurgency Field Manual 3-24

Chapter 7
Leadership and Ethics for Counterinsurgency

Leaders must have a strong sense of the great responsibility of their office; the resources they will expend in war are human lives.

There are leadership and ethical imperatives that are prominent and, in some cases, unique to counterinsurgency. The dynamic and ambiguous environment of modern counterinsurgency places a premium on leadership at every level, from sergeant to general. Combat in counterinsurgency is frequently a small-unit leader's fight; however, commanders' actions at brigade and division levels can be more significant. Senior leaders set the conditions and the tone for all actions by subordinates. Today's Soldiers and Marines are required to be competent in a broad array of tasks. They must also rapidly adapt cognitively and emotionally to the perplexing challenges of counterinsurgency and master new competencies as well as new contexts. Those in leadership positions must provide the moral compass for their subordinates as they navigate this complex environment. Underscoring these imperatives is the fact that exercising leadership in the midst of ambiguity requires intense, discriminating professional judgment.

Leadership in Counterinsurgency

7-1. Army and Marine Corps leaders are expected to act ethically and in accordance with shared national values and Constitutional principles, which are reflected in the law and military oaths of service. These leaders have the unique professional responsibility of exercising military judgment on behalf of the American people they serve. They continually reconcile mission effectiveness, ethical standards, and thoughtful stewardship of the Nation's precious resources—human and material—in the pursuit of national aims.

7-2. Army and Marine Corps leaders work proactively to establish and maintain the proper ethical climate of their organizations. They serve as visible examples for every subordinate, demonstrating cherished values and military virtues in their decisions and actions. Leaders must ensure that the trying counterinsurgency (COIN) environment does not undermine the values of their Soldiers and Marines. Under all conditions, they must remain faithful to basic American, Army, and Marine Corps standards of proper behavior and respect for the sanctity of life.

7-3. Leaders educate and train their subordinates. They create standing operating procedures and other internal systems to prevent violations of legal and ethical rules. They check routinely on what Soldiers and Marines are doing. Effective leaders respond quickly and aggressively to signs of illegal or unethical behavior. The Nation's and the profession's values are not negotiable. Violations of them are not just mistakes; they are failures in meeting the fundamental standards of the profession of arms.

7-4. There are basic leadership tenets that apply to all levels of command and leadership in COIN, though their application and importance may vary.

7-5. Effective leaders ensure that Soldiers and Marines are properly trained and educated. Such training includes cultural preparation for the operational environment. In a COIN environment, it is often counter productive to use troops that are poorly trained or unfamiliar with operating close to the local populace. COIN forces aim to mobilize the good will of the people against the insurgents. Therefore, the populace must feel protected, not threatened, by COIN forces' actions and operations.

7-6. Proper training addresses many possible scenarios of the COIN environment. Education should prepare Soldiers and Marines to deal with the unexpected and unknown. Senior commanders should, at a minimum, ensure that their small-unit leaders are inculcated with tactical cunning and mature judgment. Tactical cunning is the art of employing fundamental skills of the profession in shrewd and crafty ways to out-think and out-adapt enemies. Developing mature judgment and cunning requires a rigorous regimen of preparation that begins before deployment and continues throughout. Junior leaders especially need these skills in a COIN environment because of the decentralized nature of operations.

7-7. Senior leaders must determine the purpose of their operations. This entails, as discussed in chapter 4, a design process that focuses on learning about the nature of unfamiliar problems. Effective commanders know the people, topography, economy, history, and culture of their area of operations (AO). They know every village, road, field, population group, tribal leader, and ancient grievance within it. The COIN environment changes continually; good leaders appreciate that state of flux and constantly assess their situation.

7-8. Another part of analyzing a COIN mission involves assuming responsibility for everyone in the AO. This means that leaders feel the pulse of the local populace, understand their motivations, and care about what they want and need. Genuine compassion and empathy for the populace provide an effective weapon against insurgents.

7-9. Senior leaders exercise a leadership role throughout their AO. Leaders directly influence those in the chain of command while indirectly leading everyone else within their AO. Elements engaged in COIN efforts often look to the military for leadership. Therefore, military actions and words must be beyond reproach. The greatest challenge for leaders may be in setting an example for the local populace. Effective senior and junior leaders embrace this role and understand its significance. It involves more than just killing insurgents; it includes the responsibility to serve as a moral compass that extends beyond the COIN force and into the community. It is that moral compass that distinguishes Soldiers and Marines from the insurgents.

7-10. Senior commanders must maintain the "moral high ground" in all their units' deeds and words. Information operations complement and reinforce actions, and actions reinforce the operational narrative. All COIN force activity is wrapped in a blanket of truth. Maintaining credibility requires commanders to immediately investigate all allegations of immoral or unethical behavior and provide a prudent degree of transparency.

7-11. Army and Marine Corps leaders emphasize that on the battlefield the principles of honor and morality are inextricably linked. Leaders do not allow subordinates to fall victim to the enormous pressures associated with prolonged combat against elusive, unethical, and indiscriminate foes. The environment that fosters insurgency is characterized by violence, immorality, distrust, and deceit; nonetheless, Army and Marine Corps leaders continue to demand and embrace honor, courage, and commitment to the highest standards. They know when to inspire and embolden their Soldiers and Marines and when to enforce restraint and discipline. Effective leaders at all levels get out and around their units, and out among the populace.

Such leaders get a true sense of the complex situation in their AO by seeing what subordinates are actually doing, exchanging information with military and interagency leaders, and—most importantly— listening.

7-12. Leaders at every level establish an ethical tone and climate that guards against the moral complacency and frustrations that build up in protracted COIN operations. Leaders remain aware of the emotional toll that constant combat takes on their subordinates and the potential for injuries resulting from combat stress. Such injuries can result from cumulative stress over a prolonged period, witnessing the death of a comrade, or killing other human beings. Caring leaders recognize these pressures and provide emotional "shock absorbers" for their subordinates. Soldiers and Marines must have outlets to share their feelings and reach closure on traumatic experiences. These psychological burdens may be carried for a long time. Leaders watch for signs of possible combat stress within individuals and units. These signs include—

- Physical and mental fatigue.
- Lack of respect for human life.
- Loss of appetite, trouble with sleep, and no interest in physical hygiene.
- Lack of unit cohesion and discipline.
- Depression and fatalism.

7-13. Combat requires commanders to be prepared to take some risk, especially at the tactical level. Though this tenet is true for the entire spectrum of conflict, it is particularly important during COIN operations, where insurgents seek to hide among the local populace. Risk takes many forms. Sometimes accepting it is necessary to generate overwhelming force. However, in COIN operations, commanders may need to accept substantial risk to de-escalate a dangerous situation. The following vignette illustrates such a case.

Defusing a Confrontation

[On 3 April 2005, a] small unit of American soldiers was walking along a street in Najaf [en route to a meeting with a religious leader] when hundreds of Iraqis poured out of the buildings on either side. Fists waving, throats taut, they pressed in on the Americans, who glanced at one another in terror. . . . The Iraqis were shrieking, frantic with rage. . . . [It appeared that a shot would] come from somewhere, the Americans [would] open fire, and the world [would] witness the My Lai massacre of the Iraq war.

At that moment, an American officer stepped through the crowd holding his rifle high over his head with the barrel pointed to the ground. Against the backdrop of the seething crowd, it was a striking gesture. . . . "Take a knee," the officer said. . . . The Soldiers looked at him as if he were crazy. Then, one after another, swaying in their bulky body armor and gear, they knelt before the boiling crowd and pointed their guns at the ground. The Iraqis fell silent, and their anger subsided. The officer ordered his men to withdraw [and continue on their patrol].

© Dan Baum, "Battle Lessons, What the Generals Don't Know," *The New Yorker*, Jan 17, 2005.

7-14. Leaders prepare to indirectly inflict suffering on their Soldiers and Marines by sending them into harm's way to accomplish the mission. At the same time, leaders attempt to avoid, at great length, injury and death to innocents. This requirement gets to the very essence of what some describe as "the burden of command." The fortitude to see Soldiers and Marines closing with the enemy and sustaining casualties day in and day out requires resolve and mental toughness in commanders and units. Leaders must develop these characteristics in peacetime through study and hard training. They must maintain them in combat.

7-15. Success in COIN operations requires small-unit leaders agile enough to transition among many types of missions and able to adapt to change. They must be able to shift through a number of activities from nation building to combat and back again in days, or even hours. Alert junior leaders recognize the dynamic context of a tactical situation and can apply informed judgment to achieve the commander's intent in a stressful and ambiguous environment. COIN operations are characterized by rapid changes in tactical and operational environments. The presence of the local populace within which insurgents may disappear creates a high degree of ambiguity. Adaptable leaders observe the rapidly changing situation, identify its key characteristics, ascertain what has to be done in consultation with subordinates, and determine the best method to accomplish the mission.

7-16. Cultural awareness has become an increasingly important competency for small-unit leaders. Perceptive junior leaders learn how cultures affect military operations. They study major world cultures and put a priority on learning the details of the new operational environment when deployed. Different solutions are required in different cultural contexts. Effective small-unit leaders adapt to new situations, realizing their words and actions may be interpreted differently in different cultures. Like all other competencies, cultural awareness requires self-awareness, self-directed learning, and adaptability.

7-17. Self-aware leaders understand the need to assess their capabilities and limitations continually. They are humble, self-confident, and brave enough to admit their faults and shortcomings. More important, self-aware leaders work to improve and grow. After-action reviews, exchanging information with subordinate and interagency leaders, and open discussions throughout a COIN force are essential to achieve understanding and improvement. Soldiers and Marines can become better, stronger leaders through a similar habit of self-examination, awareness, and focused corrective effort.

7-18. Commanders exercise initiative as leaders and fighters. Learning and adapting, with appropriate decision-making authority, are critical to gaining an advantage over insurgents. Effective senior leaders establish a climate that promotes decentralized modes of command and control—what the Army calls mission command and the Marine Corps calls mission command and control. Under mission command, commanders create the conditions for subordinates' success. These leaders provide general guidance and the commander's intent and assign small-unit leaders authority commensurate with their responsibilities. Commanders establish control measures to monitor subordinates' actions and keep them within the bounds established by commander's intent without micromanaging. At the same time, Soldiers and Marines must feel the commander's presence throughout the AO, especially at decisive points. The operation's purpose and commander's intent must be clearly understood throughout the force.

7-19. The practice of leaders sharing hardship and danger with subordinates builds confidence and esprit. Soldiers and Marines are more confident in their chances of success when they know that their leaders are involved. They understand their leaders are committing them to courses of action based on firsthand knowledge. However, this concept of leaders being fighters does not absolve leaders from remembering their position and avoiding needless risk.

7-20. COIN operations require leaders to exhibit patience, persistence, and presence. While leading Soldiers and Marines, commanders cooperate with, and leverage the capabilities of, multinational partners, U.S. Government agencies, and nongovernmental organizations. Commanders also gain the confidence of the local populace while defeating and discrediting the insurgents.

Patience, Presence, and Courage

For the first two months of 2006, the Marine platoon of the 22d Marine Expeditionary Unit had walked the streets in Iraq on foot without serious incident. Their patrols had moved fearlessly around lines of cars and through packed markets. For the most part, their house calls began with knocks, not kicks. It was their aim to win the respect of the city's Sunni Arab population. Suddenly things changed. An armored HMMWV on night patrol hit an improvised explosive device. The bomb destroyed the vehicle. Five Marines were wounded and two died shortly thereafter. A third Marine, a popular noncommissioned officer, later died of his wounds as well. The platoon was stunned. Some of the more veteran noncommissioned officers shrugged it off, but the younger Marines were keyed up and wanted to make the elusive enemy pay a price. A squad leader stood up in the squad bay asserted that there would be a pile of dead Arabs on the street when the platoon went out the next day. Just then, the company commander walked in. He was widely respected and generally short on words. He quickly sensed the unit's mood and recognized the potential danger in their dark attitude. Speaking directly to his Marines, the commander urged them to remember why they were there. He reminded them that a very small percentage of the populace was out to create problems. It was that minority that benefited from creating chaos. The enemy would love to see an overreaction to the attack, and they would benefit from any actions that detracted from the Marines' honor or purpose. The commander urged his Marines not to get caught up in the anger of the moment and do something they all would regret for a long time. Rather, they needed to focus on what the force was trying to accomplish and keep their minds on the mission. They had taken some hits and lost some good men, the commander said, but escalating the violence would not help them win. It would fall for the insurgents' strategy instead of sticking to the Marines' game plan of winning the respect of the populace. The commander knew his Marines and understood the operational environment. He assessed the situation and acted aggressively to counter a dangerous situation that threatened mission accomplishment. By his actions, the commander demonstrated patience, presence, and courage.

Ethics

7-21. Article VI of the U.S. Constitution and the Army Values, Soldier's Creed, and Core Values of U.S. Marines all require obedience to the law of armed conflict. They hold Soldiers and Marines to the highest standards of moral and ethical conduct. Conflict brings to bear enormous moral challenges, as well as the burden of life-and-death decisions with profound ethical considerations. Combat, including counterinsurgency and other forms of unconventional warfare, often obligates Soldiers and Marines to accept some risk to minimize harm to noncombatants. This risk taking is an essential part of the Warrior Ethos. In conventional conflicts, balancing competing responsibilities of mission accomplishment with protection of noncombatants is difficult enough. Complex COIN operations place the toughest of ethical demands on Soldiers, Marines, and their leaders.

7-22. Even in conventional combat operations, Soldiers and Marines are not permitted to use force disproportionately or indiscriminately. Typically, more force reduces risk in the short term. But American military values obligate Soldiers and Marines to accomplish their missions while taking measures to limit the destruction caused during military operations, particularly in terms of collateral harm to noncombatants. It is wrong to harm innocents, regardless of their citizenship.

7-23. Limiting the misery caused by war requires combatants to consider certain rules, principles, and consequences that restrain the amount of force they may apply. At the same time, combatants are not required to take so much risk that they fail in their mission or forfeit their lives. As long as their use of force is proportional to the gain to be achieved and discriminates in distinguishing between combatants and noncombatants. Soldiers and Marines may take actions where they knowingly risk, but do not intend, harm to noncombatants.

7-24. Ethically speaking, COIN environments can be much more complex than conventional ones. Insurgency is more than combat between armed groups; it is a political struggle with a high level of violence. Insurgents try to use this violence to destabilize and ultimately overthrow a government. Counterinsurgents that use excessive force to limit short-term risk alienate the local populace. They deprive themselves of the support or tolerance of the people. This situation is what insurgents want. It increases the threat they pose. Sometimes lethal responses are counterproductive. At other times, they are essential. The art of command includes knowing the difference and directing the appropriate action.

7-25. A key part of any insurgent's strategy is to attack the will of the domestic and international opposition. One of the insurgents' most effective ways to undermine and erode political will is to portray their opposition as untrustworthy or illegitimate. These attacks work especially well when insurgents can portray their opposition as unethical by the opposition's own standards. To combat these efforts, Soldiers and Marines treat noncombatants and detainees humanely, according to American values and internationally recognized human rights standards. In COIN, preserving noncombatant lives and dignity is central to mission accomplishment. This imperative creates a complex ethical environment.

War Fighting versus Policing

7-26. In counterinsurgencies, war fighting and policing are dynamically linked. The moral purpose of combat operations is to secure peace. The moral purpose of policing is to maintain the peace. In COIN operations, military forces defeat enemies to establish civil security; then, having done so, these same forces preserve it until host-nation (HN) police forces can assume responsibility for maintaining the civil order. When combatants conduct stability operations in a way that undermines civil security, they undermine the moral and practical purposes they serve. There is a clear difference between war fighting and policing. COIN operations require that every unit be adept at both and capable of moving rapidly between one and the other.

7-27. The COIN environment frequently and rapidly shifts from war fighting to policing and back again. There are many examples from Iraq and Afghanistan where U.S. forces drove insurgents out of urban areas only to have the insurgents later return and reestablish operations. Insurgents were able to return because U.S. forces had difficulty maintaining civil security. U.S. forces then had to deal with insurgents as an organized combatant force all over again. To prevent such situations, counterinsurgents that establish civil security need to be prepared to maintain it. Maintaining civil security entails very different ethical obligations than establishing it.

7-28. Civil security holds when institutions, civil law, courts, prisons, and effective police are in place and can protect the recognized rights of individuals. Typically this requires that—

- The enemy is defeated or transformed into a threat not capable of challenging a government's sovereignty.
- Institutions necessary for law enforcement—including police, courts, and prisons—are functioning.
- These institutions are credible, and people trust them to resolve disputes.

7-29. Where a functioning civil authority does not exist, COIN forces must work to establish it. Where U.S. forces are trying to build a HN government, the interim government should transition to HN authority as soon as possible. Counterinsurgents must work within the framework of the institutions established to maintain order and security. In these conditions, COIN operations more closely resemble police work than combat operations.

Proportionality and Discrimination

7-30. The principle of proportionality requires that the anticipated loss of life and damage to property incidental to attacks must not be excessive in relation to the concrete and direct military advantage expected to be gained. Proportionality and discrimination require combatants not only to minimize the harm to noncombatants but also to make positive commitments to—

- Preserve noncombatant lives by limiting the damage they do.
- Assume additional risk to minimize potential harm.

7-31. Proportionality requires that the advantage gained by a military operation not be exceeded by the collateral harm. The law of war principle of proportionality requires collateral damage to civilians and civilian property not be excessive in relation to the military advantage expected to be gained by executing the operation. Soldiers and Marines must take all feasible precautions when choosing means and methods of attack to avoid and minimize loss of civilian life, injury to civilians, and damage to civilian objects.

7-32. In conventional operations, proportionality is usually calculated in simple utilitarian terms: civilian lives and property lost versus enemy destroyed and military advantage gained. But in COIN operations, advantage is best calculated not in terms of how many insurgents are killed or detained, but rather which enemies are killed or detained. If certain key insurgent leaders are essential to the insurgents' ability to conduct operations, then military leaders need to consider their relative importance when determining how best to pursue them. In COIN environments, the number of civilian lives lost and property destroyed needs to be measured against how much harm the targeted insurgent could do if allowed to escape. If the target in question is relatively inconsequential, then proportionality requires combatants to forego severe action, or seek non-combative means of engagement.

7-33. When conditions of civil security exist, Soldiers and Marines may not take any actions that might knowingly harm noncombatants. This does not mean they cannot take risks that might put the populace in danger. But those risks are subject to the same rules of proportionality. The benefit anticipated must outweigh the risk taken.

7-34. Discrimination requires combatants to differentiate between enemy combatants, who represent a threat, and noncombatants, who do not. In conventional operations, this restriction means that combatants cannot intend to harm noncombatants, though proportionality permits them to act, knowing some noncombatants may be harmed.

7-35. In COIN operations, it is difficult to distinguish insurgents from noncombatants. It is also difficult to determine whether the situation permits harm to noncombatants. Two levels of discrimination are necessary:

- Deciding between targets.
- Determining an acceptable risk to noncombatants and bystanders.

7-36. Discrimination applies to the means by which combatants engage the enemy. The COIN environment requires counterinsurgents to not only determine the kinds of weapons to use and how to employ them but also establish whether lethal means are desired—or even permitted. (FM 27-10 discusses forbidden means of waging war.) Soldiers and Marines require an innate understanding of the effects of their actions and weapons on all aspects of the operational environment. Leaders must consider not only the first order, desired effects of a munition or action but also possible second- and third-order effects—including undesired ones. For example, bombs delivered by fixed-wing close air support may effectively destroy the source of small arms fire from a building in an urban area; however, direct-fire weapons may be more appropriate due to the risk of collateral damage to nearby buildings and noncombatants. The leader at the scene assesses the risks and makes the decision. Achieving the desired effects requires employing tactics and weapons appropriate to the situation. In some cases, this means avoiding the use of area munitions to minimize the potential harm inflicted on noncombatants located nearby. In situations where civil security exists, even tenuously, Soldiers and Marines should pursue nonlethal means first, using lethal force only when necessary.

7-37. The principles of discrimination in the use of force and proportionality in actions are important to counterinsurgents for practical reasons as well as for their ethical or moral implications. Fires that cause unnecessary harm or death to noncombatants may create more resistance and increase the insurgency's appeal— especially if the populace perceives a lack of discrimination in their use. The use of discriminating, proportionate force as a mindset goes beyond the adherence to the rules of engagement. Proportionality and discrimination applied in COIN require leaders to ensure that their units employ the right tools correctly with mature discernment, good judgment and moral resolve.

Detention and Interrogation

7-38. Detentions and interrogations are critical components to any military operation. The nature of COIN operations sometimes makes it difficult to separate potential detainees from innocent bystanders, since insurgents lack distinctive uniforms and deliberately mingle with the local populace. Interrogators are often under extreme pressure to get information that can lead to follow-on operations or save the lives of noncombatants, Soldiers, or Marines. While enemy prisoners in conventional war are considered moral and legal equals, the moral and legal status of insurgents is ambiguous and often contested. What is not ambiguous is the legal obligation of Soldiers and Marines to treat all prisoners and detainees according to the law. All captured or detained personnel, regardless of status, shall be treated humanely, and in accordance with the Detainee Treatment Act of 2005 and DODD 2310.01E. No person in the custody or under the control of DOD, regardless of nationality or physical location, shall be subject to torture or cruel, inhuman, or degrading treatment or punishment, in accordance with, and as defined in, U.S. law. (Appendix D provides more guidance on the legal issues concerning detention and interrogation.)

Limits on Detention

7-39. Mistreatment of noncombatants, including prisoners and detainees is illegal and immoral. It will not be condoned. The Detainee Treatment Act of 2005 makes the standard clear: *No person in the custody or under the effective control of the Department of Defense or under detention in a Department of Defense facility shall be subject to any treatment or technique of interrogation not authorized by and listed in the United States Army Field Manual on Intelligence Interrogation [FM 2-22.3].*

No individual in the custody or under the physical control of the United States Government, regardless of nationality or physical location, shall be subject to cruel, inhuman, or degrading treatment or punishment.

7-40. In COIN environments, distinguishing an insurgent from a civilian is difficult and often impossible. Treating a civilian like an insurgent, however, is a sure recipe for failure. Individuals suspected of insurgent or terrorist activity may be detained for two reasons:

- To prevent them from conducting further attacks.
- To gather information to prevent other insurgents and terrorists from conducting attacks.

These reasons allow for two classes of persons to be detained and interrogated:

- Persons who have engaged in, or assisted those who engage in, terrorist or insurgent activities.
- Persons who have incidentally obtained knowledge regarding insurgent and terrorist activity, but who are not guilty of associating with such groups.

People engaging in insurgent activities may be detained as enemies. Persons not guilty of associating with insurgent or terrorist groups may be detained and questioned for specific information. However, since these people have not—by virtue of their activities—represented a threat, they may be detained only long enough to obtain the relevant information. Since persons in the second category have not engaged in criminal or insurgent activities, they must be released, even if they refuse to provide information.

7-41. At no time can Soldiers and Marines detain family members or close associates to compel suspected insurgents to surrender or provide information. This kind of hostage taking is both unethical and illegal.

Limits on Interrogation

7-42. Abuse of detained persons is immoral, illegal, and unprofessional. Those who engage in cruel or inhuman treatment of prisoners betray the standards of the profession of arms and U.S. laws. They are subject to punishment under the Uniform Code of Military Justice. The Geneva Conventions, as well as the Convention against Torture and Other Cruel, Inhuman or Degrading Treatment or Punishment, agree on unacceptable interrogating techniques. Torture and cruel, inhuman, and degrading treatment is never a morally permissible option, even if lives depend on gaining information. No exceptional circumstances permit the use of torture and other cruel, inhuman, or degrading treatment. Only personnel trained and certified to interrogate can conduct interrogations. They use legal, approved methods of convincing enemy prisoners of war and detainees to give their cooperation. Interrogation sources are detainees, including enemy prisoners of war. (FM 2-22.3 provides the authoritative doctrine and policy for interrogation. Chapter 3 and appendix D of this manual also address this subject.)

7-43. The ethical challenges posed in COIN operations requires commanders' attention and action. Proactive commanders establish procedures and checks to ensure proper handling of detainees. Commanders verify that subordinate leaders do not allow apparent urgent requirements to result in violations of these procedures. Prohibitions against mistreatment may sometimes clash with leaders' moral imperative to accomplish their mission with minimum losses. Such situations place leaders in difficult situations, where they must choose between obedience to the law and the lives of their Soldiers and Marines. U.S. law and professional values compel commanders to forbid mistreatment of noncombatants, including captured enemies. Senior commanders clearly define the limits of acceptable behavior to their subordinates and take positive measures to ensure their standards are met.

7-44. To the extent that the work of interrogators is indispensable to fulfilling the state's obligation to secure its citizens' lives and liberties, conducting interrogations is a moral obligation. The methods used, however, must reflect the Nation's commitment to human dignity and international humanitarian law. A commander's need for information remains valid and can be met while observing relevant regulations and ethical standards. Acting morally does not necessarily mean that leaders give up obtaining critical information. Acting morally does mean that leaders must relinquish certain methods of obtaining information, even if that decision requires Soldiers and Marines to take greater risk.

Lose Moral Legitimacy, Lose the War

During the Algerian war of independence between 1954 and 1962, French leaders decided to permit torture against suspected insurgents. Though they were aware that it was against the law and morality of war, they argued that—

- This was a new form of war and these rules did not apply.

- The threat the enemy represented, communism, was a great evil that justified extraordinary means.

- The application of torture against insurgents was measured and not gratuitous. This official condoning of torture on the part of French Army leadership had several negative consequences. It empowered the moral legitimacy of the opposition, undermined the French moral legitimacy, and caused internal fragmentation among serving officers that led to an unsuccessful coup attempt in 1962. In the end, failure to comply with moral and legal restrictions against torture severely undermined

French efforts and contributed to their loss despite several significant military victories. Illegal and immoral activities made the counterinsurgents extremely vulnerable to enemy propaganda inside Algeria among the Muslim population, as well as in the United Nations and the French media. These actions also degraded the ethical climate throughout the French Army. France eventually recognized Algerian independence in July 1963.

The Learning Imperative

7-45. Today's operational environment requires military organizations at all echelons to prepare for a broader range of missions than ever before. The Services are preparing for stability operations and post conflict reconstruction tasks with the same degree of professionalism and study given to the conduct of combat operations. Similarly, COIN operations are receiving the attention and study merited by their frequency and potential impact. This broader mission set has significant leader development, education, and training implications, especially for land forces.

7-46. Army and Marine Corps leaders need to visualize the operational and informational impact of many tactical actions and relate their operations to larger strategic purposes. Effectively blending traditional military operations with other forms of influence is necessary. Effective leaders place a stronger emphasis on organizational change, develop subordinates, and empower them to execute critical tasks in consonance with broad guidance. Commanders must influence directly and indirectly the behavior of others outside their chain of command. Leaders are increasingly responsible for creating environments in which individuals and organizations learn from their experiences and for establishing climates that tap the full ingenuity of subordinates. Open channels of discussion and debate are needed to encourage growth of a learning environment in which experience is rapidly shared and lessons adapted for new challenges. The speed with which leaders adapt the organization must outpace insurgents' efforts to identify and exploit weaknesses or develop countermeasures.

7-47. Effective individual professional development programs develop and reward initiative and adaptability in junior leaders. Self-development, life-long learning, and reflection on experience should be encouraged and rewarded. Cultural sensitivity, development of no authoritarian interpersonal skills, and foreign language ability must be encouraged. Institutional professional development programs must develop leaders' judgment to help them recognize when situations change from combat to policing. Effective leaders are as skilled at limiting lethal force as they are in concentrating it. Indeed, they must learn that nonlethal solutions may often be preferable.

Summary

7-48. Senior leaders must model and transmit to their subordinates the appropriate respect for professional standards of self-discipline and adherence to ethical values. Effective leaders create command climates that reward professional conduct and penalize unethical behavior. They also are comfortable with delegating authority. However, as always, accountability for the overall behavior and performance of a command can not be delegated. Commanders remain accountable for the attainment of objectives and the manner in which they are attained.